THE ISRAELI CAREER
OF HUMMUS

THE ISRAELI CAREER OF HUMMUS

Colonial Appropriation, Authenticity, and Distinction

—〰—

DAFNA HIRSCH

INDIANA UNIVERSITY PRESS

This book is a publication of

Indiana University Press
Herman B Wells Library
1320 East 10th Street
Bloomington, Indiana 47405 USA

iupress.org

This book was published with the support of the Israel Science Foundation.

For customers in the European Union with safety or GPSR concerns, please contact Mare Nostrum
Group B.V., Mauritskade 21D, 1091 GC Amsterdam, The Netherlands. Email: gpsr@mare-nostrum.co.uk

First Printing 2026

Cataloging information is available from the Library of Congress.
ISBN 978-0-253-07530-7 (hdbk.)
ISBN 978-0-253-07531-4 (pbk.)
ISBN 978-0-253-07533-8 (ebook)

CONTENTS

Preface: Why Hummus?   *vii*

Acknowledgments   *xi*

Introduction: Zionism and Culinary Appropriation   *1*

1. Early Culinary Contacts   *27*

2. "The East Conquers the Stomachs of the West"   *53*

3. Nationalism in a Can   *78*

4. The Gourmetization of Hummus and the Return of
   the Repressed Arab   *104*

5. Made with Love: Mass-Produced Authenticity   *127*

Conclusion   *149*

Notes   *155*

References   *243*

Index   *281*

PREFACE: WHY HUMMUS?

THIS PROJECT STARTED FROM a passion and a disagreement. The passion was not exactly mine but a collective one: Israelis are crazy about hummus. In one of the funniest parodies on Israeli masculinity I have seen on screen— Dennis Dugan's *You Don't Mess with the Zohan* (2008)—the Israeli macho protagonist dips a chicken leg in hummus, uses hummus as a hair dye, and even puts out a fire with a hummus jet. Although Israelis do not yet put out fires with hummus, the film's depiction of the Israeli obsession with hummus is accurate. It has certainly afflicted my own family: I love hummus and eat a lot of it, but Smadi, my life partner, is a real addict who will never skip an opportunity to eat in one of her favorite hummus joints, even if it takes a journey.

In fact, when Smadi wanted to win my heart back in 1994, after I returned to Israel from several years abroad, she introduced me to the legendary Abu Hassan, located just a ten-minute walk from Old Jaffa, where I grew up. Later, I discovered that in the vicinity of Abu Hassan were several other celebrated hummus joints. This left me wondering: how could I have lived so many years in Jaffa unaware of the existence of these places? I knew that as a child in a middle-class Ashkenazi family, and regardless of our leftist political orientation, we were always facing north, to Tel Aviv. Yet, how could we have been so ignorant of these culinary treasures in our immediate vicinity? It took me a while to realize that it was not so much, or not only, that *we* were ignorant but that hummus—and particularly "Arab hummus"—did not enjoy the same celebratory status that it does today. It was a popular food all right, but not one deserving any special culinary or cultural attention.

It was from the conundrum of hummus becoming such a culinary passion in recent decades that I began my journey into the history of its consumption in

Israel, and not from questions of cultural appropriation. At the same time, it is exactly the fact of hummus being a politically charged dish that made it interesting for me. I was always fascinated by the ways in which the most mundane aspects of our everyday lives—our most embodied sensibilities—are shaped by political and social structures. It was not just any dish that became an Israeli culinary passion and a national symbol but one adopted from Palestinian Arabs. When in 2009 we organized a conference on cultural contacts and conflicts in Israel to inaugurate the Graduate Program in Cultural Studies at the Open University of Israel, where I was hired to work, I decided hummus would be my topic. At the time there was not a single study on hummus and very little on the local history of food, which has occupied me ever since. In the course of my work on this project, debates about ownership and appropriation grew louder. Hummus has become synonymous with cultural or culinary colonialism—the "soft" side of the Israeli colonization of Palestinian land.

The disagreement was with a small statement made by my former professor, Itamar Even-Zohar, in a paper seeking to identify generalities in the phenomenon of cultural interference—namely, the process whereby an item from a certain source culture is "naturalized" in a recipient culture and becomes part of its generative cultural repertoire. Even-Zohar argued that once interference has occurred, the question of its source or origin is no longer relevant.[1] The example of hummus suggested that this was not always the case, especially when interference occurs against the background of political antagonism. As my research progressed, it seemed that the source not only was relevant but also played a pivotal role in shaping its sociocultural career.

Remembering that hummus has not always been the culinary and cultural hero that it is today made me skeptical about explanations that transpose a political relation onto the culinary sphere: Israel stole hummus just as it stole land and other Palestinian assets. What I seek to do in this book is not so much to discredit this perspective as to complicate it—to try to understand the Israeli appropriation of hummus as a social and historical process. Culinary appropriation is not just a battle of symbols; it is a story of changing tastes, of consumption habits, and, not least, of making a living—and sometimes a fortune—out of food. The framework of culinary colonialism tells us little about the history of consumption (and production) on the ground.

How and why taste changes are extremely difficult to reconstruct. Even when we have elaborate accounts of the experience of consumption at our disposal, which is often not the case, there is something about "the comprehensive, all-enveloping sensuality of taste," as Priscilla Parkhurst Ferguson pointed out, that exceeds the verbal.[2] What makes it all the more complicated to trace the changing experience of consuming a specific dish is that the dish itself is not always the self-same object but varies between producers and historical periods. Yet, while the experience of taste exceeds the verbal, it is by no means disconnected from it. Sense perceptions and discourses are intertwined, shaping one another, even if one cannot be reduced to the other.[3] Hence, I am interested both in substances, tastes, and consumption practices and in the discourses that lend meaning to hummus and its consumption, and how they interact and transform over time.

Tracing the historically shifting meanings of a certain food item is also not without its challenges. Food may function as an allegory for political relations, identities, and aspirations, and it is often these meanings that gain prominence in public discourses. When Israeli soldiers egregiously wrote on the walls of a mosque in the Jenin Refugee Camp, occupied West Bank, "we came to eat hummus," they were invoking the Israeli perception of hummus as a symbol of indigeneity and masculinity.[4] Yet in any given society, the meaning of a particular food is never singular, nor is it reducible to symbolism alone—especially when it comes to foods consumed on a regular basis. As Sidney Mintz had noted, "what [a certain] food is, how people come to have it, how it is prepared, whether it is plentiful or scarce, under what circumstances it is available—all of these circumstances, and many others, are integrated into what the food means."[5]

Some meanings, then, can be much more subtle, if not necessarily less political, and distinguish between different instantiations of the same food. In my childhood and adolescent years in the 1970s and 1980s, when eating in restaurants was a much less common practice than it is today, there was one Jaffa restaurant we used to visit on occasion called Younes. Younes became fashionable among Jewish diners from Tel Aviv and the vicinity in the mid-1960s as an affordable option for out-of-the-ordinary and "authentic" Arab food. In the opposite direction from where we lived, on the way to the Jaffa clock tower, was a line of simple restaurants serving similar food as Younes but owned by Jews who descended from Arab countries. In contrast to Younes, we considered these restaurants unrefined and unsophisticated and looked down on them and on the people who ate in them as anything but authentic. This is only a small example of how perceptions of taste and authenticity became entangled with the politics of ethno-class distinction.

This book, then, is about the ways in which appetites and culinary desires are historically and politically produced and reproduced although, as I argue, they are always produced by a combination of factors, never a single one, and the ways these intertwine in specific historical moments. Among the factors that have shaped the career of hummus in Israel, three structures are particularly emphasized: the settler-colonial complementary cultural dynamics of indigenization/Westernization; the expansion of Israeli capitalism; and ethno-class relations. These structures, and the ways they play themselves out in the historical process, sometimes complement and sometimes contradict each other, but what they produce is not a simple "erasure" of the Arab/Palestinian source of hummus. It is often *as* Arab that various items of Palestinian culture have been appropriated and incorporated into the cultural repertoire for the construction of Israeli selves.[6] In this regard, this book is also about Zionism and the specter of the "native."

In my academic writing, I try to find the right balance between critique and empathy. I have always felt ambivalent toward the type of critical scholarship that treats its subjects with the condescension of a historical, social, or moralistic distance and always sought—if not necessarily always succeeded—to adopt a critical perspective at eye level. Maintaining such balance has not become any easier in the period of brutal violence we are currently living through, which meets an increasingly polarized academia and public discourse. I have found myself writing and rewriting some sections many times, sometimes just to find the right tone of voice. Nevertheless, I refuse to abandon this effort, if only because it would mean abandoning the hope for a different future.

The focus of this book is Israel and Israeli society. I am well aware that an Israeli writing a book about hummus in Israel might seem like another way of claiming hummus as an "Israeli food." As much as I would have liked to write a book about the intertwined changes in hummus consumption in both Palestinian and Israeli societies, it is beyond the scope of my abilities and expertise. I can only hope readers will judge my handling of the subject as fair.

In writing this book, I aimed to use accessible language and minimize jargon. Readers who are not particularly interested in the theoretical aspects can skip the introduction and dive straight into the main content, beginning from chapter 1.

Finally, this book has no normative takeouts. Whoever looks for a condemnation of the Israeli passion for hummus or for prescriptions for how to become more ethical hummus consumers will be disappointed. When I try to imagine how the local hummus scene would look after decolonization, I suspect it would look pretty much the same, with one exception: Israelis will have learned to see the Palestinians, whose hummus they admire, as their equals.[7] But this is about so much more than hummus.

ACKNOWLEDGMENTS

WE ARE CURRENTLY LIVING THROUGH one of the darkest periods in the bloody history of this region. The October 7 Hamas massacre has given license to Israel's most right-extremist government to pursue its fantasies of ethnic cleansing and Greater Israel with extraordinary fervor and very little public protest. It is now over 650 days that Israel's genocidal war on Gaza continues unabated, while in the West Bank, displacement and land theft through settler and military violence have climbed to new extremes. In the face of so much violence, death, destruction, and indifference to human suffering, everything else appears to have lost meaning. Does it make any sense to publish a book about hummus in Israel when in Gaza people are being starved? Alas, academic scholarship has its own temporality. If anything can provide some consolation at such times of human and moral crisis, it is the circle of beautiful and caring people who are my close milieu, many of whom are in this book in one way or another.

Work on this project has taken me so long, and so many people have contributed to it along the way, that the one thing I can be certain about is that I will forget to acknowledge some of them. It is not because your contribution is unappreciated but because I failed to write down your name in my "acknowledgments" file in due course. Perhaps others who are acknowledged will not even remember that they helped at all. I assure you—you did.

Research for this book was supported by a generous grant from the Israel Science Foundation (no. 43/11). I am grateful to the foundation for its support and, no less, for daring to fund a project on hummus. This grant was complemented by a grant from the Open University of Israel's Research Authority.

Both allowed me to benefit from the help of research assistants who worked with me for longer or shorter periods or on a specific segment of the research. A big thank-you to Roii Ball, Matan Boord, Netta Cohen, Aviv Derri Weksler, Netta Avnon, Tanya Kolobov, Ronit Liberman, Nisreen Mazzawi, and Noam Soulcat Sasson. Thanks are also due to Anat Oren, the academic manager of the B. I. and Lucille Cohen Institute for Public Opinion Research at Tel Aviv University, for helping me design the survey and for administering its implementation.

The Department of Sociology, Political Science, and Communication at the Open University of Israel is probably the best academic home I could wish for, full of brilliant and big-hearted people who are always ready to read and offer valuable critique. Many of them have also become close friends who were there for me in times of need. Special thanks to Anat Ben-David, Eran Fisher, Dana Kaplan, Gal Levy, Inna Leykin, Motti Regev, and Zeev (Andy) Rosenhek. Love you all! Yoni Alsheh left the department for another continent too many years ago, but his place in my life—and heart—is firmly secured.

I was fortunate to spend my sabbatical year in 2014–15 at the Department of Nutrition and Food Studies at NYU, where I received warm hospitality and intellectual nourishment. It was during this year that I began to consider myself a "food scholar." Special thanks to Krishnendu Ray, Amy Bentley, and Scott Alves Barton.

I embarked on this research project with my longtime friend Ofra Tene. If at some point our ways parted (in research, though not in life), it is entirely due to my own failing. I thank Ofra for introducing me to the world of food scholarship and for her friendship. Ofra's husband, Zeev Tene—probably the only food technologist who is a rocker—shared with me his knowledge and some connections, for which I am grateful. Both feed us not only with knowledge but also with wonderful meals.

More than anyone else, Gadi Algazi has taught me how to read and write. Gadi is my paragon of rigorous scholarship, true critical thinking, and intellectual generosity, and I am proud to have been—and still be—his student and friend. Gadi helped me formulate this project in its early stages, read parts of the book, and sent me many sources along the way. For this and so much more—my heartfelt thanks.

Many people contributed to this project by reading parts, by listening and offering advice, by sharing their knowledge, by sending materials, or simply by being friends. I thank Safa Aburabia, Rami Adut, Nof Atamna-Ismaeel, Nir Avieli, Tamar Barkay, Bashir Bashir, Ramez Eid, Keren Elad, Ra'anan Gabay, Shooky

Galili, Trevor Graham, Omri Grinberg, Rafi Grosglik, Hadas Gur, Manar Hasan, Alma Igra, Nily Kashman, Tali Katz-Gero, Michal Kravel-Tovi, Kinneret La-had, Israel Livny, Adel Manna, Anne Meneley, Daniel Monterescu, Regev Na-thansohn, Benny Nurieli, Jennifer Robertson, Natalie Rothman, Areej Sabbagh-Khouri, Ori Schwarz, Hizky Shoham, Neta Sobol, Erela Teharlev Ben-Shachar, Alon Ten-Ami, Ronit Vered, and Michal Warshavsky. Special thanks to Naor Ben-Yehoyada, Snait Gissis, Vered Kraus RIP, Alejandro Paz, and Yuval Yonay.

This project could only materialize thanks to the goodwill of dozens of people—restaurant owners, food technologists, agriculturalists, industry workers, journalists and authors, and many others—who were willing to devote their time and share their knowledge and memories with me, and I am grateful to each and every one of them. While I cannot mention all of them by name, many of their names appear throughout the pages of this book.

I am indebted to the team at Indiana University Press for a remarkably smooth, efficient, and—no less importantly—pleasant process. I deeply appreciate their willingness to accommodate my various requests along the way. I am especially grateful to Bethany Mowry, whose trust in this project and whose kind, sensitive, and patient editorial guidance made all the difference. My thanks also go to Darja Malcolm-Clarke, Sophia Hebert, Jennifer Wilder, Sami Heffner, Alyssa Lucas, and all those whose behind-the-scenes work contributed to bringing this book to fruition and supporting its postproduction life. I thank the two anonymous reviewers for their insightful and constructive feedback, and Paul Silverstein, Susan Slyomovics, and Ted Swedenburg for first considering my manuscript for IUP. I am also grateful to Abdul Khader for managing production at Amnet; to Ursula Wokoeck for editing earlier versions of two chapters and her careful proofreading; to Hadas Blum for compiling the index; and to Maya Raanan for organizing an extremely messy bibliography and securing image permissions.

Sadly, my parents, Siona Shimshi and Jachin Hirsch, who accompanied this project from the start, did not live to see it come to fruition. My gratitude for everything they have given me, however, lives on. Their interest in my work is something I have never taken for granted. If this book would make it to the heavenly library, I know they will read it more than once. I think my father would have been happy to know that two of his beautiful photographs, of restaurants in 1950s Acre, are included in this book.

Finally, to my beloved Smadi (a.k.a. Dr. Smadar Sharon), who could live on hummus alone (almost), and to our beloved son, Omer Sharon Gabay, who acquired a taste for hummus with his mother's milk—thank you for being the wonderful, smart, and caring people who you are and the best companions in life and research. Your love and support have carried me through this journey's ebbs and flows.

Parts of this work were published as journal articles and a book chapter:

Hirsch, Dafna. "'Hummus Is Best When It Is Fresh and Made by Arabs': The Gourmetization of Hummus in Israel and the Return of the Repressed Arab." *American Ethnologist* 38 (2011): 617–30.
Hirsch, Dafna, and Ofra Tene. "Hummus: The Making of an Israeli Culinary Cult." *Journal of Consumer Culture* 13 (2013): 25–45.
Hirsch, Dafna. "Palestinian Urban Food Venues as 'Contact Zones' between Arabs and Jews during the British Mandate Period." In *Making Levantine Cuisine: Modern Foodways of the Eastern Mediterranean*, edited by Anny Gaul, Graham Auman Pitts, and Vicki Valosik, 93–114. Austin: University of Texas Press, 2021.

THE ISRAELI CAREER
OF HUMMUS

INTRODUCTION

Zionism and Culinary Appropriation

IN JULY 1908, A GROUP of men from Bar-Giora—a clandestine Zionist militia—arrived at the colony of Mescha to help defend the colonists from attacks by members of the neighboring village, Maʿdhar. A villager who was hired to guard the colony was shot on its premises in controversial circumstances, and the villagers' request for compensation was denied. Consequently, Mescha farmers were attacked in the fields and called on the nearby colonies, where the men of Bar-Giora had been employed, for help. Men came from the surrounding colonies and organized in guarding shifts until the attacks gradually stopped.[1]

Following this incidence, the colonists decided to hire the men of Bar-Giora as permanent guards. The latter conditioned their acceptance on replacing not only the Arab guards but also the Arab workers of the colony with Jewish workers who would train to become farmers.[2] Fifteen men were sent to the colony to live and work on the farms in place of the Arab *harathin* (lit. plowmen).[3] Their response was part of a shift in the Zionist settlement policy in the wake of the Zionist Organization's involvement in "practical work" in Palestine, toward greater readiness for violent confrontation in the process of land acquisition and settlement.[4] In 1909, Bar-Giora transformed into the Hashomer (The Watchman) organization, whose members are famous for "playing Arab" by adopting various Arab habits and dress forms.[5]

One of the members of Bar-Giora sent to Mescha was Ukrainian-born Gad Avigdorov, who had arrived in Palestine in the early 1900s at age fifteen. When he was recruited to go to Mescha, he reacted with enthusiasm: "I will be a worker for one of the farmers—I will now be a *fallâh*!" (Arabic for farmer). Turning into a fallâh, however, proved harder than he had expected; he could barely manage a mule. Neither was the acquisition of working skills sufficient to turn one into a fallâh: being a fallâh required adopting a certain way of life, including eating a certain kind of food. Avigdorov recounted how his "land-lady" used to feed him "*mjaddara*: for the field—a pot of lentils for the whole day, and when I return from the field—a porridge of chickpeas"—namely, hummus (probably prepared without tahini). One day, told Avigdorov, "Nathan and I were plowing a single meadow, and at lunchtime Nathan took out a latke [potato fritter], and I took off the lid from the lentil pot.—Nathan, listen, latkes are women's food. Come eat lentils, be a 'fallâh'! Nathan understands that I am right and eats the lentils with appetite. I only tasted from the latkes—a delicacy [*tsapichit*]! I swallowed another one, and the others were swallowed after the first."[6]

Avigdorov's contrasting of mjaddara and hummus—the foods of the fallâh—with the feminine food of the Eastern European Jewish Diaspora—latkes—was not coincidental. Neither was his use of the Arabic *fallâh* to denote the masculine opposite of the feminine latke consumer. Among Jewish "idealistic workers" who arrived in Palestine before WWI, the figure of the fallâh gained a mythological status not only for being considered a relic of the biblical past but primarily for its association with a set of masculine qualities that were highly valued in the context of the colonization of land and labor: physical strength, endurance, and connection to the land.[7] In other words, Arabness, indigeneity, and masculinity were part of a single—albeit modular and malleable—semiotic cluster.[8] At the same time, Avigdorov's attitude toward these foods was mark-edly ambivalent: "local" and "masculine," yet hardly the object of desire as the familiar foods of his Eastern European home.

If hummus was met with a similar ambivalence from many of Avigdorov's generation, by the beginning of the third millennium it had become one of the foods Israelis feel most passionate about. It is a regular part of institutional receptions, canteen menus, rituals of male commensality, and kindergarten meals. It is not just eaten abundantly but also talked about incessantly in vari-ous public and private communication spheres. In the discourse on hummus, which has developed since the 1990s, it appears as an indispensable dish, an in-disputable delicacy, even a sort of culinary miracle—unassuming yet sublime. It is described as the quintessential food of the region, an Israeli "obsession," and one of the main things Israelis miss when they travel abroad.[9] Numerous people describe themselves as "hummus addicts," and distaste for hummus is considered somewhat of an oddity. In short, it has become not just a dish Israelis consider part of their national food repertoire but a veritable culinary cult.[10] At the same time, hummus has become a global fad and, concomitantly, a symbol of Israeli culinary appropriation and "food colonialism" more than ever before. How has a dish from the Palestinian Arab menu become such an Israeli culinary passion and a national symbol? What is the relationship between land colonization and food consumption?

Adopting dishes and, primarily, ingredients from the Palestinian menu to signify a transformation from newcomers into "natives" was not uncommon among idealistic workers like Avigdorov. In the abovementioned incident, however, it was not the workers but the farmer's wife who prepared the dishes of mjaddara and hummus. Both lentils and chickpeas were grown in the colony of Mescha, and ways to prepare them were learned from the Arab workers who lived on the farm, often with their families, and with whom the farmers interacted on a daily basis.[11] Such performative acts of consumption, then, were predicated on a reality of contacts.

Yet the subsequent careers of hummus and mjaddara were very different, in spite of their similar symbolic value. While mjaddara is well liked in Israel, it never became an object of culinary passion and symbolic investment like hummus, nor of everyday consumption. Why their different trajectories? This book is intended as a history both of hummus consumption in Israel and of its making into a culinary cult and as a commentary on culinary appropriation in a settler society. It proceeds from the assumption that the stomach does not simply submit to the logic of colonization—itself not a unitary political and cultural project—reproducing it in the culinary sphere. Zionist settlers could have rejected Arab food just the same. That they developed a taste for this food and even claimed certain dishes as their own while simultaneously— at least in certain contexts and historical periods—attributing greater value to Arab-made instantiations of these dishes, as the case of hummus clearly demonstrates, resulted from a complex and sometimes contradictory historical process in which political aspects articulated with nutritional, economic, social, and cultural ones.

While Israeli cultural appropriation from the Palestinians could have been studied through other cultural objects (e.g., words), food provides a particularly compelling lens into this process. Food is not only a powerful semiotic device;[12] it is also an extremely sensitive social and political medium by which "social relations are manipulated and power is enacted."[13] Moreover, food, unlike words, can assume a commodity form. In fact, food is a commodity of a special kind: one that is destroyed upon consumption, thereby generating potential for more consumption.[14] Food therefore provides a platform for studying the intermingling of different logics and its effects on the career of an appropriated cultural item: the settler-colonial cultural logics of indigenization/Westernization, the social logic of distinction, and the capitalist logic of profit maximization.

CULINARY APPROPRIATION AS DISPOSSESSION

In 2009, the Consulate General of Israel in New York City posted on its website a two-minute video clip titled "How to Make Hummus!" In this clip, mostly shot in close-ups on ingredients and kitchen appliances, an appealing young woman in a not-so-appealing kitchen environment demonstrates how to cook and mash chickpeas, crush garlic, squeeze lemon, add spices, mix everything, and prepare hummus—all to the sound of swing music. At the end of the clip, hummus is served with slices of challah bread, and the caption reads, "Serve with chala [sic] bread or pita," marking hummus not just as "Israeli" but also as "Jewish."[15]

Examples like this abound. In January 2021, the Israeli Ministry of Foreign Affairs posted on its Facebook page a series of clips titled "Taste of Israel," explaining how to prepare various dishes, including hummus.[16] In "Israeli restaurants" abroad—and increasingly also in "Jewish restaurants"—hummus has become a mandatory item on the menu. Although Israelis' obsession with hummus is relatively recent, both hummus and falafel had already been nationalized in the late 1950s; in 1957, well-known Israeli songwriter Dan Almagor composed "The Falafel Song," claiming falafel as Israel's national dish.[17] Over time, a broader array of dishes that originated in the region has been variously positioned as Israeli food.

Palestinian and other critics of such representations have pointed to the political implications of what may appear as mere culinary enthusiasm. Rather than benign gestures of culinary openness and multiculturalism, as they are often presented, these acts of culinary appropriation are seen as part of a broader settler-colonial project of erasure. As Laila El-Haddad and Maggie Schmitt argue in *The Gaza Kitchen: A Palestinian Culinary Journey*, "Palestinians take great offense to such attempts at cultural appropriation, viewing them as yet another form of colonization."[18] Steven Salaita puts it more poignantly: "When Zionists (or their oblivious collaborators) claim Arabic food as Israeli, it's not a paragon of intercultural harmony but the studious destruction of Palestinian culture."[19]

This critique is rooted in the understanding that the settler-colonial logic of elimination of the native operates not only through physical dispossession of land and displacement of people and communities but also through the symbolic appropriation and erasure of indigenous cultural forms.[20] Israeli cultural appropriation, in this view, seeks to sever the connection between Palestinians and their cultural heritage, presenting Israel as the rightful bearer of indigenous culture. As Christiane Dabdoub Nasser writes in a special double issue of *Jerusalem Quarterly* on Palestinian foodways, Zionist "relentless effort to usurp Indigenous Palestinian culture and with it the formative cultural accomplishments that originated in the region, are efforts to impose settler colonists as the true bearers of Indigeneity."[21] Palestinian American author Susan Abulhawa has called this strategy "epic forgery."[22]

Food plays a particularly charged role in this dynamic, embodying an intimate historical connection to the land and its flora and fauna.[23] As Dabdoub Nasser notes, "Food culture and food production systems are the result of centuries of interacting with the land and the elements when farming communities adapted their agricultural practice to the topography, the climate, and annual rainfall," laying down "the foundation on which a society regenerates itself and evolves."[24] Other scholars emphasize food's function in sustaining cultural identity, family and social ties, and communal values such as hospitality and generosity.[25] In this context, keeping food traditions, and affirming them as "Palestinian," becomes a form of *sumud* (steadfastness)—a refusal to surrender cultural life in the face of ongoing dispossession and appropriation.

The consequences of cultural appropriation, moreover, are not confined to the symbolic realm. They are seen as entangled with material inequalities, economic exploitation, and the dehumanization of Palestinians. In a petition initiated by Palestinians working in the food industry in the US, and circulated in late October 2023, it was written that *"Israel has long weaponized food,* erasing Palestinian people while claiming their cuisine. Here in the U.S., the appropriation of Palestinian foods as 'Israeli' has led to more than Israelis profiting off of Palestinian culture; it is an erasure that has had real implications for Palestinians. It allows us to negate their cultural currency, and turn our attention away with more ease when we see Palestinian death."[26]

These critiques—deeply grounded in the Palestinian experience of dispossession—are by no means exclusive to Palestinians. Over the past two decades, they have reverberated through public and academic discourses across North America and Europe, as well as within Israeli society itself.[27]

CULTURAL APPROPRIATION AND "EATING THE OTHER"

Indeed, Israel's claiming hummus and falafel as its national dishes looks like a textbook case of cultural appropriation. But what exactly is *cultural appropriation*? Despite its present ubiquity, cultural appropriation remains an ambiguous and undertheorized concept. In its currently dominant sense of taking cultural assets from subordinated groups, it emerged in public discourse in the 1980s and began to receive substantial scholarly attention in the late 1990s.[28] Earlier uses were of a less-pejorative and even positive nature, regarding appropriation as something the powerless do or as something everybody does—an ordinary aspect of everyday life (sometimes defined, in the case of appropriation of items from other cultures, as "culture crossing," "cultural borrowing," or "transculturation").[29] Today, however, this concept is mostly used to denote the unauthorized taking of material or intellectual cultural assets by members of a dominant culture from a dominated or disadvantaged one (sometimes termed "misappropriation" or simply "theft").[30] As such, it is understood to be a motivated act, associated with power and entailing material and/or symbolic harm.[31] These may include lack of recognition of the source culture, financial profit at the expense of its creative labor, degradation of its cultural integrity and viability, and alteration or misrepresentation of the appropriated content.[32]

Regardless of its different uses, the concept of appropriation indicates something beyond simple taking. In *Economic and Philosophical Manuscripts* (1944), Marx understood appropriation (*Aneignung*) as a relation of making oneself and the external world one's own, stripping them of their alien nature, and not merely taking something as possession.[33] Appropriation is thus an active and productive act of incorporation, through which both the appropriating subject and the appropriated object are transformed. Where there is no capacity for appropriation, alienation occurs.[34] In de Certeau's work, appropriation or "reappropriation" indicates the active and creative ways in which the dominated inhabit the structures and strategies of domination ("tactics").[35] Later uses focusing on ethnicity and race (rather than class) and on hegemonic (rather than subaltern) practices conceive of cultural appropriation, especially of the type manifested in producing or consuming items that originated in dominated or "exotic" cultures, as a means of playing with and mastering Otherness.[36] As various critics argue, in certain types of appropriative acts, alterity itself is rendered an essence that can be extracted from ethnic and racial others and invested in objects, and through them in the appropriating subject.[37] In these critiques, too, the transformative character of appropriation is retained.

Although cuisine is a cultural sector that receives much attention in public debates about appropriation, it has received markedly less scholarly attention. Scholars have adopted frameworks like "culinary appropriation," "eating the Other," and "cultural food colonialism" to refer to various modes of Western (mis)engagement with indigenous or "ethnic" food and culinary traditions.[38] Following bell hooks, who formulated her ideas in other than specifically food-related contexts, "eating the Other" refers to the commodification of difference for white consumption. Whether the Other is consumed in an effort to signify pluralism and the overcoming of white prejudice or as an assertion of power and privilege—an act of incorporating and thereby mastering a threatening yet alluring Other—it is always meant to serve the ends of white desire.[39] This position is often accompanied by a critique of consumers' lack of knowledge of the culture from which the food was taken, if it is acknowledged at all; of their misrepresenting the cuisine of the Other or representing it as fixed, "authentic," and "traditional"; of the adaptation of foreign dishes to fit the Western palate; and more.[40] In a piece arguing against the inclusion of diverse attitudes toward the food of differently positioned Others under a single banner of "cultural appropriation," Krishnendu Ray characterizes settlers' approach toward the food of indigenous populations as one of erasure rather than (mis)appropriation.[41]

The frameworks of "culinary colonialism" and "eating the Other" seem particularly apt in the Israeli case, in which appropriation of Palestinian dishes can be regarded as yet another instance of Israel's swallowing of Palestinian assets and claiming them as its own. At the same time, these frameworks have been subjected to several critiques. First, as Uma Narayan has argued, the commodified interaction with an Other culinary culture seems preferable to the complete lack of acquaintance that permits the food of the Other to appear as a mark of strangeness and Otherness.[42] In many colonial contexts, it was the latter that characterized colonizers' attitudes toward indigenous food.[43] One could argue with the notion that acquaintance facilitates acceptance. However, this critique points to the possibility of more than one relation to the food of the Other and therefore raises the question of why some items are rejected and others are seen as acceptable and are even appropriated. This question calls for historical investigation.

Second, some scholars have argued that any stable notion of "the food of the Other" is predicated on an essentialized concept of culture, which regards it as a distinct, bounded, and static unit, coextensive with a national or ethnic group.[44] Yet identities and "cultures" are always formed and reformed through contacts so that no individual culture is free from the dynamic flow of cultural exchange.[45] This is certainly true of contemporary food cultures. Food items—both ingredients and dishes—travel, and they travel in all directions.[46] This critique points not only to the fact that "the food of the Other" is often a product of earlier exchanges but also to the cultural labor involved in constructing boundaries and asserting purity—in marking certain foods as "theirs" and claiming others as "our own."[47]

Moreover, in the Israeli case, any assumption of cultural purity or absolute alterity between Jews and Arabs is problematized by the fact that a significant share of the Israeli Jewish population hailed from Arab countries and shared Arab culture. Transposing the settler/native polarity from the field of politics to the field of culture replicates the symbolic violence involved in associating Israel with Western culture. While the cuisines of Arab countries vary, they share ingredients, taste profiles, cooking techniques, and dishes. Even if most Jews who originated in the Arab world were not familiar with every Palestinian dish, their attitude toward Palestinian cuisine, and Palestinian culture more generally, was hardly one of absolute alterity.

The antiessentialist critique was subject to countercriticism. First, as Nicholas Dirks has pointed out, the consequences of emphasizing the constructedness of "culture" are not the same for the colonizer and for the colonized.[48] Second, while culinary diffusion is a natural result of cultural contact (even if not all cuisines are open to external influences to the same extent[49]), it is one thing to consume and even master the preparation of dishes from other cuisines and quite another to claim them as one's own—an act that Rafram Chaddad and Yigal Nizri deem "culinary injustice."[50] Thus, while sushi and pasta are extremely popular in Israel, no Israeli will venture to claim them as "Israeli food." That Palestinian dishes in particular are appropriated as "Israeli" is directly related to the colonial situation.

A third critique concerns the subjection of the culinary to the political that these frameworks entail. Yet food's trajectory is never reducible to its being a political symbol; rather it is shaped by a number of fields, including the culinary, the cultural, the economic, and the political.[51] Among these fields, there is no necessary correspondence, even if some of them—primarily the political and the economic fields—are more likely to shape dynamics in the other fields.[52] As the case of hummus demonstrates, the culinary field neither reflects the political field nor is wholly independent of it. Rather, the two fields interact in significant ways, and processes and mechanisms that are specific to each shape their interaction.

Instead of looking at food consumption as a way of dealing with pregiven Otherness, in this book I examine how culinary appropriation produces identities, affinities, and notions of alterity within a shared, albeit contested space.[53] I look at how the meanings and identity of hummus were historically constructed and reconstructed by differently positioned groups of actors as a nexus of strategies and tactics: discursive and nondiscursive evocations of hummus's symbolic function alongside more mundane acts of consumption, where the marking of identity is an inevitable, albeit not intentional or conscious aspect.[54] To avoid the pitfalls of both essentialism and the antiessentialist critique, I replace the ideological concept of "origins" with a historically grounded concept of "source." While "origins" remains a vague and disputed concept in the case of hummus, for reasons that are both political and analytical, Israelis' adoption of hummus from Palestinian Arabs usually goes uncontested.[55] Moreover, rather than simple "erasure" of its Arab source, at various points in its career hummus gained symbolic currency from its association with the Arabs. In other words, the alternating association and dissociation of hummus and Arabness form a central aspect of its cultural biography.

In what follows I regard the Arabness of hummus as a Peircean qualisign—that is, a quality or a property that is a sign.[56] This property is not simply given; whether it is made salient or repressed and how it is interpreted (e.g., what aspects of Arabness are brought to the fore in which context) are products of social and cultural action, the "making and remaking of identities."[57] Constituting the value of Arabness in a specific context are both political ideologies (e.g., whether Arabs are constructed as "primitive" or as "close to nature") and what Webb Keane terms "semiotic ideologies."[58] The latter invest appropriated items with a capacity to confer on their consumers specific qualities associated with the Arabs. For early Zionist settlers, the most important of these qualities were an authentic tie to the land and masculinity.

My main argument is twofold. First, contrary to accounts that regard food consumption as metonymic of political relations, I argue that because food items move in several fields, both their consumption and their signification are overdetermined processes shaped by the interaction between these fields; the meanings of appropriation, however, are inseparable from the colonial process. Second, rather than considering "the food of the Other" to be a manifestation of an essential alterity that is incorporated and then erased, I argue that the source of the food may function as a semiotic resource employed by actors who are embedded in various social, cultural, political, or economic projects— ranging from intimate performances of indigenization by early rural settlers to the international strategies of the Israeli food industry.[59] Thus, whereas accounts of cultural appropriation often take for granted the identification of cultural items with their source culture, my analysis draws attention to the construction/suppression of this identification in social practice and to the processes of mediation it involves.

FRAMEWORK: SETTLER-COLONIAL NATIONALISM AND CULTURE BUILDING

Zionist settlers' attribution of authenticity and masculinity to Palestine's Arab inhabitants, and their desire to appropriate these qualities, should be understood in light of the cultural grammar of settler-colonial identity politics and of the specificities of the Zionist project. Zionism is the branch of European Jewish nationalism that sought to solve "the Jewish problem" in Europe through colonizing a territory overseas. For the founders of the Zionist movement in the late nineteenth century, colonization and settlement were a means not just for acquiring Jewish sovereignty but also for shaping a new type of Jew—for transforming the feeble, uprooted, "Oriental" Jews of the Eastern European Diaspora into stout, civilized, and masculine men who are rooted in the land.[60] In other words, Zionism is a fusion of nationalism and settler colonialism whose original goal was the mutual transformation of both the people and the land.

Understanding Zionism as a settler-colonial project does not imply that it must conform to a given set of theoretical tenets.[61] To borrow Raef Zreik's formulation, "Zionism is a settler-colonial nationalism, and, at least in part, a colonialism of refugees" who considered Palestine their ancestral homeland ("The Land of Israel"). Being late to join the colonial feast, Zionists settled amid a population that was already in the grip of modernization currents and was a part of the wider Arab world.[62] And although Zionism was essentially a European movement, a large section of the settler population hailed from the Arab world and had a stronger cultural affinity with Palestinian Arabs than with European Jews. This is not to argue that Zionism is an exceptional case of settler colonialism but a plea to attend to its specificities rather than force-fitting it into a generalized model.

From its inception, Zionist settlement in Palestine was accompanied by an intensive activity of culture building. At its core was the conviction that national regeneration required replacing the Jewish cultures of the Diaspora with a new "Hebrew" culture. Its specific content, however, was not self-evident but subject to interpretation, negotiation, and struggles between different groups of cultural entrepreneurs.[63] Although these often presented the cultural models they propagated as a "return to the authentic national culture," their activity involved, besides invention, appropriation and adaptation of items from various existing cultural repertoires.[64]

Settler narratives, write Anna Johnston and Alan Lawson, are caught between two sources of authority and authenticity, which are both desired and disavowed: the authentic imperial culture from which the settlers are separated (or, in the Jewish case, which cast them out) and an indigenous authenticity that they desire as a sign of their own legitimacy.[65] Amid the heterogeneity of the Zionist cultural sphere, two central dynamics were prominent both as orientations for action and as schemes for perception and interpretation: Westernization and indigenization. Beyond the structure of settler narratives, they derived from the Jews' location within the European metropole as an alien "Oriental race." Having internalized the European gaze on the Orient, as well as on themselves, Zionists imagined themselves both *as* and as *not quite yet* civilized settlers who have come to lift the country from its Oriental backwardness, and native to Palestine—their ancestral homeland, to which they have returned after two thousand years of exile.[66]

Establishing the authenticity of the settlers as both Western (civilized, modern, scientifically and technologically advanced) and native to Palestine became a central concern for Zionist culture builders. And also a source for tension: in the discourse of authenticity, modern civilization itself was seen as eroding human authentic existence.[67] Moreover, with its sedentary lifestyle, material comfort, and refined manners, civilized modernity threatened to render men soft and effeminate.[68] In contrast, men of subjugated groups like peasants, proletarians, and some indigenous people, with their rough physicality and "primitive" way of life, were often seen as embodying the lost authenticity and masculinity of civilized man.[69] Authenticity, as Avril Bell notes, "*is not a property of indigenous cultures, but a value attributed to them out of the concerns of European modernity.*"[70]

The figure of "the Arab" was therefore essential to all three projects of Zionist self-fashioning—Westernization, indigenization, and masculinization. For the first, it provided a foil: the backward Oriental Other of the modern, civilized settler self, from whose hands Zionists had to redeem the land in order to develop it. For the other two, it served as a prototype, especially the mythological figures of the Bedouin and the fallâh: the authentic and masculine "native" who possesses desirable qualities such as physical strength, endurance, and attachment to the land.[71] Thus, the sign of Arabness, detached from real Arabs and embodied in a selection of material and immaterial cultural products, served early Zionist settlers to index their transformation from feeble newcomers into bold and masculine "natives."

In the eyes of European Zionists, the image of Jews who descended from the Arab and Islamic world (*Mizrahim*, lit. "Easterners") was likewise ambivalent. Serving as default soldiers of the settler-colonial Judaization project, especially after the Holocaust, they were considered a fifth column and were subjected to various measures of "correction" and de-Arabization in the cultural project of Westernization.[72] Simultaneously, some of their own material and intellectual cultural assets were appropriated and served either in the compilation of an inventory of national treasures or in the construction of a cultural stratum of "folk culture" or "folklore."[73]

Importantly, Westernization and indigenization are strategic orientations; they never circumscribed the entire cultural field. Cultural engineering efforts existed side by side with spontaneous cultural flows, and planned activities of culture building encountered various tactics "from below." Probably, no other cultural sphere exemplifies it better than cuisine. While most dishes comprising the symbolic repertoire of "Israeli food" are Middle Eastern, as demonstrated in the menu of the Israeli restaurant abroad, the actual domestic culinary repertoire is much more diverse.[74] Nevertheless, these seemingly conflicting yet in effect complementary orientations constitute a powerful conceptual scheme, organizing practices, perceptions, and self-perceptions to this day.

FOOD, IDENTITY, INDIGENEITY

In the area of food, the Westernization/indigenization projects were manifested in the efforts of various cultural entrepreneurs and mediators to shape a new food culture for the heterogeneous population of the settlers. These efforts, which have been studied primarily through the lens of nationalism, although increasingly also of settler colonialism, aimed at uprooting the eating habits of the Diaspora by inculcating a new culinary repertoire more adjusted to the conditions of the land.[75] Nutrition experts conceived of this process as "rationalizing" the settlers' diet, which they sought to achieve with the help of Western nutrition science.[76]

While most of the dishes and cooking styles recommended by nutrition experts were European, some Arab dishes, such as hummus, were also included, framed as suitable for the local conditions. Granted, settlers did not simply comply. Often, they continued to eat the food they were accustomed to, when available, and sometimes adopted new dishes through social contacts or commercial channels, regardless of nutritional advice. Food consumption patterns are shaped by a complex interplay of material and symbolic factors, and the Zionist adoption of Arab dishes is no exception.[77] Yet at certain historical junctures, symbolic factors can take on heightened significance for cultural entrepreneurs and everyday consumers alike.

If the dictum "you are what you eat" seems by now a truism, it can still be true in different ways. According to Steven Shapin, until the modern era of nutrition science, the relation between food and identity was based on a logic of analogy where consumers were thought to share qualities with the food consumed.[78] In colonial settings, this logic was expressed in the rejection of native foods, which were thought to impart the undesirable qualities associated with the natives on European colonizers.[79] In modern times, Shapin argues, the analogical relation was replaced by an analytical one, focused on the effects of the food's constituents on personal health and well-being.[80] Yet, I would argue that the analogical aspect has not completely disappeared from processes of identification through food consumption, although it is manifested not so much in the qualities of the food consumed but rather in mimetic eating.

One of the most elaborate accounts of the relationship between food, embodiment, and identity is offered by Pierre Bourdieu. In *Distinction*, embodied practices of food consumption, mediated by the dispositions of the habitus, index social position—primarily the configuration of class and gender. They do this both through their actual effect on the physical body and the way it relates to the type of body most valued within the social group and through the experience of the body, which consuming a specific food induces, and the way it relates to the "practical philosophies" underlying distinctions between specific classed and gendered bodies. This experience may result from the food's (real or perceived) nutritional qualities or from its manner of consumption; it is not just *what* one eats but *how* one eats it that makes a difference.[81]

In this context, the association of hummus with masculinity in Israel seems odd, given its vegetarian composition and mushy texture, reminiscent of baby food. Outside the Middle East, where hummus was first introduced in its industrialized version, it is mostly considered a gender-neutral and even feminine food.[82] Yet there are other qualities that support the masculine gendering of hummus in Israel, primarily hummus eaten in a *hummusiya* (Hebrew for hummus joint). Hummus is a filling dish, satiating for many hours, often causing gas—qualities that are associated with masculinity. It is eaten with the hands using bits of pita bread, in broad circular gestures referred to in Hebrew as "wiping" (as opposed to Palestinian "dipping"), from a plate which is often shared. This eating manner exhibits some of the main qualities that Israelis like to associate with "Israeliness" and particularly with Israeli masculinity: roughness and informality to the point of rudeness, but also sociability.

Studies on food consumption and its relationship to identity offer several qualifications to Bourdieu's account. First, taste in food is shaped not only through habitual embodied practices but also through more discursive forms of knowledge.[83] While food habits may be extremely tenacious and difficult to change, discourses on food, and the meanings attached to specific foods, can sometimes act as powerful catalysts of transforming consumption habits and tastes. Discourses on health and ethics, for example, have participated in changing the social status of certain foods—elevating some and condemning others to marginalization and even oblivion. In the Zionist case, the functioning of specific local products as markers of indigeneity relied on discursive mediation.

Second, consuming food is never merely expressive and reproductive of social identities; it may also participate in the construction and negotiation of identities.[84] Consider the following excerpt by Yigal Alon, a member of the Jewish paramilitary organization Palmach. Alon was one of Israel's most prominent military commanders, responsible for the expulsion of tens of thousands of Palestinians in the 1948 war. Referring to the famous "coffee ritual" maintained by Palmach members, Alon writes that preparing and drinking coffee "according to the habits and manners of our Arab neighbors" ("rhythmic swallows and smacking lips") expressed "an unconscious desire to integrate into the nature of the country and the nature of its inhabitants"[85] (for Alon, "neighbors" was not a figure of speech: having grown up in Mescha, his family maintained friendly relationships with Arabs from neighboring villages, and he himself was quite attached to his father's *harathin*;[86] in his case, ethnic cleansing was not motivated by personal animosity). As his account illustrates, Palmach members did not simply drink coffee: in an act of "reverse colonial mimicry," to quote Alona Nitzan-Shiftan, they mimicked what they perceived to be the Arab way of drinking coffee, by which they aspired not to become Arabs but to appropriate Arabs' indigenous authenticity, with coffee serving as a vehicle for performing a new kind of self—one "naturally" rooted in the land.[87] What made food consumption particularly effective as a technology of the self was its ability to index a veritable bodily transformation achieved through the repetitive act of consumption—the acquisition of a taste for the local.

As various sources demonstrate, such acts of mimetic consumption were not just performative but also affective.[88] In the scene described by Avigdorov with which I opened, the potential of food consumption to transform one into a fallâh induces appetite. Or think about the adjective *unconscious* in Alon's account: How can this experience be unconscious if Alon reports it? It seems to me that *unconscious* here betrays the elusive quality of the affect produced by consuming food as a technology of the self: felt but not reflected on, or reflected on only in retrospect.

Finally, the logic of associations and dissociations that food promotes seems more complex than Bourdieu allowed for when he distinguished food preferences along the axes of class and gender, neglecting religion, ethnicity, and nationality.[89] Thus, aversion toward the taste of others is conceived as forming a barrier between the classes, although revulsion, disgust, and other forms of rejection are no less common reactions toward the food of subordinate ethnic, racial, or religious others.[90] Alternatively, in certain contexts a taste for specific food may come to embody a sense of national belonging, crossing class, gender, religious, and ethnic divisions. These two contradictory dynamics can mutually reinforce each other, as the "nationalization" of specific dishes might give rise to strategies of distinction between groups within the national collective, manifested in no less embodied notions of how they should be prepared and how, where, and when they should be consumed.

Where does all this take us? Food is integrated into consumption patterns whose meanings are contingent and contextual (eating hummus in a hummusiya at a Friday noon male gathering does not carry the same meaning as spreading factory hummus over bread at breakfast, which itself can mean different things in different contexts of consumption). Yet some meanings can attain a symbolic value and be formalized in discourse. Such is the case with hummus as an index of indigeneity and masculinity. For certain groups of self-styled Zionist "new men," Arab food was instrumental in the affective performance of an authentic, indigenous masculine self, and this lent it prestige among wider circles. Once hummus became naturalized in the culinary repertoire of Israelis, due to reasons that are not merely symbolic, these meanings were appropriated by other types of mediators who continued to promote them, even while their importance in motivating consumption may have waned.

So far, my discussion has focused on the semiotic aspects of consumption. Yet in reducing food consumption to a circulation of signs, as Michael Dietler cautions, we risk ignoring the crucial materiality of the food consumed and its embeddedness in economic systems of production and exchange.[91] The sociocultural career of hummus in Israel, and its relation to processes of identification and to attributions of authenticity, cannot be understood apart from its career as a commodity, which is contingent on its specific materiality and its affordances.

MATTER AND AUTHENTICITY

Numerous times have I been asked about the origins of hummus—a question more often than not motivated by political rather than culinary interest. But what do we mean by *origins*? A search for a genealogy of hummus immediately begs another question: with or without tahini? On the face of it, tahini is an essential ingredient, given that *hummus* is in fact shorthand for *hummus bi-tahine*, literally chickpeas with tahini.[92] Yet various speculations about the origins of the dish have ignored this question altogether. For example, when in 1957 journalist and Orientalist Menachem Kapeliuk suggested that the *hometz* in which biblical Boaz had invited Ruth to dip her bread[93] was not vinegar—the contemporary meaning of the Hebrew word *hometz*—but probably hummus, he described it as "that delicacy made of crushed pulses, thickened with oil and seasoned with spices," but no tahini.[94] (When in 2001 writer Meir Shalev repeated this thesis, he received much more attention than Kapeliuk.[95] But although it is occasionally taken up by various commentators, on the whole it remained marginal to the discourse on identity and appropriation.[96])

It is difficult to determine when chickpeas and tahini united for the first time. The earliest known recipe for a mash of cooked chickpeas, tahini, wine vinegar, pickled lemons, nuts, herbs, and spices appears in a Syrian cookbook from the mid-thirteenth century: *Kitāb al-wusla ilā l-habīb fī wasf al-tayyibāt wa-l-tīb* (*Winning the Beloved's Heart with Delectable Dishes and Perfumes*).[97]

Yet we do not know what the historical relationship between this dish and contemporary hummus bi-tahine looks like, or when mashed chickpeas with tahini became typical of the Levant (present-day Syria, Lebanon, Jordan, and Palestine/Israel). According to James Grehan, toward the end of the nineteenth century, hummus was sold on the streets of Damascus, especially in the cold winter months. Known recipes include *hummus bi-zayt*—mashed chickpeas mixed with olive oil, thyme, and cumin—and what Grehan defines as a variation of *musabbaha*: mashed chickpeas and tahini sprinkled with lemon or pomegranate juice, melted butter, and pistachios or pine nuts.[98] Yet he notes that earlier sources make no mention of these dishes, and even toward the end of the nineteenth century, they were virtually unknown outside of Damascus and must have been latecomers to local kitchens.[99]

Are all the dishes described above hummus? Are any of them? And does it make a difference? Questions regarding origins, identity/difference, and authenticity may become significant in the context of debates over ownership, especially where a politically charged dish such as hummus is concerned. Yet historical evidence is unlikely to conclude them. The answer to the question "is this the same dish?" can never be a neutral one but is a function of classification, which is always pertinent to specific ideological projects.[100]

This is not to argue for the primacy of meaning over matter. In recent decades, a perception of matter and material objects as generative and "agentive," rather than as inert objects of discourses and meanings, gained traction across the humanities and the social sciences.[101] Given that the material forms with which social actors interact "circumscribe, encourage and test their discourses," material objects do not lend themselves to completely arbitrary semiosis.[102] This is also true of symbolic objects, sites, and substances: rather than simply representing something other than themselves, their cultural power and social resonance are crucially shaped by their relational materiality and its affordances.[103] From this follows that the materiality of the sign vehicle in which the qualisign "Arabness" is embodied matters for its social and cultural career.

As my historical examples demonstrate, the name *hummus* can potentially be applied to substances that differ in their ingredients and preparation methods. Authenticity aside, hummus can be considered a *type* with different materializations. These materializations are produced not only through the application of preparation techniques to ingredients but also through other types of qualification processes—by producers, consumers, and other mediators.[104] Beyond simple tokens of the type hummus, they constitute a nexus of substances, models of consumption, and meanings.[105] What interests me here are both the perceptible properties of these materializations and the processes of qualification, differentiation, and claims/assumptions of identity/commensurability, which allow signs, meanings, and models of consumption to flow between them. It is through the conjunction of material and discursive qualification processes that matter becomes significant for attributions of authenticity and for the sociocultural career of hummus in Israel more broadly.[106]

For example, as the popularity of hummus increased and it became an object for distinction practices, it gained certain qualities, such as thickness, texture, and level of acidity. Such qualifications are contingent on the affordances of its specific materiality: the fact that the combination of a small number of ingredients allows producing a vast number of variations, differing in the type of basic ingredients (chickpea variety, tahini brand), their relative amount, grinding smoothness, additions, type and quality of olive oil, and so on and yet relatively similar in their substance (in this sense, the category hummus is more similar to the category wine than to the category cheese). Yet although these differences are "out there," they become discernible only through discursive mediation.

Among the affordances of the materiality of hummus, which have shaped its sociocultural career in Israel, one can mention the fact that hummus is *parve*—neither meat nor milk, making it permissible to eat at any time and with any food under Jewish dietary laws. But probably the most significant is its amenability to industrial replication in the form of a dish ready to eat, which can pass—at least with a sufficient number of consumers—as "hummus." The success of the industrial version makes hummus particularly susceptible to "authenticity tests."[107] There is no "authentic falafel/tahini/labaneh/ful" as there is "authentic hummus." These tests, which classify both the products and their consumers,[108] are related to the fact that most of the hummus consumed by most Israelis most of the time comes in a prepackaged container, which is nevertheless considered inferior to the "real thing"—hummus prepared in a hummusiya.

Authenticity is a complex and often contradictory predicate when applied to food. As a central value-granting attribute in contemporary consumer culture, it is highly cherished and sought after but also dismissed by many, primarily on the grounds of its constructed and unstable nature.[109] While scholarship on contemporary food discourse contains various definitions of authenticity, two general conceptions can be discerned. In the weaker first sense, "authenticity" indicates that something is true to its "type" (or category of classification), conforming to a set of expectations regarding how it should look, feel, or taste. The stronger second conception of authenticity, which is tied to specific values and carries moral connotations, refers to something being a true and sincere expression of individual or social nature.[110] In food discourse, these two conceptions are often intertwined. As Fabio Parasecoli writes,

> Authenticity denotes the expected adherence of ingredients, dishes, and customs to an idealized supposedly original form built on genuineness and the lack of artifice and pretension. It allows consumers to have direct access to the true nature not only of what they eat but also of the people that produce, cook and serve food to them. Its roots are to be found in time (the past), and in space (specific places). It can also refer to skills and techniques that are embedded in a world of artisans and producers with unique personalities and stories: the opposite of mass production. Despite the sophistication that "authentic" products may display, connotations of "simplicity" and "straightforwardness" remain important, especially when they are identified as exotic and "other."[111]

Applied to hummus, the adjective *authentic* at first usually stood for handmade, as opposed to industrially produced. With the emergence of a new gastronomic discourse in the second half of the 1980s, and increasingly in the following decades, authenticity became much more strongly associated with Arab producers. Indicative of this process is the establishment in Hebrew of the phrase *hummus asli* (Arabic for "authentic hummus," *asli* meaning "original") in this period (the word *hummus*, however, is pronounced in Hebrew as khumus, as opposed to the guttural *h* and the emphatic *m* in the Arabic).

However, while the association of "Arab hummus" with authenticity as provenance and sincere expression is based on the values of tradition and historicity, in relation to the first conception, authenticity is established based on material qualities. In 2015, I participated in a panel on hummus in the framework of a festival of Levantine food in Haifa, where two Palestinian chefs from Northern Israel, Habib Daud and Mu'in Halabi, held very strong opinions as to what "real hummus" should be like, with their definitions centering mainly on ingredients, taste, and texture (leaving many contemporary artisanal producers aspiring). As Daud recounted, he had been experimenting with hummus for the past fifteen years—the type of water, the type of chickpeas, the cooking time—and he contrasted the professionalism it takes to make "real hummus" with Arab women's home preparation (at the same time, he replicated the conception of authenticity as sincere expression when he stated in our conversation before the panel that genuine hummus existed in Palestine's cities before 1948; "the truth of hummus left in 1948," he said).[112]

Webb Keane suggested thinking about physical properties and qualities in terms of "bundling"—that is, specific combinations of qualities that may be contingently bound up in a specific object. "In any given practical or interpretative context," writes Keane, "only some of these properties are relevant and come into play. But other properties persist, available for promotion as circumstances change."[113] Thus, for Halabi tahini is essential for a dish of mashed chickpeas to be considered hummus (to wit, hummus bi-tahine). For claiming an ancient origin for hummus—it might not be. But the presence of tahini (and how much of it) may become significant in other ways and contexts—for instance, in the context of health discourse, when nutritional qualities are emphasized, or in contexts where reducing costs is a primary objective (since tahini is the most expensive ingredient in hummus, industrial hummus contains less tahini than homemade hummus, often supplemented by less-healthy vegetable oil). Specific projects or circumstances of production/consumption produce specific materializations.

The aforementioned panel on hummus also hosted Yaron Tzur, a food technologist working for one of the leading hummus brands, who brought with him three samples of hummus fresh out of the factory for tasting: one containing preservatives, one without any, and one with less acidity than the standard hummus product. His aim was to demonstrate that fresh industrial hummus tasted just like homemade hummus, since it was produced from the same ingredients; that contrary to popular belief, the preservatives in hummus had no discernible taste; and that the main perceptible difference between mass-produced and artisanal hummus resulted from the level of acidity required by the Israeli standard. While many hummus aficionados still vocally reject industrial hummus, such a move would not have been thinkable several decades back. As I will show, transformations in the substance of mass-produced hummus opened up a new terrain of semiotic possibilities.

HUMMUS BETWEEN THE ARTISANAL AND THE INDUSTRIAL, THE LOCAL AND THE GLOBAL

The symbolic value of hummus in Israel is linked to its perception as a quintessentially local dish, eaten in the region for generations. As I noted, in the differentiating discourse that has developed around hummus, the prototype for "real hummus" is hummus produced and consumed in a hummusiya (certainly not in a factory, but neither at home). The most basic distinction in this discourse is the one between industrial and artisanal hummus, which is itself an internally divided category. Yet the culinary and cultural career of hummus in Israel—its becoming a national symbol and a culinary cult—is inseparable from its industrialization and from global flows of people, discourses, commodities, and capital.

The contrast between artisanal and industrial hummus taps into a larger symbolic universe, which currently supports the growing popularity of hummus around the globe: that which contrasts authenticity and tradition to mass production, health to industry, slow to fast food, local production to global trade circuits.[114] As Anne Meneley writes, "[It] was when industrial food became readily available and cheap—and viewed with some derision and suspicion—that 'the Mediterranean' became the positive Other for the North Atlantic, largely defined in terms of food that was imagined to be artisanally, instead of industrially, produced."[115] True, most of the hummus consumed outside the Arab Middle East comes from a prepackaged tub; yet the success of industrial hummus is to a large extent dependent on the industry's ability to align its products with the concepts that occupy the positive pole of these oppositions.[116]

Meneley and others have complicated this picture, showing how the artisanal and the industrial, the local and the global are intertwined and mutually constitutive spheres of food production and consumption. First, what is considered "local," "traditional," and "artisanal" often incorporates phases of industrial production and various manifestations of global flows.[117] Second, as global models and commodities are embedded in local contexts, they are "localized" through the particular ways they are appropriated, qualified, and perceived by social actors.[118] Alternatively, various industrial and global commodities owe their prestige to their association with a particular locale.[119] Thus, industrially produced food from distant lands may bear the signature of authenticity, regardless of its being mass-produced. As Richard Wilk writes, the global/industrial food system includes simultaneous movements toward generification, homogeneity, and mass production, and new kinds of localization.[120]

Hummus in Israel is an interesting case study for the entanglement of the artisanal and the industrial, the local and the global. Unlike industrial-born commodities (like Coca-Cola), industrial hummus is a mass-produced replica of a dish that was previously consumed in its artisanal or homemade versions and became globally spread through mass production. And unlike localized global commodities (kosher McDonald's is a case in point), hummus embarked on its global career after it was already established in Israel as a local and "national" dish. While the globalization of hummus is beyond the scope of my discussion, I examine the effects of the industrialization and globalization of hummus, and of the firms producing it in Israel, on its culinary and cultural career.

Yet beyond merely highlighting the local/global and the artisanal/industrial entanglements, my analysis pays attention to the practical and the semiotic labor involved in constructing the relationship between the poles of these oppositions—sometimes bringing them closer to one another and at other times keeping them apart. These constructions, which graft material qualities, practices, and meanings, differ between historical periods and social actors. For example, if the first generation of industrial producers mainly tried to distinguish their hummus from that of "Oriental restaurants," contemporary producers are seeking to assimilate their hummus to that of hummus joints, appropriating the discourse on artisanal hummus and co-opting artisanal producers to their campaigns.

Moreover, the "local" in food discourse is never a simple factual descriptor, and hummus is no exception. First, given that the origins of hummus cannot be traced to a single nation-state, "local" remains an ambiguous attribute that can refer to a state, a region, even the entire Middle East. Second, over the years, both chickpea varieties and much of the ingredients used to produce hummus in Israel have been imported into the country. As Rachel Laudan writes, what makes a food or a cuisine "local" is not geography or agriculture but culture.[121] The Israeli food industry, for its part, capitalized on and promoted the perception of hummus as a distinctly local staple, advancing its nationalization on both practical and symbolic levels.

But if the process of constructing the "authentically local" is neither simple nor straightforward but based on highlighting certain relations and suppressing others,[122] how did the globalization of hummus-producing companies affect their localization strategies? What kind of strategies did these companies adopt in different contexts? Outside of Israel, "localization" of hummus is fraught with complications, given that hummus was consumed across the Levant before it spread to other regions and with the rise of the discourse on Israeli culinary appropriation, which is tightly related to the success of Israeli companies abroad. But inside Israel too, localization does not always reproduce a purely Jewish national imaginary. As I will show, industrial companies seeking to tie their products to the values of locality and authenticity reproduce both the discourse on hummus as an Israeli dish and the discourse that ties authenticity to its Arab source.

METHOD AND SOURCES

Although this study, like many before it, is devoted to a single comestible, consumption patterns do not occur in isolation but as part of a much broader and changing culinary landscape.[123] To date, the history of Israeli foodways has received little scholarly attention. Hence, to reconstruct the biography of hummus in the context of culinary transformations, this study draws on historical, sociological, and anthropological methods including archival research, analysis of published and digital sources, interviews, participant observation, and a random sample survey.

Archival materials include sources on varied topics, ranging from Arab and Jewish food venues during the Mandate period, through data on Israeli importation of chickpeas and nutrition education after the foundation of the state, to data on the sales of Telma's industrial hummus and Telma-filmed commercials.[124] Published sources included books containing descriptions of food consumption patterns in both Jewish and Palestinian societies; cookbooks; guidebooks on hummus restaurants in Israel and the Occupied Territories; publications of industrial companies; literary works; articles pertaining to hummus cultivation, trade, and production from professional and semiprofessional journals; and publications of the Israel Central Bureau of Statistics. A wealth of additional sources related to hummus were collected from the internet and social media, including articles from online food journals and news portals, blog entries, institutional sites, Facebook groups, and Instagram pages. A most valuable source were digitalized archives of daily newspapers published in Palestine and Israel—fourteen relevant newspapers, all but one in Hebrew, were available for keyword search, some dating back to the Mandate period, and one extending from 1939 to the present.[125]

I conducted forty-nine semistructured face-to-face and phone interviews with owners of restaurants and hummus joints; with food experts in general and "hummus experts" in particular; with writers and journalists; with different actors in the food industry; with agronomists and agriculturalists involved in chickpea cultivation and experimentation; and with elderly Palestinians and Mizrahi Jews.[126] Face-to-face interviews, which usually lasted between one and two hours, were recorded, transcribed, and analyzed. Beyond formal interviews, I held numerous conversations with restaurant owners, journalists, industry people, and others and documented each of them afterward, in as much detail as I could remember. Film director Trevor Graham has kindly shared with me recordings of interviews he conducted in the framework of research for a documentary on hummus (fifteen interviews with culinary experts, food journalists, chefs, small food producers, and industry people—Palestinian, Lebanese, Israeli, and others).[127] In addition, I conducted participant observation at various hummus-related events such as hummus tours, the hummus record event at Abu Ghosh, and hummus festivals and events organized by industrial companies. I was also given tours of the Strauss factory in Karmiel and the Tzabar factory in Kiryat Gat.

Finally, I conducted a random sample phone survey of the adult Jewish population on hummus consumption habits and perceptions about hummus (n = 502).[128]

The survey contained fifty-five questions, primarily multiple choice, with several open-ended questions. Most questions pertained to present-day hummus consumption and preparation habits as well as to perceptions about hummus, but there were also several questions about food and cultural consumption habits more generally. The purpose of the survey was to assess the prevalence of certain hummus-related practices and perceptions and to test the relationship between hummus consumption patterns and cultural capital.

CHAPTER-BY-CHAPTER OUTLINE

This book is organized both chronologically and thematically. Each chapter is dedicated to a different period (except for the last two chapters, which cover approximately the same period) and highlights a specific phase in the culinary and cultural career of hummus in Israel. In chapter 1, "Early Culinary Contacts," I discuss culinary contacts between Jews and Arabs prior to the foundation of the Israeli state in 1948, focusing on four channels of culinary mediation: social encounters in Palestine's "mixed cities"; labor relations in the agricultural colonies; commercial venues; and nutritional advice. As this chapter shows, before 1948, European Jewish settlers' most common attitude to local food—usually marked as "Oriental" and sometimes as "Arab"—was either disinterest or outright rejection. Nevertheless, several ingredients and dishes from the Palestinian menu did make inroads into specific European Jewish sectors, and some—primarily falafel—even gained popularity, especially among the young.

Chapter 2, "'The East Conquers the Stomachs of the West,'" is devoted to the establishment of hummus in the food repertoire of Israeli Jews during the first decade of statehood, albeit at this stage mostly as an "exotic" element, not yet enjoying a special status or prestige. Two main processes contributed to the growing consumption of hummus in this period: food rationing and meat shortage; and the arrival of a mass immigration of Jews from North Africa and the Middle East. The chapter examines both the sphere of commercial food venues, focusing on Middle Eastern restaurants and food stalls, where most Jews encountered hummus, and the sphere of nutrition education, where hummus, falafel, tahini, and other Arab staples were integrated into suggestions for an Israeli menu as a "culinary mosaic." Finally, I discuss a specific group of cultural entrepreneurs—self-styled Zionist "New Men"—who mediated the consumption of various Arab foods as signifiers of indigeneity and masculinity to a wider circle of consumers.

Chapter 3, "Nationalism in a Can," focuses on the Israelization of hummus between the late 1950s, when hummus was first industrialized by an Israeli company, and the early 1980s. This chapter shows how, in a period of heightened state investment in industrialization on the one hand and institutionalized efforts to shape a unique Israeli culture and Israeli style on the other hand, the food industry played a pivotal role in marking and marketing hummus as an Israeli national dish and in facilitating its penetration into the Ashkenazi domestic menu. The chapter discusses various initiatives intended to shape a symbolic Israeli national cuisine in the context of the growing consumer culture and tourism industry. It then examines the role of the food industry in the production and dissemination of both products and meanings related to hummus. The final sections examine the Israeli "discovery" of Palestinian restaurants and hummus joints in the wake of the 1967 occupation of the West Bank and the Gaza Strip. The spread of industrial hummus in this period, and the encounter with Palestinian hummus, led to the emergence of a concept of "authentic hummus" as well as to the Israeli adoption of the model of the hummus restaurant and hummus as a meal.

Chapter 4, "The Gourmetization of Hummus and the Return of the Repressed Arab," focuses on the period between the late 1980s and the present. In this period of culinary transformations, consumption of hummus increased, and it became the object of a passionate discourse and a medium for distinction practices, leading to the "gourmetization" of certain versions. As I show in this chapter, developments outside and within the culinary field led to the revaluation of hummus made by Arabs as better and more authentic than hummus made by Jews. This chapter examines the transformation of the culinary field in this period, the differentiation between hummus versions, and the association of Arabness with quality and authenticity. It also discusses the role of various cultural mediators in promoting Israeli-Palestinian "coexistence" through food consumption in the context of the "peace process." I will also briefly discuss what seems like a gradual decoupling of Arabness and attributions of authenticity in recent years.

Chapter 5, "Made with Love: Mass Produced Authenticity," focuses on the entry of powerful and globally active food corporations into the packaged salads market and their central role in turning hummus into a national symbol and a culinary cult. As this chapter shows, the development of hummus products commensurable with artisanal hummus supported the transfer of signs from the artisanal to the industrial domain, prioritizing those related to national localism but also to Arab authenticity. The chapter discusses the changes in the hummus market following the entry of these corporations and their competing branding strategies. It then discusses the "hummus wars" between Israel and Lebanon in the context of the competition over global markets. Finally, it examines how the companies' branding and marketing strategies, particularly their blending of the industrial and the artisanal domains, enhanced the ubiquity of hummus in the lifeworld of Israelis, both as a culinary element and as a subject of endless discourse.

A NOTE ON TERMINOLOGY

If terminology is often a complicated and controversial issue in the context of Palestine/Israel, it is only because this history itself is complicated and controversial, replete with politically contested concepts and porous and partially overlapping categories of affiliation. Throughout the book, I have adopted a context-specific use of terms while acknowledging that any choice of terminology is politically informed and inflected.

One terminological challenge arises out of the ambiguity of identity categories in the Israeli-Palestinian case. When speaking of national groups, the obvious designations would be *Israelis* and *Palestinians* (some of the latter are citizens of Israel and therefore, strictly speaking, Israeli, yet the term *Israeli* usually refers to Israeli Jews—part of the distortions of citizenship in the settler state). However, prior to the foundation of the Israeli state in 1948 there were no Israelis, and therefore the accepted national designation is *Jews*. Yet *Jews* may also refer to religion and ethnicity (sometimes understood as "race"). The term *Palestinians* is also not without its complications. During the Mandate period, the term *Palestinian* was not yet used to denote a national identity and could refer to Palestine's Jews as well (some of whom were indigenous to Palestine). When discussing the Mandate period, I therefore use the collective designations of *Jews* and *Arabs* (and sometimes *Palestinian Arabs*). After 1948, I generally use *Israeli / Israeli Jews* and *Palestinians / Palestinian Arabs*, except when I refer to sectors within the Israeli citizenry, when I often use *Arabs* to avoid the more cumbersome *Palestinian citizens of Israel*.

Given the salience of the East/West division in Israeli society, which usually tramples the subdivision into countries of descent, I use the overarching categories of *Mizrahim* (singular Mizrahi) and *Ashkenazim* (singular Ashkenazi) to refer to Jews of Asian and North African descent and to Jews of European descent, respectively. Importantly, the distinction between Ashkenazim and Mizrahim, understood in Israel as an ethnic distinction, refers to relative and racialized positions within the Israeli social space rather than to coherent groups sharing a set of common traits.[129] While most Mizrahim descended from Arab countries, some descended from non-Arab countries such as Turkey, Iran, India, Georgia, and Uzbekistan. Nevertheless, in Israel they were lumped together under the title of *the Eastern communities* (ʿedot hamizrah), which was later replaced with the more affirmative self-designation *Mizrahim*.

I use the term *Oriental* as an equivalent to the Hebrew adjective *mizrahi* (lit. eastern), especially in culinary contexts (the Hebrew word for Oriental—*orientali*—is usually used to refer to the Middle East rather than to Southeast Asia; and like the term *Oriental*, it usually carries derogatory connotations, albeit less so in culinary contexts). Thus, the term *Oriental cuisine* (*mitbach Mizrahi*) refers to an overarching category of the food of the Middle East. Likewise *Oriental restaurant* (*mis'ada mizrahit*) refers to a restaurant serving Middle Eastern food (usually a selection of grilled meat and fish, vegetable dishes, and a selection of salads, with local variations).

When it comes to cuisine, complications abound. Priscilla Ferguson defined cuisine as the "cultural construct which systematizes culinary practices . . . into a stable cultural code."[130] Yet given the lack of overlap between political units and culinary practices, categorization of foodways into cuisines is not always that stable. The cuisines of the Arab Middle East share ingredients and dishes, yet there are also differences between them.[131] I use the overarching category *Middle Eastern food* either to reflect a contemporary designation or to highlight the family resemblance between cuisines. At other instances, a more specific category is appropriate—for instance, when referring to the cuisine of Palestinian Arabs. Palestinian cuisine is considered part of a broader category of Levantine cuisine. In some contexts, however, it would make no sense to refer to *Levantine cuisine*—for example, when seeking to convey the emic Jewish perception of Palestinian food. In this context, I alternately refer to *local food, Palestinian Arab cuisine*, or *food from the Palestinian menu*. The cuisines of Mizrahi Jews were those of their specific countries of descent, adapted to Jewish dietary restrictions. Thus, when I speak of *Mizrahi dishes*, I do not mean to suggest that these dishes were specific to Jews but to point at Mizrahi Jews, rather than Palestinians, as their source.

Finally, to remain faithful to the language of the sources, I use a range of terms throughout the book to describe hummus, including *dish, salad, dip, spread*, and *puree* (when highlighting its texture). These varied descriptors reflect the versatility of hummus and its diverse modes of preparation and consumption.

ONE

—◊—

EARLY CULINARY CONTACTS

Chickpea (Hummus): Peel the cooked chickpeas, mash it and mix in the salad tahini, oil and lemon.

—Lilian Cornfeld, How to Cook at Times of War, 1942[*]

IN WINTER 1941, JOURNALIST DOROTHY KAHN BAR-ADON complained about the Jewish avoidance of cheap, nourishing, and tasty local products, "popular with the Orientals," that domestic science institutions had been advocating since the outbreak of the war. Predating critiques of "cultural food colonialism" by half a century, she wrote, "There are people who have lived in Palestine for decades without ever tasting the dishes prepared by Arabs and Oriental Jews. There are others who slip into an Oriental restaurant once in a while for a lark, like you go to a Chinese restaurant in New York for a bit of chop suey and gumquats [*sic*] on sticks. But the foods are never taken seriously as food." Kahn Bar-Adon predicted that "only the sheerest necessity will make a dent in the wall of resistance" and added, "Food habits cling. There are many Eastern Europeans who have never learned to eat olives!"[1]

By comparing Oriental restaurants in Palestine to Chinese restaurants in New York, Kahn Bar-Adon suggested that for Jews of European descent, Middle Eastern food, if noticed at all, was at most "exotic."[2] Indeed, most Jews who arrived in Palestine in the first half of the twentieth century treated the local food, to which they were exposed primarily through commercial channels, with suspicion. Various ingredients used were unfamiliar; tastes were strange and sometimes repellent; such food was often considered dirty and even dangerous, especially food sold on the street or in simple eateries.

If European Jews adopted anything at all from the Palestinian menu, it was mostly vegetable ingredients rather than dishes. Yet by the end of the Mandate period, some local dishes had become familiar and even popular, mainly among the young. First among them was falafel. Hummus, too, was beginning to gain traction, although it took longer to strike roots among the population of the settlers.

In this chapter, I discuss several spheres of culinary contact and culinary mediation prior to the establishment of the Israeli state. These ranged from the commercial sphere to the arena of nutrition education and circles of sociality, where food moved in more than one direction. Although this book's protagonist is hummus, given that most Jewish settlers had not yet discovered hummus in this period, I discuss their encounters with a broader range of Arab foods as well as the experiences and meanings attached to specific acts and practices of consumption.

While correct in some respects, Kahn Bar-Adon's analogy missed an important point: in certain Zionist circles, the symbolic value and affective resonance of Palestinian food derived not only from its perception as exotic but also, predominantly, from its being native to the land. True, necessity created by war and food shortage served as a catalyst for trying and sometimes adopting new foods.[3] Yet for certain groups of Zionist settlers, it was food's capacity to index transformation within performances of an indigenous self that made various Arab dishes and ingredients worth incorporating into their menu and learning to like. The Israeli career of Arab food in general, and hummus in particular, was not shaped by these "inside meanings" alone, not even primarily.[4] Yet, such affective acts of consumption by a small group of cultural mediators shaped the meanings attached to them for years to come.

HUMMUS IN PALESTINIAN FOODWAYS

Palestinian Arab cuisine is part of the highly elaborate cuisine of the Levant (*al-Sham*).[5] It is based on the rich variety of plants and animals native to the region—the western part of the Fertile Crescent. Since the last decades of the nineteenth century, the growth in foreign trade and the flow of capital into the country have led to an expansion of the range of available products.[6] The majority of the country's inhabitants, however, were fed mainly on local crops, which formed the mainstay of the cuisine—primarily cereal grains, vegetables, and legumes. The consumption of animal products was limited, although demand for meat increased in the cities throughout the Mandate period (1918–48), as did the demand for imported foods—both signs of distinction—among the burgeoning middle class.[7]

Chickpea was one of the most prevalent crops in the country and consequently an important ingredient in the Palestinian kitchen. According to Jewish agronomist Aaron Aaronsohn, chickpea was "one of the most valuable legumes grown in Palestine," which was "excellently adapted for use as a rotation crop before wheat."[8] Its advantages were many: it did not require a too careful preparation of the soil; its yield was high—twelve bushels to the acre in a good year; and it sold for as much as wheat and often for more. It was also resilient in arid environments and provided hay for the animals for the dry season. Hence, chickpea was cultivated in the upper Galilee and central and southern Palestine—each area with its typical varieties.[9]

Chickpeas were prepared and eaten in multiple ways: fresh or dry, cooked or roasted, whole or pounded into small pieces, mixed with spices and fried (falafel), or, less frequently, ground into flour, which was added to sorghum or barley flour to create a special kind of thick flatbread (*talami*).[10] Half-raw seeds were eaten straight or roasted in the oven, sometimes wetted and covered with salt, or crushed and mixed with sugar and eaten as a candy. Powdered roasted chickpeas were also mixed with olive oil, crushed Za'atar (hyssop) leaves, sesame, sumac, and salt to create a dip for bread.[11] Whole cooked chickpeas were either part of vegetable, rice, or bulgur dishes; served in olive oil, lemon juice, garlic, and spices (*balila*); or mashed into a puree and seasoned.

Although what we call hummus today is shorthand for hummus bi-tahine, in the Mandate period *hummus* could stand for mashed cooked chickpeas prepared without tahini, which was the more expensive ingredient. In his extensive ethnography of Palestinian rural life during the 1920s, German theologian and Orientalist Gustaf Dalman mentions a beloved chickpea dish called *madmūsa*, *mahrus* (boiled, mashed)—chickpeas soaked for a day, cooked, pounded with a wooden pestle (*medakka*), and seasoned with salt, lemon juice, olive oil, and garlic.[12] In 1925, the British government lifted the customs on sesame, which lowered the price of tahini, but it was still relatively expensive and therefore not always used.[13]

More often than not, hummus was prepared and consumed at home; several interviewees described Saturday as hummus and falafel day.[14] Gloria E. (b. 1925) recalled how the entire family participated in the preparation of the weekly hummus, falafel, and salad meal. In a counter-nostalgic moment, she noted that since there were no food processors, the hummus was not as good as it is today.[15] Writing about his youth in the 1940s, Palestinian writer Hisham Sharabi tells about the magnificent rooftop dinners he used to have with his friend in Acre: the friend's mother prepared fish they had caught on the same day, together with tahini, hummus, baba ghanoush, and fried bread.[16]

Figure 1.1 Palestinians eating hummus, 1935. Photo by Elia Kahvedjian, Elia Studio Jerusalem.

Hummus was also served in restaurants, where it was usually eaten before or alongside meat dishes, and in "hummus restaurants," where it was either consumed on the spot, as a meal in and of itself, or bought in bulk for home consumption. In some smaller restaurants and hummus restaurants, chickpeas were mashed, mixed with tahini, and seasoned for each individual customer, and for regular ones, the dishes were prepared according to their taste.[17] With the proliferation of restaurants and Western-style cafés in the 1930s and especially in the 1940s, hummus could be found on the menus of more upscale restaurants or of cafés serving food. In the mid-1940s, a serving of hummus in a simple restaurant cost between 20 and 25 mils—the same as mjaddara, a bit more than *ful* (a dish of fava beans cooked to a porridge), which cost 15–20 mils, a bit less than stuffed vegetables or stuffed intestines (30 mils and 33 mils, respectively).[18] It was not the food of the poor, as is sometimes assumed, but rather simple food that was nevertheless considered a treat.

CHANNELS OF CULINARY CONTACT AND CULINARY MEDIATION

According to Sami Zubaida, Middle Eastern foodways, while far from homogeneous, are nevertheless describable in a vocabulary and set of idioms that are "often comprehensible, if not familiar, to the socially diverse parties" and within which "differences and boundaries are drawn and redrawn, negotiated and altered."[19] For Jews who arrived in Palestine from across the Middle East, Palestinian Arab food and foodways were "comprehensible, if not familiar," even if some of the dishes were previously unknown to most of them, as was the case with hummus bi-tahine, given that only a minority arrived from the Levant.[20] There was nothing extraordinary or exotic in the consumption (and sometimes preparation and selling) of local Arab food.

For those who hailed from Europe, in contrast, many ingredients and tastes were unfamiliar (or familiar but disliked, such as tomatoes). Others were not necessarily unfamiliar or disliked but were prepared in unfamiliar ways, using ingredients that were unpalatable for Europeans, such as specific spices or the strong-tasting olive oil. This was the case with chickpeas, which back in Europe were consumed in small amounts and mostly eaten boiled.[21] In 1936, it was reported in *Davar* that Jewish prisoners suffered greatly because they could not get used to the prison menu: for breakfast, pita bread "from very bad flour" and halva or twenty olives; for lunch, two pita breads and "porridge of chickpeas or lentils," sometimes with additional eggs.[22] Today these foods are well liked in Israel, even if not necessarily in their prison versions.

Yet, far from being merely a matter of habit, differences of taste are strongly affected by hierarchies of prestige: most Jewish newcomers did not find Middle Eastern cuisines worthy of attention or appreciation.[23] Writing about Palestinian food and foodways in 1901, surgeon and scholar E. W. G. Masterman reflected this attitude when he noted that "the preparation of many of the most popular native dishes is long and tedious, and the result, it must be confessed, does not usually impress the western palate as being worth the trouble taken over it."[24]

Nevertheless, as I will show, ingredients, recipes, and dishes did flow between ethnic and religious groups through several channels of contact and mediation, including social and commercial encounters and nutritional advice. I divide my discussion of social encounters into two types, which occurred in different social settings: social encounters between neighbors and friends in ethnically diverse neighborhoods, and labor encounters in the colonies. In each of these settings, culinary transfer attained different functions and different meanings.

SOCIAL ENCOUNTERS AND CULINARY TRANSFER

In her family memoir, Rachel Seri recounts the lives of her parents, Badur al-Naddaf and Suleiman al-Seri, who, after their marriage, made their home in the Jerusalem neighborhood Nachlat Zion. Badur's family had arrived in Palestine from Yemen in 1882, when she was still a child.[25] They were part of a growing Jewish migration in the second half of the nineteenth century, both from Europe and from the Middle East, that turned the country's small Jewish minority of ten thousand into a larger minority of sixty-five to eighty-five thousand (around 10 percent of the general population) on the eve of WWI.[26] Nachlat Zion had recently been founded by an Iraqi Jewish businessman and offered cheap housing with convenient payment terms outside the Old City walls.[27] It attracted an ethnically diverse population, mostly of Jews from all over the Middle East, including Syria, Yemen, Persia, and Turkey, but also Sephardi Jews from the Balkan and some Ashkenazim. Within this milieu, social and neighborly encounters were accompanied by an exchange of dishes, recipes, and sometimes cooking and eating models.[28]

Treating neighbors to whatever one cooked that came out well was a common habit among the neighborhood's women.[29] Badur began to incorporate into her Yemenite menu dishes she had learned from neighbors from diverse ethnic backgrounds, including Ashkenazi noodle kugel, Sephardic *pastelicos*, and Aleppo pickles.[30] Every day, Arab and Jewish food vendors came into the neighborhood, offering their merchandise in several languages (Hebrew, Arabic, Ladino, and Yiddish).[31] Badur's menu diversified, and she started to cook a different dish every day, as she had learned from her Sephardi neighbors.[32] New dishes also came from the Palestinian Arab kitchen: her husband tried to teach her to prepare his beloved dish, *siniya* (meat, vegetables, and spices placed on a copper tray and cooked in the oven), which he may have encountered through interacting with Arabs or Sephardi Jews in the public sphere.[33] Sometimes men who played games together in a café bought the ingredients, placed them on a tray, and asked the delivery person to carry it to the neighborhood oven.[34] Rachel's uncle Haim, who was in the milk delivery business, bought his milk from various Arab families, with whom he also maintained social relationships, including mutual hosting and sometimes sleepovers.[35] As was customary wherever Jews and Arabs lived side by side, his Arab friends used to bring the family large trays of butter, cheese, milk, *laban*, honey, and hot flatbreads, decorated with flowers, on the last day of Passover.[36]

Recent scholarship challenges the view—shaped retrospectively through a nationalist optic—of Palestine's Jews before Zionism as a separate and homogenous community, antagonistic to the Arab majority, highlighting instead the cultural and organizational differences between Jewish communities and the existence of a public sphere of interaction between Jews and Arabs and between members of different Jewish ethnic and religious groups.[37] In cities like Jerusalem and Jaffa, Jews and Arabs often lived in the same neighborhoods and maintained business, trade, social, and neighborly relations.[38] While it was mainly Sephardi Jews who integrated into the country's rapidly expanding economic and cultural sectors, sections of the Ashkenazi communities did too.[39] Several scholars argue for the existence of a distinctly local identity of "Arab Jew" that became extinct with Zionism's rise to hegemony among the majority of Palestine's Jews.[40]

According to Jacob Yehoshua, Arab villagers who came to Jerusalem to sell their produce demanded higher prices from Ashkenazi women, since they considered them "strangers."[41] Yet Ashkenazim residing in ethnically diverse cities also maintained business, leisure, and sometimes social contacts with Arabs and with Sephardi Jews, which led to the exchange of dishes.[42] Ita Yellin, who arrived in Palestine from Russia in 1879, at the age of twelve, describes in her memoir the Lag Ba'Omer celebration and pilgrimage to the tomb of Shimon HaTzadik as an arena for the exchange of food between ethnic groups: people used to bring food from home and share it with children, friends, and neighbors. The celebration was well attended by wealthy Muslim and Christian Arabs as well as by Arab vendors who sold food and drink.[43] In general, Jews and Arabs often participated in each other's religious festivals.[44] Yellin herself used to cook both dishes she had learned from her Russian mother and Iraqi dishes she had learned from her mother-in-law.[45] Yet marriage between Ashkenazi and Sephardi Jews was relatively rare.[46]

In sources on the early transfer of food through social contacts, hummus bi-tahine is hardly mentioned. One exception is found in a book by Howard Sacher, where he notes the adoption of various items of Arab culture by the Sephardi Castel family, including "churned *humus* and *techina*."[47] Two other cases came up in oral testimonies: in both, present-day hummus makers were using a recipe they obtained from one of their parents, who had learned to prepare it from Arab neighbors in the Old City of Jerusalem.[48]

With the advancement of Zionist settlement after the institution of the British Mandate and the intensification of Palestinian resistance to Zionism, which led to several waves of violent clashes, the social and spatial realities in Palestine became increasingly divided. Contacts between Jews and Arabs never stopped, but residential patterns became more segregated, and everyday encounters were more limited to specific sectors or to specific spheres of life, such as commerce.[49] The growing influx of Jews from the Middle East, against the backdrop of Zionist Westernization, enhanced the internal division between Ashkenazim and Mizrahim, with the latter being viewed by Ashkenazi Zionists as the "Orient within." This distinction, which had social, spatial, and cultural manifestations, was reflected in Ashkenazi reactions to Mizrahi food and eating habits. Polish-born Ora Shem-Or describes in her memoir a meal at the home of a Mizrahi childhood friend: "The way they moved their hands, their jarring voice, the ragged clothes, the animalistic manner of eating [sitting on the floor and dipping their hands in a bowl of ful], the blinking eyes and smacking lips, the scratching under the arm, I have never seen anything like that in my entire life."[50] Shem-Or recounts how she tried to mitigate her gut reaction through rational argumentation, but in vain. Her reaction calls to mind Kristeva's definition of the abject as "above all a revolt against an external menace from which one wants to distance oneself, but of which one has the impression that it may menace us from the inside."[51]

CULINARY CONTACTS IN THE AGRICULTURAL COLONIES

The Jewish agricultural colonies were also sites of culinary contacts between Jews and Arabs. Colonists' adoption of ingredients and dishes from the Arab menu often occurred as a matter of course and necessity, even as it was invested with symbolic meaning. Regardless of its underlying motivations, it persisted primarily where interactions—mainly in the context of labor relations—were regular and frequent.

The first colonies were established in the late 1870s by Orthodox Jews, among them descendants of Jerusalem's Ashkenazi community. They were part of a wider international movement seeking to turn Jews into productive and rooted people through "return to the soil."[52] They were soon followed by colonies established by groups of nationally minded Jews from Eastern Europe. The colonies came under the patronage of Jewish philanthropists and depended on Arab labor: both day laborers and *harathin*, who lived on the farm, sometimes with their families, and maintained intensive interaction with the farmers.[53]

Until 1900, most colonies were based on plantations and a minority on field crops. Following the economic crisis at the turn of the century, the Jewish Colonization Association (JCA), which took over the responsibility for the colonies, instituted a more varied agricultural scheme comprising plantations, field crops, and auxiliary farms of vegetables and livestock.[54] Chickpea became one of the most prevalent crops in the colonies, and experiments were carried out with different varieties in order to increase its yield.[55] Locally cultivated crops like wheat, lentils, and chickpea became central items on the menu of the colonies, and ways to prepare them were often learned from the wives of the *harathin*.

The culinary repertoire that developed in the colonies was a pastiche of European and local Arab foods and preparation methods. In his memoir,

Mescha-born Yigal Alon (1918–80) lists the products his family used to buy on their shopping trips to Haifa, to stock up for the winter: sugar, halva, small barrels of herring, and cans of smoked fish, sardines, and Australian bully-beef. Olive oil was bought from the neighboring Arab village. The *taboon* (a dome-shaped clay oven) was used to bake both bread and flatbreads, and milk was used to prepare butter, cream, cheese, and laban as well as *labaneh* in olive oil. Vegetables and legumes common in the Palestinian kitchen, such as marrows, eggplants, tomatoes, chickpeas, and lentils, were used for cooking soups and stews. Wild plants and herbs, such as Za'atar, *hubeiza* (mallow), and *akkoub* (gundelia), were also picked and cooked.[56]

An Arab dish frequently encountered on the menu of the colonies was mjaddara, made of bulgur and lentils. Lentils were eaten in abundance: when it turned out that the first Jewish worker who was sent to Mescha did not like lentils, his hostess reacted with indignation.[57] According to Tzvi Nadav, a meal at a Metula farmer's home contained cooked lentils with oil, green olives, and "tasty Galilee bread," baked in a taboon, whereas a meal he ate in Mescha consisted of mjaddara, followed by cooked pigeons and, finally, noodle soup.[58] Chickpeas were more often eaten boiled than mashed, although mashed chickpeas were sometimes prepared, most likely without tahini.[59] These dishes supplemented though did not replace Eastern European dishes like borscht, chicken soup with *kneidlach*, and cholent baked in the taboon.

Adopting items of Arab culture in the early colonies was not limited to food, although it was usually confined to the more mundane and nonprestigious registers of culture.[60] The colonies were a laboratory for cultural experimentation intended to shape an indigenous Jewish national culture. Although culture-building initiatives in the colonies did not congeal into a coherent and unified repertoire, a consciousness of indigeneity and a set of shared public and private cultural practices to manifest it did develop among the locally born generation.[61] Within that set, various items of Arab culture functioned as indices of rootedness and often also masculinity. In many stories of the period, the image of the Arab-looking Jew on horseback marked the transformation from foreign settlers into rooted "natives."[62] The Arabs themselves, however, were often depicted as lazy and primitive.[63]

Appropriation of Arab cultural items continued among the "idealistic workers" of the "second immigration wave" (1904–14). The first workers arrived in Palestine with the intention of becoming agricultural proletariat in the Jewish colonies. Yet the colonists preferred to hire Arab workers, who were cheaper and more experienced. The workers' predicament was solved through the establishment of collectivist agricultural settlements (kibbutz and moshav), which guaranteed the Jewish hold of purchased land and monopoly over labor.[64] Among the workers, the group most associated with the appropriation of Arab cultural practices and products was the Hashomer paramilitary organization, which operated between 1909 and 1920. Hashomer members adopted Bedouin and Circassian forms of dress, practiced various Arab customs (such as performing a "fantasia" on horseback), and used Arab words and expressions in their spoken Yiddish.[65] The earliest case I came across of eating hummus bi-tahine and roasted meat in an Arab restaurant was written by a former member of Hashomer and refers to the early 1910s.[66] Gur Alroey describes the confrontational attitude of Hashomer, which often provoked violence rather than defended against it.[67] Not only Arabs but also colonists who employed Arab workers were subject to violence and threats.[68] In Hashomer, the principle of masculine revival through struggle with the "natives" in order to inherit and *become* the natives received its most lucid expression.[69]

In various texts by idealistic workers, consuming local products that were shunned at first, like olives and tomatoes, appears as an index for "striking roots."[70] Tzvi Nishri wrote, "We were told that whoever wants to strike roots in the country has to get used to eating olives, the more the better." He described how they used to eat many green olives before every meal.[71] Sara Malkin tells how during lunch break in a Petach Tikva orchard Arab and Jewish workers had the same food for lunch: bread and olives, cheese and onion.[72] Town dwellers were called "herrings" (though herrings, when available, never vanished from the workers' tables).[73]

Such symbolism was grafted on a reality of shortage. Beyond anything else, the menu of the early workers' collectives was shaped by availability and scarcity. Cereals, legumes (chickpeas, lentils, and beans), and cheap vegetables like eggplants were the main ingredients, which were prepared as soups, porridges, or simple stews (sometimes barely edible, for lack of cooking knowledge) and eaten with bread.[74] Golda Meir recalled how in early 1920s Merchavia, chickpeas were eaten as soup (cooked with onion), as porridge, and in the evening as "salad" (ground with onion).[75] Occasionally, wild herbs and mushrooms were also picked and cooked, following the Arab example.[76] The growth and institutionalization of the labor movement went hand in hand with the Europeanization of its diet. On most Jewish farms, except for those that continued to employ Arab workers, chickpea was abandoned: its picking was one of the most arduous agricultural tasks, and the local variety was unsuitable for picking with a combine harvester, which was widely used in the Jewish agricultural sector since the 1930s.[77] By the early 1940s, consumption of legumes decreased significantly and came to resemble the amounts consumed by urban Ashkenazim.[78]

In her 1941 article on Jewish avoidance of "Oriental food," Kahn Bar-Adon quoted a former kibbutz member, who told her that for the past twenty years she had been trying to introduce tahini into the communal settlements but without success.[79] Only as late as the early 1960s, several Middle Eastern dishes were served once a week in some kibbutzim, to "spice up" the European menu. According to a report in the Labor newspaper *Davar*, this change was met with enthusiasm only by the younger generation.[80]

ENCOUNTERS IN THE COMMERCIAL SPHERE

Despite the symbolic and practical significance of the agricultural sector for the Zionist project, its demographic share was small. Most Zionist settlers encountered local food in urban commercial settings. The Mandate years were a period of accelerated urbanization: among Palestinian Arabs, the share of urban dwellers increased from 21 percent in 1880 to 36 percent toward the end of the Mandate, mostly due to labor migration from the countryside, while the Jews were a predominantly urban population throughout the period.[81] In both communities, a middle class had developed, showing an increasing inclination toward consumption and leisure.[82] Consequently, the commercial food scene expanded and diversified, with establishments such as street stalls, eateries, cafés, and restaurants catering to a diverse clientele—from single men seeking sustenance to middle-class individuals in search of recreation as well as tourists, British officials and soldiers, and various other groups.

From the early 1930s to the end of British rule, half of the Palestinian urban dwellers lived in what the government defined as "mixed cities"—cities and towns with significant Arab and Jewish populations. Among Jewish urban dwellers, the percentage living in mixed cities decreased from 78 percent to 48 percent between 1922 and 1946.[83] Out of the seven mixed cities, it was mainly Jaffa, Haifa, and Jerusalem that were characterized by a modernizing, capitalist, and cosmopolitan urbanity. In these cities, the trends of spatial and social segregation, exacerbated in the wake of violent confrontations, coexisted alongside shared neighborhoods, intercommunal interactions, commercial partnerships, and other forms of collaboration.[84] Yet, even in places and periods where trends of separation prevailed, ethnic and religious boundaries were constantly crossed.[85] Indeed, food was a realm in which such boundary crossings took place on a regular basis.

The most common channel for commercial culinary encounters between Jews and Arabs was street vending. Arab street vendors sold food and foodstuffs in shared commercial spaces such as the Hamra Square in Haifa, or, since the early 1920s, the Carmel market area in Tel Aviv, but many also sold their merchandise in exclusively Jewish neighborhoods.[86] Street vendors sold either raw products or prepared foods such as falafel, ful, hummus, *mashawi* (roasted meat), *hamle malan* (roasted chickpea pods), *ka'k* (ring-shaped pastry with sesame or Za'atar), and sweets, including a candy made from a mix of thinly crushed chickpeas and sugar. Some sold drinks from big kettles or flasks, like *sahlab, sus* (a sweet drink made from licorice roots), tamarind juice, and lemonade.[87]

Restaurants were few and far between in the late Ottoman period and typically confined to urban commercial centers. The early restaurants catered primarily to hungry men—bachelors or married men working away from home—and travelers. The main establishment for (male) sociality and recreation in Palestinian society, as in the rest of the Middle East, was the café, where men went to drink coffee or tea, smoke, play dice, read newspapers (or listen to them being read aloud), and, beginning in the 1930s, listen to radio broadcasts where a device existed.[88] Since the beginning of the British Mandate, and most notably in the 1930s and 1940s, the number of cafés and restaurants in major cities steadily increased. Alongside the "humble" cafés a fancier variety developed, with a capacity to serve sometimes up to several hundred people and space for dancing and performances. The more upscale cafés were visited by women as well, and there were even cases of women managing cafés.[89] Some of the fancier cafés served alcoholic beverages and food.[90] The simple cafés did not serve food, but people sometimes bought foods like hummus and ful from other vendors and ate them in the café.[91]

Restaurants of the period can also be categorized into simple eateries, some of which specialized in one or two dishes such as hummus, ful, or roasted meat versus more elaborate establishments with fuller menus that included a variety of meat and vegetable dishes.[92] In both types, the cooking was done by men, in contrast to home cooking, where women were in charge.[93] A 1927 article titled "*Mata'em*" (Restaurants) in *Filastin*—the most widespread, nationalistically minded Palestinian newspaper of the time—mentioned the growing number of restaurants in Jaffa. Writing in a modernizing vein, the author reprimanded restaurant owners for their poor hygiene, lack of food safety, and exaggerated prices. If Jewish food had been palatable to Palestinians, he wrote, those who wanted to indulge would undoubtedly visit Jewish restaurants.[94] This suggests that the notion of eating in restaurants as a form of recreation was already underway, although it took longer to arrive in smaller towns.[95] Nevertheless, in the mid-1940s recreational restaurant dining was still much more common among Jews than among Arabs.[96]

In Haifa, which became the major city in northern Palestine following the opening of the Hijaz railway in 1905, many shared spaces of leisure existed.[97]

One of them was the drinks and *buza* (ice cream made with resin of *Pistacia lentiscus*) shop of Mustafa al-Haj in the northern corner of Hamra square—a popular recreation spot for Jews on Friday evenings, when Jewish businesses were closed.[98] Sources mention different types of friendly or at least benign interactions between Jews and Arabs in cafés, including conducting business meetings and playing billiards and card games, as well as less benign ones, like fist fighting.[99] The city expanded in the 1930s and 1940s, following the establishment of the refineries and the expansion of the port, emerging as a cultural hub that drew visitors from across Palestine and neighboring countries. In the early 1940s, the Jewish paramilitary organization Haganah (defense), whose intelligence unit prepared meticulous documentation of the Arab assets in the country, listed seventy-eight cafés and fifty-eight restaurants owned by Arabs in Haifa, mostly downtown.[100] Many of these restaurants were patronized by Jews as well.[101] According to Mordechai Ron, the morning fare was ful with olive oil, sometimes alongside hard-boiled eggs, served with two flatbreads, a plate of pickles, and a jug of cold water while hummus reigned during the day. The cook prepared the hummus on the spot and scooped it onto a plate, wiping the edge with his thumb. The dish would then be topped with fava beans and olive oil.[102] Janet M. (born 1937 in Haifa) noted in an interview how she and her friends used to mock Jews who came to eat hummus and ful in the restaurants near the entrance to the port, quoting the Arabic saying, "what do donkeys understand about ginger?"[103] Jewish customers did not limit themselves to hummus and ful; according to Ron, they also ordered a variety of vegetable and meat dishes.

A café and restaurant culture was also developing in Jerusalem around the same time, and particularly in the 1930s: the presence of the British army led to a growth in the service sector, which attracted both Palestinian and Jewish labor migrants.[104] Many food and drink establishments became sites of Arab-Jewish interaction, such as the ones located at the periphery of the new neighborhoods around the area of Musrara, Jaffa Gate, and the Russian Compound, which were home to a particularly cosmopolitan milieu.[105] Yet Jews sometimes visited simple Arab eateries as well.[106] Dorothy Kahn Bar-Adon described an Oriental restaurant inside the Damascus gate, "which displays its wares most temptingly" and served "humas salad" (prepared without tahini)—at the time unknown to most of her readers: "a symphony of colour and taste, if it suits your taste. It is made of a bean which is grown in most parts of the country, the beans that vendors sometimes roast on the street. But after the beans [are] crushed and mixed with oil and lemon and properly garnished in the leisurely Oriental fashion, they are hardly recognizable."[107]

In Jerusalem, the Haganah counted sixty-two Arab-owned cafés, restaurants, and canteens and at least nine "hummus kitchens."[108] On the whole, however, eating out as a form of recreation was more prevalent in the coastline cities of Haifa and Jaffa than in more conservative Jerusalem.[109]

A different situation prevailed in Tel Aviv, which grew out of a neighborhood established by some of Jaffa's Jewish residents seeking to separate from the Oriental city and establish a modern and Western, exclusively Jewish town.[110] By the late 1930s, Tel Aviv was home to a third of the county's Jewish population.[111] The arrival of bourgeois Jewish immigrants in the 1920s and 1930s and the growing presence of British security forces in the country since the outbreak of the Great Arab Revolt (1936–39) accelerated the development of a vibrant scene of restaurants, cafés, and bars, with its hierarchies of fashion, in Tel Aviv. A city of some 160,000 residents, Tel Aviv had more than four hundred cafés and restaurants by 1939.[112] Yet in spite of the aspirations of its founders, Tel Aviv was never entirely separate from Jaffa: several Jewish neighborhoods, which were part of the Tel Aviv urban sequence, were under the jurisdiction of the Jaffa municipality while much of the mixed Jaffa neighborhood of Manshiyeh was encircled by Tel Aviv's municipal border. Until the 1930s, Jaffa remained the urban center for Tel Aviv's residents, and even later Jews continued to go to Jaffa for administrative, commercial, and recreational purposes.[113] In neighborhoods on the border zone between Jaffa and Tel Aviv, populated predominantly by Mizrahi Jews, Arab and Jewish stores, workshops, restaurants, and cafés existed side by side and served members of both groups.[114]

Pace the author of the piece from *Filastin* cited above, commercial culinary encounters went both ways: Arabs, typically those of higher social status, did visit Jewish cafés and restaurants, though less frequently, owing to their generally lower rates of restaurant attendance. Members of the new Palestinian middle class were often attracted to European restaurants, with their foreign aura, although Arabs visited Jewish-owned Oriental restaurants as well.[115] Some Jewish establishments that sold alcohol and hosted entertainment shows like cabarets and belly dancing even attracted Arabs from neighboring countries. *Filastin* itself published advertisements for Jewish-owned cafés and restaurants.[116]

Outbreaks of political violence, coupled with economic bans, disrupted commercial encounters between Jews and Arabs. The bloody clashes of 1921 and 1929, followed by an Arab ban on Jewish businesses in Jaffa, and the Great Revolt, which started with a six-month commerce and labor strike, slowed down intercommunal commerce and promoted greater spatial separation.[117] In 1946, an article on an Oriental café near the Carmel market complained that before the revolt, Mizrahi Jews used to spend time in cafés in Jaffa, but after the revolt they "transferred the atmosphere [of Jaffa] to the heart of Tel Aviv."[118] Arabs who vended in Jewish neighborhoods were sometimes beaten.[119] Nevertheless, Arab vendors continued to sell in Tel Aviv, and many Jews continued to visit Jaffa in the years after the revolt, especially during the "quiet" years of WWII.[120] Heavy traffic of Tel Aviv residents to Jaffa's restaurants was noted especially on days when Jewish businesses were closed, such as Saturdays and Yom Kippur, or on Passover, when people went to Jaffa to look for bread.[121] Author Haim Gouri (1923–2018) mentions a row of Arab restaurants in Manshiyeh where he would sometimes eat in the 1930s and 1940s (he specifically mentions hummus). Gabriel Strassman (b. 1931) wrote in 1955 that Jews looking for "Levantine dishes" in the 1940s would go to Wadi Nisnas in Haifa, the Old City of Jerusalem, or Arab Jaffa.[122] According to author and restaurant critic Menachem Talmi, the restaurant of Abu-Laban in the Carmel market became a trendy spot among Tel Aviv's bohemian circles in the second half of the 1940s.[123]

Yet not only Arabs but also Mizrahi Jews mediated Arab dishes to Ashkenazi consumers. Yehoshua Zalivansky (b. 1919), a son of an Ashkenazi family from Tel Aviv, describes in his memoir from the late 1920s and early 1930s an elderly Mizrahi woman who used to sit on the sidewalk in Tel Aviv's Shabazi Street next to a giant pot cooking on a Primus stove, preparing hummus. When the chickpeas were soft, she would pound them to a puree in a pottery vessel, add olive oil, lemon, and spices, and hand it to her customers, who ate standing. After a customer finished eating, she would wipe the plate, refill it, and hand it to the next one. Zalivansky first tried the hummus out of curiosity but later ate it whenever he had the chance because it was tasty and he liked the atmosphere in this "standing restaurant for beggars."[124] Other Mizrahi vendors sold falafel, which by the late 1930s had become quite popular in Tel Aviv. In an article from 1939 titled "Seaside Temptations," nutritionist Lilian Cornfeld described "the filafel man" [sic] as the most popular in the "unending gastronomic procession" along the shore of Tel Aviv: "He seems to give you an almost unlimited amount of food for next to nothing. . . . Unhappy the person who does not know the delights of filafel."[125] In 1940 there were seven licensed falafel vendors in Tel Aviv and many others who sold falafel without a license, most of them Mizrahim.[126] Many of the vendors were of Yemenite origin, although falafel was unknown in Yemen.[127]

Jewish immigrants from Arab countries and the Balkan also opened restaurants serving Middle Eastern food. Several such restaurants published newspaper advertisements announcing the serving of "Oriental food," sometimes alongside "European food." The dishes featured in the advertisements were usually hummus, ful, falafel, shashlik, and kebab. Several of these dishes restaurant owners were likely to have first encountered in Palestine.[128] Some of the advertisements stressed that the food was not only kosher but also clean and fresh, attesting to the common European perception of Oriental restaurants as dirty and to their desire to distance themselves from such stereotypes.

Jewish customers seeking local cuisine might have chosen Jewish-owned restaurants due to kashrut—the Jewish dietary laws. In fact, until the 1930s, many Jewish restaurants in Tel Aviv did not observe kashrut. Meat butchered by Arabs, including prohibited animals like camels, found its way into restaurants and homes in Tel Aviv.[129] In the course of the 1930s nationalist and religious interests coalesced, and serving kosher meat butchered in the Tel Aviv slaughterhouse became the norm in Tel Aviv's restaurants and institutional kitchens.[130] In any case, for the observant nonorthodox section of the Jewish population, kashrut was a flexible norm centered mostly on meat while vegetable dishes prepared by non-Jews were tolerated.

By the late 1930s, the number of Jewish-owned Oriental restaurants in Tel Aviv increased due to Mizrahi migration into the country or out of Jaffa.[131] For the Jewish refugees from Jaffa, selling food was one of the most accessible options for creating income from a small initial investment. Those who were granted a permit to open a food establishment received some initial financial help.[132] Most of these restaurants were clustered in the southern neighborhoods, on the border zone between Tel Aviv and Jaffa.[133] In May 1939, two months after the end of the revolt, a reporter of the sensational *Iton Meyuchad* (*Special Journal*) wrote about the restaurant of Yosef Batito, who moved from Jaffa to Tel Aviv after the outbreak of the revolt: "Here the people of Nazareth and the descendants of Albion drink together with the daughters of Tel Aviv, without a hint of racial hatred. Here hatred and anger disappear with the appearance of arak on the tables and everyone drinks to the sounds of a gramophone, which sometimes mix with sounds of a very different kind: smashing of bottles, yelling, swearing and the sounds of vocal fights."[134]

It is hard to know how the author of this column viewed such interracial sociability. Both the Jewish and the Palestinian national movements tried to exert control over various types of border crossings and particularly opposed "our women" mingling with "their men."[135] At the same time, this excerpt describes the situation in not entirely negative terms ("hatred and anger disappear"), although it may have been written with a pinch of irony, as the facilitator of this amicable interaction is the bottle. What is clear from this excerpt, however, is that such places were perceived as strongholds of uncivilized behavior ("smashing of bottles, yelling, swearing") from which middle-class Ashkenazim from "good homes" better stay away.

Sources suggest that for the first generation of Ashkenazi settlers, local food sold in restaurants and in street stalls was generally unappealing. Dorothy Kahn Bar-Adon expressed a much wider sentiment when she wrote that "the majority of the Oriental restaurants do not tend to stimulate one's appetite."[136] Moreover, in a city that sought to fashion itself as modern and Western, it was often perceived as "out of place." Many letters to the Tel Aviv municipality, by both residents and merchants, complained about various nuisances created by the presence of Arab as well as Mizrahi Jewish vendors and restaurants: litter, shouting, foul odors, and suffocating smoke.[137] While expressions of repudiation of Oriental food and food establishments were often couched in hygienic and sanitary terms, the discourse of hygiene itself reflected nationalist, racial, and cultural assumptions.[138]

Children, in contrast, were much more enthusiastic about Oriental street food, particularly falafel, and hence a popular spot for food vendors was near schools, where they aroused the concern of parents, school managers, and school physicians. In a 1947 piece written by a Jerusalem pupil, falafel and hummus are described as temptations lurking outside the school gate, which only the fortunate managed to buy.[139] Author David Shacham (b. 1923) tells how he used to buy falafel from a Yemeni vendor next to his school in Tel Aviv in secret, since his mother was sure that it was full of germs.[140] In 1944, the municipal Inspection Department in Tel Aviv declared a war against falafel vendors, particularly against those who sold near schools, but all measures taken were in vain: the vendors continued to sell, and schoolchildren continued to buy from them.[141] It is likely that children's attraction to street food like falafel and hummus in large part derived precisely from authority figures' admonitions to avoid it.[142]

Yet there were also Ashkenazi men who were attracted to Arab food and food establishments for the affective, no less than culinary experience they offered. One example is a 1929 column written by journalist Itamar Ben-Avi (1882–1943), son of famous Hebrew lexicographer Eliezer Ben-Yehuda. Ben-Avi described to the readers of the newspaper he established and edited, *Doar Hayom*, his experience of eating falafel in the following words: "Oh, how I enjoyed them in this mountain-morning, with the sweet sunrays erupting from the East. . . . How I ate them, how I ate them, how I chewed them and how I swallowed them in my vibrant 'Easternness.' Indeed, it is only the sons of Arabia, and their brethren—Sephardi Jews—that may prepare such a spicy dish, which is so delicious."[143]

פָּטֶנט חָדָשׁ בְּתֵל אָבִיב

„אַנְטִיפַלַפְלוֹן" — תְּרוּפָה בְּדוּקָה נֶגֶד רֵיַם הַפַּלַפֶל שֶׁפָּשַׁט בְּתֵל אָבִיב.

Figure 1.2 "A New Patent in Tel Aviv: Anti-falafelon—a
Tested Remedy against the Smell of Falafel That Spread in
Tel Aviv," *Haaretz*, September 2, 1940. The writing on the
cart says "*falafel á lá kefag*"—a faulty (Frenchified?) version
of the Arabic *'ala kaifak*, meaning "however you want."

For Ben-Avi, the experience of being or becoming "Eastern" was part of an
explicit political-*cum*-cultural agenda. In a programmatic article that opened
the first issue of *Doar Hayom* he associated the Jewish national revival and the
rejection of the Diaspora with an Eastern cultural orientation, "like our forefathers, and as all our sons will probably be tomorrow," albeit without forsaking
Western progress.[144] The pleasure involved in eating falafel—which the repeti-
tions in this text are clearly meant to convey—seems to derive not only from its
delicious taste but also from its ability to confer "Easternness" on its consumer
(note the image of the sunrays erupting from the east). This excerpt provides an
exceptionally revealing example for the way food consumption could function
as an affective technology of the self.

Other sources betray a sense of exoticism, sensuality, and sometimes also
danger that the visit to Arab places elicited. Gabriel Strassman described how

Figure 1.3 Restaurant in the lower city of Haifa, 1928. Photo by Dr. Edward Elkan. Courtesy of Bitmuna.

"tahini-hummus-kebab-shashlik meals" at Arab restaurants, albeit cheap, were regarded as festive meals and as a kind of luxury. "Devouring them had something of the Oriental charm," he wrote, noting that he and his friends were willing to eat in these restaurants in spite of some of the preparation methods, such as spitting on the roasting meat to improve its taste.[145] As this excerpt shows, the "exotic" allure of Arab restaurants could act as an antidote for potential feelings of disgust. According to Yehuda Litani, a journalist and coauthor of a guidebook to Israel's hummus joints and olive-oil producers, members of the Jewish paramilitary organization Palmach used to visit Arab restaurants as an act of heroism in the early 1940s.[146] Yet sources suggest that more than "heroism" was at stake in the consumption of Arab food. I end this section with two literary accounts of Palestinian Arab urban spaces involving food, written by Palmach warrior Haim Gouri. The first is the poem "A Journey to Haifa's Lower City," which he likely wrote during the war of 1948, shortly before Arab Haifa was demolished.[147] The second is an account of his visits to Arab Jaffa—"that loved or hated world"[148]—during the Mandate period, which appears in *The Crazy Book* (1972). In both of these texts, the Arab city is described in similar terms: full of smoke, smells, noises, shouts, and teeming crowds. It is a space that is decaying, malicious, and threatening (Gouri mentions in his poem a "knife in the back"—obviously intended for the Jewish visitor; in *The Crazy Book*, there is a voice that keeps warning the protagonist "Don't go to Jaffa! Don't go to Jaffa, crazy!" and also "They slaughter there, don't you know?"), but it is also alluring, with its aura of exoticism, historicity, and sensual abundance (coupled with the very sense of danger it incurs). In the poem, Gouri explicitly mentions an Oriental restaurant that "assaults his senses" with the smell of roasting meat. In *The Crazy Book*, he provides lengthy descriptions of the food in Jaffa, including the "Za'atar powder, which carries the smell of mountains at the end of the summer" and hummus and ful in a puddle of thick olive oil.[149] For Gouri, Arab spaces offered an unmediated connection to an authentic and ancient Orient, its sounds, smells, and tastes—an authenticity that modernized Jewish settlers will always strive for but never fully possess. We will come back to Gouri and his recollections of an authenticity lost in 1948 in the next chapters.

NUTRITION EDUCATION

One group of mediators encouraged Jewish settlers to adopt ingredients and dishes from the Palestinian menu not as exotic food to consume in public venues but as food to integrate into the repertoire of home cooking. These were nutrition experts, most of whom were affiliated with the Zionist women's organizations Hadassah and WIZO (Women's International Zionist Organization). Both organizations were active in the fields of public health and social welfare and engaged in health-education activities, including in the area of nutrition.[150]

When Zionist physicians and ideologues in early twentieth-century Europe were framing "the Jewish problem" in terms of physical and mental deterioration, food habits were sometimes mentioned as one component in a wider set of habits that had to be corrected as part of a comprehensive project of reform. Yet, until the second half of the 1930s, nutrition did not receive much institutional attention from the main Zionist bodies. Institutionalized efforts to reform eating habits were mainly undertaken by Hadassah and WIZO, sometimes in cooperation with the workers' Sick Fund, in the framework of their health-educational activities.[151] Physicians and "dieticians" working in these organizations presented the Ashkenazi diet in Palestine as "irrational" and unadjusted to the conditions of the land, particularly its climate and produce. "In no other area of our lives does conservatism reign as in the area of eating-habits," lamented Dr. Yosef Me'ir; "the herring and the conserves are not getting off our table."[152] Indeed, by 1939, Palestine's Jews spent a third of their food expenditure on imports, half of which was used to buy "luxury" products such as meat and fish conserves, thickened milk, and dry fruits.[153]

Nutrition experts viewed their role as guiding women in how to nourish their families with a diet that was not only healthy but also "rational" and "in harmony with local supplies and with the demands of our climate."[154] According to the prevailing nutrition discourse, national or racial diets developed over centuries in harmony with local climate and produce. However, as civilization progressed, the balance was disrupted when people began replacing "natural" foods with processed ones and local ingredients with imported ones.[155] According to Zionist nutrition experts, this problem was particularly grave in Palestine, where large numbers of new arrivals were unfamiliar with the food traditions of the country and continued to practice the nutritional habits of their countries of origin. These habits were not only ill suited to local conditions but also economically irrational as they led to a dependence on imports.[156] Science, however, was capable of facilitating, within just a few years, the adjustment to the environment that "racial empiricism" had achieved over generations.[157]

The interwar years were a period of significant developments in the knowledge and practical applications of nutrition science. Toward the end of the nineteenth century, European and American scientists began to investigate the energetic contents of food and the body's energy expenditure, measured by "calories."[158] Since the early twentieth century, the discovery of vitamins led to studying the connection between food and disease prevention and to the development of the "newer knowledge of nutrition" in the 1920s, with its emphasis on "protective foods" (primarily meat, milk, cheese, eggs, fruits, and vegetables).[159] With the discovery of vitamins and deficiency diseases, the emphasis on quantity was replaced by biochemical emphasis on the nutritional qualities of the food consumed.[160]

These changes affected the study of food and populations. The invention of the calorie as a measurement unit allowed standardization of value across diets, time periods, and populations, making human diets seem less diverse than had previously been assumed.[161] The "newer knowledge of nutrition" reintroduced a connection between diet and race. Students of nutrition traveled to colonial territories, which offered a laboratory for comparative nutritional research, with their variety of races in their "natural" habitats consuming their "natural" diets. Research showed that nutritional health was a matter not only of environmental conditions but also of the different diets followed by populations within the same environment.[162] By the late 1930s, scientists agreed that differences of nutrition could explain some of the physical differences between races; that the same nutritional requirements could be met in many ways; and that different national and racial food traditions, albeit adapted to their environment, were nonetheless often deficient in terms of people's nutritional needs and hence should be improved with the help of science.[163]

The shifting perspective on indigenous food traditions within the discourse of nutrition science, coupled with a growing Western openness toward ethnically diverse cuisines in this period, allowed Zionist nutrition experts to view Arab and Mizrahi Jewish diets as potential sources from which to borrow to enhance the diet of Ashkenazi newcomers.[164] As Sarah Bromberg noted in a preface to a 1931 survey on the diets of various population sectors in Palestine, the survey included the food habits of the Bedouin and the fellahin, since "these people, being indigenous to the soil for generations, have presumably reached an adjustment to their environment, and their racial experience as expressed in their food habits should contain much of value to the newcomer seeking a proper habituation to the country."[165] Moreover, some components of their diet coincided with the recommendations of contemporary nutrition science, such as the abundant consumption of fresh vegetables and fruits, or "the proper appreciation of the nutritive value of milk and its derivatives."[166] Nutrition experts praised various real or imagined Arab cooking and eating habits, like subsisting on local plants, roasting meat instead of frying, and "patient chewing" as healthier than Jewish ones.[167]

Granted, "Oriental diets" were not exempt from criticism. For example, in an article on "purposeful nutrition in Eretz Israel," nutritionist Sarah Bromberg noted that in the countries of the Near East there is typically a collision between the dispositions of the "natural sense" and the disposition for gluttony. It is known, Bromberg wrote, that in hot climates appetite tends to be lower. Over many generations people have tried to overcome this deficiency by adding excessive amounts of hot spices and by frying, rather than by giving a good shape and taste to the food. With time, the disposition for gluttony prevailed. Bromberg also pointed out another harmful habit: finishing the meal with black coffee to stave off the drowsiness that usually follows a large meal (and "all Oriental meals are too large"). This practice, she explained, redirects the blood flow to the head instead of the stomach, hindering digestion.[168]

From the early days of Zionist nutrition advice, experts recommended a shift to a diet based on more vegetables and fruits and less meat. Milk, eggs, and white cheese were recommended as cheaper and more easily digestible sources of animal protein, which were more suitable for the local climate, and tahini was recommended as a nutritious and healthy source of fat.[169] The importance of consuming local produce rather than imported food was also emphasized. In the introduction to the first comprehensive cookbook published in Hebrew, *How to Cook in Eretz Israel* (1936), WIZO nutrition instructor Erna Meyer wrote that replacing the European cuisine with a healthy Eretz-Israeli cuisine was "one of the most important means for striking roots in our old-new homeland."[170]

The growing tendency to regard nutrition as part of governance on both the national and international levels after WWI, and the shortage of various products in the Jewish market due to the Arab Revolt, triggered a more systematic Zionist engagement with the problems of nutrition.[171] In 1936, a Nutrition Committee adjacent to the Institute for Economic Research of the Jewish Agency was established in order to coordinate the institutions active in the field of nutrition, make policy suggestions, conduct research, and promote public interest in nutrition through educational campaigns.[172] One of the committee's main tasks was to coordinate Jewish agricultural production and food consumption, with the goal of reducing dependence on Arab produce and increasing Jewish production.[173]

It was mainly during WWII that nutrition education received more focused attention from both Zionist and British bodies. On the one hand, the war years were marked by economic prosperity: Palestine served as an important base for the British in their Middle East campaign, creating jobs for the local population and boosting local industries and agriculture.[174] On the other hand, as the war progressed and transportation became precarious, some products almost disappeared from the legal market (most notably beef, but also eggs and cheese) or were in short supply (wheat), and food prices soared, especially of imported foodstuffs (apart from milk, vegetables, and fruits, all food supplies depended on supplementary imports).[175]

Starting in August 1939, the government inaugurated a series of control measures intended to deal with the problem of food shortage and combat the emergence of black markets. A point scheme for rationing was introduced, similar to the one adopted in Britain and elsewhere in the empire.[176] This scheme was a source for much confusion and distress, and Zionist organizations expanded their educational activities. This period saw the production of a plethora of educational material in the form of newspaper columns, recipe booklets, exhibitions, radio programs, and cooking demonstrations and courses aimed at teaching women how to manage with the point system and make do with the available products.[177] In particular, nutrition experts stressed the importance of replacing imported with local products (namely, products from Jewish farms), which were often more expensive, and called for the consumption of plenty of vegetables and more legumes (213–240 grams per person per week was the recommended amount).[178] As Erna Meyer stated in her column in *Haaretz*, "She, who can adjust her cooking to the conditions of the land, will never miss points," referring to the fact that vegetables and legumes were not rationed.[179]

While most recipes were European, nutritionists usually incorporated into their suggested menus Middle Eastern dishes and ingredients such as mjaddara, eggplant in tomato sauce, stuffed vegetables, and bulgur. Tahini, either

Figure 1.4 Erna Meyer, *How to Cook in Eretz Israel* (Tel Aviv: WIZO, 1936).

used as a sauce or eaten as "salad," was celebrated as a cheap, accessible, nutritious, and easily digested substitute for liquid oil. According to nutrition experts, Middle Eastern diets, albeit deficient in some respects, were the most suitable for times of emergency, since they made the most out of cheap, nourishing local products.[180] "If we compare our nutrition with that of the people of the Orient," stated an article in *Davar* on "Nutrition in Times of War," "we will see that their diet, which is composed of local products with much nutritional value, is usually healthier, cheaper and suitable to the climate. In this context we must remember that the bulgur, lentils, peas, beans, fruit and vegetables comprised the main nutrition of the ancient Hebrew" (note the exclusion of Mizrahim from the collective "we").[181]

One of the most prominent advocates for the introduction of Arab and Mizrahi dishes into the Ashkenazi menu was Canadian-born nutritionist Lilian Cornfeld, who since 1933 worked as a nutrition adviser to various British and, later, Israeli bodies.[182] Cornfeld published many cookbooks and numerous articles on nutrition and cooking in the English and Hebrew press. In 1939 she wrote, "While there is much in the diet of the Oriental communities which is not commendable and could be improved—such as the excessive use of frying—their diet on the whole is valuable for its cereals, fats, sugars and generous use of vegetables and fruit, and there is much to learn from it."[183] In another article she emphasized the use of whole grain cereals and legumes, the combination of which constitutes a complete protein; the use of small pieces of meat as a "spice"; and many other nutritional habits. She also wrote that Orientals know how to fry in a "scientific manner": with much hot oil.[184] In her 1942 cookbook *How to Cook at Times of War*, which appeared in both Hebrew and German, I found the first Hebrew recipe for a "hummus and tahini salad," under the section "grits, legumes, and peanuts."[185] Dispersed throughout the book were recipes for other Middle Eastern dishes such as shashlik, mjaddara, okra with tomato sauce, tahini salad, and kibbe (bulgur and meat dumpling).

After the war, nutrition educators continued to promote the consumption of legumes as food prices remained high and animal products—particularly meat—were in short supply.[186] In her *Haaretz* column, "Shulamit" suggested peanuts, almonds, and baked beans—which she defined as "royal delicacy" and recommended serving mashed to ease digestion—as "meat substitutes."[187] In fact, legumes were signifiers of ethno-class distinction: poor Mizrahim consumed the largest amount per capita (which was the amount recommended by nutritionists), followed by wealthier Mizrahim, while poor Ashkenazim consumed very little, and wealthy Ashkenazim hardly consumed legumes at all.[188] Given the Ashkenazi tendency to avoid legumes, hummus and falafel had the advantage of providing chickpea in a form in which it was "hardly recognizable."

It is hard to estimate to what extent women heeded the advice of nutrition experts. According to a 1964 study on changes in food consumption habits along three generations, 50 percent of the new food items adopted by first-generation Ashkenazim were learned from the media—newspaper columns and radio broadcasts—but these were mostly vegetable ingredients rather than dishes.[189] Studies indicate that first-generation Ashkenazim incorporated new foods into their diet only slowly, partially, and reluctantly. When they did, it was primarily foods associated with wealth in Europe, such as white instead of dark bread and citrus fruits.[190] Possibly the main role of nutrition educators with regard to Arab food was to familiarize Ashkenazi women with it and lend legitimacy to its consumption.

Nevertheless, some changes in the direction of the local diet did take place among Ashkenazim. Perhaps most noteworthy was the growth in the consumption of fruits and vegetables, which agronomist Akiva Ettinger attributed to the success of nutrition propaganda.[191] Some hitherto unknown or disliked vegetables, which were common in the Palestinian diet, such as olives, tomatoes, eggplants, and marrows, eventually found inroads into the Ashkenazi kitchen, often prepared to match familiar dishes (such as "chopped liver" made of eggplant or chicken soup with squash).[192] Halva became a popular sweet, and by 1931 coffee consumption already slightly exceeded tea.[193]

Whole dishes, however, seem to have hardly penetrated the urban Ashkenazi menu. To the extent that the Tnuva restaurant in Tel Aviv, which opened in 1945, was indicative of mainstream Ashkenazi taste, then only a single Arab dish appeared on the menu: eggplant with tahini.[194] In 1937, a Jewish bakery in Tel Aviv began to bake pita bread, yet it entered Ashkenazi homes only much later.[195] Arab foods that were striking roots among Ashkenazim were primarily those available as street food: falafel, often served with tahini, and to a lesser extent, hummus. The single chapter on Arab food in the series Nutrition Cycles—an educational radio series that presented the cuisines of different Jewish ethnic communities, aired in late 1944—described hummus as "the simplest and most prevalent dish, also among some of our Mizrahi communities, and becoming popular among others as well. It is excellent as appetizer and also to satisfy one's hunger."[196] Yet, it was not before the early to mid-1950s that hummus became popular among a broader Ashkenazi public.

TWO

"THE EAST CONQUERS THE STOMACHS OF THE WEST"

Hummus with Tahini Salad: Soak the chickpeas overnight with a pinch of baking soda, the next day strain and rinse, cook until very soft. Grind twice, add some salt, a bit of the cooking water, tahini, lemon juice, minced garlic and crush the peas while stirring well. Serve a thin layer over a flat plate, spread some paprika on top, drip some oil and decorate with parsley.

—WIZO Instructors, Thus We Shall Cook, 1956

IN THE BOOK *NOT BY HUMMUS ALONE* (2000), Yehuda Litani tells a story of conversion: in late 1948 or early 1949, when he was only five years old, he joined an army battalion on an excursion to the area of the battles in the Jerusalem corridor (the battles were just over; the war itself was to officially end only in July 1949). At lunchtime, they entered a small café in the conquered Palestinian village of Abu Ghosh.[1] One of the dishes they received was a murky-yellowish puree, decorated with green leaves and dark oil, which the soldiers happily devoured. The child did not dare to taste it, but the soldiers urged him to try this delicious dish. His first reaction was an urge to vomit, but soon his face lit up: "This is actually tasty! Very tasty! More—much more—than the chicken soup, cutlets, mushed potatoes and boiled chicken to which he was accustomed until the siege of Jerusalem."[2]

If it had been a decade later, five-year-old Litani would have probably known what hummus was, although he was more likely to eat it as one of several first courses in an urban Oriental restaurant, or from a can. In the first years of statehood, hummus became much more visible in the Israeli public foodscape than in previous decades. It appeared in food columns and cookbooks intended for a Jewish readership and on the menus of Oriental restaurants (and sometimes

53

of European restaurants as well), which had grown in number considerably throughout the decade. The growth in the Jewish consumption of hummus was mainly the result of two interrelated processes: the arrival of hundreds of thousands of Jewish immigrants from the Middle East and a food-rationing scheme inaugurated in the first half of 1949. Nutrition aside, more than ever before hummus became an instrument in the performance of a new Israeli masculinity as "non-Diasporic" and rooted in the land.

The Jewish triumph in the 1948 war and the Palestinian Nakba (catastrophe) brought about a dramatic transformation in the country's physical and social landscape. Most Palestinian Arabs who resided in the territories that became Israel were expelled or fled for their lives and were barred from returning to their homes and lands. Palestinian society was shattered, most of its social elites had fled the country, and its urban culture was destroyed.[3] Nazareth alone survived as an Arab town; in five other cities only a fragment of the Arab residents stayed put: Haifa, Jaffa, Acre, Lydda, and al-Ramla.[4] Out of more than 500 villages, only some 100 survived; the rest were evacuated and later demolished.[5] An impoverished population of 160,000—many of whom were internal refugees—remained under Israeli sovereignty as a colonized minority within a state that defined itself as Jewish.[6] They were subjected to military rule, which lasted until 1966, and their civil liberties and freedom of movement were severely curtailed.

Simultaneously, hundreds of thousands of Jews from Europe and the Middle East, many of them refugees, arrived in the newly established state (in the years 1948–51 alone, 687,000 Jews entered the country; of them, 312,900 arrived from Arab and Muslim-majority countries[7]). In the course of only three years, the Jewish population of Israel doubled itself. By the end of the decade, the number of Jewish new arrivals amounted to 900,000. The ethnic composition of Jewish society had changed too: from Ashkenazim being a decisive majority of 75 percent in the late 1940s, they became a small majority of 55 percent by the end of the 1950s.[8] Most Mizrahi immigrants hailed from Iraq, Yemen, and North Africa, but there were also immigrants from Turkey and Iran. Only a small minority of approximately 3,500 immigrants arrived from the Levant between the years 1948 and 1954.[9]

In the eyes of Ashkenazi veterans, Mizrahi immigrants were culturally and even racially inferior and threatened the modern and Western nature of the new society. They suffered discrimination and marginalization and were the targets of various "rehabilitative" actions, including attempts to modify their foodways. Despite nutrition educators' attempts to introduce various Mizrahi dishes into the diet of the new nation, their cuisines largely remained confined to the private sphere of domestic cooking. At the same time, the establishment of restaurants and eateries by immigrants, most of whom shared a core of common Middle Eastern dishes, supported the popularization—and later Israelization—of some of these dishes, among them hummus.

This chapter focuses on the establishment of hummus in the food repertoire of Israelis in the 1950s, albeit at this point as a food consumed mostly in the public sphere, predominantly as a restaurant first course ("a salad"). After delineating the Israeli foodscape of the period, I delve into the realm of commercial food establishments where Israelis encountered hummus as a culinary option that not only was inexpensive and satiating but also had a distinct allure, particularly among Ashkenazi consumers. I then discuss nutrition educators' incorporation of Mizrahi and Arab dishes into their recommended (mostly Ashkenazi) menus, and finally, I address the promotion of hummus, and several other Arab dishes, as the foods of the "Sabra" by a group of cultural entrepreneurs.

As I will show, on the one hand hummus was subsumed under the increasingly conspicuous category of "Mizrahi" (Oriental)—a category that encompassed both Arab and Middle Eastern Jewish items (with time it would come to refer primarily to Jews of Middle Eastern descent and their cultural productions). On the other hand, during most of the decade, it retained its Arab identity and was considered an exogenous element that was, at the same time, quintessentially local. The Hebrew name for hummus—*himtsa* or *humtsa*—gradually gave way to its Arab name, except in agricultural contexts. Hummus, then, was a flexible signifier that could be incorporated into different, albeit interrelated identity projects.

THE ISRAELI FOODSCAPE OF THE 1950S

In *Sweetness and Power*, Sidney Mintz shows how the pervasive consumption of sugar in nineteenth-century Europe had both a cultural and a nutritional aspect: it had to do not only with its prestige as a formerly rare and expensive product consumed by the aristocracy but also with its nutritional quality of being a source of quick energy.[10] Hardly a basic food like sugar, the growth in the Jewish consumption of hummus and falafel in the early 1950s likewise had a nutritional, no less than a cultural aspect. It should be understood in light of the reality of widespread poverty, scarcity, substitutions, and hunger for variety and for filling, nourishing, and tasty food, which prevailed in the years following the foundation of the state.

In April 1949, the government inaugurated an austerity regime (*tzena*), which included strict supervision of prices and rationing of food, other basic commodities, and foreign currency.[11] Its goals were to fight the raging inflation and keep the expenditure of foreign currency in check so as to secure the funds required for the state's military and civilian goals, foremost among them handling the masses of new arrivals.[12] It was designed to guarantee minimal consumption standards to the citizens, many of whom could not secure their own food.[13] The allocation of products to consumers was implemented through a book of coupons, which people had to submit when buying rationed products.[14] Besides consumption, production and import were also placed under government control.

Given the shortage of various basic products, most notably meat, the austerity menu was based on substitutions: egg and milk came in powders, margarine replaced butter, and frozen fish filet took the place of meat.[15] Legumes—long considered "poor men's meat" due to their high protein content[16]—were rationed but did not require coupons: 250 grams per person per week in summer 1950 and half a kilo a year later.[17] In July 1948, Cornfeld suggested replacing the missing meat with eggs for the main course and noted that "there are also hummus and falafel as a vegetable dish."[18] In October 1949, *Maariv* reported on an Arab *sulha* (peace-making ceremony) that was celebrated in Jaffa with several eggs, pickles, hummus, and beer rather than the usual rice and lamb, although these, as one of the participants whispered to the district deputy inspector, could have been fixed. As this excerpt suggests, hummus, albeit relatively cheap and accessible, was at the same time sufficiently festive to function as a meat substitute in a sulha meal.[19] Among Ashkenazim, however, consumption of legumes, most of which came from import, remained relatively low.[20]

While food rationing burdened the majority of the population, those who suffered most were dependent and marginalized populations: new immigrants, mainly Mizrahim, and Palestinians who remained under Israeli rule. Out of the new Jewish immigrants, those who did not find settlement solutions were sent to "immigrant camps" and, as of May 1950, to "transitional camps" (*maʿbara*, pl. *maʿbarot*) where they lived in temporary dwellings, sometimes for many years.[21] In immigrant camps, where food was provided by the Jewish Agency, food quantities were often insufficient, and in camps where no communal kitchen existed, much of the food was spoiled.[22] On top of that, the government used deprivation of food cards as a form of punishment to disobedient immigrants.[23] In transitional camps and depopulated Palestinian villages settled by immigrants, provision of fresh produce was slow and deficient. Moreover, food provisioning was tailored to Ashkenazi tastes.[24] This was also true for the rationing scheme, despite official declarations that rationing would be adjusted to accommodate the consumption habits of different ethnic groups.[25]

Palestinians who remained under Israeli rule were also severely hit by food shortage. The military rule not only restricted Palestinian freedom of movement but also provided the infrastructure for further expulsions and massive land expropriation, leaving many impoverished.[26] Those who succeeded in holding onto some land could usually manage,[27] but for others, such as internal refugees and town dwellers who were cut off from their rural hinterland, the situation was much graver: many suffered severe shortage and distress, sometimes to the point of hunger.[28] Ration coupons were distributed only to those who received Israeli IDs, and the IDs, when granted, often took time to issue.[29] In the Negev desert, registration of Bedouins was completed only in 1954, and a hunger crisis emerged.[30] The rations allotted to Arabs were smaller than those allotted to Jews, and Bedouins received even smaller portions.[31] Moreover, the conditions of dependency and the arbitrariness of military rule in a context of food scarcity gave rise to much disorder, corruption, and sometimes sheer abuse: there were cases where military officers and government officials stole or delayed provisions or forced Arabs to accept products that were discarded from the Jewish inventory.[32] Military government officials and police officers often exploited Arab conventions of hospitality and invited themselves to dine. This habit, widely employed as a form of bribery, was so rampant that in May 1951 the military governor issued an edict requiring officials to receive government approval for dining in Arab places.[33]

Initially successful, the rationing system eventually faltered, with shortages, decreased ration sizes, declining quality, and rising prices undermining the system from early 1950.[34] Escalating demand fueled a massive black market, which gave rise to an extensive supervision apparatus.[35] Protests broke out throughout the country.[36] In October 1950, the government resigned, and the Ministry of Supplies and Rationing was disbanded.[37] Immigration from Arab countries also dwindled due to a governmental selection scheme.[38] After the 1952 elections, most of the regulations of the rationing were lifted, retaining primarily price control.[39] Foreign currency also began to flow into the country.[40] A key state objective during this period was strengthening the agricultural sector to meet food demands and safeguard Jewish control over conquered territories.[41] With much new fertile land and improvements in water supply, the main expansion of agricultural production was achieved by the middle of the decade.[42]

In 1954 a new immigration policy came into effect, and the selection criteria were relaxed; between 1954 and 1957, an additional 114,000 immigrants arrived in the country, mainly from the Maghreb.[43] New arrivals were sent directly to rural settlements and "development towns," established to provide a settlement solution to the immigrants and to create "facts on the ground" in conquered territories.[44] By the end of the decade, Judaization of most of the country's territory had been completed.[45] Since the mid-1950s, emphasis was placed on developing a local industry, which owed its growth to, besides governmental investment, the availability of cheap labor power provided by Mizrahi immigrants.[46] Food became one of the main industrial branches, and it embraced Arab foods like tahini, falafel, and hummus.[47] A Jewish society and economy were built over the ruins of Palestinian society, with a clear ethnonational division of labor: white-collar professional jobs were mainly in the hands of Ashkenazim and low-skilled, low-paying jobs were allocated mainly to Mizrahi Jews and Arabs.[48]

THE RISE OF THE "ORIENTAL RESTAURANT"

Although recipes for hummus and other Arab dishes occasionally appeared in newspaper food columns and Hebrew cookbooks, hummus hardly entered Israeli homes before the arrival of the industrial version but was consumed in commercial venues. While the growth in the Jewish consumption of hummus, falafel, tahini, and other Arab staples can be partly attributed to the change in the ethnic composition of the consumers, it is insufficient as an explanation. In early 1956 journalist Ruth Bondi defined "shashlik, kebab, and hummus with tahini *'a-la-kaifak*" as "the favorite foods of Ashkenazim."[49] Rather, it should be understood in the context of the changing place of Oriental food and the Oriental restaurant in a period of shortage. In this process, Mizrahim functioned not only as consumers but also as producers and mediators.

During the austerity years, restaurant attendance rose whenever people had more money to spend than products to spend it on. The difficulties of home cooking under conditions of rationing also increased the attraction of dining out for those who could afford it.[50] In Tel Aviv—a city of approximately 340,000 people—the number of restaurants in 1951 was 1,150, most of them serving European food.[51] However, restaurants, too, suffered shortages in supply, and therefore the quantity of the food was often insufficient and the quality poor.[52] The food controller determined the food categories that restaurant meals could include and their prices, and they, too, were obliged to comply with meatless days.[53]

According to Anat Helman, consumers' predicament in the austerity period stemmed not only from the lack of sufficient food and its low quality but also from lack of variety and "depressing monotony."[54] This can explain the new Ashkenazi attraction to Oriental restaurants, which offered a variety of unfamiliar foods. Moreover, compared to European restaurants, Oriental restaurants were less dependent on meat, used more vegetables and spices, and often served fried instead of boiled food, which was richer in calories and more flavorful.[55]

Arab cities became a destination for Jewish tourists searching not just for Oriental exoticism but also for culinary variety, particularly meat. Orit Rozin describes the craving for meat during the austerity years: even those who received a sufficient quantity of animal protein felt they were "hungry" when they did not get their share of meat.[56] While the Arab residents of these cities often suffered severe food shortages and even hunger, smuggling and other ways of tricking the system ensured that at least in restaurants that catered to a Jewish clientele, meat could often be found. The encounter between the country's new rulers and the colonized population in these restaurants was shaped by the power relationship between them and was therefore fraught. It was further complicated by the combination of hostility and hospitality that Arab restaurant owners and employees were forced to display to Jewish customers, on whom they relied for their livelihood.[57]

The Arab city that became a foremost destination for Jewish tourism was Nazareth.[58] The only Arab city to have survived the war, Nazareth was home to the largest Palestinian community that remained under Israeli rule.[59] In the months following its occupation, it suffered from overcrowding, housing shortages, and unemployment due to the numerous refugees who streamed into the city, as well as shortages of basic foodstuffs and electricity and an inadequate water supply.[60] In May 1949, journalist and MP-to-be Yosef Tamir hyperbolically stated that in spite of the dire economic situation and unemployment, there was no austerity in Nazareth: the shops and the restaurants were overflowing with merchandise, and the city was crowded with Jewish tourists looking for cheap consumer goods and cheap and abundant food. The signs on the restaurants stating in Arabic "open to IDF soldiers—by military command" suggested that at least some of the restaurants refused to serve them.[61] Nevertheless, Nazareth's restaurants survived on Jewish customers.

In 1950, meat was missing from Nazareth's restaurants, too, so that people who came there looking for shashlik and kebab ended up finding fish filet or the vegetarian alternatives: hummus and falafel.[62] Yet by early 1951 journalist Amos Elon reported that in the city's dozen restaurants meat was available throughout the week and was sold in controlled prices but without coupons. Although Nazareth is undoubtedly one of the most beautiful cities in the country, wrote Elon, when someone returns from Nazareth people do not ask him "what did you see?" but rather "what did you eat?"[63] Some of the reports reveal the patronizing attitude of Jewish tourists who flooded the city on Sabbaths and holidays and especially on Christmas Eve, when the city's supply of meat was increased.[64] On Christmas 1950, Elon described the Jewish tourists who raided the city's restaurants, decorated with photos of Herzl and the Israeli flag, in the hundreds, demanding to be fed—kebab, shashlik, steak, schnitzel, and even ham—as if they had not eaten since the previous Christmas.[65] In light of these raids, on Christmas 1953 the military governor banned the entry of Jews into the city, to the detriment of local restaurant owners and the relief of the city's residents.[66]

Another popular destination for Jewish tourists was Acre. Previously an almost exclusively Arab town, after the occupation it was being quickly settled with Jewish immigrants. In contrast to Nazareth, most of the original residents had fled the city—some of them after the conquest of Haifa, which brought to Acre many refugees and others due to heavy shelling.[67] When the Israeli army had entered the city, hardly any services were functioning. In a short vignette on a visit to an Acre restaurant, written in July 1949, Rachel Hoter-Yishai, wife of Chief Military Counsel Aharon Hoter-Yishai, described how several months earlier she and her family had entered Acre, still closed by a military edict, and found a dead city: the streets were empty and the shops closed. They managed to find a single open restaurant in the Old City. Although the owner served them with servility and all the other Arab customers were friendly, the atmosphere felt artificial and tense. "There was excess in their desire to please us. There was a feeling of the defeated fawning in front of the governor," she wrote, and told how despite their effort to deface the power relations, the submission and self-deprecation of the Arab customers cast an unpleasant and distressful air on the encounter. At some point we learn that her husband was dressed in an officer uniform.[68] Later reports also mention the scant number of restaurants in Acre, although several of the existing ones seem to have thrived on Jewish customers.[69]

Some restaurants survived in nearby Haifa, which was also dramatically transformed in the war: the Old City was destroyed, and out of the seventy-five thousand Arab residents, only three thousand remained. These were concentrated in the Wadi Nisnas area and subjected to military rule.[70] Haifa's restaurants also became a destination for food tourists. In December 1949, D. Nahum suggested to "he who wants to drink a fragrant and refreshing coffee" and to eat a dish of hummus swimming in oil to go to Edward café in Haifa. The author wondered about the existence of products missing from the Jewish market, like coffee and chickpeas, in the Haifa café. Yet it was something else that raised his indignation: "It is very nice that the Arabs who stayed with us

Figure 2.1 The Sea café, Acre, 1958. Photo by Jachin Hirsch.

Figure 2.2 Man eating, probably hummus, in an Acre restaurant, 1958.
Photo by Jachin Hirsch.

feel themselves at home: drinking coffee and dipping pita in hummus, but how is it possible that in a café, which is a public meeting place, there will not be anything of the signs of the Israeli state? Since the menu . . . is printed in Arabic and English alone, like in the old days."[71]

Nahum was willing to tolerate the owner's insubordination when it came to serving controlled foodstuffs, given that he, too, had enjoyed them. It was the owner's failure to submit to the insignia of state power that turned Nahum from a customer into a patronizing supervisor who held the authority to determine under what conditions the Palestinians should "feel at home" while eating their own food in their homeland.

The city of Jaffa was also shattered in the war. The number of its Arab residents decreased from 70,000 to only 3,647—both original Jaffa residents and refugees from the area. They were concentrated in a fenced area known as "the ghetto" and were placed under military rule that lasted from May 1948 to July 1949.[72] Simultaneously, Jaffa was settled with Jewish immigrants, mostly from the Balkan and North Africa. The Judaized Old City became known as the Big Territory and was considered a site of poverty, crime, and prostitution.[73] In April 1950, a merger was announced between Tel Aviv and Jaffa, turning Jaffa into the "Oriental backyard" of Tel Aviv. At the same time, Jaffa became a space of leisure, which offered Tel Aviv's Ashkenazi residents an exotic visual, auditory, and culinary experience.[74] Next to simple venues patronized primarily by Arabs and Mizrahi Jews sprang up food, drink, and music establishments that served a commercialized "Orient" to a more heterogeneous clientele, including middle-class Ashkenazim.[75]

Several Arab cafés and restaurants survived the war; some were operated by their original owners while others moved to Jewish hands, and there were also immigrants who opened cafés and restaurants.[76] Anat Helman brings a story of a Polish Jew who opened a restaurant in the city that served only Arab food, since this was what Jewish customers were looking for in Jaffa.[77] In June 1952 Tikva Weinstock noted that there were still "a few Arab restaurants" in the Big Territory that had "not yet spoiled" and that served hummus with a generous amount of oil and a bean soup that actually contained beans, suggesting that an internal differentiation between "authentic" Oriental restaurants (implicitly Arab) and "spoiled" ones was beginning to emerge.[78] Writing in 1953, Israel Goldschmidt-Paz noted that during the austerity years Jaffa's cafés attracted visitors from all echelons of society, from near and far, since they served hearty meals that contained meat, including at nighttime. The meat came from smuggled and illegally slaughtered animals and was served only after ensuring that the customer was not an undercover government inspector.[79]

Most of the Palestinian restaurant sector, however, was destroyed in 1948. Into this gap entered Mizrahi immigrants. Opening a food and drink establishment, often as a family-run business, was a way to convert skills into income in conditions of little or no economic, cultural, or social capital.[80] Some of these establishments were opened in immigrant settlements, with or without a license, and catered to a local clientele.[81] In a short story by Avner Treinin, the Ashkenazi protagonist accidentally reaches a transitional camp and searches for something to eat. When he comes across an old man and asks him whether there was a place where one could eat for money—as he was unable to utter the word *restaurant*—the man tells him that the place where they were standing was a café. Assuming his customer was dismayed to see the place empty, he added that whoever had means went to "their cafés," pointing at the space behind the sandy hills that surrounded the camp like a fence. The man ordered hummus—the only food left.[82]

Most immigrants who opened food and drink establishments did so in major cities like Tel Aviv and Jerusalem or in Judaized Arab towns like Be'er Sheva (Bi'r a-Saba') and Ashkelon (Majdal). The number of these restaurants increased significantly in the first half of the 1950s.[83] For some of the immigrants, primarily in the major cities, opening a food establishment was not just an act of survival but a route to upward economic and social mobility. Ezra Sherfler, who arrived in Israel from Turkey in 1948 at age twelve, first worked as a dishwasher in one of the restaurants in the Machane Yehuda market in Jerusalem. From there, he moved to the kitchen of the famous Rachmo restaurant, and in 1952, he opened his own restaurant in the market, Azura. With time, Azura became a trendy venue for meals of home-cooked food known, inter alia, for its hummus.[84] Janet, who arrived in Israel from Egypt in 1950, was invited by an Arab coworker in a restaurant where she used to cook to join as a partner in the fish restaurant he had opened at the Jaffa port, together with another Arab and a Jew. The restaurant, which received the name Che Janet, served Middle Eastern and Italian dishes and became one of Jaffa's famous dining spots, attracting both a lowbrow and a highbrow clientele.[85] Albert Majar, who arrived in Israel from Bulgaria in 1948, borrowed some money from his wife's family and opened a place for falafel and Oriental cakes in the Jerusalem border neighborhood Mamila, but it was unsuccessful. After working as a taxi driver for several years, he opened the Ta'ami restaurant with one of his relatives. Ta'ami became one of the most popular Oriental restaurants in Jerusalem, also famous for its hummus.[86]

The term *Oriental restaurant* (*mis'ada mizrahit*, lit. Eastern restaurant) became established in Hebrew in the 1940s and widespread in the 1950s.[87]

It indicated a restaurant, either Arab or Jewish owned, that served food from the "Oriental cuisine": usually a selection of mezze, grilled meats, and various vegetable dishes (there were also restaurants that served a combination of Middle Eastern and European dishes[88]). The category Oriental cuisine, which was also used in Hebrew cookbooks from the period, partly reflected the lumping together of people from different countries of descent, with different cultures and different cuisines, under a single "Oriental" label.[89] But partly it reflected the reality of culinary kinship and culinary (and sometimes social and economic) contacts on the ground: Mizrahi immigrants often served in their restaurants dishes from across the Middle East. Thus, Janet served in her restaurant the Libyan-Tunisian dish *hraime*, and Indian-born Moshe El Natan opened a falafel place in Jerusalem.[90] Ezra Sherfler served in Azura rice and beans, mjaddara, and hummus, which he had learned to prepare by watching Abu Shukri in his Haifa restaurant.[91] Albert Majar learned to prepare hummus from his father-in-law—a member of Jerusalem's Moroccan community who had probably learned to prepare it from his Arab neighbors.[92] Other restaurant owners also learned to prepare hummus from Arab cooks, neighbors, and friends.[93] But there were also Jewish-owned Oriental restaurants that hired Arab cooks. In a piece on Oriental restaurants in Jerusalem from 1954, the author noted that the popular Shemesh restaurant employed a cook from Nazareth, and therefore the taste and quality of the dishes were guaranteed.[94]

Already in 1951, Tikva Weinstock described the flow of Ashkenazi customers to Oriental restaurants, which she defined as "the only ones in which you can eat." Everyone ordered hummus and tahini as the first course, she wrote.[95] Hummus was indeed a staple on the menu of Oriental restaurants, although it is difficult to tell what the dish was actually like: occasional periods of chickpea and tahini shortage resulted in hummus that was sometimes rather watery and bland.[96] In 1954, a dish of hummus cost 0.300 Israeli liras (IL), compared to 1–1.5 IL for a meat dish in an average-priced restaurant.[97] In advertisements for Oriental restaurants, the items that were usually mentioned were shashlik, kebab, hummus, tahini, and sometimes steak, ful, and fish, suggesting these were the most popular items on the menu. The actual menus were more diverse. Weinstock noted that Oriental restaurants usually served eight to nine vegetable dishes. Typical dishes besides hummus and tahini, shashlik, and kebab were bean soup, baked and spiced potatoes and eggplant, bulgur, rice, string and baked beans with tomato sauce, vegetable stew, baked or grilled fish, and even herring (according to Weinstock, ordered as a first course only by Sephardi Jews; Ashkenazim claim, "This we have at home").[98] When necessary products were missing from the legal market, restaurant owners often turned to the black market as a solution.[99]

For members of the Ashkenazi elite, the growing presence of Oriental restaurants and street stalls in Jewish or Judaized cities, and their success among Ashkenazi diners, embodied the threat of "levantinization" associated with the immigrants, which fed on both ethnic and class antagonisms. In 1950, Y. H. Tenev described his experience of visiting an Oriental restaurant off Allenby Street in Tel Aviv as a veritable culture shock. Using a no less scathing metaphor than "valley of death," he described the restaurant as an uncivilized inferno, the epitome of the way of life of the backward, immoral, "filthy and polluted" Orient: wrapped in thick smoke of roasting meat; people shouting, swearing, gorging food, eating with their hands; and two drunkards threatening to murder Prime Minister Ben-Gurion if he would not give away free beer. "Had I not received a recommendation about the food, and had I known what was expecting me, I would never have gone there," wrote Tenev, implying that he was going out of his way.[100] Letters of complaint about Oriental restaurants and food stalls arrived in the Tel Aviv municipality throughout the decade. "I do not mean to be taken by hyperbole," wrote the son of Orientalist Menachem Kapeliuk, "but this smoke is like poisoning gas and it is thrown by the wind directly into the homes and has already caused severe headaches and various allergies."[101] In a 1946 piece titled "Falafel—Israel's National Dish?" journalist Uri Keisari (born Keizermann) demonstrated the class bias inherent in elitist attitudes toward Oriental food when he wrote that "while in Arab cities the smell of falafel pervades the alleys of the poor, here it penetrated all the main streets and fancy boulevards."[102]

Nevertheless, despite the lower culinary and cultural prestige of Oriental restaurants, and their "lowbrow" image regardless of their level, they became a viable option in the restaurant repertoire of Ashkenazi Jews, including Ashkenazim of means, which had previously tended to avoid them. In fact, dishes like hummus, tahini, and grilled meats entered many European restaurants, including upscale ones.[103] In 1957 N. Ben-Isser wrote in *Yediot Ahronot* that "the struggle over the Israeli stomach between the forces of the 'Asian East' and those of the 'European East' was concluded mostly in favor of the Orient."[104]

NUTRITION EDUCATION, THE ISRAELI MENU, AND MIZRAHI FOODWAYS

In the 1950s, hummus, together with other Middle Eastern dishes, was also integrated into institutional efforts to shape the foodways of the new nation through education. The inclusion of Arab dishes in suggested recipes and menus in this period should be understood in the context of educators' acknowledgment of the importance of preserving ethnic food traditions, at least in part, and their striving to diversify the Ashkenazi menu. Among their recommended dishes, they included Arab foods that were already becoming popular among Israelis, like hummus, tahini, falafel, and mjaddara, normally defined as Oriental but occasionally as Arab.[105]

While the main concern of educators in this period was to teach women how to prepare nutritious food with the available products rather than to shape a "national cuisine," they were not unconscious of their role as cultural entrepreneurs. Although the title of the most widespread cookbook in this period represented the authoritative certainty of institutional rhetoric—*Thus We Shall Cook*, published by the WIZO (Women's International Zionist Organization), was reprinted ten times between 1948 and 1965—institutions, too, were not always so certain when it came to shaping the foodways of a society in flux. Yet most educators held onto the opinion that a homogenous menu based on European food was not only impossible to achieve but also inadvisable and that the menu of the new nation had to include both European and Middle Eastern elements.

In an article on food, identity, and nation building, Orit Rozin describes two contrasting approaches to the issue of homogenizing the national menu that prevailed in the 1950s. One, represented by Pinchas Lavon, who replaced Dov Yosef as the minister responsible for food provisioning, objected to the idea that rations should be adjusted to ethnic tastes, not only on organizational and budgetary grounds but also on the grounds that eating habits were tools for shaping a homogeneous nation. The other approach was that of women's organizations, supported by Prime Minister Ben-Gurion. According to Rozin, they, too, were in favor of homogenizing the national diet, but in contrast to Lavon, they promoted a model of a "culinary mosaic" in which Ashkenazi food predominated while other ethnic groups made their contributions.[106] Other studies also mention educators' goal of homogenizing the national diet.[107]

Yet promoting a "culinary mosaic" was not tantamount to "homogenization." The issue of "cultural homogenization" was frequently discussed in Israel in this period.[108] It was tightly related to, yet not synonymous with, the issue of crafting a unique national culture (to be discussed in the next chapter). Although assimilating the immigrants into ostensibly modern and Western Israeli culture was a main goal of the "educating state" and its loyal elites in the 1950s, "Israeli culture" itself was not a consolidated entity, and the question of homogenization remained contentious.[109] It was also sector-specific: in cultural sectors such as language and manners, homogenization was deemed essential, but the case of food was more complex. The first edition of WIZO's cookbook voiced an unambiguous commitment to homogenizing Israeli nutritional habits, and so did the 1957 edition, albeit with the disclaimer "if possible."[110] Nevertheless, nutrition experts' statements often ran counter to this goal. Although they imagined the Israeli menu as essentially Ashkenazi with "ethnic contributions," adjusted to the local conditions and demands of nutrition, they did not think that members of different ethnic groups had to eat the same food. Dr. Sarah Bavly, Israel's chief nutritionist and director of the Institute for Nutrition Education, expressed this sentiment when she stated that "we should not aspire, under any circumstances, to create a homogenous Israeli menu."[111]

During the austerity years, and especially in the difficult years of 1950–51, cooking became much more than a survival skill—it attained economic, political, and consequently moral implications more than ever before.[112] Thus, minister of rationing Dov Yosef had written in his preface to Cornfeld's *What Shall I Cook with the Rationing Portions? A Guide* that the public's satisfaction with the rationing menu was dependent on its ability to use the available products efficiently.[113] This was one of the main goals of nutrition education in this period, with its different strategies and information channels aimed at women, on whose shoulders the success of the system allegedly rested.[114] In another place, Yosef defined Israeli housewives' "ignorance of vital facts about nutrition and food uses" the "weak link" in the Israeli food chain.[115]

If women in general were seen as ignorant about the demands of nutrition, the highest ignorance was attributed to Mizrahi women. As I noted, the mass immigration of Jews from Arab countries after the foundation of the state caused a veritable fear of "levantinization" among Ashkenazi veterans.[116] Descriptions of the immigrants, which appeared in the Hebrew press, depicted them as a different race from Ashkenazi Jews, uncivilized and unhygienic, passive and apathetic, who procreated too much (yet cared too little for their children) and hence one day would become the majority.[117] Popular perceptions were backed by the discourse of social scientists and educators, who lent scientific approval to the need to "de-socialize" and "re-socialize" the immigrants.[118] As Sarah Bavly wrote, Mizrahi immigrants arrived in Israel "from underdeveloped countries without even the barest knowledge of proper nutrition" and with "the most abominable food habits imaginable."[119] Examples of habits that commentators described as abominable were eating with the hands while seated on the floor, eating whenever appetite arose instead of at fixed meal times, and giving the best parts of the food to men and the lesser parts to women and children.[120]

Mizrahi immigrants became targets of a massive educational apparatus intended to "raise the civilizational level of family life" through teaching women "proper habits" in hygiene, home economics, childcare, cooking, and eating.[121]

Figure 2.3 WIZO instructors teach Mizrahi immigrants how to cook.
WIZO Archive; Central Zionist Archive, PHWI\1246431.

While educators targeted all Jewish women, educating Mizrahi immigrants was seen as the most pressing task. An army of instructors, both professionals and volunteers, went to immigrants' settlements to teach women how to adjust their foodways to Western standards and how to prepare "balanced menus" with the available rationed products, many of which were unfamiliar to them.[122] Nevertheless, in a 1955 report on the food habits of "Oriental Jewish communities" following their immigration to Israel, Dr. Walter Strauss of the Hebrew University's Hygiene Department stated that out of the sixty-four families interrogated, only a few were reached by teaching institutions, and "no noticeable impression has been made on them."[123] Nutrition education of the younger generation through the schools was somewhat more successful: many of the schools had a lunch program that was often accompanied by cooking and nutrition lessons.[124] In 1960, Bavly stated that having children who attended an Israeli school was the single most important factor accounting for the integration of European dishes into the menu of Mizrahi families.[125]

Regardless of educators' aspirations, the chances of converting Mizrahi immigrants to the Ashkenazi diet were close to nil. Studies show that food habits are one of the last cultural sectors to change among migrants, partly due to food being a powerful means for reconstructing a lost sensory environment and (re)producing "home" and community in a new country.[126] Many Mizrahi immigrants hailed from countries where variety was much more substantial than in 1950s Israel and meat was abundant and relatively inexpensive, such as Iraq, Morocco, and Yemen.[127] Whatever hierarchies of culinary value educators were trying to impart to them, most of them did not find Ashkenazi food particularly appealing.[128] Although Mizrahi foodways were changing in the wake of immigration,[129] when they were no longer dependent on communal kitchens, they made efforts to reconstruct familiar dishes using available substitutions for the missing products or buying them in Arab localities.[130] Some immigrants brought with them various foods, spices, and even seeds of vegetables that did not grow in Israel.[131]

Yet it was not simply failure to convert Mizrahi immigrants to Ashkenazi tastes that explains nutrition experts' support for preserving parts of their culinary heritage, which they expressed from early on. Rather, it reflected an accepted tenet of the prevailing nutrition discourse, which attributed increasing importance to cultural factors and assumed that any nutritional change should take ingrained habits and cultural meanings into account.[132] In the US, with which Israeli nutrition experts maintained educational and institutional ties, reformers started to promote a modified version of various ethnic foods as part of the American diet already in the 1920s.[133]

Furthermore, culinary hierarchies did not simply mirror sociopolitical hierarchies, although the assignment of culinary value is not altogether detached from global power dynamics.[134] Whichever hierarchy of culinary value nutrition educators followed, they did not regard Ashkenazi cuisines as inherently superior to the cuisines of Mizrahi Jews and Arabs. As I showed in the previous chapter, while Middle Eastern cuisines were praised for their resourceful use of simple local products, Ashkenazi food was considered unsuitable to the local climate and produce and its Israeli variant dull and monotonous, especially in times of scarcity and meat shortage but also later. Consequently, nutrition experts regarded Middle Eastern dishes as a spice that can "liven up the dull dish" of Ashkenazi cooking, to paraphrase bell hooks.[135]

In October 1950, the Institute for Nutrition Education held its third bi-monthly conference on the question of how to mediate between Yemenite and North African food traditions and the Israeli food reality. Three hundred women attended the conference.[136] According to Cornfeld, who reported on the conference for the readers of *Haaretz*, the pending question was how to teach the immigrants the foundations of a healthy national nutrition without offending their sense of taste. As we adjusted the austerity dishes to Mizrahi communities, she wrote, we had to deal with more than just the five senses: "tradition and religion, psychological and physiological factors, all partake in the habits of nutrition. The memory of a food eaten hot or cold, spicy or delicate—these affect the pleasure of eating. How much of this pleasure is spoiled when, for instance, people who have dipped a piece of pita bread in their food their entire lives have to use forks? How to get used to the nutritionally standard bread, when the memory of hot and steaming 'kubaneh' and the smell of cumin brings with it yearnings?"[137]

Cornfeld did not shy away from expressing her appreciation for the cuisines of North African Jews, although she found them not entirely suitable to the Israeli climate (too much oil and not enough fresh vegetables). In spite of the title under which her piece appeared—"One Cuisine to the Ingathering Exiles"—she ended her report with the statement "It seems to me that we have a lot to learn, even while we teach." The conference concluded with several policy suggestions intended to facilitate Mizrahi immigrants' preservation of their traditional cuisines. Another report on this conference, by journalist and scholar Henrietta Boas, was concluded with the sentence "While Israel [sic] nutritional experience may help to create a healthier population from Yemen and North Africa, the care and variety of the Oriental cuisine may add more color to the frequently indifferent Israeli cooking."[138]

A similar position was expressed in Strauss's report, which suggested a "liberal" approach to a national food policy that would facilitate the development of an Israeli kitchen as one in which "adaptation" would work both ways: "When it is seen with what eagerness children of European origin eat falafel, humus, tchina and other food preparations unknown to their family circle, it can well be imagined that the Oriental kitchen, with its rich palette of spices can give taste to European dishes which become monotonous when the wide choice of foodstuffs on which they depend for variety, is missing."[139]

Through exhibitions, cookbooks, and food columns educators labored to acquaint Ashkenazi consumers with a variety of Middle Eastern dishes. This was the purpose of a 1953 exhibition at the Seligsberg vocational school in Jerusalem, where women in traditional costumes presented dishes from their countries of origin.[140] This was also the purpose of a booklet published by the College of Nutrition and Home Economics at the Ministry of Education, marking the tenth anniversary of the state. The booklet was titled *Thou Shall Make Your Guests' Heart Happy* and included recipes of five Mizrahi communities, with one chapter dedicated to Eastern Europe and one to the United States. The foreword stressed the importance of shaping a common style of hospitality through cultural exchange between the ethnic communities, just as the different Diasporas were being made into a single nation.[141] A 1958 study on Iraqi and Yemenite foodways even proposed considering serving Oriental food in school lunches in order to raise the prestige of this food, suggesting that in spite of the popularity of various Middle Eastern dishes, overall the status of Middle Eastern food was still relatively low.[142]

While government publications focused mainly on the cuisines of Jewish ethnic groups, in various cookbooks and food columns the Oriental category included staples from the Palestinian Arab kitchen. In January 1950, Lilian Cornfeld wrote in her *Haaretz* column, "Why is it that the Arab cuisine is so much better than ours? Especially that the Arabs use the simplest materials at our disposal. I have recently dined at the table of the mayor of Nazareth and all the dishes which were served deserve that we try to imitate them and compete in their preparation." Cornfeld mainly praised the Arab method of slow cooking over low fire and the addition of very little meat to simple dishes, which turned them into "real delicacies."[143] In various columns, she tried to convince her readers to integrate Middle Eastern dishes into their repertoire of home cooking. "Why should your children always buy this food on the street," she wrote in a column devoted to tahini, "when you can easily prepare it yourself at home."[144] In a later column, titled "Secrets from the Oriental Kitchen," she noted that "the foods of the east are already popular in many Ashkenazi circles, who know to appreciate the special merits of this kind of cooking: piquant spicing, healthier mode of cooking (except overly fried foods), usually over open fire, and aesthetic serving with decorated plates." She suggested her readers prepare the provided recipes, including hummus, at home rather than eating them in Oriental restaurants and paying prices that are no less "spicy" than the dishes.[145]

The establishment of hummus, falafel, and tahini in the culinary repertoire of Israelis, and educators' attempt to naturalize them in the Israeli kitchen, were manifested in a suggested menu for an Independence Day dinner that appeared in 1957 in *Davar*.[146] Previous suggestions by governmental agencies offered both familiar and invented dishes, the rationale for which was mainly symbolic. Especially the 1955 suggestion, devised by the Nutrition Department of the Ministry of Education, offered two menus that combined Western and Eastern elements (e.g., a mallow salad with tahini together with *klops* [meat loaf] with a hard-boiled egg), but it failed to catch on.[147] The 1957 suggestion, which was published anonymously in the column "For the Woman and the Family," included two separate menus: an Ashkenazi "cold meal" (hard-boiled eggs filled with chopped liver, corned beef, or sausage, and potato salad) and an "Oriental style meal" (vegetable salad with hard-boiled eggs, hummus, tahini, falafel, spicy fish, and Turkish coffee). "The dinner we offer you is at once festive and informal," it was stated; "it is meant to create the special atmosphere which would lift the spirit of the diners but not chain them in festive formality."[148] As this suggestion attests, hummus and falafel were seen as suited for an occasion that was both festive (since they were popular yet "special") and informal (since they were considered relatively "low" in status). In order to achieve the same combination of festivity and informality, the European meal had to be cold.

The symbolism of including Arab food in a dinner marking the Jewish triumph in the battle over the land is hard to miss. However, in the same year Cornfeld suggested to include hummus in Purim dinner and, in fact, in any party—served either as "dip" or as bread or cracker spread.[149] "Guests always welcome hummus and tahini, especially at young people's parties," she wrote elsewhere.[150] *Thus We Shall Cook*, which included only two Middle Eastern recipes in 1948 (kebab and *kibbe*), by 1957 had a separate "Oriental" section with eleven recipes including falafel, "hummus and tahini salad," "tahini salad," and "mayonnaise from tahini." However, throughout most of the decade, Middle Eastern foods hardly entered the Ashkenazi kitchen.[151] When Ashkenazim consumed them, they usually did so in the public sphere.

THE FOOD OF NEW MEN

In early 1954, two newspapers reported on the Purim holiday party at the shack of Reuven and Shulamit Aloni (former Palmach and later parliament member) in Kfar Shmaryahu (at the time Reuven—formerly a commander in the Haganah[152]—was busy sorting out lands in order to place evacuated Arab land under a single administrative body, which he would later help establish). Among the guests were "all the folks from the Palmach," military men (including Chief of Staff Moshe Dayan), journalists and bohemians, and "dozens of girls."[153] According to journalist Dahn Ben-Amotz, who covered the party for *Davar* readers, one of the rooms featured an electrical bonfire (!) surrounded by mattresses and mats where guests sat cross-legged, playing Arab. Among the few items of refreshment served were falafel and hummus.[154]

So far, I have discussed the "infrastructure" for the spread of hummus, falafel, and other Palestinian staples among Israeli consumers after the foundation of the state. Yet to understand the attraction of these dishes for a growing Israeli public, it is necessary to examine the way they have been appropriated and mediated by a group of cultural entrepreneurs, best defined as self-styled Zionist "New Men"—former warriors, primarily Palmach members, who partook in the cultural project of crafting a new Jewish-indigenous ("Sabra") cultural repertoire. In the 1950s, this repertoire, which originated in earlier decades, spread among broader circles through their work.

The elite Jewish combat units known as Palmach (an acronym for Plugot Machatz—Hebrew for Assault Companies) formed in 1941 to help defend the country from German incursions and evolved into the primary Jewish fighting force in the war of 1948 (it was dismantled after the foundation of the state). Playing Arab was a favorite activity among Palmach members, whose culture and style profoundly influenced the development of the Sabra cultural archetype in the 1950s. Embodying masculine values such as boldness, combative spirit, shrewdness, and directness, Palmach culture provided the generation of native-born Israelis with a set of models that could be adopted to mark one's distinction from the Jews of the Diaspora (and their representatives in Israel) and from the generation of their parents. Regardless of the number of those who embodied this archetype, its cultural influence was far and wide.[155]

The function of Arabness within the culture of the Palmach is captured in the following excerpt from the 1981 book *1948—Between the Countings* by famous (female) Palmach warrior Netiva Ben-Yehuda: "We were dying to be like them, only this preoccupied us: to talk like them, to walk like them, to behave like them, in the sun, in the wind, in the field, at night, to dress like them . . . the keffiyeh, the moustaches, the finjan, the chizbat. Everything we took from them. We regarded them as the model of the native [*bney ha'aretz*], and we—perhaps we did not even come close to something definite, but we were certainly 'not Diaspora Jews.'"[156]

In the introductory chapter we saw how Palmach members' mimicking what they perceived to be the Arab way of drinking coffee allowed them to perform a self that was "naturally rooted in the land." Rather than eating the Other, it was eating to *become* the Other, or perform, and thus inhabit, the Other's indigenous authenticity (obviously becoming something other than the Other[157]). The association of Arabs (and, to a lesser extent, Mizrahi Jews) with authenticity, which modernized Ashkenazi Jews have presumably lost, was a recurrent theme in the discourse of Ashkenazi cultural entrepreneurs on Arab/Middle Eastern food. In the theater of authenticity, food consumption had a uniquely powerful affective resonance, engaging all senses and bodily faculties and, through the act of incorporation, transforming the body of the consumer from the inside.[158]

I would like to focus on the writings of two former Palmach members who were instrumental in promoting the consumption of hummus and other Arab dishes as indices of indigenous authenticity and masculinity: Dahn Ben-Amotz and Haim Gouri. Both were born in 1923 and were twenty-five years old when they fought in the 1948 war. Both were journalists and authors: Ben-Amotz was a novelist, a translator, a scriptwriter, a radio broadcaster, and an actor, and Gouri was a poet, a novelist, a songster, a translator, and a filmmaker. Both played pivotal roles in shaping and spreading the Sabra cultural repertoire. While their public personas differed significantly—Gouri embodying the solemn voice of the national ethos and Ben-Amotz representing down-to-earth, coarse Israeliness—both associated the Orient with authenticity, which they found lacking among Ashkenazim.

Of the two, it was mainly the bohemian gastronome and omnivore avant la lettre Ben-Amotz (d. 1989) who often wrote about food in his popular column What's Up.[159] Born in Rovno (present-day Ukraine), Ben-Amotz arrived in Palestine with the Youth Aliyah at age fifteen.[160] He was considered by many the quintessential New Hebrew, which he became by force of a self-willed transformation: he changed his name from the exilic-sounding Moishe Tehilimzuger to the Hebrew and biblical sounding Dahn Ben-Amotz; he made up a biography of a native for himself; he lived on a kibbutz for a while and served in the Palmach. And, like many others of this social circle, he was a bold and direct man who cultivated an image of unruliness and independence. He was also an avid womanizer, notorious for his predatory attitude. In his later days, he used to wear an Arab *jellabiya* and walk barefoot, which became his trademark.

Several of Ben-Amotz's columns from the 1950s contained references to eating hummus. For instance, in May 1955, he described a hummus, shashlik, and beer meal at the Kings Restaurant in Haifa, "one of the most authentic places we have seen in the country."[161] In October that year, he described in detail a visit to the restaurant Pninat Hamizrah (Pearl of the East) by the Tel Aviv shore:

> What do you do when there is nothing to do in the evening in Tel Aviv? You go down to Allenby [Street] by the shore. . . . First we entered Pninat Hamizrach and ordered hummus ʿalakaifak, a big glass of soda water and a dish of kebab with shashlik half-half mixed. The waiter turned to the counter . . . and announced with a loud hoarse voice: "hummus ʿalakaifak, okiya mshakala salaha!" The customers around us were young guys, with black moustaches and white shirts, sleeves folded, and their girls with black and shiny hair, slightly transparent white silk blouses and cheap jewelry. At the next table sat four guys, and once the waiter brought them a dish with fresh pita bread, each grabbed a pita, tapped both sides on his palm to remove the extra flour. When their hummus arrived, they tore a piece and picked the hummus between their forefinger and thumb.[162]

Were these guys Arabs? Mizrahi Jews? Ben-Amotz does not say. In his writings, hummus and other Arab staples appear as the food of "real" (read: authentic) and simple men and simultaneously as the opposite of the dull, repetitive, and unexciting Eastern European ("Diasporic") cooking, and Diasporic culture more generally.

Figure 2.4 Dahn Ben-Amotz in his Old Jaffa home. Photo by Rachel Hirsch. Courtesy of the photographer.

They were common and familiar foods yet still exotic enough to merit a detailed description—not just of the food but of the entire scene of its consumption (audaciously accompanied by the meaningless words "okiya mshakala salaha," probably intended to convey the author's proficiency in Arabic). In other columns he made sure to position himself as an expert on Arab food. For instance, in his first *Maariv* What's Up column from 1956, he addressed the "housewife who doesn't know how to prepare kugel" (an Eastern European dish), telling her that he, too, did not know how to prepare it but that he could teach her how to prepare hummus—thus marking himself as both masculine and "local."[163]

As the popularity of hummus, tahini, and other Arab staples became widespread among Jewish consumers, "Arab"—as distinct from "Oriental"—could serve as a means of distinction not just between "old Jews" and "new Hebrews" but also between the speakers—members of the cultural elite—and the unenlightened Jewish "masses." For example, in a 1958 column on the opening ceremony of the Karawan restaurant in Abu Ghosh, Ben-Amotz contrasted the "hummus-tahini-kebab-shashlik-tempo" served in Oriental restaurants with authentic Arab food, which even Arab restaurants catering to Jewish customers failed to serve. Citing some dozen dishes, which he called by their Arabic names, he stated that for ten years he has been waiting for a "real Arab restaurant" that would serve "the splendor of Arab cuisine," but to no avail. According to him, he tried to convince the owner to prepare these dishes "which our audience has already forgotten," but the latter stated that the Jews mainly liked kebab, shashlik, hummus, and tahini.[164] In this excerpt, Ben-Amotz positions himself as a mediator of Arab authenticity not only to Jews, who have allegedly "forgotten" it, but also to the Arab restaurant owner. To his detriment, his cultural mission encountered the market-oriented approach of a real Arab seeking to make a living by selling food.

A similar association of Arab hummus with authenticity, in contrast to hummus made by Jews, is found in a 1956 article by Haim Gouri (although he attributed a higher degree of authenticity to hummus made by Mizrahim, compared to Ashkenazim[165]). Gouri (d. 2018) was born in Tel Aviv as Haim Gurfinkel, to a father who was one of the founders of the labor Zionist Mapai party. He was educated in the School for Children of Working Parents in Tel Aviv, which was affiliated with the labor movement, and later in kibbutz Beit Alfa and in the agricultural school Kadoorie—a breeding ground for Zionist leaders. In 1941 he joined the Palmach, and in 1947 he was sent by the Haganah to Europe, where he commanded the first IDF paratroopers' class. He fought in the war of 1948 as a deputy platoon commander (and later in the wars of 1967 and 1973). After the war, he studied Hebrew literature, philosophy, and French culture at the Hebrew University of Jerusalem and contemporary French literature at the Sorbonne. Between 1954 and 1988 he worked as a journalist, wrote poetry, prose, and essays, and served as an editor, translator, and filmmaker. A recipient of the prestigious Israel Prize (1988), Gouri is considered one of Israel's most acclaimed poets.[166]

As we saw in the previous chapter, for Gouri Arab food was metonymic of Arab space, which he associated with historicity and sensual abundance as well as danger. Gouri's most elaborate descriptions of eating (Arab) hummus appeared after the 1967 occupation of the West Bank and Gaza, but there are also a couple of mentions of eating hummus in Arab restaurants, which appeared in the journal *LeMerchav* in the 1950s. In a 1956 piece on his visit to Nazareth, Gouri contrasted the "real hummus" he had eaten there to the "European hummus" served in Jewish restaurants.[167] In this article, Nazareth is an Other space within the Israeli space: filthy, reclusive, and hostile but also full of character, folklore, history, and memories, with "an atmosphere of holiness and mystery" that he contrasted with Israeli architectural modernism: "gray houses, light, cubist, straight-lined, without a long life-burden, which lends a city yearning and power." Nazareth, with its Oriental mystery, historical depth, and sensuality, is that thing that "belongs not to us" and that will never be ours because it is "unoccupiable." In a 1957 article in which Gouri related some Haifa adventures from the days of the Palmach, he wrote, "Without even slightly offending the Israeli hummus experts, we must note that only our cousins know how to make *real* hummus, hummus which is served in clay bowls with greenish, heavy olive oil."[168]

Anna Johnston and Alan Lawson note the doubleness of settler narratives, concerned with acting out not only the suppression or effacement of the indigene but also the indigenization of the settler.[169] Through consuming Arab food—especially street food eaten with the hands—"civilized" Jewish settlers striving to constitute themselves as New Men and "natives" could perform an authentically local and masculine self. At the same time, Arab indigenous authenticity—both quintessentially local and "exotic"—was repeatedly reaffirmed in their writings as that thing Jewish settlers will always desire but will never entirely possess. Enter the electrical bonfire.

The marking of hummus and falafel as "Oriental" (Mizrahi) facilitated their "Israelization" since the late 1950s, which will be discussed in the next chapter. Yet in various discursive contexts, they were simultaneously marked as "Arab" throughout the decade. Thus, a 1953 piece on Be'er Sheva described a Jewish restaurant that served only "Arab dishes" and a 1957 satirical piece from *Davar* noted that in spite of the Arab ban on Israel the Israelis allowed themselves to eat falafel, tahini, hummus, and shashlik, *"national Arab foods by all accounts."*[170] But I also came across a few cases from the second half of the 1950s—usually while discussing an Oriental restaurant opened by an Israeli abroad—where they were defined as "Israeli foods."[171]

THREE

—ɯɯ—

NATIONALISM IN A CAN

Preparing hummus—a children's game! Just add water and the hummus is ready for immediate serving. No need to cook.

—Advertisement for Telma's hummus, 1958

BY THE LATE 1950S, HUMMUS became a viable option in the food repertoire of Israelis, and the models organizing its consumption diversified. It broke out of the bounds of the Oriental restaurant and entered other non–ethnically marked food establishments, and since 1958, the domestic kitchen, through the food industry. After the occupation of the West Bank and the Gaza Strip in 1967, another model began to gain ground among Israeli consumers: that of hummus as a meal. On the symbolic level, hummus was branded an Israeli "national dish," and its Arabness mostly suppressed—a process reinforced by a reality of spatial segregation. After the termination of the military rule in 1966 and the 1967 occupation, Jewish attendance of Arab-owned restaurants increased, and so did the prestige of certain Palestinian hummus joints. A differentiating discourse on hummus has developed, mainly around the distinction between artisanal and industrial versions of the dish and between "real hummus" and hummus catering to "common taste."

With a dire economic situation, massive immigration from countries deemed "backward," and lack of international recognition of Israeli sovereignty in all the territories conquered in 1948, the first years of Israeli statehood were characterized by much uncertainty concerning the viability of the new state. By the late 1950s, Israeli confidence had grown. The conquest of the Gaza Strip and the Sinai Peninsula in 1956, although short-lived, reassured Israel of its military might. The economic situation was also ameliorated, and the austerity

78

regime was officially lifted in 1959. Israel became more open to the world: the exit permit, which limited citizens' ability to travel abroad, was abolished in 1961, and more emphasis was placed on tourism.[1] During the first nine months of 1960, ninety-three thousand tourists visited the country, and some of the biggest luxury hotel chains opened local branches.[2] Both incoming and outgoing tourism had a decisive influence on the local culinary sphere.

Economic growth and industrial development, coupled with the expansion of the private sector and the middle class, led to the consolidation of consumer culture in the 1960s. While the dominant ethos continued to stress restraint and identify "excessive consumption" with decadence, this state-made middle class began to mark its distinction through way of life and style, signified, inter alia, through consumer goods.[3] Between 1958–59 and 1968–69, per capita expenditure on consumption increased by almost 70 percent, and the standard of living rose considerably.[4] But so did social gaps: the reparations from Germany, the making of Mizrahi Jews into an industrial proletariat, and the further dispossession of Palestinian citizens under the military rule tightened the correlation between ethnicity and class.[5]

The budding consumer culture was accompanied by efforts to develop an aesthetic language of "Israeliness" in various fields of material culture, among them food. Some of these efforts were state sponsored, but the symbolic currency of the "uniquely Israeli" made it a central objective in many grassroots cultural initiatives as well. While the building blocks for the new language of Israeliness were drawn from a variety of cultural sources, its syntax was usually symbolic, intertwining elements that indexed ties to the place, "ingathering of the exiles" (i.e., the Zionist ideal of Jews leaving the Diaspora to settle in Israel), or a synthesis between East and West. Hummus, alongside several other Arab dishes, was integrated into some of these initiatives as a beloved local staple, even if its insertion into constructions of symbolic Israeliness did not go uncontested.

But probably the most significant force in the process of nationalizing hummus in this period was its industrialization. The food industry not only made hummus much more easily accessible for Israelis but also mediated emerging discourses on hummus through its publicity campaigns, lending them authority and volume. Simultaneously, the rise of industrial hummus contributed to elevating the hummus produced in specific restaurants and hummus joints, both Jewish and Arab owned.

This chapter focuses on the Israelization of hummus since the late 1950s and in the following two decades. After a short introduction to the culinary field of the 1960s, I discuss the integration of Arab and Mizrahi dishes into symbolic constructions of "Israeli cuisine." Subsequently I examine the essential role of the industrialization of hummus in shaping and propagating consumption patterns and meanings. The next two sections look at the changes brought about by the 1967 occupation of the West Bank and the Gaza Strip: Israelis' encounters with Palestinian restaurants and hummus joints and their adoption of the model of hummus as a meal. As I will show, industrialization gave rise to a dialectical process of nationalization and distinction: on the one hand, the food industry played a pivotal role in domesticating and de-Arabizing hummus; on the other hand, it gave rise to a differentiating discourse on hummus, emphasizing quality and authenticity. Alongside the encounter with Palestinian hummus joints after 1967, it set the stage for the association of Arab-made hummus with authenticity and better quality in later decades.

CULINARY TRANSFORMATIONS

The rapid economic growth since the mid-1950s, coupled with substantial state investment in agricultural and industrial development, markedly shaped the culinary landscape. The range of products available to consumers expanded, including luxury products, food prices dropped, and local demand grew and diversified.[6] A widening selection of industrially processed and packaged foods as well as new appliances (e.g., mixers and gas stoves) entered middle-class kitchens.[7] Specialty stores sprang up on the streets of the main cities, and a new institution—the supermarket—promised to bring the American shopping experience to Israeli consumers.[8]

The increased availability of a diverse range of products was accompanied by a growing number of books teaching women how to use them. In the 1960s, at least fifteen cookbooks were published, including specialized ones, compared to two in the 1950s and six in the 1940s.[9] A few of them were even authored by men, including professional chefs or food experts, attesting to the rising legitimacy of gastronomy as a worthy occupation. Professional cooking had developed,[10] and so had "professional" consumption: in 1968, the international association of gastronomy Confrérie de la Chaîne des Rôtisseurs opened its Israeli branch, which was headed by Jerusalem mayor Teddy Kollek and joined by prominent politicians such as Moshe Dayan and Shimon Peres.[11]

Restaurant attendance also rose in the 1960s; in 1965, Menachem Talmi mentioned the restaurant trend, discussed "in every decent social circle."[12] By 1968, there were 1,400 restaurants in Israel, in which 7,000 people were employed (besides 2,400 cafés and cafeterias and 1,700 kiosks and falafel stands).[13] The selection of cuisines available for consumers in the main urban centers, primarily in Tel Aviv, diversified, with French, Italian, and Greek food, American-style fast food, and even two Chinese restaurants supplementing the more traditional Central European and Middle Eastern fare.[14] Since the early 1960s, daily newspapers began to publish restaurant reviews, whose authors ranged from the amateur to the professional.[15] Most of them covered both highbrow and lowbrow restaurants, among them Oriental ones. Nevertheless, for most middle-class families, recreational dining in a restaurant was still a rare practice.[16]

The expansion and diversification of the restaurant sector prompted its stratification—between high and low as well as within the low. On the whole, Oriental restaurants were still considered relatively low in status, but once they became popular with Ashkenazim, derogatory references to such restaurants were less on account of their "Oriental nature," and more on account of their association with "common taste" and low culinary and sometimes sanitary standards.[17] Yet there were some Oriental restaurants that gained reputations among Ashkenazi elites as authentic alternatives to the ordinary options— namely, to restaurants that were associated with an exclusive Mizrahi clientele or those perceived to have compromised their authenticity to cater to Ashkenazi or broader Jewish preferences (obviously restaurants had to appeal to Ashkenazim to be deemed "authentic").[18] Abu Christo's fish restaurant in Acre, Abu Skander restaurant in Haifa, Ta'ami in Jerusalem, and a few of the restaurants in Tel Aviv's Yemenite Quarter (the Kerem neighborhood) are several examples.[19] In Jaffa, the Younes restaurant opened in 1965 by Suleiman Mahmoud Nassar from the northern village of Tur'an and soon became trendy among Jewish restaurant-goers. According to restaurant critic Menachem Talmi, who referred to Younes as an "eatery" (*mizlala*) although it was a restaurant tout court, many Tel Avivis stood on line there despite the unsanitary conditions and its location in the heart of the "Arab ghetto," notorious for being a dilapidated area of poverty and crime.[20] Most Jews, however, tended to avoid Arab places beyond the usual tourist routes, so some Arab restaurants that sought to attract a Jewish clientele opened in liminal spaces such as gas stations or on the periphery of Arab villages and towns.[21] Greek restaurants, which also served popular Middle Eastern dishes, became a fashionable "Mediterranean" option for the country's bohemians and social and political elite—a "third-space" that was not quite Western nor entirely Oriental.[22]

In this period, hummus—usually consumed as a first course, a "salad" or a "spread"[23]—continued to penetrate new types of food establishments, ranging from swimming pool cafeterias to wedding halls—a process likely to have been precipitated by the arrival of the industrial version.[24] Similar to the institution of the Oriental restaurant, hummus lost its status as a special or exotic food and became simply a popular food that Israelis liked to eat; as of the mid-1960s, "hummus-tahini" was sometimes invoked by food connoisseurs as synonymous with "common taste."[25] The sense of familiarity, even intimacy with the dish, was manifested in two ostensibly opposing practices: one was improvisation (e.g., "Colorful hummus or hummus with vegetables" recipe for Purim breakfast[26]); the other was authoritative judgment. For example, when a reader named Gisela Ardosh wrote *Maariv* in 1969 requesting recipes for hummus, tahini, and falafel, "which are so popular in Israel," she noted that although these could be bought everywhere, only a few places prepared them properly.[27]

Sidney Mintz defined *cuisine* as the food of a community that eats it frequently enough so as to consider itself expert on it: "They all believe, and care that they believe, that they know what it consists of, how it is made, and how it should taste."[28] Ardosh's letter betrays a different approach to hummus and falafel: presumptive judgment on how they should "properly" taste, combined with little knowledge of their ingredients or how they are actually made.

EAST/WEST AND THE MAKING OF AN "ISRAELI CULTURE" AND "ISRAELI CUISINE"

Hummus, accompanied by pita bread, did sometimes appear in more elevated culinary contexts, such as on the menu of a fancy hotel restaurant or in an official festive dinner for distinguished guests, especially when the "Israeliness" of the meal had to be conveyed. For example, when Jerusalem mayor Teddy Kollek hosted Baron Edmund de Rothschild for dinner in 1966, he served him a meal "based only on Oriental dishes," including hummus. And when Israel hosted the International Gastronomic Congress in November 1968, the meal served to the guests of the congress—members of the Confrérie de la Chaîne des Rôtisseurs and of the country's social and cultural elite—included hummus alongside tahini, eggplant, cucumbers and tomatoes, and tilapia fish "our style."[29]

The integration of hummus, falafel, tahini, and other Arab staples into a repertoire of "Israeli food" was part of a much broader effort to shape a symbolic "Israeli culture" and "Israeli style" that permeated many fields of cultural production, including music, dance, fashion, interior design, even beauty—each with its distinct dynamics, discourses, and timelines.[30] This effort intensified in the late 1950s in the context of economic growth and industrial development, and with them the expansion of consumption, the export of Israeli products, and the growth of the tourism sector. The latter two granted the "uniquely Israeli" an economic and not just a symbolic value, especially in light of the growing curiosity toward "ethnic" and foreign cuisines among European and North American consumers.[31]

A central feature of the symbolic "Israeli style," especially when designed with an international audience in mind, was the fusion of East and West.[32] This trend was particularly discernible in cultural domains categorized as "folk culture" or "folklore." It could take different forms, such as the integration of Eastern elements and techniques into Western genres or combining Eastern and Western items into a larger whole.[33] The increased presence of Arab and Mizrahi cultural elements within symbolic constructions of "Israeli culture" was not always well received by Ashkenazi gatekeepers. Yosef Carmel denounced it in the pages of the leftist daily *Al Hamishmar* as "our Oriental mania."[34]

The term *Oriental* (Mizrahi), which was increasingly applied to Mizrahi Jews and their cultural production, was a racialized category associated primarily with social and cultural backwardness in hegemonic discourses.[35] Yet the sign of the Oriental could also stand for authenticity, historicity, and connection to the Oriental space. Thus products of Mizrahi traditional cultures, often rejected as nonmodern by Mizrahim themselves, served to give the symbolic "Israeli" culture an authentic aura, as items of a quintessentially Oriental culture extending back to the ancient Hebrews.[36] Among Mizrahim, the figure of the Yemenite carried the strongest symbolic weight as a pristine incarnation of an ancient past, although its symbolic prominence declined in the course of the 1960s.[37]

In the meantime, real Mizrahim continued to suffer poverty and institutional neglect in urban slums, in "development towns," and in immigrant moshavim (cooperative settlements) on the periphery, and some still in transitional camps. Their lived cultures were degraded by the Ashkenazi cultural elites and were considered synonymous with low aesthetic value and vulgarity.[38] In fact, cultural consumption among Mizrahim in this period was characterized by what Oded Erez termed "cosmopolitanism-from-below"—a fusion of cultural products from a variety of Western and Middle Eastern sources. Since Mizrahim underwent a process of de-Arabization, cultural sources perceived as "non-Arab Oriental" or "Mediterranean" held significant sway, including Greek and Turkish music; Indian, Persian, and Turkish cinema; and food from across the Middle East and the Balkans.[39]

Much of the incentive to develop an Israeli culinary specificity in this period came from tourism.[40] The absence of an Israeli cuisine or unique Israeli dishes usually came to the fore when Israeli food culture was scrutinized by Western eyes.[41] According to commentators, tourists complained that the food they received in Israeli hotels was dull, monotonous, and especially not "Israeli."[42] In 1960, Wilta Bar-Ilan, an American nutrition expert and the wife of an Israeli pianist, arrived in Israel in the framework of the American Technical Assistance

Program, to advise the Governmental Tourism Company on how to improve the level of food served in hotels and restaurants.[43] Her report was devastating. Among Bar-Ilan's lengthy list of deficiencies was the lack of a typical Israeli dish, which she suggested inventing to draw tourists from around the world.[44] She also recommended organizing a cooking contest and giving dishes Hebrew names—two recommendations that were indeed implemented.[45]

Efforts to shape a repertoire of "Israeli food," which involved state institutions, commercial bodies, various food professionals, and laypersons, relied on two main strategies. One was invention: new dishes concocted either by home cooks or by experts and consecrated by other experts. Here the main principle that made dishes eligible to contend for the title was "locality": local ingredients, local cooking techniques, Hebrew names (often local place names—e.g., Ne'ot Mordechai veal rolls, Eilat Beach fish soup). The second was the appropriation of various Jewish and Arab dishes popular with Israelis or considered worthy of promotion from the ethnic niche into the national repertoire under the banner of "ingathering of the exiles." These two strategies were sometimes combined so that when Knesset Chef Rafi Strauss was invited by the Israeli embassy in Paris to prepare a meal celebrating the 1967 victory, he prepared hummus, fish with tahini, chicken "new wave" in orange sauce, and avocado mousse.[46]

The most conspicuous example of the first strategy was the biannual Queen of the Kitchen recipe contest, which took place between 1963 and 1972. It was part of a broader culinary initiative, the March of Israeli Delicacies, which was sponsored by the Prime Minister Office and the Hotel Owners Association, among others.[47] According to Arieh Avisar, the manager of the Instruction Department in the Governmental Tourism Company, the main goal of the contest was to develop an Israeli cuisine, or at least an Israeli dish, to stave off tourists' complaints. A secondary goal was to infuse "culinary consciousness" in the Israeli public and improve the Israeli menu. Another goal mentioned by Avisar was to bring about an ethnic culinary fusion.[48] The winning recipe was to be distributed to all restaurants and hotels in the country.

Submitted recipes had to be kosher and had to focus on specific local ingredients as their theme. Traditional Jewish foods were prohibited, as were imported products.[49] More than thirteen hundred women submitted recipes to the first contest.[50] According to the reports, the main line was a combination of Iraqi, Greek, and Middle Eastern dishes.[51] Arabs, too, were called on to participate, given "the excellent quality of the Arab kitchen,"[52] but when Abela Mazzawi, a Palestinian from Nazareth, won the first contest with her lamb-stuffed artichoke, not everyone rejoiced. An article in the right-wing newspaper *Herut*

Figure 3.1 Recipe booklet based on recipes from the
Queen of the Kitchen contest. Bella Almog, *Israeli
Delicacies 1965* (Tel Aviv: March of Israeli Delicacies).

argued that tourists searched for traditional Jewish foods and that the win-
ner was a woman whose culinary concepts derived from a nonkosher cuisine,
which was alien to thousands of Jews. The author also argued that neither the
winning dish nor its expensive ingredients were eaten in many Jewish homes.[53]
Another winning recipe was "new wave chicken"—chicken with olives and
orange juice. For a while, it became associated with Israeli cuisine, especially
in foreign contexts, but it hardly struck roots in Israel itself.[54]

It was existing dishes already popular with Israelis—primarily Arab ones—
that were much more frequently appropriated as Israeli foods in various official contexts. Already toward the tenth Independence Day celebrations, Dan

Almagor had written "The Falafel Song" ("and we have falafel, falafel, falafel…"), claiming falafel—only a decade earlier vilified by many professional and public figures—as *the* Israeli national dish.[55] Appropriated Arab dishes were usually incorporated into the genre of "ethnic diversity," which featured the Israeli culinary riches.[56] Several books of this genre appeared starting in the late 1950s. One of them was Molly Bar-David's *Folkloric Cookbook* (1964).[57] The book was organized around Jewish holidays, opening with the most nationalist holiday of them all: Independence Day (which is where a hummus recipe appears, alongside recipes for falafel, tahini, shashlik, and other Middle Eastern and European dishes). In the opening of the Hebrew edition, Lyons Bar-David, a culinary adviser to the Israeli national airline El Al, describes her work interviewing immigrants from more than eighty countries, who contributed to the culinary "melting pot," as having led to the book's publication. The book, distributed free of charge to El Al passengers, features the first hummus recipe to include a blender—possibly due to the wealthy audience for which it was intended.[58]

As we saw in the previous chapter, in 1957 hummus, falafel, and tahini were already integrated into suggestions for an Independence Day dinner, and they continued to appear in similar suggestions in later years. For example, in 1970, Dafna Mor suggested to the readers of *Maariv* an "ingathering of the exiles" style meal for Independence Day, which included hummus, tahini, and eggplant alongside potato salad, gefilte fish, and "seven species cake."[59] While attempts to standardize an Independence Day dinner failed, a ritual of roasting meat on this day, and eating it together with hummus, tahini, pita bread, and vegetable salad, developed "from below" starting in the 1970s.[60] By natural selection, Ashkenazi dishes associated with the Eastern European Diaspora were completely shunned, leaving appropriated Arab dishes and the masculine practice of roasting meat—largely considered an Oriental practice in Israel— to mark the reinvigoration of the Jewish nation.

Once appropriated Arab dishes entered into the more official cultural registers, their Arab identity was often suppressed, and they were associated either with a general Oriental category or with a specific Mizrahi Jewish community (or both). For instance, Lilian Cornfeld, in her *Israeli Cookery*, defined falafel as a dish "of Middle Eastern and Yemenite origin."[61] Hummus, however, Cornfeld defined as an "Arab food."[62] At other times, they were defined as relics of the biblical era. For instance, Bar-David wrote in her *Folkloric Cookbook*, "Many Israelis hold a picnic on Independence Day—they roast shishlik [shish kebab] on coals, according to the custom of our ancient forefathers. . . . Many people hold a special dinner at home. . . . Falafel, hummus, and other favorite lentil dishes from the time of the bible will not be absent from many tables."[63]

The embrace of Arab foods as Israeli symbols, however, did not go uncontested. The myth of Palestinians being the keepers of ancient Jewish assets notwithstanding, some argued that they could not symbolize Israeli particularity exactly *because* they did not originate in Israel.[64] In 1973, in the wake of the last March of Israeli Delicacies, a debate broke out between two of Israel's leading chefs—Chef Nikolai (Yitzhak Niran) and Chef Uri Gutman—as well as the reigning "King of the Kitchen," Yaʿacov Lishanski, regarding which of two options, invention or appropriation, best represented "Israeli cuisine." Chef Nikolai, who addressed the audience at the Gastronomic Congress, stated that "in contrast to common opinion, falafel, hummus and tahini are not Israeli foods." An avid supporter of culinary ingenuity, Nikolai urged Israelis to develop a comprehensive Israeli menu suited to the climate, to recent culinary innovations, and to the correct rules of nutrition.[65] In response, Lishanski stated that before one defined what was not Israeli, one had to define what was: "Who said hummus is not Israeli? Perhaps our ancestors who lived here had eaten it? In our sources, there is much information on eating, and we should check it and learn from it. The Jewish cuisine of our grandmothers is ours too, and it should be a part of the Israeli cuisine."[66] For Lishanski, the culinary patrimony of the Jewish people stretched from close to ancient ancestors whose real or imagined food repertoires could be legitimately claimed as "ours," regardless of contemporary dietary patterns. Both, however, agreed that "Israeli food" should be based on local produce.

Lilian Cornfeld, in her *Israeli Cookery*, described "Sabra cooking" as neither entirely Middle Eastern nor entirely European: "One finds kugel and zimmes, latkes and borsht on the menus with pilaffs, mousakas, machshee, kouftas and goulash. In many cases they have become an Israeli 'daisa' [porridge] of one sort or another. In common is a love for a meat soup with rice or noodles, eggplant in all forms, salads, hamoutzim (pickles), lamb shalik or kebab on [a] spit, houmous, tehina, falafel, cottage cheese and lebenia in countless combinations."[67]

At the same time, Cornfeld emphasized the preference of Ashkenazim, and mainly Ashkenazi youth, for Oriental food.

> With the blending of food habits in Israel, the national preferences seem
> to be mostly for oriental foods. This is true not only of Orientals but of
> most of the youth of European extraction as well. This is sound ecology;
> foods which have been eaten here for centuries and on which countless

generations have survived and thrived, are low in cost, highly nutritive and well-balanced foods. These are: burghul, lentils, chickpeas (houmous), leben, olives, honey, grapes, the unsaturated oils of seeds and nuts, lamb, and fresh and saltwater fish. On the whole, the European eating habits are not as good as those of the Oriental.[68]

Studies conducted by Sarah Bavly in the early 1960s revealed that at least in some respects, Ashkenazi and Mizrahi eating habits were drawing closer.[69] WIZO (Women's International Zionist Organization) cooking courses, which served as an important platform for crafting and disseminating a symbolic Israeli culinary style, featured a blend of Western and Middle Eastern dishes or elements ("Oriental strudel," sponge cake with halva cream, etc.).[70] In early 1967, El Al announced its intention to make its menu more Jewish and Middle Eastern by incorporating eggplant, tahini, and chopped liver.[71] Nevertheless, in most institutional contexts, Middle Eastern food continued to be the marked option and was seldom served, if at all.[72] This was true of school meals,[73] Kibbutzim menus,[74] hotel restaurants, and military dining halls (in 1958, industrial hummus and tahini were added to the repertoire of dishes, but their place on the menu remained marginal at least for another decade[75]). Restaurants opened by Israeli émigrés abroad serving "Israeli food," however, clearly tilted to the Middle Eastern side.[76]

THE CANNING OF AUTHENTICITY

The signs for mother's acclimatization / in the Mediterranean space / first appeared / when on the lunch table / "Hummus Telma" from a can / (decorated with tomato slices and sweet paprika) / replaced chopped liver.

—Zeev Tene[77]

The 1960s saw the development not only of gastronomic culture in Israel but also of industrial cuisine. Studies have shown how industrialization of food production, beyond its far-reaching implications for human nutrition, social organization, and relationship to the environment, had significant cultural effects. More than any other factor, industrialization contributed to standardizing diets across vast geographical regions, leading to the development of "national" cuisines as well as to the "domestication" of foreign foods.[78] In the United States, as Donna Gabaccia has shown, it was the food industry that introduced various immigrant foods to wider publics, eventually making them part of the American diet.[79] In Israel too, the food industry played a pivotal role in shaping the menu of the new nation, including in the introduction of Middle Eastern staples into Ashkenazi kitchens.

In the latter half of the 1950s, the Israeli food industry thrived. Production output increased, and a wider variety of products appeared. The quality of the products also improved, and producers began to look for opportunities beyond the domestic market.[80] On the side of consumption, the rise in the standard of living and the growth in the rate of women's employment made canned and packaged food an essential component of the daily menu in many homes.[81] In 1960, food constituted the largest industrial sector in terms of revenue and employees.[82] "The improving living standards and an increased readiness to spend more money on food is also noticeable in our food business, and especially in our mayonnaise business," it was stated in a business review of the Palestine Edible Products Ltd. (Tozeret Mazon Eretz Israelit)—the first large producer of canned hummus.[83]

Palestine Edible Products was established in 1938 by Dr. Arnold Hildesheimer, a refugee from Nazi Germany, as a company specializing in the production of margarine. In 1947, the company began to produce bread spreads and a salad dressing under the newly established Telma brand. In the mid-1950s, Telma spotted the growing popularity of hummus, tahini, and falafel and decided to integrate them into its repertoire.[84] In charge of developing these products was Avraham Oser, an émigré from Vienna and an autodidact food technologist. The development process of hummus was long and arduous, since there were several technical problems Oser had to solve, such as the change in the texture and taste of tahini once heated and the change in the taste of lemon.[85] Eventually he managed to find solutions, and in mid-1958, Telma's hummus hit the market.

The first hummus product launched by Telma was a jar of paste that had to be mixed with water before serving.[86] When chickpea prices went up, Telma replaced a third of the quantity of chickpeas with beans.[87] In 1962, it came out with canned hummus ready to eat—a thick and granular puree with a distinct sour taste that came in three sizes and was its most successful product. Other versions followed: instant hummus "Yemeni style" (1969), which joined the "Yemeni style" falafel powder, and "Hummus 'ala kaifak" (1974)—instant hummus in a plastic bag.[88] It continued to sell canned, powdered, and condensed hummus into the 1980s.

The chickpea used in Telma's hummus was sourced from local growers.[89] Before 1948, chickpeas were primarily cultivated on Arab farms.[90] Their meager yield, labor-intensive harvesting, and unpopularity among Ashkenazim made Jewish farmers reluctant to grow them.[91] With the influx of immigrants from the Middle East and the burgeoning popularity of falafel and hummus, demand surged. Through experimentation with sowing schedules and a new variety brought into the country by an immigrant from Bulgaria, yields were

Figure 3.2 Advertisement for hummus from a
Telma publicity booklet, 1958.

significantly augmented, and hand picking gave way to mechanized harvesting.[92] By the time Telma launched its hummus, the cultivated chickpea area in
Jewish farms came closer to that in Arab farms, and it continued to expand:
further experimentation with breeding, sowing distance, watering, and pest
control resulted in even higher yields, making chickpeas more lucrative for
farmers.[93] Over the 1960s, the cultivated chickpea area on Jewish farms nearly
tripled that on Arab farms, whose cultivable land was anyway shrinking due to
expropriation, and the yield per acre was much higher.[94] Thus the Israelization

of hummus and falafel was accompanied by the Judaization of chickpea cultivation within the 1948 borders.

The success of Telma's hummus was spectacular: in 1962, Telma advertised the production of its five hundred thousandth hummus can; by 1968, the company had produced its fifteen millionth can! (Israel's population at the time amounted to less than three million people.)[95] In the mid-1970s, it even erected a separate wing dedicated to its "Oriental line," to meet the huge demand.[96] According to company surveys, its hummus was consumed across the board—by secular and religious Jews, Ashkenazim and Mizrahim, men and women, even Arabs. Telma was also successful in exporting its hummus, including, indirectly, to Arab countries;[97] yet most consumption was local.[98] In 1968, writer Yoram Kaniuk humorously described the New Year's shopping of "Mrs. Ashkenazi": on her list were, among other things, four cans of Telma's hummus as well as three cans of prepared tahini and one can of tahini paste.[99] In Sarah Bavly's 1964 study, it was found that among the new foods introduced to the domestic kitchen among families of new immigrants, mainly in the second generation, hummus belonged to the category of foods encountered in supermarkets and grocery stores.[100]

While Telma sometimes defined its hummus as a "first course" (and tahini as a "sauce"), more often than not, it was used as a spread, either on bread or inside pita bread.[101] In the 1970s, when production of pita bread became mechanized and the product more easily accessible to Israeli consumers, half a pita with Telma's hummus and canned pickles became the standard refreshment at school trips and children's birthday parties.[102] Given that the majority of Israelis did not eat out frequently or prepare hummus at home, it seems safe to assume that at least until the mid-1970s Telma's hummus was the predominant form in which most Israelis consumed most of their hummus.

Following Telma's success, several other companies began to produce hummus for the retail market, both canned and powdered.[103] However, none of them was as successful as Telma, which became synonymous with industrial hummus—at least until the appearance of the refrigerated type.

In Telma's advertisements and filmed commercials, hummus was constructed as both Oriental (though not Arab) and Israeli.[104] Some of Telma's advertisements included figures marked as Oriental, but many others featured "all-Israeli" figures, which were implicitly Ashkenazi. They presented hummus as a healthy, easy-to-prepare dish that could be consumed either at home or outdoors and that was appropriate both for casual meals and for special events such as parties and dinner parties. Many of the advertisements featured children or targeted children. Its slogan was "Clean. Fresh. Healthy" (implicitly

Figure 3.3 Telma advertisements, 1958–70.

alluding to the perception of handmade Oriental food as dirty). And it was Telma that first crowned hummus as a "national dish" in the framework of its publicity campaign: "Knish or verenikas. Not all your guests are familiar with these eastern European dishes. But everybody eats hummus enthusiastically—hummus, the Israeli national dish."[105] In this advertisement, the popularity of hummus marks the successful integration of the Jews into the local space and the shedding of the old culture of the Eastern European Diaspora.

Figure 3.4 Advertisement for Friman's hummus, *Maariv*, February 7, 1963.

Evident in Telma's advertisements from the 1960s and 1970s, and in those of other companies, is the gendering and ethnicizing of both consumption and production. When advertisements featured consumers, they were usually Ashkenazi and often female, in their capacity as food providers for their families. When they featured producers of hummus, they were exclusively male and usually Oriental—either "general Orientals" or Mizrahi Jews, mostly Yemenites.[106] Thus the Israelization of hummus advanced by the food industry promoted the association of hummus with Mizrahi Jews rather than with Arabs.

Figure 3.5   Osem advertisement: "When you open a packet of Osem's hummus it is as if you opened an Oriental kitchen at home," *Maariv*, May 12, 1978.

At the same time, Mizrahim in these advertisements are clearly outsiders. Characterized by "visual display of excessive corporeality,"[107] what signifies Mizrahi identity is either hair (mustache and sometimes sidelocks) or "traditional clothes" (or both). These render Mizrahi identity a "costume" consisting of a set of external characteristics that may be shed at will. A particularly striking example is a 1961 filmed commercial showing a Yemenite couple in their traditional attire entering a fancy hotel restaurant, ordering a couple of pitas, and taking out a can of Telma's hummus from their satchel (the only commercial I came across where Mizrahim are in the role of the consumers).[108] As this commercial betrays, the only place where the authentic Yemenite attire needed for the authentication of the hummus could be tolerated and even normalized is a hotel. If the Yemenite couple has to be dressed in their authentic dress, they must at least be placed in a space that in itself renders them guests. Obviously, placing the Yemenite couple in a luxury hotel restaurant where they order probably the most expensive pitas one could get in Israel obscures the fact of proletarization of Mizrahim with the process of industrialization, which the couple are depicted as nothing but enjoying.

A few of Telma's commercials placed industrial production at their center. Like many other commercials from this period of rapid industrialization, they presented images of the sophisticated and efficient production process, associating the Israeli industry with technological modernity, rationality, and progress. For instance, a 1964 filmed commercial for a raffle among buyers of Telma's Oriental products was comprised mostly of shots of the assembly line, showing the "new and sophisticated machines" in Telma's factory.[109] Another example is an advertisement for tahini from 1963, where a bold caption reads "We made it!" and, underneath it, "After many comprehensive researches and experimentations, our experts have managed to solve the problem of producing tahini ready to eat—of the same exquisite quality which characterizes the famous hummus Telma."[110] Note that Telma's tahini was exquisite not like handmade restaurant tahini but like Telma's hummus! Although in one of its late 1960s advertisements Telma argued that its hummus was "just like in the best of Oriental restaurants," generally, it did not pretend to produce a product that came close to restaurant hummus (neither did other contemporaneous industrial producers of hummus).[111] Rather, its advertisements suggested that this was the modern and sanitary alternative to handmade hummus. Even as late as 1984, Telma still presented its hummus, this time refrigerated, as "clean work," untouched by human hands.[112]

According to Richard Wilk, canned food imported from Britain allowed British settlers in Belize to experience a "piece of home" in the new environment. Even when the food encapsulated in the cans was readily available in its fresh and much cheaper version, canned food was preferred.[113] Anat Helman describes a similar predilection for imported canned food in 1920s Tel Aviv, which began to wane toward the end of the decade, with the development of Jewish farming.[114] Yet as the case of industrial hummus demonstrates, just as cans could provide settlers with a piece of a longed-for elsewhere, they could provide them with technologically produced and sanitized "locality."

The industrialization of hummus facilitated its incorporation into official presentations of "Israeli food." As we have seen, the period of state-directed industrialization coincided with governmental and public efforts to shape an

Israeli national cuisine.[115] Hence, industrial products had pride of place in various official presentations of "Israeli food." Starting in the late 1950s, industrial hummus and falafel and sometimes gefilte fish represented "Israeli cuisine" in food exhibitions and "Israel weeks," which were held in various countries, as well as in displays of "Israeli food" at home.[116] Most presentations were organized by the Israeli Company for Exhibitions and Fairs, which was sponsored by both governmental and commercial bodies. The state project of forging a national culture, then, was fused with the economic interests of Israeli industry.

Data collected by Palestine Edible Products Ltd. demonstrates both the absolute growth in food consumption (even when population growth is accounted for) and the change in the status of hummus over two decades. In 1960, Telma estimated its sales of hummus at 11 percent of its mayonnaise sales (26 and 235 tons, respectively). In comparison, in January–July 1979, it sold 854 tons of hummus, which constituted 83.6 percent of the 1,021 tons of mayonnaise it sold.[117] Since both canned hummus and mayonnaise could serve the same culinary function as a base for other ingredients, it seems reasonable to assume that for many Israelis, hummus came to replace mayonnaise as a favorite bread spread, which could be eaten with either meat or dairy.

The food industry, then, advanced the nationalization of hummus in two main ways: first by making hummus much more easily accessible to Jewish consumers, facilitating its introduction into a wide range of food spaces, from cafeterias and military dining halls to the domestic kitchen; and second by framing hummus as an Israeli national dish, associating it with Mizrahi Jews rather than with Arabs. This is well demonstrated in *Israeli Cookery*: Cornfeld defined falafel and hummus, "Oriental in origin," as "the national snacks of Israel," with the accompanying photo showing industrially produced hummus and falafel.[118]

On another level, canned hummus, in offering packaged and sanitized locality, produced with modern industrial methods and sanitary standards, may be regarded as the perfect embodiment of the paradoxical nature of Jewish settlers' efforts at indigenization, described succinctly in Tene's poem: the very act that signifies Tene's Polish-born mother's "acclimatization" also renders her a stranger: eating hummus from a can.

OCCUPATION

According to Yehuda Litani, the 1967 occupation of the West Bank and the Gaza Strip was a watershed in the history of hummus consumption in Israel; until that point, hummus had been "a little sheepish, on the margins."[119] Writing in the year 2000, Litani associates hummus with handmade Palestinian hummus consumed in a hummusiya. Yet many sources testify that by 1967 the symbolic Israelization of hummus had been completed, even if falafel held the primacy as *the* Israeli "national dish." An article on the food provided to the athletes at the Tokyo Olympics in 1964, for instance, stated that "if anyone will wish to dine his heart in *pure Israeli dishes*, like hummus, tahini and falafel—he will be able to fill his stomach."[120] Nevertheless, the occupation did contribute to changing the status and modes of consumption of hummus among Israelis.

In the 1967 war, Israel more than tripled the territory and the Palestinian population under its control.[121] Soon after the war, Israelis began flocking to the occupied territories in search of touristic excitements and cheap consumer goods.[122] Already on June 9, before the war officially ended but limitations on the movement between the two parts of Jerusalem were lifted, Mayor Teddy Kollek wrote to Defense Minister Dayan, "There is an atmosphere of festival in the city. All the Arabs are in Zion Square and all the Jews are in the bazars" (on June 27, East Jerusalem was officially annexed to Israel).[123] Two weeks after the war ended, Amos Kenan ironically wrote, "When we arrived in Bethlehem we saw the whole of Dizengoff Street [at that time, the trendiest recreation street in Tel Aviv] eating hummus with pickles. How did they know that it was our national dish? And so quickly?"[124] Gaza restaurants, too, were filled with Israeli diners, in spite of occasional warnings from the Ministry of Health.[125]

Consumerist tourism to the Occupied Territories became an accepted practice, at least until the 1987 Intifada (uprising). Israeli newspapers published occasional accounts of such trips, some of which included recommendations on where to eat ("'The municipal garden of Ramallah' restaurant. . . . Something similar probably existed only in the time of the bible, since where and when is it possible to dine amid roses, lilies, oleander and other flowers?"[126]). Reviews of various West Bank restaurants also appeared in the restaurant review columns in the daily newspapers from time to time ("It was a pigeon not too young and not too old, not too stuffed and not too starved, not crumbling and not sticky. In short—exactly as a roasted pigeon should be"[127]). Particularly the Old City of Jerusalem, with its winding alleys, sprawling market, restaurants, and cafés, became a popular destination for Israelis seeking exoticism close to home.[128] The Old City was where many Israelis first encountered the institution of the hummus joint. Jerusalem became the country's hummus capital. "Jerusalem exceeds the other cities of this country in many areas. One of these areas is the way of preparing hummus," wrote Menachem Talmi.[129] "It became apparent to me that ten measures of the art of preparing hummus descended to the world, and Jerusalem took nine of them," wrote Danny Rubinstein a decade later.[130]

The Occupied Territories provided Israeli tourists with a "time machine,"[131] transporting visitors not only to the ancient national past but sometimes to the recently experienced past of pre-1948 Palestine. Thus Haim Gouri described the "real" hummus of Abu Shukri in East Jerusalem as his "madeleine cookie," which conjured his entire childhood and adolescence years—the hummus he had eaten in Jaffa and Haifa in the 1930s and 1940s.[132] This is the first account I came across where hummus attains such a transcendental quality. This is also the first time I encountered the verb *to wipe* in relation to hummus. Gouri— then a supporter of Greater Israel—also predated the "hummus coexistence" discourse of the 1990s. In this column, he argued with the thesis that holding onto the Occupied Territories would turn Israel into a security state, a "community of detectives and persecutors and investigators and prison guards," since "reality breeds a thousand and one ways of life in common."[133] One of these ways was eating hummus together, as he wrote in a later text: "The effect of a single Jerusalem is working in thousand[s] of open and hidden ways. Because peace is coming into being every minute, because thou shalt not always eat sword, but we will always eat hummus, together, us and our neighbors."[134] The assumption that increased interactions between Palestinians and Israelis in contexts of commerce and service were a sign of peaceful coexistence between them was shared by many Israelis.

However, the discourse on the hummus in Jerusalem, and Palestinian restaurants more generally, did not yet express the assumption that would become prevalent in culinary discourse beginning in the 1990s: that hummus prepared by Arabs was categorically better and more authentic than hummus prepared by Jews. Thus Talmi's piece focused on a Jewish hummus maker ("The restaurant of M. Cohen is one of the places which grant Jerusalem the status of hummus glory"[135]), and Rubinstein, too, described Jerusalem's best and most famous hummus joints on both sides of the green line.[136] And while the phrase *real hummus* appeared in several accounts, it did not refer to the identity of the cooks but rather signified hummus that was handmade as opposed to hummus produced in a factory.[137] For example, Buki Na'e wrote that "whoever wanders in Samaria can find there, among the antiquities and the ruins, another rare archaeological finding, which is called 'real hummus *'ala kaifak*,' without cans and without instant."[138]

Nevertheless, signs for this imminent discourse could be found in this period as well. For example, Talmi wrote in his review of Abed's restaurant in Haifa that although the hummus there "compromises with the taste of 'Ashkenazim,'" after adding some salt and pepper, the hummus became "better than the one you get, in most cases, in the Hebrew Oriental restaurants."[139] Rubinstein, too, defined Abu Shukri's hummus as "the Jewel in the crown" of hummus restaurants and, in contrast to the other hummus places he surveyed, provided a detailed description of its color and texture ("very bright and finely crushed, in the center of the plate a drizzle of green olive oil"). According to Rubinstein, the Palestinians had serious grievances against the bland and watery "modern" Israeli vegetables. Any self-respecting restaurant, he wrote, would serve vegetables from dryland farming in their season. Thus Abu Shukri's tomatoes had not been chemically treated, and the hard-boiled "baladi" eggs came from "real chicken, in all colors, who roam the yards collecting grains, not these white creatures, densely squeezed in long coops ... receiving artificial food and injections."[140] Here, too, the Palestinian territories functioned as a time machine that could transport the diners to an era when food was not yet spoiled by modernization and industrialization.

In fact, soon after the occupation, Israel embarked on a large-scale project aimed at modernizing Palestinian agriculture, in which almost half of the population had been employed.[141] It initiated agricultural research, planning, and instruction, introduced advanced agricultural methods intended to increase production, and encouraged the cultivation of some crops while discouraging others. The goals of this project were to raise the Palestinian standard of living so as to pacify the population, to prevent competition with Israeli farmers, and to introduce to the territories crops that were otherwise imported.[142] Among the crops that were designated for the industry as import substitutes were chickpeas and sesame, which at the time were imported to Israel in large amounts.[143] Both were previously grown by West Bank farmers but were replaced with more profitable crops.[144] By 1969, the area of chickpeas and sesame was increased by 30,000 dunams, and the yield of chickpeas increased from 70 kilograms to 150 kilograms per dunam.[145] In the same year, production of sesame amounted to 1,700 tons, compared to 700 tons in 1968.[146]

Israel became the main market for Palestinian produce: two decades after the occupation, 68 percent of the Palestinian exports went to Israel.[147] More importantly, the Occupied Territories (OT) soon became a captured market for Israeli products, making it the second most important market for Israel after the US.[148] By 1988, the OT derived 90 percent of its imports from Israel, including industrial and agricultural products.[149] Although I have no data on the sale of specific Israeli products to the OT, judging from a 1968 story about a West Bank resident who was stopped at the border crossing by Fatah people for carrying an Israeli hummus can, it can only be assumed that industrial hummus was among the Israeli canned goods that overwhelmed the Palestinian market.[150]

The Israeli investment in Palestinian agriculture was short lived. The economic crisis in the second half of the 1970s, the realization that Israeli growers could profit from restricting Palestinian agriculture, and primarily the growing political orientation toward land grab and settlement led to a shift in the official policy.[151] The increased productivity of Palestinian agriculture in the 1970s, coupled with the decrease in the area under cultivation, diminished the number of Palestinians employed in agriculture and boosted labor migration to Israel.[152] Tens of thousands of Palestinians entered the Israeli labor market, providing Israeli employers with cheap labor power.[153] This process had an indirect effect on the Israeli culinary field: although the majority worked in construction and agriculture (around 70 percent), many also worked in services (10.9 percent in 1973 and 18.8 percent in 1993).[154] One of the sectors that thrived on Palestinian labor migrants was the restaurant sector, which Palestinians entered as service workers and cooks.[155] As celebrity chef Israel Aharoni noted, in the 1970s, "there were no kitchen workers, there were Arabs. . . . Restaurant workers did not say 'my cooks,' they said 'my Arabs.'"[156]

On a different level, the expanded sphere of contact between Israelis and Palestinians following the occupation (and the termination of the military rule over Palestinian citizens of Israel a year earlier) increased the presence of Arab culture in the Israeli public sphere. The Israeli Television, which inaugurated its general broadcasts in 1968, targeted the occupied population from the start and broadcasted a daily Arabic slot; soon some of its programs became highly popular with Israelis—Mizrahim and Ashkenazim alike.[157] Palestinian handicrafts entered Israeli homes, and Palestinian products and forms were integrated into the industry of symbolic Israeliness, primarily through the mediation of Maskit—a governmental company established in 1954 to produce and market handicrafts by immigrants.[158] And although various Arab foods were already established in the Israeli food repertoire, the broader, if still limited, encounter with Palestinian food culture affected Israeli food culture in general and hummus culture in particular.

HUMMUS BECOMES A MEAL

In the mid-1970s, thirty-five-year-old Amnon Tzaban and twenty-four-year-old Asher Bitansky, both in the music business, were looking for a source of extra income and decided to open a hummus restaurant in Tel Aviv.[159] Both encountered the model of the hummus joint in the Old City of Jerusalem after 1967. In fact, Tzaban's favorite hummus was Ta'ami's, in the western part of the city, but the owner refused to share his recipe, so Tzaban asked for and received the recipe of Abu Shukri. A Moroccan Jewish acquaintance who used to work as a baker at the King David Hotel experimented with the recipe, which quickly came out well and, at least according to Tzaban, resembled the original version. In 1976, the two opened their place on Yermiyahu Street in Tel Aviv, and Bitansky named it Ashkara—a slang word that entered Hebrew through Arabic, meaning "clearly/just like that."[160] The name, which rang peculiar at the time, was chosen both to signify authenticity and for its resemblance to Abu Shukri. According to Tzaban, Ashkara was the first Jewish-owned restaurant dedicated to hummus, and people warned them that they would fail. Yet with growing public openness to culinary novelties during a period of economic recession, the time was ripe for the new establishment, and Ashkara became a big success. Unlike the Palestinian hummus joint, which opened in the early morning and closed when the hummus finished, usually at midday, Ashkara served hummus around the clock. Although it took a while before the new model became pervasive—in 1978, Ashkara was still dubbed an Oriental restaurant; the Hebrew term *hummusiya* was coined only in the 1990s[161]—gradually other entrepreneurs followed suit.

Between 1967 and 1973, the prewar recession gave way to an economic boom. The development of a military-industrial complex after the war and the growth of the private sector due to economic liberalization led to the emergence of a new bourgeoisie that became a player in the global market.[162] Private consumption increased, including food consumption. More Israelis traveled abroad, where they became acquainted with new cuisines, and new food items appeared on the Israeli market.[163] Books such as Amos Kenan's *The Book of Pleasures* (1970), which introduced pleasure-seeking "modern" women and men to a variety of foreign luxuries, and Joel Marcus's *The Book of Wine* (1972), together with Dahn Ben-Amotz's columns, which tied together food and sex, inaugurated a hedonistic eating-for-pleasure ethos.[164] Such publications found an echo in a society that was becoming increasingly individualistic and consumerist.

Cookbooks addressing "housewives" also became more oriented toward culinary pleasure and diversity: in 1970, Aviva Goldman published the first Hebrew cookbook with chromo photographs, *The Cookbook*.[165] But the real landmark in this period was Ruth Sirkis's *From the Kitchen with Love* (1975), which mediated post-WWII American food cosmopolitanism to a wide Israeli readership.[166] Both books contained mostly Western recipes and a small number of Middle Eastern ones, among them hummus (Goldman recommended pressing the cooked chickpeas through a sieve; Sirkis recommended using a meat grinder).[167] While Goldman's recipe included only four lines of succinct instructions, Sirkis's recipe included twelve lines of detailed instructions and a short preamble: "There are many versions as to the exact taste and the level of coarseness a hummus should have. Try the recipe for home-made hummus and you may reach the conclusion that your version is better than the hummus served in many restaurants."[168] As this preamble demonstrates, the object "hummus" became increasingly differentiated, not only along the machine-made/handmade axis but also according to more refined distinctions of taste and texture.

This process was influenced by the increased prominence of Mizrahi culture in the Israeli public sphere and the post-1973 recession. The entry of Palestinians from the West Bank and the Gaza Strip into the Israeli labor market allowed a measure of mobility to some Mizrahi and, to a lesser extent, Arab sectors. Overall, social and economic gaps between Ashkenazim on the one hand and Mizrahim and Arabs on the other hand only widened after 1967, giving rise to the largest Mizrahi protest since the foundation of the state. At the same time, the turning of Palestinians from the OT into the new industrial and agricultural proletariat pushed some Mizrahim and Arabs into more professional and better-paying jobs and gave rise to small middle-class and entrepreneurial strata among them, with increased buying power.[169] Although I have no systematic data at my disposal, it can be assumed that the food sector continued to serve as an important channel for economic mobility for Mizrahim and Arabs.[170]

After the 1973 war, Israel entered a long period of economic recession, which was accompanied by a skyrocketing yearly inflation rate (reaching its 400 percent peak in 1984). In 1974, government subsidies on various basic foods decreased. Food prices climbed, and meat became too expensive to afford for many. "People eat more hummus—and less meat," a Yemenite restaurant owner was quoted as saying in an article on the situation of restaurants in the face of the crisis.[171] In the same month, the price of a steak with side dishes was four times higher than the price of a dish of hummus, which itself increased more than 45 percent from the previous year.[172] Many of those who could afford to eat in restaurants from time to time opted for cheaper alternatives, such as restaurants serving inexpensive "ethnic food" and Oriental restaurants.[173] Toward the end of the decade, Arab restaurants, especially the ones located in mixed cities or on the outskirts of Arab villages, also attracted a growing Jewish clientele.[174] Thus an article on entertainment venues in the villages of the triangle in central Israel noted that recently several restaurants "for Oriental food" had opened in Tira and Taybeh, where one could enjoy an Oriental band, good food, alcoholic beverages, and cheap prices, which attracted many Jews from the area. The title of this section was "The Jews Come to Eat."[175]

The heightened presence of Mizrahi cultural elements at the heart of Israeli public culture spurred Ashkenazi discourses and practices of distinction. The elitist association of Mizrahi products with "common taste" and low cultural value, and the emergence of a differentiating discourse on lowbrow culinary options in general and on hummus in particular, made eating hummus at specific, often Arab-owned hummus joints a means of distinction for people high on cultural and low on economic capital. The soldiers of the Jaffa-based IDF radio station (Galei Tzahal)—a production line for journalists and other key figures in the Israeli media industry[176]—are a case in point. In the early 1970s, several soldiers from the station discovered the hummus restaurant of Abu Hassan—today one of the most celebrated hummusiyot in Israel[177]—as a nearby venue for cheap, filling meals. By the second half of the decade, Abu Hassan gained the status of a shrine for the station's soldiers, and eating there became a well-established social ritual.[178] Yet another decade would pass before much longer lines of worshippers gathered at Abu Hassan's doors.

FOUR

—⁓—

THE GOURMETIZATION OF HUMMUS AND THE RETURN OF THE REPRESSED ARAB

Hummus recipe of "The Brothers" (for half a kilo of dry chickpeas)

Soak the dry chickpeas in a bowl with plenty of cold water for at least 12 hours. Every 3–4 hours we strain, rinse, and change the water.

After soaking, we transfer the grains to a sieve and rinse well with cold water.

We transfer the chickpeas to a pot and cover with water, about 5 centimeters above the chickpeas. We add a teaspoon and a half of baking soda and stir well.

We bring the pot to a boil and, using a spoon, remove the foam that rises to the surface. The foam will rise several times.

After completing the process, we reduce the heat to a gentle simmer and cook the chickpeas for about an hour, until they are completely soft. Once fully softened, we strain the chickpeas but save the cooking liquid. We keep one cup of chickpeas in the cooking liquid for use when serving and chill the remaining chickpeas well in the refrigerator.

We place the chilled chickpeas and half a cup of the cooking liquid in a food processor. We turn on the food processor and grind into a smooth puree. We add three garlic cloves and the juice of two lemons, and we continue processing well.

When the mixture is very smooth and liquid, we add one cup of high-quality tahini and continue blending in the food processor. The mixture should thicken and reach the consistency of a stable hummus paste. If it is not thick enough, we add more tahini; if it is too thick, we add a little cooking liquid to thin it out.

We add salt and continue blending for another two minutes. We taste and adjust the seasoning if necessary.

We heat the chickpeas we set aside in the cooking liquid. We spread the hummus paste on a plate and top it with warm chickpeas and plenty of olive oil. It is recommended to serve with pita or challah from The Brothers, and of course, with our zhug as well.

—Handout from The Brothers' delicatessen in Tel Aviv

NINE O'CLOCK ON A CHILLY Saturday morning. Ofra and I were waiting in front of the Jerusalem municipal building for the tour to start. This was not an ordinary tourist excursion, however, but a tour of Palestinian hummus joints in East Jerusalem, organized, curiously, by Beit Shmuel—the Jerusalem branch of Progressive Judaism. Our friendly young guide seemed more like the backpacker type than the average gourmet type. But like many other Israelis, he was a self-appointed hummus expert. The tour opened with a question: "So . . . who does hummus belong to? Is it *ours* or *theirs*?" Except for a couple of dissidents, group members agreed that it is "theirs." "Hummus for Arabs is a different matter than it is for us," explained our guide. "We would describe any hummus as delicious. The Arabs have developed a taste for it for 2,000 years. In their mind, one must keep high standards." By citing the number two thousand—a constitutive number in the Zionist narrative of exile and return—our guide invoked the symbolic function of hummus as an emblem of locality. The tour progressed as a pastiche of history, mythology, folklore, and hummus lore. Accompanied by an armed security guard, we walked from one hummus joint to the next, sampled the hummus, discussed its qualities, and compared it to the others we had tasted.

This tour of East Jerusalem hummus joints exemplifies two interconnected processes: the "gourmetization" of hummus in Israel since the 1990s and the re-emergence of its Arab identity, which has been submerged for several decades. At the same time, the hummus hype of which this tour is part owes much to and simultaneously reinforces the perception of hummus as "the most Israeli dish of all."[1] What made the Arab identity of hummus resurface in culinary discourse? As this chapter argues, this shift in the discourse on hummus resulted from the interaction between developments in several different fields.

The 1980s was a decade of profound social and cultural transformations. The process of economic liberalization that began after the 1967 war continued apace with the rise to power of the liberal right-wing Likud party in 1977 and received its formalization in state policy in the 1985 Emergency Economic Stabilization Plan. It expedited the integration of the Israeli economy into the global market, as did the 1990s "peace process," which opened the Israeli market to multinational corporations that hitherto refrained from operating in Israel due to the Arab boycott.[2] In a relatively short span of time, the Israeli economy experienced several radical transformations: from an industrial to a postindustrial knowledge economy; from Keynesian state intervention to privatization, deregulation, and neoliberalization; and from an ethos of frugality to an outright celebration of consumerism.[3] These processes brought about a profound transformation of the culinary sphere.

Figure 4.1 Participants in the hummus tour in front of Uncle Moustache, Old City of Jerusalem, October 3, 2009. Photo by the author.

This chapter focuses on the making of hummus into a food cult and an object for distinction practices and the consequent return of its Arab identity, associated with quality and authenticity. After an introduction to the cult of hummus, I discuss the transformations in the culinary field since the mid-1980s and then examine their interaction with the search for authentic "ethnic cultures." I then discuss the differentiating discourse that has developed around hummus and how the value placed on authenticity and locality in foodie discourse raised the prestige of hummus made by Arabs. The following section looks at how the Oslo Accords and the "peace process" of the 1990s opened up new (real or imagined) spaces of consumption and gave rise to a discourse of coexistence through food, making Palestinian food culture more present in the Israeli public sphere. Finally, I discuss the recent phase of increased "Israelization" of hummus, manifested in quality assessments and in subsuming Arab food and food culture under the heading of Israeli "multiculturalism."

THE CULT OF HUMMUS

Until the late 1980s, hummus was in the shadow of falafel—at least as a national symbol, even if not necessarily as food. Yet among a certain group of cultural

Figure 4.2 Yehuda Litani and Naʿim ʿAraidi, *Not by Hummus Alone: Hummus, Olive Oil, References* (Tel Aviv: D. Dinur and Modan, 2000).

mediators, hummus was becoming an iconic dish, an institution of male commensality, and a fledgling cultural hero.[4] In the 1990s, a quantitative as well as qualitative change in hummus consumption took place. While reliable data for the growth in consumption is available only for barcoded hummus (discussed in the next chapter), hummus restaurants, too, have become much more conspicuous than previously, especially in Jewish cities.[5] The rise in consumption went hand in hand with a proliferation of the discourse on hummus, which became increasingly more passionate. Hummus-related items abound in the Israeli media and social media (as of late 2024, the "Hummusologists Inc." Facebook group had 82.7k members), and heated debates over which hummusiya serves the best hummus are a common male ritual. Hummus lovers will often boast about their going out of their way to try out a new hummusiya with good reviews.[6] Since the year 2000, several guidebooks on the best hummusiyot in Israel (and sometimes also in the Occupied Territories) have appeared, alongside several hummus apps and a hummus blog.[7] In light of this hype, hummus has entered Israeli artistic and popular-cultural production, with songs, works of literature, films, TV series chapters, and artworks portraying various aspects of the dish and its consumption.[8]

The elevation of hummus to the status of a culinary cult in Israel cannot be understood apart from the competition among large producers over market

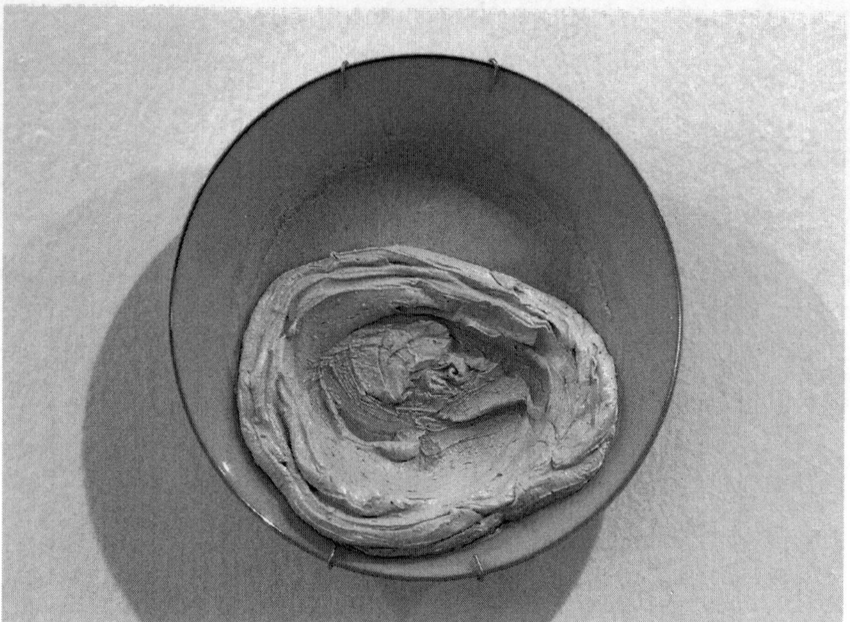

Figure 4.3 Eliyahu Fatal, *Hummus*, 2001–03, plate with oil paint, diameter 19 cm. Courtesy of the artist.

shares, which I discuss in the next chapter. But the rise of hummus in the 1990s was supported by several other global trends, primarily the growing importance attributed to "health" in food consumption and the consequent popularity of the "Mediterranean diet,"[9] the expansion of vegetarianism and veganism,[10] and the value attached to "local food" in foodie discourse. Thanks to these qualities, hummus was also adopted by various movements of ethical and spiritual consumption, such as the organic movement and Zen inspired cooking.[11]

In the early 2000s, the nutritional virtues of hummus began to surface more frequently in media representations of the dish. Articles delved into hummus's dietary benefits, showcasing its richness in protein, dietary fiber, calcium, folic acid, vitamins, and minerals. With twice the iron content compared to other legumes, hummus earned the status of a superfood. When combined with tahini and eaten with bread, hummus provides a complete protein in a form that is relatively easy to digest, making it an ideal substitute for meat (and more flexible with regard to the Jewish dietary laws).[12] In 2007, a study by four Israeli researchers claiming that the domesticated chickpea varieties contain the highest levels of the amino acid tryptophan, which determines brain serotonin synthesis, received wide publicity in the Israeli media.[13] Hummus was deemed good not only for the body but also for the soul.

It should be noted that in contrast to the Israeli hype around hummus, the place of hummus in Palestinian culture is more mundane. It is certainly an essential part of the cuisine and a beloved dish, eaten on a regular basis and on different occasions—at breakfast or lunch, as part of the mezze table, at different kinds of gatherings and celebrations—but it was never the object of so much fuss as it is in contemporary Israel. As Reem Kassis writes, "As a child, we regularly ate it, but I never thought much of it; it was just something that was always around, like labaneh, and I didn't care much for it."[14] Hummus is not considered the epitome of Palestinian cuisine and does not enjoy a special status as a symbol of "Palestinianness" like *msakhan*, za'atar, or olive oil.[15] If hummus gained some symbolic traction in Palestinian food discourse, it is primarily in response to its appropriation and the desire to reclaim it as a Palestinian rather than an Israeli dish.

THE CULINARY FIELD RESTRUCTURES

The passionate discourse on hummus is related to the changing place of food in Israeli culture more broadly. The growth of the private sector and service economy gave rise to a new middle class that developed a cosmopolitan cultural orientation with a strong emphasis on consumption and leisure.[16] Among the new middle class, an individualistic ethos has developed stressing self-reliance, personal achievement, creativity, and enjoyment.[17] Since the mid-1980s, the "creative class," largely congruent with Bourdieu's cultural intermediaries, has expanded.[18] For this sector, aestheticization of the body, the home, and everyday life, inter alia through consumption, became part of an ethic of self-improvement.[19]

Out of this sector emerged the mediators of a new culinary model in the 1980s, which eventually restructured the entire culinary field. This model emphasized refinement, professionalization, variety, creativity, and "cosmopolitan authenticity."[20] It constructed food as an object not only of sensual pleasure but also of intellectual engagement. Most of its mediators—chefs, restaurant critics, and food connoisseurs—were exposed to it during an extended stay abroad. Newspapers associated with the creative class began to feature growing food sections that embarked on an educational mission, and restaurants specializing in a specific "exotic" cuisine or offering an Israeli version of nouvelle cuisine targeted a wider stratum of consumers than previously.[21] While gourmet food was popularized, some popular foods were "gourmetized": the democratization of culinary knowledge, further advanced by food TV and social media, supported an omnivorous ethos, which in turn expanded processes of differentiation within the culinary field.

A gastronomic field has developed, with its own experts, institutions, discourses, and practices. Since the 1990s, the number of chef restaurants, gourmet

Figure 4.4 Boaz Arad, *Hummus* (installation), 2012, mixed technique. Courtesy of Rosenfeld Gallery, Tel Aviv.

food stores, and artisanal food and wine industries in Israel has steadily increased, and so has the discourse surrounding food. Food preparation and consumption, including the consumption of food-related knowledge and entertainment, have become central components of the leisure culture.[22] Food writing has prospered in many digital and printed media channels, and so have food and cooking-related TV shows.[23] The preoccupation with food is also manifested in the flourishing of cooking workshops and culinary tours to local and international destinations.[24]

More than ever before, food became a medium for personal identity construction and self-expression.[25] Cookbooks and food blogs have become personal texts, and the injunction to "be yourself" or "cook yourself" is often heard in cooking reality TV.[26] With talent and competence in cooking believed to be a class-blind art of the everyday, cooking seems to be the creative medium that best supports the ideology of universal creativity promoted by cultural intermediaries.[27] As a site for the creative articulation of the self, food discourse fuses the languages of art and therapeutic culture: the relationship of food and cooking to the person—both as a unique individual and as part of a collective—is often conceived in psychological and emotional terms.[28] These processes shaped the discourse on hummus, giving rise to the hummus expert and to the hummus addict as well as to "gourmet hummus."

THE RISE OF "ETHNIC CULTURES"

The second process that is relevant to the sociocultural career of hummus is the rise of identity politics and the search for authentic "ethnic cultures." Liberalization and privatization went hand in hand with the erosion of the ideology of cultural unification. The triumph of Likud marked the end of the political and cultural hegemony of the Labor Party. Traditionally an opposition party, Likud presented itself as a champion of hitherto marginalized Jewish groups, most notably Mizrahim, lending legitimacy to the discourse on ethnic discrimination, if not necessarily effecting a real change in resource allocation along ethnic lines.[29] Since the early 1980s, a mild version of multiculturalism became part of an explicit state agenda. Simultaneously, several political and economic developments, such as the integration of Palestinians from the OT into the Israeli workforce, the expansion of the welfare state, and the change in the structure of the higher education market, gave rise to a substantial Mizrahi middle class, with increased buying power.[30] In this period, culture came to occupy center stage in the discourse on ethnic discrimination.[31]

Members of the second and third generations of Mizrahi immigrants, most of whom had grown up in an atmosphere of contempt toward manifestations of "Oriental culture," began to articulate their sense of difference through practices and products, conceptualized either as part of an encompassing Mizrahi identity or as part of a specific culture of descent.[32] If made-in-Israel "Mizrahi music" became associated with a generalized Mizrahi identity, cuisine became central to the representation of specific ethnic cultures. The cuisines of the parents or grandparents became a resource for the construction of nostalgic identities and authentic selves for members of marginalized ethnic groups.[33] Food also entered the market for ethnic commodities through the work of various Mizrahi entrepreneurs such as cookbook authors, founders of various food businesses, and chefs.

No less important in this context was the development of a cosmopolitan pattern of cultural consumption among the new middle class, especially among cultural intermediaries.[34] The new appreciation for cultural diversity in the realm of food created a market not only for foreign or "exotic" cuisines (French, Italian, Chinese, etc.) but also for different Jewish ethnic ones.[35] This process was apparent in the food columns of newspapers associated with the creative class like *Ha'ir* and *Hadashot,* whose educational mission involved introducing readers to a broad spectrum of cuisines. As Ofra Tene has shown, in the new middle-class culinary culture, "the ethnic," alongside "the foreign" and "the local," became a commodified option in a repertoire available for the construction of a "cosmopolitan self."[36]

The process of lending culinary and cultural value to ethnic cuisines also affected Arab restaurants in Israel. The revaluation of local food in the 1990s increased the reputation of Palestinian food. The local trend entered the Israeli culinary field less as a social movement resisting globalization, industrialization, and large-scale agribusinesses and more as a global discourse in translation. Various chefs and food experts, primarily left leaning, proclaimed Palestinian food the quintessential local cuisine since it formed locally over generations, uses mostly local ingredients, and is adapted to the conditions of the land.[37] In the words of food writer Eli Landau, "The Arab cuisine may not be as perfect as the French or Italian one, but it is perfect in its connection to the land, its climate and fragrance."[38]

Although more often defined as Arab rather than Palestinian, the cuisine of Palestinian Arabs became the authentic option within the generalized Oriental category, which Ashkenazi elite consumers associated with lack of sophistication and mediocre quality.[39] Since the late 1990s, new types of Palestinian restaurants have appeared, such as restaurants serving dishes from the domestic menu or personal interpretations of familiar dishes, and have attracted a growing foodie clientele. Products from Palestinian small producers have also gained a growing market among Israeli foodies, who associate them with the values of authenticity, artisanal production, and connection to the place or *baladi.*[40] If most Palestinian food establishments were previously appreciated mainly for their use value, they now gained a stronger potential of being appreciated as gastronomic institutions.

DISTINCTION STRATEGIES AND GOURMET HUMMUS

Before the 1990s, the Israeli gastronomic discourse primarily centered on upscale restaurants and highbrow cuisine. Hummus, in contrast, stood for popular taste and a lack of creativity and sophistication—a meal that politicians would often indulge in before Election Day to signal their being "one of the people."[41] Thus, in a 1987 advertisement for the fashionable restaurant the Pink Ladle—a pioneer of Israeli nouvelle cuisine—hummus was listed as one of several dishes "we do not have." Under the heading "what we do have in the menu" was written "things you have never eaten before."[42] Demonstrating the educational thrust of late 1980s gastronomic discourse, the type of potential customers this advertisement targeted were not those who were already in the know but rather the unenlightened—those whose culinary horizons had to be expanded.

Since the mid-1990s, the gourmet discourse has been increasingly applied to lowbrow cuisine and ethnic food, including hummus. For instance, in 1997, Israel Aharoni, a celebrity chef and one of the leading mediators of the new culinary discourse, described the hummus in the Nazareth restaurant A-Sheikh in the following terms: "The hummus, it should be stated immediately, was the best hummus I have ever eaten in my life. A pure hummus, very fresh, which had never seen a refrigerator, light and tasty—I have almost forgotten how tasty a good hummus can be. In the center of the plate was a pile of ful, which wasn't cooked to a mushy texture . . . and the puddle of excellent olive oil on the plate completed the whole affair."[43]

A later example comes from journalist Alon Hadar's restaurant review blog. In a post titled "Journey to the Best Hummus in the World," Hadar relates his experience in a Jerusalem restaurant whose identity remains obscure: "The quality of the dish was enhanced from bite to bite. The concentrated taste of the fresh hummus slowly filled the mouth, combining in one base memories from the soft Abu Hassan and the boldness of Galilean hummus. Like dishes served in masterful restaurants, no foreign flash entered the dish. Only a perfect extraction of the raw ingredients, but still the furthest from a sterile taste. A powerful, earthy, mineral plate. Keeps meticulous proportions of fresh tahini (Nablusi), water and salt. This hummus was a stunner."[44]

The concept of cultural omnivorousness emerged in the sociology of culture in the 1990s, to mark a new pattern of cultural consumption among privileged groups. According to the omnivore thesis, members of high-status groups no longer consume only highbrow or "legitimate" culture but show openness toward a wide range of cultural products and genres, including lowbrow ones.[45] Here is Aharoni again, in what can be considered an omnivore's manifesto: "I can't stand it when somebody says, 'a simple hummus is much better than delicate goose liver.' Why either this or that? Why not this and that? I want to eat a wonderful hummus, and a great sandwich, and delicious pasta and delicate goose liver."[46] Although the exact nature and scope of this phenomenon, and the social composition of omnivore consumers, are subject to debate among scholars, they are commonly associated with the new middle class, and particularly with cultural intermediaries.[47] According to Josée Johnston and Shyon Baumann, omnivorous cultural consumption is a way of negotiating the tension between social distinction and exclusion on the one hand and democracy—namely, inclusionary social, cultural, and ideological trends—on the other hand, which characterizes contemporary Western societies.[48]

The switch to omnivorousness, then, does not mark the end of distinction through cultural consumption. Omnivores will not simply consume anything. First, omnivores tend to reject the most routinized and mass-produced forms of popular culture.[49] Second, not all lowbrow cultural products are considered equally worthy of consumption. As Omar Lizardo and Sara Skiles argue, at stake in omnivorous consumption is the transposition of the aesthetic disposition—the appreciation of things according to their aesthetic rather than their use value—to products from all registers of culture.[50] Third, since omnivorousness functions not only as vertical but also as horizontal differentiation from those higher on economic and lower on cultural capital, distinction is marked not only through consumption of specific things but also through demonstrations of knowledge about the things consumed.[51]

A central concept anchoring distinction in foodie discourse is "authenticity."[52] As Johnston and Baumann argue, authenticity does not inhere in an object's objective qualities but is generated through perceptions of how it negotiates a set of standards and values.[53] As they show, in contemporary foodie discourse, authenticity stands for a range of other values—such as geographic specificity, "simplicity," personal connection, "historicism" (i.e., food grounded in tradition), and "ethnic connection"—or the notion that in order to be authentic, food has to be prepared by members of the ethnic group in which it originated. These values are not self-evident. The ability to tell the difference between authentic and inauthentic food requires the kind of knowledge and skills that usually go with cultural and economic capital.[54]

The elitist rejection of mass-produced culture was reflected in my survey in the form of a negative correlation between cultural capital and consumption of packaged hummus.[55] However, distinguishing between artisanal and industrial hummus does not require any special knowledge or skills. Thus, making hummus an object for distinction practices resulted in internal differentiation of artisanal hummus, which assumed two distinct forms. One was the integration of hummus into gourmet cooking. The flagship dish of the restaurant Chan Manoli, which operated in Jaffa between 2014 and 2016, was hummus made of chickpeas cooked in olive oil and sage and mushed to a puree on the spot. Its chef, Felix Rosenthal, claimed to have "set out on a journey to prepare the best hummus in the world," no less.[56] It offered hummus with various toppings such as chard leaves and garlic, chopped lamb with wild herbs, pickled onion and sumac, and a mix of liver, hearts, and spleen. While Chan Manoli was not the only restaurant to serve a specialty hummus, overall these attempts have not been very successful and in any case were exceptions rather than the norm.

Far more significant in terms of its influence on both culinary discourse and consumption practices was the differentiation of plain hummus, both along geographical lines—namely, by associating styles of hummus with specific regions[57]—and along quality lines. In terms of quality, the hummus served in a standard Oriental restaurant—either Arab or Jewish owned—was distinguished from "gourmet hummus" produced by a top hummusiya, which itself became an internally divided category, with attributes like freshness, lightness, texture, and ingredient quality as the main distinguishing criteria. Previously unfamiliar chickpea and tahini preparations, like *msabbaha/mshawsha*, entered the menus of many Israeli hummus joints.[58] Finally, Arab-made hummus was distinguished from Jewish-made hummus and deemed better and more authentic. For example, food writer Sherry Ansky described in one of her columns how her friend Litani had tried in vain to prepare "real hummus, like the Arabs."[59] Shooky Galili, an internet consultant and founder of a popular hummus blog called *Hummus for the Masses*, wrote that "hummus is best when it is fresh and made by Arabs."[60] In a post in the "Hummusologists Inc." Facebook group, Erez Tikolsker, one of the authors of a 2022 hummusiyot guidebook, included in his "ten commandments" for hummusologists the following: "If there is an Arab hummusiya within a radius of one kilometer (if you're on foot), or ten kilometers (if you drive), don't eat Jewish hummus. . . . The relationship between Jewish hummus and hummus is like the relationship between Israeli football and football. You consume it only if there's nothing better. The best Jewish hummus will win the Maccabiah. The Maccabiah is not the Olympics."[61]

The main concept anchoring the distinction between authentic Arab and inauthentic or less authentic Jewish hummus in food discourse is historicity, as demonstrated in the introduction to the hummus tour quoted at the beginning of this chapter. In *Not by Hummus Alone*, Yehuda Litani writes that "a copy is never exactly identical to the original, and close as it may be, there will still be differences, sometimes even essential differences: not only in the long tradition, where Palestinians have a clear advantage over most of the descendants of various Diasporas in Israel, but in skills and patience."[62] Later in the book, in an interview with his Palestinian coauthor Na'im 'Araidi, Litani states, "It's a matter of generations and for this I envy you. You have 'it' naturally and we don't."[63] While the distinction between hummus made by Arabs and hummus made by Jews is rooted in Orientalist discourse—the identification of the Arabs with tradition, their closeness to nature, their patience—this discourse serves to account not only for the Arabs' better skills at food preparation but also, on occasion, for their presumably stronger connection to the land.

In contrast to the exclusivity implied by the elitist notion of "gourmet food," in the case of lowbrow-food-turned-object-of-distinction strategies, apparently everyone can join the distinction game. Yet those who promoted a gourmet discourse on hummus, including the association of Arab hummus with authenticity, were mostly cultural intermediaries, predominantly of a leftist political orientation, with or without culinary expertise. Thus, meditations on hummus by such "hummus experts" are often accompanied by erudite discussions on the history of the dish, its nutritional qualities, or the sociology of its consumption (in terms of culinary discernment, however, this discourse remains relatively limited).[64]

Obviously, the claim that Arabs make better hummus than Jews never goes uncontested. In discussions on hummus on social media, participants occasionally refuse this dictum or deny the Arab provenance of hummus.[65] Nevertheless, the assumption that hummus made by Arabs is superior to hummus made by Jews became so commonplace in culinary discourse that in a 1997 newspaper column that offered an Independence Day hummusiyot tour, all seven recommended hummusiyot were Arab.[66] In my survey, conducted almost two decades later, 44 percent of the respondents agreed with the statement that hummus made by Arabs is better and more authentic than hummus made by Jews (however, when asked to choose from a given list of adjectives the three they most strongly associated with hummus, 57.2 percent chose "Israeli," and only 32.1 percent chose "Arab"; out of those who chose "Israeli," 29.6 percent also chose "Arab").[67]

As we have seen in previous chapters, certain Palestinian hummus restaurants, especially in mixed cities, have attracted a substantial Jewish clientele in earlier decades, but from the mid-1990s, the prestige of some of them soared. Abu Hassan's hummus restaurants are a case in point. In the 1950s, the late founder, Ali Karawan, began selling homemade hummus from a cart in Jaffa. In 1959, he opened his own place in Sixty Street, which later moved to the Dolphin Street, near the Jaffa port.[68] Karawan's hummus has always been popular with Jaffa's Palestinian residents and in the 1970s also with soldiers from the nearby IDF radio station. But only in the late 1980s was it discovered by a broader Jewish public. In 1986, a short paragraph in the restaurant section of the Tel Aviv weekly *Ha'ir* referred to Abu Hassan's hummus under the heading "Secret." A decade later, no Israeli hummus aficionado was unaware of Abu Hassan. In a 1996 ode to Abu Hassan, comic artist Dudu Geva—a doyen of the Israeli hummus cult—described his experience of first trying Abu Hassan's msabbaha as "an orgasmic experience, which tied the depth of the soul with the palatal glands and ended with a song of halleluiah accompanied by up and

Figure 4.5 Abu Hassan restaurant in Jaffa, 1 the Dolphin Street, January 2008. Photo by Shomroni. Licensed under CC BY-SA 4.0 (https://creativecommons.org /licenses/by-sa/4.0/).

down blowing of the shofar."[69] In 2000, Abu Hassan opened a second restaurant in Jaffa. A third one was soon to follow (interestingly, a branch opened by his sons in Tel Aviv's fancy Sarona food market was short lived, from 2015 to 2016). Especially on Friday at noon, one could expect long lines in front of Abu Hassan's restaurants. For years, Abu Hassan had won every poll on "the best hummusiya in Israel." Shortly before Independence Day 2010, *Ha'ir*, together with the Tzabar Company, came up with the idea of mapping the best hummusiyot in Israel (including East Jerusalem). A group of "hummus experts" compiled a list of hummusiyot, and people could vote for their favorite one. Out of the ten hummusiyot that got the most votes, seven were Arab, with Abu Hassan topping the list.[70] As of the mid-2020s, Abu Hassan remains highly popular, although its reputation as the best hummusiya in Israel has somewhat diminished.

The logic of distinction through consumption of lowbrow food propels "hummus experts" to perpetually search for yet undiscovered hummusiyot in "authentic" places, preferably Arab towns and neighborhoods. Thus Yehuda Litani, in his *Ha'ir* column, structured his account of the hummusiya of Abu al-'Abed in Palestinian North Jerusalem as a story of persistent revelation: "I took

Eyal Shani there, the owner of Ocean restaurant in Jerusalem [at present one of Israel's top celebrity chefs]. He finished the dish hurriedly . . . and said immediately: I prefer the hummus here to a three-Michelin-star restaurant in Provence. I took Sherry Ansky, the writer of the *Maariv* food column, she dipped and exclaimed: 'That's it! This is the best hummus I have ever eaten in my life!' Writer Eyal Meged said after the first bite that he is enslaved to this place forever and ever."[71]

Food consumption has probably been the main occasion for Jews to visit Arab localities in Israel.[72] Although many celebrated Arab hummusiyot are located in impoverished areas—Arab localities being among the poorest in Israel—they attract visitors from all social strata. However, most Israelis will seldom, if ever, enter an Arab village or town.[73] Those who do are likely to opt for a well-known hummusiya in one of the mixed cities or in a town considered friendly like Abu Ghosh. Many hummusologists, on the other hand, report eating hummus in Arab villages, towns, and neighborhoods beyond the destinations considered safe for food tourism.

If food is the main occasion for Jews to visit Arab localities, for Arabs the main occasion to visit Jewish homes in Israel is labor. As the following excerpt from a nutrition column in *Haaretz* by Limor Evron Gilat demonstrates, the discourse on superior Arab hummus brings forth a type of Othering based on the notion that Arabs, in general, are inherently better able than Jews to produce good hummus: "For years I have been trying to prepare hummus at home, with no success. . . . And then several men came to my home to install new doors. I was in the middle of another failed attempt to prepare hummus . . . and suddenly I had a great idea, I asked which of these excellent men prepares the best hummus. They all pointed at Ibrahim Abu al-Nasser from Yafiʿa, the hummus champion of the area."[74] Evron Gilat does not write "several Arab men," although for anyone familiar with the Israeli social field it is obvious that the only point of asking random men who came to install new doors about preparing hummus is that these men were Arab. That none of them would know how to make hummus, or how to make good hummus, seems to be a nonoption for Evron Gilat.

The assumption that Arabs are inherently more capable than Jews of producing good hummus, and its complementary assumption that Arab chefs should only cook Arab food,[75] are instances of what Patrick Wolfe termed "repressive authenticity"—the settlers' appropriation of a determinative authority over indigeneity and its approved iterations ("everything that 'we' are not").[76] The mirror image of the Arab producer of authentic hummus is the Jew who fails to produce "real hummus" no matter how hard she tries. Rather than merely reflecting Palestinian historically acquired expertise in making hummus (and

Israeli lack thereof), this opposition is rooted in a settler-colonial structure, which renders the Israeli quest for indigenous authenticity a relational and hence ongoing project—at least as long as this structure remains intact.[77]

HUMMUS COEXISTENCE

The rise in the prestige of Arab-made hummus was also affected by the so-called peace process in the 1990s. In fact, "authentic Arab hummus" first entered Israeli consciousness in the context of war rather than peace—during the Lebanon War of 1982. The Hebrew press reported on soldiers and politicians flocking to restaurants in the Christian section of Beirut after it came under Israeli control and celebrating "terrific hummus" and "real olive oil."[78] In such contexts, where food consumption appears as a means of domesticating an otherwise alien and threatening space, the framework of "eating the Other" seems most pertinent. At the same time, it was because, by 1982, hummus had become an established part of Israelis' culinary repertoire that a newspaper piece about Israeli soldiers and civilians eating at the Emile restaurant in Beirut could describe them as feeling "at home" there.[79]

As Rebecca Stein shows, the Oslo Accords and peace process brought about a change in practices of tourism to Palestinian sites in Israel, including food tourism. Israelis did not hasten to return to restaurants in the Occupied Territories, but visits to Palestinian towns and villages within the 1948 borders increased significantly and were no longer limited to restaurants and other businesses on the margins.[80] Stein specifically mentions Israeli pilgrimages to Abu Ghosh—a hummus Mecca, which has since fallen from grace. This process was accompanied by a growing number of articles on Palestinian food in the Hebrew press. Various left-leaning writers promoted the idea that the Jewish taste for Arab food in general and for hummus in particular was a sign of cultural closeness and sought to further acquaint Israelis with Palestinian food culture. Prominent among them was Yehuda Litani, who, over the 1990s, published erudite articles on Palestinian restaurants and food businesses in the local newspapers *Ha'ir* (Tel Aviv) and *Kol Ha'ir* (Jerusalem).

It seems that no less than real trips to Palestinian localities in Israel, it was imaginary trips to neighboring Arab countries that boosted the reputation of "Arab-made hummus." The peace accord with Jordan in 1994 and the peace talks with Syria in 1999 opened new spaces for the projection of food fantasies—hummus fantasies in particular. As the logic of distinction determined that the more authentically Arab the hummus, the better it was, the Orientalist logic conferred greater authenticity on unknown regions. During the talks, items on food in Jordan and Syria appeared in the Israeli press from time to time.[81]

Figure 4.6   Campaign poster for the One Voice peace movement, Tel Aviv, 2010. Photo by the author.

Writers stated that "the best hummus in the world" could be found in Damascus and Beirut.[82] "Hummus in Damascus" became such a common trope for peace with Syria that several right-wing ideologues wrote that the Israeli Left was willing to forgo the material and spiritual assets of the Jewish people in return for a bowl of hummus.[83] The idea that hummus in unknown (i.e., yet inaccessible) regions was better carried into a 2010 street poster of the One Voice peace organization, which forecast the headlines of a January 1, 2018, newspaper titled "Israel." The headline above a close-up photo of a hummus plate reads, "The victims of peace." The subheading continues, "Tel Avivis are flocking to Nablus, Abu Hassan goes bankrupt."

This discourse is predicated on the Orientalist assumption that the only thing worthwhile in Nablus, Damascus, or Beirut is food (as many writers noted, one could go to Damascus, eat hummus, and return home on the same day). As in the case of the Lebanon war, here, too, hummus seems to function as a means for domesticating a threatening space. It ensures that although everything in that space is different (the hummus is taken to have qualities Israelis have never encountered before), it is still familiar (and in a world where the touristic experience is structured by discourses of consumption, this may be read as a commentary on the necessity of peace[84]).

The discourse on hummus as "the real broker in the Middle East" continued after the collapse of the Oslo process in the late 1990s, which culminated in the Second Intifada (2000–2005).[85] For example, travel writer and journalist Tzur Shezaf wrote in an article, "This dish has become the cement that connects Jews and Arabs, right-wing and left-wing, and is the real foundation on which true peace will be established—contented, smiling, with a swollen stomach—between the Euphrates and the Nile."[86] In the preface to a bulky, award-winning English volume dedicated to hummus recipes, photographs, and tales from across the Levant, Israel, and Egypt, it is written that "in the end, it is all about humanity, and food can only bring hearts closer together."[87] Food in general and hummus in particular became central to the Israeli "genre of coexistence"[88] and its accompanying industry, manifested in various culinary peace initiatives and educational tours focusing on food[89] and reflected in cookbooks intended for a foreign readership.[90] Naturally, this "consumer coexistence"[91] or "coexistence of hummus joints" draws much Palestinian criticism, as coexistence between service givers and service receivers that crops up primarily when food is involved.[92]

The prestige of hummus made by Arabs notwithstanding, attendance at Arab localities is strongly affected by the political situation. After the outbreak of the Second Intifada in 2000, Jews refrained from visiting Arab villages and towns. At that time, many new hummusiyot were opened in Tel Aviv, some of which were owned by Arabs or employed Arab cooks. Similar withdrawal from Arab localities—out of fear, revenge, or both—usually occurs whenever violence breaks out, for example, during Israeli airstrikes on Gaza or during the "Knife Intifada" of 2015–16.[93]

If hummus is unlikely to lead to peace, peace activism often leads to hummus. Arab-Jewish political activities that take place in Arab localities will often end in a restaurant. Amos Noy has termed the tendency of the Israeli Left to translate any Arab-Jewish encounter into meals and recipes "the culinary left."[94] On another level, the well-intentioned metaphor of hummus as "the cement that connects Jews and Arabs" is predicated on the culturalization of the conflict—on turning a struggle over land and lives into a struggle between

Figure 4.7 In front of Abu Hassan's: "But this is a sacred place for both people." Caricature by Amos Biderman, *Haaretz*, October 8, 2015. Courtesy of *Haaretz*.

cultures. In this context, *culture* appears no less an agent of depoliticization than a site of political struggle.

THE PENDULUM SWINGS AGAIN?

Two developments in recent years suggest that another wave of Israelization is underway.

The first is the growth in the number and reputation of Jewish-owned hummusiyot, including several chains, where hummus is prepared by Jewish cooks. The most conspicuous example is Hummus Eliyahu, which grew from a hummusiya in the northern town of Yokneʿam to a chain with seventy-three branches throughout the country, including in some West Bank settlements, as well as its own brand of tahini, halvah, and olive oil.[95] The founder, a repentant Breslover named Eliyahu Shmu'eli, tells the story of a divine intervention that brought him the perfect tahini for his hummus after he discovered that the one he had been using was not kosher and could not find a kosher substitute that would give the same results.[96] With the mottos of "Love thy neighbor" and "The wipe with the groove" betraying his Breslover and Rastafarian inspirations, Hummus Eliyahu defines itself as "Israeli hummus."[97] In the current Hebrew discourse on hummus, the claim that the best hummus is made by Arabs is more frequently contested, and articles containing rankings of hummusiyot include more Jewish-owned and -operated ones than previously, sometimes prevailing over Arab ones (Eliyahu itself was twice named "the best hummus in Israel" by an online food magazine).[98] Nevertheless, the discourse attributing better quality and greater authenticity to hummus made by Arabs simultaneously persists. Although there are some Jewish-owned hummusiyot that specifically mark themselves as Jewish through linguistic or visual signs, much more prevalent is the use of Arab signs, such as an Arab word for a name or the Arab prefix *Abu* (*Inti, Jum'a*, Abu Dabi), to signal authenticity. And while some Jewish hummusiyot have come up with variations on standard hummus (e.g., hummus with shakshuka or "hamshuka"), most of them adhere to the basic model of the Palestinian hummus joint.

The second development is the inclusion of Palestinian food within a broader category of "Israeli cuisine" or "Israeli food culture" without necessarily ignoring its Arab provenance and sometimes even celebrating it, in the service of a reconfigured Israeliness—one that presents itself as multicultural and inclusive. This trend is manifested in the "new Israeli cuisine" concocted in the kitchens of chef restaurants, both in Israel and abroad, and its accompanying discourse, as well as in various culinary initiatives and cookbooks presenting "Israeli cuisine" to foreign audiences.

The central place of Arab food in Israeli culinary culture, and the importance of "locality" and "local authenticity" in contemporary foodie discourse, led to a growing presence of Palestinian food in what came to be known as the "new Israeli cuisine."[99] In the 1980s, some of the harbingers of the gastronomic revolution were trying to develop a local version of nouvelle cuisine by integrating ingredients associated with the local food culture into mostly French dishes and cooking techniques (the Pink Ladle's most famous dish was halvah parfait). In the following decades, ingredients and dishes from the Palestinian and Mizrahi kitchens began to occupy a much more prominent place on the menus of chef restaurants seeking to develop a new Israeli culinary style (many of these chefs are Mizrahi themselves, given that cuisine is a cultural sector where Ashkenazi gatekeeping is lax). Ingredients like tahini, eggplant burned on an open fire, okra, and various local wild herbs became integral parts of their repertoire, and so did personal interpretations of Palestinian dishes previously unfamiliar to Israelis, like *shish barak* and *kibbeh nayyeh*.[100] Many of these chefs acknowledge the Arab and rarely even the Palestinian provenance of their dishes on their menus and websites.[101] The narrative that accompanies this style of cooking presents "Israeli cuisine" as based on ethnic rather than regional variation, with Middle Eastern cuisines taking the lead, since they are better suited to the local biosphere.[102]

Dishes and ingredients from the Palestinian menu also occupy pride of place in many restaurants offering "Israeli cuisine" (sometimes defined as Jerusalem or Tel Aviv cuisine but sometimes as Levantine or Middle Eastern), which have sprung up in many European and American urban centers over the last decade.[103] It is often the case that dishes from Levantine cuisine are mediated to Western consumers through these restaurants. Unlike their counterparts in Israel, Israeli chef restaurants abroad often serve variations on plain hummus, suggesting an even stronger claim of ownership. For example, the Neni restaurant in Berlin serves a "hummus trilogy": a three-tiered dish with curry mango hummus, beetroot hummus, and "classic" hummus, and Eyal Shani's Seven North in Vienna serves hummus topped with prawns in beurre noisette.[104] Some of these chefs profess an explicit gastrodiplomatic mission, intended to show foreign diners that Israel has other sides than "the monster that conquers the Palestinians," in the words of celebrity chef Assaf Granit.[105]

These restaurants, as well as the many cookbooks introducing Israeli cuisine to foreign audiences—between the years 2000 and 2016, twenty-one Israeli cookbooks appeared in English—are part of what Ilan Zvi Baron and Galia Press-Barnathan define as "culinary Zionism": representing the success of the Zionist cultural project and normalizing the occupation through food and food narratives.[106] Typical of this genre are the familiar nationalist tropes of the bond between the people and the land and "ingathering of the exiles" but with a twist: Arabs are presented as one of the many ethnic communities that contribute to the multiethnic Israeli social landscape in general and foodscape in particular.[107] An early example is Janna Gur's *The Book of New Israeli Food* (2007). In the introduction, which tells the story of the development of Israeli foodways along the structure of exile and return, Gur presents the Arabs as keepers of many of the biblical culinary traditions and as a source of (superficial) inspiration for early Zionists seeking to distance themselves from the traditions of the Diaspora. It was only in the 1980s, as Israelis became more cosmopolitan and sophisticated diners, that they discovered the "local ethnic food traditions"—the richness both of Palestinian cuisine and of the Jewish ethnic groups. The book includes many recipes for Arab dishes as well as photos of Palestinians preparing and selling food.[108] A similar discourse recurs in food writing and culinary initiatives, such as food tours and cooking courses.[109]

Probably the most blatant expression of gastronationalism and "food washing" is the harnessing of the vibrant Israeli culinary scene in the service of the state project of promoting Israel as "normal" and fun.[110] In the face of mounting critique of Israeli settler colonialism, occupation, and apartheid, various state agencies and NGOs began to organize food tours in Israel as a form of *hasbara* (lit. "explanation"—a combination of propaganda and state PR) focused on the area of "lifestyle." Vibe Israel is an NGO dedicated to "sharing Israel's story" online, primarily by organizing tours for social media influencers.[111] These tours are dedicated to promoting Israel's image as a tolerant multicultural society and a sanctuary of creativity, innovation, and entrepreneurship. According to Channel 2 reporter Ilan Lukach, who accompanied a food tour for food bloggers, "the world for the most part believes that we live on a dune, progressive like Afghanistan and feed on hummus and Palestinian children," whereas the tours show other sides of "our charming country." On the fourth day, said Lukach, the bloggers toured the Old City of Jerusalem where they ate hummus and falafel at "some Abu Shukri" and then Zalatimo's famous *mutabak* for dessert. During their visit to Zalatimo's, famous food blogger David Lebovitz broke into an excited monologue: "You can't define Israel because there's Arabic Culture, there's Israeli Culture, there's Palestinian culture, it all works together, it seems like it's a . . . wonderful sort of mélange of foods and cultures existing together, everyone's in this small space, and you must live together, you have to make it work somehow. It's kind of . . . beautiful."[112] Vibe Israel's mission seems to have been completed. Food trips presenting a similar narrative of culinary mixing have even reached Birthright Israel (*Taglit*)—a project dedicated to taking young Jews on a free trip to Israel. While these trips include visits to Druze or Bedouin settlements and a Palestinian hummus joint, needless to say, a similar "birthright" is denied to exiled Palestinians.[113]

Rather than necessarily erasing the Arab provenance of hummus, then, these gastronationalist initiatives ground the perception of hummus as an essential component of the Israeli menu—an instance of Israeli tolerance and inclusivity. In fact, hummus has become so associated with Israeli food culture that, given the conflation of Israeliness with Jewishness, it has penetrated some "Jewish" culinary institutions, such as restaurants serving "Jewish food" (a code for Eastern European Jewish food) or the Sabbath table of American Jews.[114] Ironically, this process owes much to the global spread of hummus through the food industry, in which Israeli companies have played an important role. The contemporary Israeli hummus industry is the topic of the final chapter.

Figure 4.8 The Klezmer-Hois Jewish restaurant in Krakow, 2016. Photo by the author.

MADE WITH LOVE

Mass-Produced Authenticity

Hummus Salad
  Ingredients: cooked chickpeas 63% [water, chickpeas, acidity regulator (sodium bicarbonate-baking soda)], water, raw tahini paste 16% (sesame), salt, acidity regulator (citric acid), seasoning mix, preservative (potassium sorbate), garlic.

—List of ingredients, Achla's basic hummus

SEVEN MONTHS AFTER THE EAST Jerusalem hummus tour, in response to a request to participate in a survey that Ofra and I had posted on the *Hummus for the Masses* website, I received an email from Yaron Tzur (then Bornstein), a Strauss development technologist, inquiring about the results of the survey. I wrote back and explained why I wouldn't want to share the results with someone working for the industry. In response, we received an invitation to visit the Strauss factory in the northern town of Karmiel, where Yaron enthusiastically guided us through the production process. Throughout the tour, Yaron made an effort to persuade us that when the difference in scale is accounted for, there was no essential difference between the production of industrial hummus and that of artisanal hummus—that no trickery was involved. It seemed that one of Yaron's main motivations for inviting us to the factory was to personalize the production process, which he also did through a blog he opened on the women's portal Saloona that he presented as a direct channel to the heart of the food industry. As he noted in our tour, and repeated in one of his blog posts, industrial hummus was never meant to replace the "traditional hummus with friends on Friday": "Hummus in a hummusiya is eaten warm, with fresh pita bread and olive oil. Let's tell the truth, hummus in a hummusiya, when eaten fresh, is simply tastier."[1] Three years later, Yaron participated in a campaign in which Strauss opened a makeshift hummusiya in Tel Aviv. In one of Strauss's commercials, happy customers were seen surprised to find out that the excellent hummus they had been enjoying at "Avi's Hummusiya" arrived directly from the factory. What this campaign was designed to convey was that the difference between artisanal and industrial hummus, when eaten fresh, consisted not so much in the substance's taste but in aspects such as temperature, additions, and setting of consumption.

While the passionate discourse on hummus centers on artisanal hummus produced in a hummusiya, most of the hummus most Israelis eat is produced in a factory.[2] And while the discourse on hummus still posits mass-produced hummus as the inferior Other of "the real thing," the relationship between industrial and artisanal hummus is better conceived as one of increasing commensurability and interrelationship. To no small extent, this process is due to the entry of powerful and globally active food companies into the packaged salads market.

At first glance, nothing seems further from the values of authenticity and locality that hummus conjures in Israel than an industrial product produced by globally active companies. The contemporary valorization of these values in foodie discourse itself emerged in response to multinational corporations' command of the food market. Yet the meanings of hummus in Israeli culture—the ways it is consumed, talked about, craved, and perceived as central to the Israeli sense of self as well as the way it came to figure in political arguments about possession—cannot be understood in isolation from industrial production (of material commodities and signs) and global processes.

The leading hummus-producing companies sought to reduce the perceived gap between their hummus and the hummus of hummusiyot. To achieve this, they developed new hummus products and launched marketing and publicity campaigns that centered on concepts and images related to the realm of artisanal production. Behind their campaigns stand two ostensibly opposed ideas: the idea that industrial hummus is becoming closer to hummus produced in a hummusiya and the idea that industrial and artisanal producers do not compete over the same market segment but complement each other, and therefore the more hummus people eat, the better it is for everyone.

This chapter examines the crucial role of Israeli companies in turning hummus into a local culinary cult. By appropriating and amplifying the passionate discourse on hummus, and by permeating the lifeworld of consumers, these companies enhanced the salience of hummus not only in the domestic menu of Israelis but also in Israeli public culture as a whole.[3] At the same time, as I will show, contemporary large producers, in their quest to qualify their hummus as "authentic," resort to both Zionist symbols of connection to the land

and discourses on Arab authenticity. In their symbolic universe, Arabs occupy the pole of tradition and craftsmanship, whereas Israelis occupy *both* poles of tradition and craftsmanship *and* of modernity and industry. If brands allow a circulatory object "to act as a 'condensed space-time,' with respect to both economic and political imaginaries," as Manning and Uplisashvili argue,[4] the branding of hummus by the leading Israeli companies is legible within a political imaginary where Israeli goodwill, multicultural tolerance, and Western progress legitimate the taking of what was anyway "ours" all along.

CORPORATE HUMMUS

In the 1990s, the Israeli economy became more integrated into the global market: a growing number of foreign companies opened Israeli branches, multinational corporations formed partnerships with or took over successful local companies, and the Israeli business sector augmented the share of its activities abroad.[5] Neoliberal privatization led to the concentration of much power in the hands of several groups.[6] Israeli capitalism shifted from a national-Fordist factory-centered production model to a transnational post-Fordist one, characterized by flexible and diffuse production and market segmentation.[7] These processes were evident in the food sector in general and in the salad sector in particular. In 2021, for example, five globally active companies were responsible for 38 percent of the Israeli processed food market, among them the two leading producers of packaged hummus—Strauss and Osem.[8] These companies, and the competition between them, revolutionized the entire field.

Already in the 1970s, various small factories began to produce chilled hummus for the wholesale market, most notably for restaurants, many of which served industrially produced hummus rather than self-made versions of the dish. The poor sanitary conditions in some of these factories, and the poor quality of the products, presented an opportunity for more aspiring entrepreneurs.[9] According to Zvi Dreizin, who founded Shamir Salads in 1974, the growing competition between producers toward the end of the decade served as an incentive to invest in more advanced machinery, which allowed a higher degree of control over the production process.[10] Telma, too, had moved to producing chilled hummus in the early 1980s. In the course of the decade, consumption of packaged salads rose considerably, partly due to the growing participation of women in the labor force.[11] By 1985, the turnover of the packaged salads market was $27 million per year, with hummus accounting for 50 percent of the category, selling four thousand tons annually.[12]

For the large food companies, salads increasingly seemed like a good investment. When in 1987 the investigative TV program *Kolbotek* exposed exceptionally high levels of coliform bacteria in the hummus of several popular restaurants, the outrage it caused contributed to a favorable reception for hummus with a sanitary aura.[13] Four years later, the Strauss Company—which developed from a small family dairy farm started by refugees from Nazi Germany into the second largest food corporation in Israel, currently active in more than twenty countries—purchased a small and successful salads factory.[14] Soon after the purchase, it was approached by a team of three experts—food engineer Sam Saguy, marketing expert Ron Antonovsky, and the Jewish American sensory scientist Howard Moskowitz—who offered to improve its hummus based on a method developed by Moskowitz. Moskowitz was the originator of "horizontal segmentation" in product development—namely, the idea of developing different varieties of the same product, catering to different taste profiles. His method for "product optimization" consists of presenting a large group of consumers with different variations of the product systematically changed and asking them to score their reaction to different features of each variant. By the time the three had approached Strauss, Moskowitz had already worked with companies such as PepsiCo and Campbell's Soups.[15] Strauss was reluctant at first but eventually agreed to try. About twenty-five variations were prepared in the company's laboratories according to Moskowitz's instructions and were tasted by a large sample of consumers from around the country.[16]

According to Antonovsky and Saguy, the hummus they eventually presented to Strauss based on Moskowitz's formula was nothing like the other hummus products available in Israeli supermarkets at the time: it was less acidic, and its texture was smoother and resembled mayonnaise. At first, Strauss was skeptical and even hired another company to test the results. Eventually it adopted the new recipe, and within a couple of years, Strauss's hummus—which later received the brand name Achla (an Arabic word for sweet/sweetest or good/best, which was naturalized in Hebrew as "great" or "excellent")—became a huge success.[17]

Strauss invested a fortune in product development, publicity, and marketing.[18] During the 1990s, it was the leading hummus manufacturer in Israel: by the end of the decade, Strauss's share of the salads market amounted to almost 60 percent, with other companies lagging far behind.[19] In 1997, another large food company, Osem, purchased a successful salads company—the Yanko family's Tzabar. In 1995, Osem entered a partnership with Nestlé, which became its largest shareholder in 2000 and full owner in 2016.[20] With the capital and expertise of both Osem and Nestlé, Tzabar was able to surpass Achla in 2001 and became the leading hummus brand in Israel until 2017, when the premiere returned to Achla.[21] While Tzabar presented its success as owing to quality and taste,[22] its ascendancy owes much to the marketing strategies brought into the company by Nestlé (such as the need to constantly innovate) and its award-winning publicity campaigns created by the global advertising agency McCann-Erickson.[23] As Matti Yahav, the Tzabar marketing manager, told me, Nestlé gave Tzabar a "marketing school," while Osem wanted "to be the number one" in every category.[24]

One of the steps that contributed to the success of Tzabar was the differentiation it introduced into its hummus products. Until that point, the hummus market was based on a single type of product—plain hummus. In 2000, Tzabar started to produce hummus with toppings (such as whole chickpeas, pine nuts, hot pepper sauce, and Za'atar). Three years later, it inaugurated a new series of products containing a higher percentage of tahini and named it the Hummus King. By 2010, the company had seventeen different hummus products.[25] Strauss followed suit, developing its own hummus with toppings and a series of upgraded products—"the hummusiya."

Since the early 2000s, then, the packaged hummus market has been dominated by two powerful companies. As of 2023, Strauss and Tzabar together account for 62 percent of the market share.[26] Their economic power enables them to invest substantial capital not only in product development, publicity, and marketing but also in advanced production infrastructure. Their dominant position in the local food market also gives them considerable leverage, allowing them to influence every link in the production and distribution chains, from farmers and traders to retailers. Moreover, their corporate strategy of brand consolidation enables them to negotiate for prime shelf space in supermarket chains, often pushing out smaller brands.

Although I heard from more than one person affiliated with the industry that industrial hummus will never be exactly like the hummus of hummusiyot, especially when eaten fresh, industrial companies increasingly make an effort to develop products that come as close to it as possible. There are several challenges involved, which make the production of industrial hummus an entirely different matter from the production of artisanal hummus. First, industrial hummus has to last for a long time (currently over a month), during which it must not change its taste or texture (artisanal hummus, in contrast, not only spoils much faster but also hardens in the refrigerator).[27] Second, it must conform to a standard of acidity (pH) set by the National Food Service, which results in a relatively sour hummus.[28] The lines of products that are closer to homemade hummus contain more tahini and are therefore more expensive than the standard hummus, albeit still 20–30 percent cheaper than hummus sold in a hummusiya, which does not last as long and is much less accessible than industry hummus, which can be found in any grocery store.

As I noted in the previous chapter, foodies and hummusologists like to dissociate themselves from mass-produced hummus, even if many of them confess to eating it from time to time when no better alternative is at hand. In my survey, most people who stated that they avoid packaged hummus cited taste and health as the two main reasons, whereas the vast majority of those who buy it cited factors like accessibility, durability, hygiene, and price (however, several respondents stated that there is hardly any difference between mass-produced hummus and hummus from a hummusiya, and two even stated that they liked packaged hummus better). In a survey conducted by Strauss, "dislike for the taste" was mentioned as the main barrier to expansion.[29]

Where does all this take us in respect to the question of taste? Establishing objective hierarchies of taste, especially in the post-Bourdieusian age, is an untenable endeavor.[30] Yet at least one argument can be made with certainty: the hummus currently produced by industrial companies has come closer to hummus prepared in a hummusiya than its early predecessors. In other words, industrial companies established a plane of commensurability between mass-produced and artisanal hummus through both material and semiotic means—a fact that had a marked influence on the landscape of consumption.

According to the marketing manager of the salads department at Strauss, between the mid-1990s and 2001, consumption of mass-produced hummus in Israel almost doubled, and it continued to grow in the following decades.[31] In 2010, the revenue of the packaged hummus market was higher than the rest of the salads category taken together (384 million shekels compared to 360 million shekels).[32] Two years later, it had already reached 450 million shekels.[33] In my survey, 41.3 percent of the respondents stated that they bought packaged hummus at least once a week, and 75.5 percent stated that they bought it at least once a month.[34] Industry hummus is also consumed by many foodies and hummusologists, although they often make sure to dissociate themselves from it—for example, by defining it as "emergency hummus," in the words of one food journalist.[35]

If the coliform bacteria contributed to the ascent of packaged hummus in the early 1990s, two decades later, the spotlight of consumer journalism has increasingly turned toward the industry, indexing the growing power of corporations, which became the main addressee of consumer struggles.[36] Several investigative TV programs exposed various health hazards in the products of certain companies, and articles discussing the unhealthy composition of certain hummus products—their large amount of oil, saturated fat, and sodium—also appear from time to time.[37] Such criticism, along with occasional recalls of certain products, contributed to the stagnation and even decline of the salads category in recent years.[38] Public trust has thus become a central concern for companies, prompting them to invest heavily in branding strategies that emphasize values such as health, naturalness, and authenticity.[39]

BRANDING AUTHENTICITY

When I sample the plain hummus of Tzabar and Strauss, I sense little difference between them (in fact, the difference between each company's simple and upgraded hummus is bigger). Neither is their basic hummus different in any substantial way from that of smaller companies (some of which hummusologists hold in higher esteem[40]). In spite of the companies' official discourse stressing quality and taste, on various occasions, company people themselves concede the crucial role of publicity and marketing in creating their market value.[41] Indeed, if the main product produced by their Fordist predecessors was hummus (be it canned, powdered, or chilled), Strauss and Tzabar are no less producers of signs. Taken together, their branding practices reflect the double logic of what Hall defined as "the global postmodern," merging an appeal to a specifically local universe of meanings and sentiments with global culinary trends like authenticity, health, and localism itself.[42] Given their effort to tie their products to values associated with artisanal hummus, images related to production feature in their campaigns no less prominently than images related to consumption.

When the people of Osem entered Tzabar in 2000, they set themselves a challenge: to turn Tzabar from a "weak number two-three" in the salads category to a "strong number two." According to their strategic plan, the effort had to be concentrated on a single narrow sector, which is nevertheless relevant to a wide circle of consumers and with high potential for profit. With half of the revenue in the salads category coming from hummus, and with relatively low production costs—production of hummus, unlike some of the other salads, is completely mechanized—hummus seemed like the natural candidate.[43]

First Tzabar had to distinguish itself from Achla. Strauss's publicity was rooted in the perception of hummus as an "all Israeli" food (albeit with Mizrahi and masculine resonances). Its commercials sought to tie hummus to sentiments like joy of life, familialism, and patriotism (e.g., by showing soldiers) and hardly dwelled on the qualities of the product itself.[44] The most important aspect in which Tzabar sought distinction was "taste perception." Tzabar's research into consumers' perceptions taught the company that the entire category of industrial hummus was perceived as "synthetic"—as a substitute for "the real thing": authentic hummus, produced in a hummusiya, "personally and from the heart." Tzabar decided to build its strategy around the concept of authenticity. The values that were chosen to represent the brand, besides "authenticity," were "taste," "expertise," and "love for the work (of preparation)."[45]

To associate its products with authentic hummus, Tzabar developed its hummus with toppings, as a reference to the toppings placed on hummus in hummusiyot, and hired Mizrahi Jewish actor Jacques Cohen to lead the campaign. Years back, Cohen played the leading role in the Israeli Broadcasting Authority's Arabic series *The Big Restaurant*, which garnered him widespread popularity among Jewish and Arab viewers in Israel and beyond. By casting Cohen, Tzabar also sought to appeal to Arab consumers.[46] As the trend of considering Arab-made hummus better and more authentic than Jewish-made hummus grew stronger, Tzabar started to integrate Arab hummus makers into its campaigns.[47] For example, in 2004, after it inaugurated its Hummus King series, it released a TV commercial in which Jewish Cohen persuades two Arab restaurateurs and family members from Abu Ghosh who fought over the question of who was entitled to use the name Abu Shukri to make peace with each other ("*yalla sulha!*"). Epitomizing Israeli colonial *chutzpah*, Cohen tells the Abu Shukris, "Hummus is made with love, with soul, like in Tzabar" (the company's slogan being "Hummus is made with love, or not made at all").[48] In another commercial, however, Cohen and the team of the Big Restaurant visit the famous Saʿid hummusiya in Acre to "learn the secrets of his hummus," but while this commercial conceded expertise to Saʿid, Jewish Cohen was nevertheless the ultimate judge of quality.

Tzabar sought to associate its products with authentic hummus prepared in a hummusiya in other ways as well—for example, by organizing an annual hummus festival in Tel Aviv, where hummusiyot from all over the country sold their hummus. Twenty-five tons of hummus were sold in the first festival; of them, eight were produced by Tzabar.[49] It also changed its packages from square to round, simulating hummusiya takeaway.[50] Tzabar's focus on authenticity played a major role in its success in surpassing Achla as the leading hummus brand.[51]

It was not long before other hummus-producing companies adopted the concept of authenticity in their marketing strategies—for example, by coming out with a non-branded line of products that they marketed as "homemade."[52] In response, Tzabar sought to "re-break the record of authenticity": it sent a team to Jordan in order to find a hummus maker "with a story" with whom it could cooperate in developing a new hummus recipe[53] (of course, the precondition was that he would be willing to cooperate with Tzabar, which was often not the case). They eventually found Nehad al-Han, the owner of Al-Awaysi restaurant in Amman (his "story" was that the king had eaten in his hummusiya[54]). Tzabar bestowed al-Han with the title "the king of Jordanian hummus" and came out with a new product: "Nehad's hummus."[55] Tzabar even opened a makeshift hummusiya for Nehad in the bona fide stronghold of fabricated authenticity: the artists' colony of Old Jaffa, established in the 1960s over the ruins of the Arab old city. The opening of the hummusiya, which included a staging of an "Arab *hafla*" (party), replete with belly dancers, celebrities, and a drink bar, received much media attention. According to Matti Yahav, eighty thousand people had eaten in Nehad's hummusiya in Old Jaffa. Nehad's campaign was extremely successful, and Tzabar continued to collaborate with Arab hummus makers to create new lines of upgraded hummus products carrying their names.[56]

In the meantime, Strauss's attempts to regain its primacy were unsuccessful. In 2005, it launched a campaign that used the British Royal Family to publicize its hummus. This was a big mistake. As Strauss's investigations later revealed, Israelis perceived hummus as a simple, unpretentious, and "all-Israeli" (if emphatically masculine) dish, with strong emotional resonance. Strauss's campaign marked its hummus as elitist and detached in contrast to the more popular image advanced by Tzabar.[57] In order to restore to its hummus the values of simplicity and all-Israeliness, Strauss hired Mizrahi singer and actress Raymonde Abecassis as presenter, but its commercials mostly showed unappetizing scenes of home consumption, and the campaign did not take off. [58] Some improvement was registered following Strauss's incorporation of "health" into its set of brand values in 2008: it moved Achla to the company's "health and lifestyle" division, replaced soybean with canola oil, and reduced its amount from 30 to 16 percent. Strauss's share in the salads market rose 8 percent, but it still did not surpass Tzabar.[59]

The move that began to diminish the gap between Achla and Tzabar in earnest and eventually returned the lead to Achla began in 2010, following another restructuring in Strauss: salads were split from dairy products and came under the "fresh foods" division. Now it was Strauss that decided to put taste at the center of its branding strategy. Building on consumers' desire to know where their food came from, and echoing foodie discourses of locality and terroir, Strauss focused its campaign on different facets of authenticity: local cultivation and personal connection.[60] Although hummus is considered a quintessentially local dish, a large share of the chickpeas used by the industry are imported, given the higher price of local chickpeas (the tahini is produced in Israel but from imported sesame, mainly from Ethiopia).[61] At the time, all the chickpeas used by Strauss were imported.

Strauss appointed an agronomist, Pini Gottlieb, as the manager of agricultural procurement and agronomy of its fresh food division. Gottlieb started working directly with farmers, guiding them on how to produce chickpeas that would best fit the company's needs, signing advance contracts, and sometimes giving them down payments and loans. He also began working with Ethiopian growers, who provided the sesame to the local (Arab) companies that produced the tahini used by Strauss. Each passing year, the percentage of locally grown chickpeas that Gottlieb integrated into the production line increased, with the aim of eventually reaching 100 percent.[62] The implications of Strauss's shift to locally grown chickpeas go beyond the price of ingredients. Chickpea varieties differ in degree of sweetness, texture, water absorption, percentage of moisture, elasticity, and color, so that every change of variety requires adjustment of the production line (soaking time, cooking time, ratio of ingredients, etc.) in order to match consumers' expectations. Besides an agronomist, Strauss also hired a chef, Yaniv Gur Arye, as a culinary consultant for its salads division, whose goal was to eliminate the dichotomy between industrial and artisanal hummus and bring Strauss's hummus as close as possible to hummus from a hummusiya—for example, by disposing of the oil in the company's hummus products.[63]

One of Strauss's strategies for creating an authenticity effect in the context of its turn to local agriculture is to personalize production by integrating people who work with or for Strauss in its publicity campaigns. For example, Strauss produced various TV commercials and promotional videos featuring farmers who work with the company, including a hearty Yemenite chickpea grower, Avi Mevorach. In one of the videos, Mevorach is shown inspecting the fields, digging in the earth with his hand to pull out a chickpea plant, telling about his father who arrived in Israel from Yemen and became a farmer, and relating his sense of joy and pride that through Strauss, so many people enjoy the chickpeas that he grows.[64] The campaign was titled "Achla taste starts in the field" (with "achla taste" also meaning "great taste"). This campaign turned out to be extremely successful, and by September 2013, Strauss's share of the hummus market increased by 18.3 percent, while Tzabar's decreased.[65]

When I asked Gottlieb whether it was taste or the concept of local produce that motivated the shift to locally grown chickpeas, he insisted it was taste that came first, since "Israeli chickpeas are considered the best chickpeas, both in Israel and in the world." According to Gottlieb, he made samples of hummus using chickpeas from almost every possible country, and versions made from Israeli chickpeas were always the best. He then added, "There are candidates . . . There are stronger candidates. No, not stronger, but no less . . . but we prefer to go with the Israeli." When I asked him why the Israeli chickpea was better, he repeated several times that it was simply good and that it even responded better to the water. "It goes back to the water that watered it," he said jokingly. Although the concept of terroir has broadened to include products other than wine in recent

Figure 5.1 Achla's "Hummuseriya." The inscription on the stand reads
"The Hummuseriya: Rediscovering Hummus!" Sarona Market, Tel Aviv, 2022.
Photo by the author.

years, this was the first and only time I encountered anything close to the notion of terroir applied to hummus.[66]

Strauss also began to play the artisanal card by developing a line of hummus products with a higher percentage of tahini or by opening its own makeshift hummusiya close to Israel's Independence Day, when more packs of hummus are sold than on any other day. In 2022, the company sponsored a hummus festival that centered on the idea of hummus as a basis. During the days of the festival, several chef restaurants served unique hummus dishes, and Strauss itself opened a hummus stand in a fancy Tel Aviv food mall, serving fresh hummus out of a special dispenser developed for this purpose, with various original additions.[67] Yet in contrast to Tzabar, it adopted an ironic stance toward the discourse of searching for the best and most authentic (usually Arab) hummusiyot, invoking and parodying it at the same time, thereby interpellating a reflexive consumer who knows—just as Strauss does—that industrial hummus will never be as good as the hummus of a good hummusiya, but it can nevertheless serve as a worthy substitute.[68]

I dwelled on the campaigns of Tzabar and Strauss at some length to show how in order to requalify their hummus as authentic, their strategies combined attempts to attain authenticity in the iconic sense (developing hummus "true to its type") with tying their products to signifiers of the indexical authenticity of provenance and sincere expression.[69] Unlike their predecessors, their gastronationalism is not predicated on suppressing the Arab provenance of hummus but on fusing national and foodie discourses, including the discourse on authentic Arab hummus. Once foodie discourse was appropriated by industrial companies, appreciation for Arab cuisine was replaced with a patronizing attitude toward the Arabs, who were positioned as the masters of craft ("tradition") rather than of industry ("modernity"), with Jews being the ultimate authority to judge on quality. The source of this authority is not tradition and provenance but rather the technological and economic power of production.

"HUMMUS HAS NO BORDERS": THE HUMMUS WARS

The moment that ostensibly epitomizes the attempt to fix a national identity to hummus was the Guinness record competition in the years 2009–10, also known as "the hummus wars" between Israel and Lebanon.[70] Yet this competition is inseparable from another no less serious competition: that of industrial companies over global markets.

Over the past few decades, hummus evolved into a truly global fad. In many countries in Europe, the Americas, and the Asian-Pacific, packaged hummus is by now a regular product on the shelves of almost any supermarket. In the United States, the market for packaged hummus has grown exponentially, expanding from $5 million a year in 1995 to $325 million in 2010 and $1.82 billion in 2023.[71] In the same year, the revenue of the global hummus market was estimated at $3.85 billion and growing.[72] In most of the countries where hummus has made inroads in recent decades, consumers became acquainted with the industrial version first, which was often followed by homemade hummus entering the menus of many restaurants and cafés.[73]

Israeli companies have fared well in this process, either by exporting their hummus or, more substantially, through subsidiaries abroad. The largest hummus brand in the US is Sabra.[74] Established in 1986 by an Israeli-American cab driver in partnership with the founders of Tzabar, in 2005 it was bought by Strauss, who sold half of the company to PepsiCo two years later.[75] By mid-2023, Strauss Group was involved in the hummus market, besides in Israel and the US, in Canada, Mexico, and Australia, which made it one of the largest hummus manufacturers worldwide.[76] Osem-Nestlé, too, had purchased a successful American hummus brand, Tribe, in 2008, which it held for ten years.[77]

Given the importance of geographic specificity in establishing the value of global food commodities, qualifications of food products by companies producing for the global market often include various localization strategies, ranging from the use of visual and verbal markers to the legal tools of geographical indications.[78] In the case of hummus, localization is both geographically complicated and politically fraught. While companies may resort to a national idiom in their competition over markets, localization is not a simple and straightforward attachment of a national identity to hummus. Examined at close range, this is aptly demonstrated in the hummus wars.

In fact, the first record battle was waged between Israeli companies (Tzabar and Sabra) rather than states. Signaling their power of production through gigantic hummus dishes, they broke each other's records in the framework of their publicity campaigns, beginning in 1995. In 2008, Tzabar broke its own record with a 420-kilo dish presented at the Tel Aviv stand at the World Travel Market in London, where its hummus was marketed by the British kosher food distributor Yarden GB (in the following year, Yarden was purchased by Osem).[79]

In light of the success of Israeli companies in the international market, the head of the Association of Lebanese Industrialists (ALI), Fadi Abboud, appealed to the Lebanese Ministry of Economy and Trade in 2008, to request from the European Commission protected status for hummus and several other dishes as uniquely Lebanese foods. If granted, Israel would be banned from selling these foods in the EU under their original name, like the example of feta cheese and Champagne.[80] In the context of ALI's campaign, 250 Lebanese chefs prepared an over-two-ton dish of hummus in October 2009 and broke the record set by Tzabar. According to press reports, after preparing the gigantic dish, which was decorated with the Lebanese flag, the chefs gathered to sing the Lebanese national anthem. The title of the event, which was described by the organizers as a "patriotic demonstration of an international scale," was "Who Owns Hummus?"[81]

Several weeks later, businessman and restaurant owner Jawadat Ibrahim, a Palestinian citizen of Israel, announced his intention to break the Lebanese record in his hometown Abu Ghosh and "bring back the honor to the state of Israel."[82] Ibrahim, a well-connected lottery millionaire, has always been a man of "hummus coexistence": he used to sponsor hummus preparation workshops in the Jewish holiday of Hanukah for Arab and Jewish kids and even planned to live on a kibbutz.[83] In January 2010, Ibrahim broke the Lebanese record with a dish containing over four tons of hummus. In May, Lebanon broke the record again with a dish of 10,452 kilograms, which represented Lebanon's total area in square kilometers.[84] Currently Lebanon is still registered as the Guinness

Figure 5.2   Preparing the world's largest hummus serving in Abu Ghosh, 2010.
Photo by the author. Jawadat Ibrahim in front.

record holder. However, a request to the European Commission, to my knowledge, has not been filed.

Although these displays of culinary patriotism did not directly serve the interests of specific corporations, the fact that both Abboud and Ibrahim were involved in the hummus industry in their respective countries—Abboud as the owner of the first company to have produced chilled hummus in Lebanon and Ibrahim as then a new partner in an Israeli salad company—speaks volumes to the fact that something more than sheer patriotism was at stake.[85] As Ari Ariel writes, with the rise of global hummus consumption, authenticity takes on an economic value.[86] While Abboud's anger at seeing Israeli companies present hummus at international food exhibitions as an Israeli dish may not have stemmed exclusively from a sense of economic loss, at the least the "hummus wars" represent the fusion of nationalist sentiments with economic interest in the context of competition over global markets.

However, although media representations of the Abu Ghosh event, including by Ibrahim himself, constructed it as an Israeli refutation of the Lebanese claim of ownership, the most pronounced meanings conveyed by the staging of

Figure 5.3 Setting a Guinness record for the world's largest hummus serving in Abu Ghosh, 2010. Placed at the center of the dish is a flag with the logo of Ibrahim's restaurant. Photo by the author.

the event itself were other than Israeli patriotism or an Israeli claim of ownership. First, all over the site was publicity for the sponsoring companies, primarily for the Israeli salads manufacturer Miki Delicatessen, where Ibrahim had become a partner.[87] When we arrived at the scene, we saw some dozen men dressed in white robes and chef hats, decorated with the Miki logo, pouring the contents of Miki plastic cases into the huge satellite dish, which served as the container for the hummus. The cases, we were told, came from the Miki factory, whose facilities were used to prepare the hummus. In the center of the dish, on top of the hummus, the organizers placed not the Israeli flag but a flag with the logo of the Abu Ghosh Restaurant, owned by Ibrahim. The only Israeli national symbols on-site were the Israeli flags that decorated the village lampposts and a batch of blue and white balloons, which were blown into the air at the end of the ceremony.

Second, the identities emphasized during the event were both above and below the nation-state. On the one hand, hummus was presented as a Middle Eastern dish, which has the capacity to breach the gaps between Jews and

Figure 5.4   A singer at the ceremony, Abu Ghosh, 2010. Photo by the author.

Arabs. As famous soccer broadcaster Zouheir Bahloul, a Palestinian citizen of Israel who moderated the event, stated, "Hummus is the real mediator in the Middle East." Ibrahim even invited the Lebanese to break the new record together. On the other hand, the staging of the event was replete with local-patriotic messages: it was presented as a festive day for Abu Ghosh, and all participants in the ceremony spoke or sang its praise. Indeed, for the residents who gathered on-site, this was mainly a local feast of a village that owes its existence in Israeli consciousness mainly to hummus and that received for a moment the attention of world media.[88]

It seems that no less than promoting Israeli hummus abroad (or at least claiming the right of Israeli companies to sell "hummus" abroad), the event was staged to promote the hummus of Abu Ghosh, and particularly of Ibrahim's restaurant, at home. When Ibrahim said that "the Lebanese can claim whatever they want, but the hummus is ours, Israelis; we, in any case, prepare it better,"[89] no Israeli in their right mind would have read this as referring to Miki Delicatessen. In the context of the discourse about hummus, neither would most Israelis feel the dissonance of a *we* coming from a Palestinian citizen. By breaking the Lebanese record at Abu Ghosh, Ibrahim attempted to mark

Figure 5.5   Celebrating the record with flags of Abu Ghosh. Photo by the author.

himself, no less, and even more than hummus, as Israeli.[90] At the very least, this requires a very big dish.

Ironically, while the "hummus war" helped to establish an Israeli claim of ownership in the international public consciousness, Israeli companies that export or produce hummus abroad do not usually market hummus as Israeli, with very few exceptions.[91] With the growth of the BDS (Boycott, Divestment, and Sanctions) movement, these companies stand to lose from associating their products with Israel. If any geographical indication is at all included in their qualifications, which is often not the case, it is likely to be "Middle Eastern" or "Mediterranean." Another irony is that the "hummus war" conjoined Israelis and Palestinians in objecting to the Lebanese claim of ownership. Various Palestinian commentators responded to the attempt to nail down a national identity of hummus with much dismay. It seems that Abboud himself was aware of the incongruity of the Lebanese claim, which is why he stated that Lebanon was the first to produce *industrial* hummus and export it abroad.[92]

Perhaps the bitterest irony is that hummus produced by Israeli companies has done quite well in the captive markets of the OT, except for periods of effective boycott of Israeli products. When filmmaker Trevor Graham asked

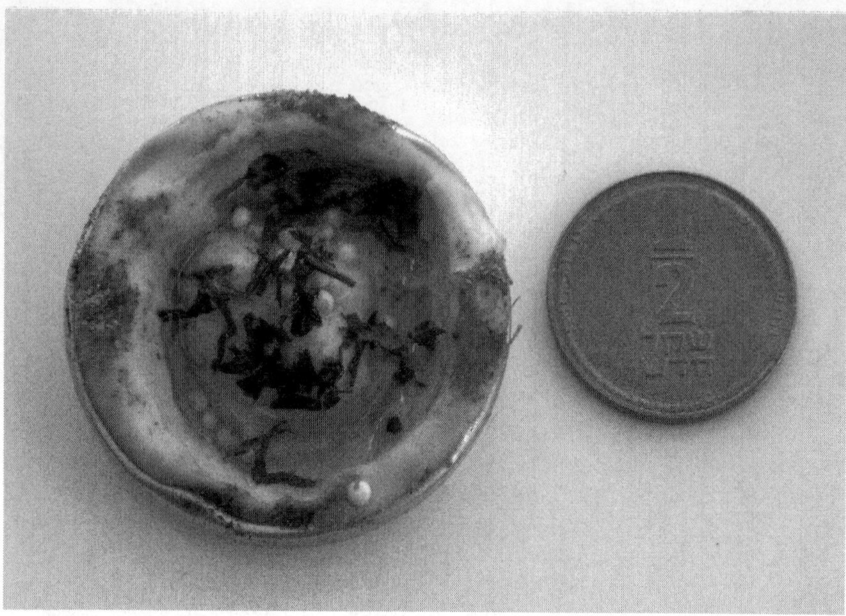

Figure 5.6 "A new Guinness record for the world's smallest hummus plate."
Shooky Galili, *Hummus for the Masses* blog, November 22, 2009, https://humus101
.com/1335. Courtesy of Shooky Galili.

Matti Yahav "who owns hummus," Yahav mentioned the success of Tzabar's
hummus in the West Bank and the Gaza Strip, stating, "Hummus has no
borders."[93] Yahav even claimed that Tzabar's hummus has been more successful in Gaza with Hebrew rather than Arabic labels. But while Israeli companies seeking to sell their hummus to Palestinians may encounter no borders,
Palestinian companies seeking to compete successfully in the Palestinian
market, let alone export their products, have to cross many.[94]

BETWEEN INDUSTRIAL AND ARTISANAL HUMMUS

As I discussed above, the development of upgraded hummus products went
hand in hand with companies' adoption of values associated with artisanal
hummus, such as authenticity, localism, and health, in their brand positioning
strategies. Yet the role of industrial companies in turning hummus into a culinary cult lies not so much, or not primarily, in the realm of representation but in
permeating the lifeworld of Israelis through their publicity and marketing practices.[95] By blurring the distinction between industrial and artisanal hummus,
and by amplifying the emotional discourse on hummus—any hummus—they

increased the ubiquity of hummus in the public sphere, turning consumers' sociality around it into an instrument for generating profit.[96]

As some of my examples thus far demonstrated, industrial companies do not simply incorporate artisanal producers in their campaigns; some of their branding practices *center* on artisanal hummus and artisanal producers, such as the mapping of the best hummusiyot toward Independence Day 2010, mentioned earlier.[97] A previous version of the Tzabar website contained a search engine for hummusiyot all over the country.[98] Another example is a series of five clips, coproduced by Strauss and the popular news portal Walla. In each clip, food journalist Noa Rozin and chef Yaniv Gur Arye visit a different hummusiya and analyze its hummus. The series, which is titled *In Search for the Perfect Hummus*, featured two Arab hummusiyot and two Jewish ones, and finally—Yaniv Gur Arye's kitchen at Strauss.[99]

Another way for companies to augment the presence of hummus, and their own presence, in the lifeworld of consumers is by having company people participate in social media platforms, such as blogs and Facebook groups dedicated to hummus (Gur Arye's post on industrial hummus received more responses than any other post in the Hummusologists Inc. Facebook group[100]) or by creating "news" related to hummus (or chickpeas). Many items on hummus in various web portals present content generated by the companies, some of which cover company-initiated or company-sponsored activities and events, such as a visit to Avi Mevorach's farm, culinary tours related to hummus, and even sending hummus to space for experimental purposes, sponsored by Strauss.[101]

In the discourse promoted by the large companies, emotionalization of hummus, its consumption, and its production is paramount, as well as references to hummus as an Israeli national dish or an Israeli "obsession." This strategy is intended not only to augment the authenticity effect (e.g., by featuring people affiliated with the industry who are motivated by the search for emotional rewards rather than for profit[102]) but also to raise the interest in the hummus category as a whole, as I was told by one of Tzabar's senior employees. The companies' propagation of an emotional discourse on hummus creates a feedback and "feed-forward" cycle where emotionalization breeds more talk, which breeds more emotionalization and so on.[103] Never before have so many Israelis *craved* hummus—any hummus. Neither have so many artisanal producers made hummus "with love."[104]

On one level, eating mass-produced hummus at home and eating hummus in a hummusiya are completely different experiences. Apart from the objective material differences between these two instantiations of hummus, taste perception is shaped by the entire context of consumption and by the consumer's knowledge about the mode of production of the food they eat.[105] Regardless of the companies' branding strategies, industrial hummus is still largely considered a mass-produced, impersonal product made not with love, pace Tzabar, but with automated machinery. On another level, quality perception is relational. While most consumers consider mass-produced hummus to be inferior to "authentic" hummus, it can safely be argued that it is still more similar to restaurant hummus than what most Israelis are able to prepare at home. In fact, Israelis do not prepare their own hummus all that often, although it has become more common than it used to be several decades ago.[106]

That the distinction between industrial and artisanal hummus may potentially be blurred for at least some consumers is illustrated by a lawsuit filed against a small company that presented its product as "homemade" (*beyti*). In a petition for a class action, the plaintiff explained that she had regularly purchased this hummus under the impression that it was "real hummus." Upon discovering that competitor brands contained less than 50 percent chickpeas, she inferred that the product she had been buying likely contained even less, since the company refrained from marking the percentage on the package, as required by law. She concluded, therefore, that it could not be considered homemade.[107] Clearly, this woman knew that she was not buying "homemade" hummus but hummus made in a factory. Still, she believed that had its chickpea content matched that of homemade hummus (approximately 70 percent), it would have qualified as "real hummus."

A different kind of testimony to consumers' perception of commensurability between industrial and artisanal hummus lies in the common practice of adding toppings to the hummus; according to a survey conducted by Strauss, this is done by more than 50 percent of the consumers.[108] The most common addition is olive oil, but also common are tahini, pine nuts, and Za'atar. While the practice of personalizing and "improving" mass-produced products is hardly exceptional,[109] what is interesting in the case of hummus is that the most common additions are intended to "authenticate" it—make it more like the hummus served in a hummusiya. One exception is Za'atar, which is normally not added to the hummus in hummusiyot but serves to authenticate the hummus in another way—namely, by adding to it "a touch of Arabness."

—〰—

I end this chapter with two consecutive Tzabar campaigns, in which the company had "opened a hummusiya" in people's homes. In the first, titled "Marhaba Festival" (Arabic for welcome), ten Arab homes located by Tzabar were turned into a hummusiya for two days. The men and women who prepared the

Figures 5.7, 5.8 Tzabar's Marhaba Festival, Jaffa, 2011. Photos by the author.

hummus were defined by Tzabar as "hummus experts" who normally prepared hummus only for their close circle of family and friends.[110] This campaign reflected the assumption that the most authentic hummus was prepared in Arab homes—that is, not accessible to the Jewish public and devoid of commercial interests.[111] In the second campaign, which marked the launch of a new product—hummus with separately packed additions—people could apply to Tzabar to open a home hummusiya. Tzabar taught the chosen families how to prepare and serve an authentic-looking plate and publicized the names and opening hours of the hummusiyot. The hummus itself was provided by Tzabar, and people could come and eat for free.[112] If hummus prepared at Arab homes was by definition "authentic," in the case of Jewish homes, authenticity was industrially produced. No wonder that some hot dudes on the Hot Dudes and Hummus Instagram page—created by four Israeli students to show the world "the best of what a little country in the Middle East has to offer," namely, muscular males and appropriated hummus—were content to photograph themselves eating hummus produced in a factory.[113]

—⑆—

CONCLUSION

"WHEN PEOPLE EAT TOGETHER, THEY don't shoot one another" is a sentence I have often heard in the context of debates over the Israeli appropriation of Palestinian dishes. True, but sometimes they still shoot each other after the meal is over. As I hope to have shown in this book, food is a highly complex medium of communication and sociality. It can serve to dismantle some borders between people and groups and simultaneously erect others. Culinary preferences, too, are rarely straightforward reflections of social or political relations. While disgust toward the food of the other indicates a greater probability of not including this other in one's framework of civic toleration, as Krishnendu Ray argues, this does not necessarily work in the opposite direction.[1]

In this book, I explored the history of hummus in Israel to understand not only how an Arab dish became an Israeli culinary passion and a national symbol but also how the dish itself, the way it is perceived, and the experience of its consumption have changed over the years and why. While hummus is just one example in a broader repertoire of Arab dishes that were appropriated and rebranded as "Israeli food," none of these dishes became a cultural icon and an object of emotional investment and everyday consumption like hummus. Hummus thus presents a particularly compelling case of gastro-politics, where processes of settler-colonial appropriation, national culture building, and capitalist commodification intersect.[2]

Another argument that frequently comes up in debates over the Israeli appropriation of Palestinian dishes is that food always moves between national and ethnic groups; that Jews have historically adopted (and adapted) the cuisines of the countries in which they lived; and that many Israeli Jews arrived from Arab countries, where at least some of these dishes were part of the local food culture. This is also true, except that Israelis are seldom denounced for liking these foods, not even for adjusting or "spoiling" them, but rather for calling them "Israeli food" or "Israeli national dishes."[3] Although the actual culinary repertoires of Israelis are quite diverse, the symbolic category of "Israeli food" is dominated by Arab dishes. This is hardly a coincidence.

The Israeli appropriation of dishes from the Palestinian menu is not only a form of cultural expropriation but also instrumentalized against the Palestinians, by serving as a vehicle for state propaganda aimed at normalizing or whitewashing the Israeli regime and its actions.[4] This propaganda ranges from overt military messaging—such as food-centered posts by the IDF spokesperson—to more subtle forms, such as the Hot Dudes and Hummus Instagram page, "international hummus day," public relations campaigns showcasing "Israeli cuisine" abroad, or portrayals of the Israeli fondness for Arab food as an evidence of cultural openness and coexistence.[5] Because such propaganda is explicitly designed to deflect or discredit critiques of colonial domination and the systematic oppression of the Palestinians, it is, by definition, anti-Palestinian.

Some critics opt for terms like *theft, cultural erasure,* even *cultural genocide* in place of the more ordinary *appropriation.* For example, Steven Salaita, who regards the Israeli appropriation of Palestinian food as part of "a project of erasure, a portent of nonexistence, a promise of genocide," suggests replacing the word *appropriation,* which "doesn't adequately capture the dynamics of Israel's voracious appetite for anything that can be marked 'Indigenous,' which it needs to shore up an ever-tenuous sense of legitimacy" with the more accurate *theft.*[6]

Yet at the present genocidal moment—which includes the destruction of Palestinian cultural institutions and monuments in Gaza—the application of the term *cultural genocide* to the Israeli appropriation of hummus and falafel seems misplaced. Concepts like *cultural erasure* and *cultural genocide* extend Wolf's thesis of the elimination of the native into the cultural domain of cuisine. Yet assuming an Israeli "voracious appetite for anything that can be marked 'Indigenous'" as part of a "studious destruction of Palestinian culture" not only reifies both Israeli and Palestinian cultures but also overlooks the dynamic cultural effects of the struggle against colonization and appropriation.[7] I suggest that at least some instances of Israeli appropriation of Palestinian cultural items are better understood as forms of exploitation rather than erasure—namely, using these items in the service of Israeli political, cultural, and economic projects, without necessarily effacing their Arab—and at times even Palestinian—source.

The fact that dishes from the Palestinian menu, in particular, are deemed "Israeli dishes," even "Israeli national dishes," while other contenders have faded, reflects the settler-colonial logic of indigenization of the settlers. Given food's capacity to not only symbolize connection to the land but also transform the body of the eater, food has served as a powerful instrument for shaping an "authentic" indigenous self for Zionist "new men" from early on. Moreover, the Zionist myth of return, which posits the Palestinians as keepers of "what is always already ours," combined with a racial regime of ownership that ties property ownership to a racialized conception of the human render everything Palestinian as "there for us to take."[8]

However, as I have sought to demonstrate throughout this book, the Arabness of hummus is not exactly erased in Israel. At times, it is suppressed, challenged, or dismissed; at others, it is acknowledged, foregrounded, and even celebrated—by both laypeople and institutional actors. In general, Israelis do not pretend to have invented hummus. "Maybe because we're . . . surrounded by food persons, I don't know a single person around me who claims that hummus is ours," said food journalist Efrat Enzel, who wondered in a podcast on hummus how it came to be that hummus is considered Israeli.[9] That Enzel could make this statement is telling, regardless of whether it was entirely genuine. I have suggested viewing the Arabness of hummus as a qualisign that is sometimes repressed and at other times made salient in the service of specific sociocultural, political, or economic projects—from elite distinction strategies to the industrial appropriation of culinary trends.

Tracing the historically shifting association of hummus with Arabness in Israel revealed three broad chronological stages. During the Mandate period and early years of statehood, Ashkenazi Jews perceived hummus as an Arab or "Oriental" dish. If they were at all familiar with hummus—sometimes through the mediation of Mizrahi Jews—it did not garner any particular attention or appreciation, although its popularity began to rise amid the constraints of the rationing regime. In the late 1950s, with the industrialization of hummus and growing efforts to construct an "Israeli cuisine," hummus was nationalized and its Arab identity suppressed. Finally, from the late 1980s onwards, the Arabness of hummus reemerged in culinary discourse, not replacing but coexisting with its perception as an Israeli dish. Rather than simply reflecting political relations, these shifts resulted from the interplay of transformations in several different fields.

Moreover, as I sought to demonstrate, the meanings of a food item are inseparable from its consumption patterns, and these cannot be explained based on the food's symbolic charge alone. Hummus became an attractive culinary option for a wide Jewish public during a period of food, and primarily meat, shortage and an object of regular consumption once it began to be industrially produced—probably the most important force in shaping its sociocultural career in Israel and currently around the world. As I showed, while the first stage of industrialization resulted in nationalizing hummus and suppressing its Arab source, in the second, post-Fordist stage, industrial companies mediated hummus as a dish that is simultaneously Israeli and authentically Arab, with Arab authenticity used to mark some products as superior to the regular supermarket brand.

The food industry's pivotal role in shaping the culinary and cultural trajectory of hummus is evident when compared to the case of falafel. Until the 1990s, falafel was considered Israel's foremost national dish, yet it never became an object of everyday consumption or achieved the cult status of hummus. While other factors—such as health trends and the rejection of fried food—may have contributed to rise of hummus to prominence, its greater amenability to industrial reproduction as a ready-to-eat dish was key. Although falafel was also industrialized around the same time, the conversion rate of symbolic to economic value in the case of falafel is much higher than in the case of hummus, for reasons that are primarily material. By making hummus the object of enormous capital investment, the Israeli food industry produced not just hummus but Hummus—namely, a food icon.

—◊◊◊—

At this point the reader may rightly wonder what my position on the Israeli appropriation of hummus, and other Palestinian dishes, is. Although I am not a fan of placing national copyrights on dishes and think that policing the flow of culture has its perils, I sympathize with the criticism of Israel's claiming of dishes from the Palestinian cuisine as Israeli. Israelis defining hummus and falafel as their national dishes under conditions of colonial domination and relentless dispossession of land is in no way comparable to Trinidadians defining Coca-Cola as a Trinidadian drink.[10] Moreover, as Sidney Mintz argued, for subjugated groups, cuisine can function as a domain where exercising some freedom and autonomy is possible.[11] In this vein, Laila El-Haddad notes that living under occupation for so many years renders the home and kitchen the only places where Palestinians can have independence, and Vivien Sansour adds that given that Israel is always stealing Palestinian time, cooking becomes a way of reclaiming it.[12] Culinary appropriation signals that even this domain of autonomy and creativity is not outside the gamut of Israeli domination.

At the same time, there is a fundamental difference between appropriation of intangible cultural assets, like culinary traditions, and the seizure of finite resources, like land. Unlike tangible resources, the cultural appropriation of intangible assets does not necessarily deprive the source culture of what has been appropriated. In some cases, the opposite may occur: the struggle against appropriation can lead to a heightened cultural flourishing within the source culture itself as it reclaims and reaffirms its identity and traditions.[13] This is indeed the case with the mediation of a distinctly Palestinian food culture to audiences overseas: to my knowledge, before 1993, there was not a single English cookbook with the words *Palestinian* or *Palestine* in its title; in contrast, between 2010 and 2024, more than ten such books appeared.[14] Though this shift cannot be attributed solely to the struggle against appropriation, its impact is unmistakable.[15] And in contrast to land theft, which is backed by military and judicial power, in contesting cultural appropriation Palestinians are better equipped for making faster gains.

In fact, the Israeli acknowledgment of the Arab provenance of hummus allows Palestinians to reclaim cultural authority and pay Israelis back their condescension. One example I have in mind is a brilliant short video by author and journalist Ala Hlehel, titled "Come to the Hummus."[16] In this video, a Jewish family arrives in Wadi Nisnas—one of the main Arab neighborhoods of Haifa and a magnet for Jewish food tourists—looking for "hummus asli." Unable to find an open hummus restaurant and intimidated by any contact with Arabs who do not serve them hummus, they are eventually directed to a small restaurant where they are fed Glatt Kosher industrial hummus disguised as homemade hummus, which they enthusiastically devour. Mocking Israelis' quest for authenticity and simultaneously their inability to tell the difference between artisanal and industrial hummus, this video can be read as a commentary on both "Israeli hummus" and "Arab authenticity" as Israeli fabrications.

The meanings of Israeli culinary appropriation cannot exist in isolation from the very material process of Palestinian dispossession. As scholar of cultural appropriation James Young argues, "Appropriation will tend to be morally suspect when it occurs in the context of unequal power caused by the appropriation of land."[17] For this reason, gestures of symbolic recognition will not do, and sometimes might even be read as offensive, if they are not accompanied by a substantive process of decolonization. If culinary appropriation and the question of origins continue to hold symbolic valence—and exercise symbolic violence—it is because decolonization is not yet on the horizon.

Finally, as the current starvation in Gaza so starkly and horrifyingly demonstrates, culinary appropriation is among the least harmful ways in which Israel is weaponizing food. Even in less catastrophic times, the ramifications of colonization and ethnic cleansing for Palestinian nourishment and food culture extend well beyond questions of symbolic appropriation. They encompass the shrinking of land available for cultivation due to perpetual land grab; the systematic uprooting of Palestinian olive trees by settlers; draconian restrictions on the entry of foodstuffs into the besieged Gaza Strip, including restrictions on fishing; the treatment of the West Bank and Gaza Strip as captive markets for Israeli goods (often of lower quality than those sold in Israel or sold at inflated prices to Gaza); myriad direct and indirect impediments to Palestinian trade; and other ways in which food—and the bodies it sustains—become colonized terrains.[18] While Salaita is right to argue that cuisine is not just an ethnic signifier but also a valuable commodity—and that, therefore, "the problem isn't who cooks or eats, but who controls the branding and profitability of food"—the profit that Israeli companies and chefs derive from hummus is less a matter of its branding as Israeli and more of Israeli economic power, acquired, inter alia, on Palestinians' backs.

I reserve the final words for Abu Hassan al-Baghdadi, an elderly Palestinian whose small hummus restaurant in the Muslim quarter of the Old City of Jerusalem—currently off-limits for Israelis—was one of the highlights in the Beit Shmuel hummus tour. In yet another TV item on hummus, titled—what else—"The Journey after the Perfect Hummus," al-Baghdadi, who still pounds his hummus with a wooden pestle, tells reporter Ohad Hemo that he uses chickpeas from a kibbutz, since they are cleaner. "It's a Zionist hummus," says Hemo. "It's a Palestinian hummus!" exclaims al-Baghdadi. "Why do you tell me Zionist, what Zionist? This is hummus from our land." But when Hemo asks him whether there is no nationality to hummus, al-Baghdadi decisively answers in the negative. "Hummus is not Arab or Jewish? What is it?" insists Hemo, to which Baghdadi answers, "Hummus belong only to God, it is from *Allah*."[19]

NOTES

PREFACE

1. Itamar Even-Zohar, "Nine Hypotheses on Cultural Interference," *Journal of Turkish Studies* 48 (2017): 388.

2. Priscilla Parkhurst Ferguson, *Accounting for Taste: The Triumph of French Cuisine* (Chicago: Chicago University Press, 2004), 187.

3. Ferguson, *Accounting for Taste*; Shannon Lee Dawdy, "A Wild Taste: Food and Colonialism in Eighteenth-Century Louisiana," *Ethnohistory* 57, no. 3 (2010): 390.

4. New Arab Staff, "Israeli Soldiers Storm Jenin Mosque, Mock Muslim Call to Prayer," New Arab, December 15, 2023, https://www.newarab.com/news/israel-forces-storm-jenin-mosque-mock-muslim-call-prayer.

5. Sidney W. Mintz, *Tasting Food, Tasting Freedom: Excursions in Eating, Culture and the Past* (Boston: Beacon, 1996), 8.

6. See also: Yonatan Mendel and Ronald Ranta, *From the Arab Other to the Israeli Self: Palestinian Culture in the Making of Israeli National Identity* (Farnham: Ashgate, 2016).

7. My understanding of "decolonization" aligns with Raef Zreik's perspective in his article "When Does a Settler Become a Native?": dismantling all mechanisms designed to secure Jewish supremacy and expansionism, ending Jewish individual and collective privileges, addressing past injustices, and working toward a political solution that would guarantee freedom, justice and equality for all the inhabitants of the land. See Raef Zreik, "When Does a Settler Become a Native? (With Apologies to Mamdani)," *Constellations* 23, no. 3 (2016): 356–58.

INTRODUCTION

1. M. T., "Chronicle," *HaPo'el HaTza'ir*, July 30, 1908, 25–26 (Hebrew); Ever Hadani, *Settlement in the Lower Galilee: Fifty Years of its History* (Ramat Gan:

Masada, 1955), 209–10 (Hebrew); Ben Zion Dinur, ed., *Book of the History of the Haganah*, Vol. 1, *From Defensiveness to Defense* (Tel Aviv: Zionist Library, 1954), 209–12 (Hebrew). See also Daniel DeMalach and Lev Luis Grinberg, "The Violent Struggle over Land: The Beginning of the Zionist Armed-Settlement Strategy, 1908–1914," in *Entangled Histories in Palestine/Israel: Historical and Anthropological Perspectives*, ed. Dafna Hirsch (London: Routledge, 2024), 33.

2. Izhak Ben-Zvi, "Hashomer," in *Kfar Tavor (Mescha), 1901–1976*, ed. Meir Hareuveni (Kfar Tavor: Yovel, 1976), 90 (Hebrew).

3. *Harathin* (s. *harath*) were Arab farm workers who used to live on the farm and perform all the agricultural tasks in exchange for a share of the crop. Hadani, *Settlement in the Lower Galilee*, 195; Yair Seltenreich, "Jewish or Arab Hired Workers? Inner Tensions in a Jewish Settlement in Pre-state Israel," *International Review of Social History* 49, no. 2 (2004): 230.

4. DeMalach and Grinberg, "Violent Struggle over Land."

5. Here I borrow from Philip Joseph Deloria's *Playing Indian* (New Haven, CT: Yale University Press, 1998).

6. Gad Avigdorov, "Stations," *Davar*, December 27, 1936 (Hebrew).

7. Itamar Even-Zohar, "The Emergence of a Native Hebrew Culture in Palestine: 1882–1948," *Studies in Zionism* 2, no. 2 (1981): 172–74; Israel Bartal, "Cossack and Bedouin: A New National Imagery," in *The Second Aliyah: Studies*, ed. Israel Bartal (Jerusalem: Yad Izhak Ben-Zvi, 1997), 482–93 (Hebrew); Yael Zerubavel, "Memory, the Rebirth of the Native, and the 'Hebrew Bedouin' Identity," *Social Research: An International Quarterly* 75, no. 1 (2008): 322–23. "Idealistic workers" refers to those Zionist settlers who engaged in manual labor for ideological reasons. See Gershon Shafir, "The Meeting of Eastern Europe and Yemen: 'Idealistic Workers' and 'Natural Workers' in Early Zionist Settlement in Palestine," *Ethnic and Racial Studies* 13, no. 2 (1990): 172–97.

8. Stuart Hall, "Signification, Representation, Ideology: Althusser and the Post-Structuralist Debates," *Critical Studies in Mass Communication* 2, no. 2 (1985): 104.

9. According to a survey commissioned by the Tzabar company, the largest share of respondents (18%) mentioned hummus as the dish they miss the most when they go abroad (second was falafel, with 17%). However, the majority thought that falafel, rather than hummus, was "the most Israeli dish" (47% compared to 27%). Ruth Ofri Taub, "Prefer Falafel, Miss Hummus, and Want to Wipe It with Yair Lapid," Datili, May 6, 2008, https://bit.ly/42TRc3j (Hebrew).

10. When I embarked on this research project, there was not a single study on hummus from a sociocultural perspective. Since then, several articles and chapters have appeared that address various aspects of hummus consumption or discuss hummus as part of Israeli cultural appropriation. See Rafi Grosglik, "Organic Hummus in Israel: Global and Local Ingredients and Images," *Sociological*

Research Online 16, no. 2 (2011): 88–98; Grosglik, "Global Ethical Culinary Fashion and a Local Dish: Organic Hummus in Israel," *Critical Studies in Fashion & Beauty* 2, no. 1–2 (2011): 165–84; Ari Ariel, "The Hummus Wars," *Gastronomica* 12, no. 1 (2012): 34–42; Zeynep Sertbulut, "The Culinary State: On Politics of Representation and Identity in Israel," *HAGAR Studies in Culture, Policy, and Identities* 10, no. 2 (2012): 49–76; Ronald Ranta and Yonatan Mendel, "Consuming Palestine: Palestine and Palestinians in Israeli Food Culture," *Ethnicities* 14, no. 3 (2014): 412–35; Ranta, "Re-Arabizing Israeli Food Culture," *Food, Culture and Society* 18, no. 4 (2015): 611–27; Nir Avieli, "The Hummus Wars Revisited: Israeli-Arab Food Politics and Gastromediation," *Gastronomica* 16, no. 3 (2016): 19–30; Claudia Prieto Piastro, *Eating in Israel: Nationhood, Gender and Food Culture* (London: Palgrave Macmillan, 2021), 139–64.

11. Ever Hadani, *Settlement in the Lower Galilee*, 158.

12. Arjun Appadurai, "Gastro-politics in Hindu South Asia," *American Ethnologist* 8, no. 3 (1981): 494.

13. Heather Paxson, *The Life of Cheese: Crafting Food and Value in America* (Berkeley: University of California Press, 2013), 4.

14. Michael Dietler, "Culinary Encounters: Food, Identity, and Colonialism," in *We Are What We Eat: Archaeology, Food, and Identity*, ed. Katheryn C. Twiss (Carbondale: Center for Archaeological Investigations, Southern Illinois University, 2006), 222.

15. The clip is available from https://www.youtube.com/watch?v=t4_JFHGyUpU, accessed February 12, 2023. Chala is a type of braided Jewish bread eaten on Sabbath and holiday meals. On the leap from "Israeli" to "Jewish" food, see Zeina B. Ghandour, "*Falafel* King: Culinary Customs and National Narratives in Palestine (I)," *Feminist Legal Studies* 21 (2013): 291.

16. https://www.facebook.com/IsraelMFA, posted on January 20, 2021.

17. Dan Almagor, "The Falafel Song," 1957, https://www.nli.org.il/he/items/NNL_MUSIC_AL990002405730205171/NLI (Hebrew).

18. Laila M. El-Haddad and Maggie Schmitt, *The Gaza Kitchen: A Palestinian Culinary Journey* (Charlottesville, VA: Just World Books, 2016), 86.

19. Steven Salaita, "'Israeli Hummus' Is Theft, Not Appropriation," *The New Arab*, September 4, 2017, https://www.newarab.com/opinion/israeli-hummus-theft-not-appropriation.

20. For example, Ahmad H. Sa'di, "Catastrophe, Memory and Identity: Al-Nakbah as a Component of Palestinian Identity," *Israel Studies* 7, no. 2 (2002): 185; Omar Jabary Salamanca et al., "Past Is Present: Settler Colonialism in Palestine," *Settler Colonial Studies* 2, no. 1 (2012): 1–8; Ghandour, "*Falafel* King," 289; Luma Zayad, "Systematic Cultural Appropriation and the Israeli-Palestinian Conflict," *DePaul Journal of Art, Technology and Intellectual Property Law* 28, no. 2 (2018): 81–125; Reem Kassis, "Here's Why Palestinians Object to the Term 'Israeli

Food': It Erases Us from History," *Washington Post*, February 18, 2020, https://
www.washingtonpost.com/lifestyle/food/heres-why-palestinians-object-to-the
-term-israeli-food-it-erases-us-from-history/2020/02/14/96974a74-4d25-11ea
-bf44-f5043eb3918a_story.html; Jamal Kanj, "Israel's Largest Surface Cultural
Heist: Palestinian Cuisine," *Palestine Chronicle*, July 26, 2023, https://www
.palestinechronicle.com/israels-largest-surface-cultural-heist-palestinian
-cuisine; Amanny Ahmad, "Freekeh and Fellahin: A Symbiotic Relationship
of Sumud," *Jerusalem Quarterly* 98 (2024): 33–50; Christiane Dabdoub Nasser,
"Introduction: Food and the Transmission of Culture: Linking Past, Present
and Future," *Jerusalem Quarterly* 99 (2024): 12; Reem Farah, "Ottolenghi and
Tamimi's Cookbook, Jerusalem: Israel as Frame and Palestine as Subject," *Jerusalem Quarterly* 99 (2024): 110. On settler colonialism's logic of elimination of the
native, see Patrick Wolfe, *Settler Colonialism and the Transformation of Anthropology: The Politics and Poetics of an Ethnographic Event* (London: Cassell, 1999).

21. Nasser, "Introduction: Food and the Transmission of Culture," 11.

22. Susan Abulhawa at the Oxford Union debate concerning the motion to
declare Israel an Apartheid State Responsible of Genocide, November 28, 2024,
https://www.youtube.com/watch?v=2ZCWCGebAuU&t=7s&ab_channel
=OxfordUnion. See also Ahmad, "Freekeh and Fellahin," 46.

23. "Editorial: Refusing Extermination," *Jerusalem Quarterly* 99 (2024): 5.

24. Christiane Dabdoub Nasser, "Discussing Food and Foodways: No Better
Time than the Present," *Jerusalem Quarterly* 98 (2024): 7–8.

25. Hanine Shehadeh, "Nourishing Resilience: The Palestinian Kitchen Table
and the Healing of Generational Trauma," *Jerusalem Quarterly* 98 (2024): 55; Lila
Sharif, "How Dough Rises in Gaza: Palestine's Foremothers and Recipes against
Genocide," *Jerusalem Quarterly* 99 (2024): 65; Nicholas Bascuñan-Wiley and
Jessica Schwalb, "Binding Identity: Chilean Palestinian Cookbooks and the For-
mation of a Diasporic Cuisine," *Jerusalem Quarterly* 99 (2024): 25; Mona Dorani,
"From Kitchen to Community: Food and Palestinian Marriage Rituals in the
Ethnography of Hilma Granqvist," *Jerusalem Quarterly* 99 (2024): 81, 83; Kassis,
"Here's Why Palestinians Object to the Term 'Israeli Food.'"

26. Hospitality for Humanity, "An Appeal to Our Food & Hospitality Community to Take Action Now for Gaza," accessed December 12, 2023, https://
www.hospitality-for-humanity.com/pledge.

27. See, for example, Lawrence Davidson, "Food Theft as a Form of Cultural
Genocide," *Counterpunch*, August 8, 2018, https://www.counterpunch.org
/2018/08/08/food-theft-as-a-form-of-cultural-genocide; Ben White, "Israel's Obsession with Hummus Is about More than Stealing Palestine's Food," *The National*,
May 23, 2015, accessed July 16, 2023, https://www.thenationalnews.com/opinion
/israels-obsession-with-hummus-is-about-more-than-stealing-palestines
-food-1.131371; Nesrin Yavaş, "Safeguarding Traditional Palestinian Food Culture:

The Case of the Arab American Play *Food and Fadwa*," *Millî Folklore* 135 (2022): 148–59; Samia Madwar, "Much Ado about Hummus: The Fight for Bragging Rights over a Middle Eastern Dip," *The Walrus*, May 1, 2023, https://thewalrus.ca/what-is -hummus; Alon Hadar, "Israeli Chefs Did Not Invent Anything," *Yediot Ahronot*, October 5, 2019 (Hebrew); Nissan Shor, "The 'Israeli Cuisine' Does Not Like to be Reminded of Who It Stole Its Hits From," *Haaretz*, October 22, 2019 (Hebrew); Rafram Chaddad and Yigal Nizri, "How Shakshuka and Other Middle Eastern Dishes Turned into Iconic 'Jewish Food,'" *Haaretz*, November 21, 2019, https://ti- nyurl.com/ydfyxnan; Ronald Ranta and Daniel Monterescu, "Decolonizing Israeli Food? Between Culinary Appropriation and Recognition in Israel/Palestine," in *'Going Native'?: Settler Colonialism and Food*, ed. Ronald Ranta, Alejandro Colás, and Daniel Monterescu (London: Palgrave Macmillan, 2022), 147–72; Lorenzo Veracini, "The Predicaments of Settler Gastrocolonialism," in *'Going Native'?*, 247–59.

28. Christian Huck and Stefan Bauernschmidt, "Trans-Cultural Appropria- tion," in *Travelling Goods, Travelling Moods: Varieties of Cultural Appropriation*, ed. Christian Huck and Stefan Bauernschmidt (Frankfurt: Campus, 2012), 229; Michael F. Brown, *Who Owns Native Culture?* (Cambridge, MA: Harvard Uni- versity Press, 2003), ix.

29. Bruce Ziff and Pratima V. Rao, "Introduction to Cultural Appropriation: A Framework for Analysis," in *Borrowed Power: Essays on Cultural Appropria- tion*, ed. Bruce Ziff and Pratima V. Rao (New Brunswick, NJ: Rutgers University Press, 1997), 5; Kathleen M. Ashley and Véronique Plesch, "The Cultural Pro- cesses of 'Appropriation,'" *Journal of Medieval and Early Modern Studies* 32, no. 1 (2002), 1–15; Huck and Bauernschmidt, "Trans-Cultural Appropriation," 229–51.

30. The Writers' Union of Canada defines the second type of appropriation as the "taking—from a culture that is not one's own—of intellectual property, cultural expression or artifacts, history and ways of knowledge and profiting at the expense of people of that culture." Ziff and Rao, "Introduction to Cultural Appropriation," 1. For the use of misappropriation, see Krishnendu Ray, "Culi- nary Difference: The Difference It Makes," *Graduate Journal of Food Studies* 5, no. 2 (2018): 2–10; Kevin Nute, "Toward a Test of Cultural Misappropriation," *International Journal of Critical Cultural Studies* 17, no. 2 (2019): 67–82. For the use of theft, see Eric Lott, *Love and Theft: Blackface Minstrelsy and the American Working Class* (Oxford: Oxford University Press, 1993); James O. Young, *Cultural Appropriation and the Arts* (Malden, MA: Blackwell, 2008), 63–105.

31. Ashley and Plesch, "The Cultural Processes of 'Appropriation,'" 2–3; Christy Desmet and Sujata Iyengar, "Adaptation, Appropriation, or What You Will," *Shakespeare* 11, no. 1 (2015): 13.

32. Ziff and Rao, "Introduction to Cultural Appropriation," 8–16; Young, *Cultural Appropriation and the Arts*; Erich Hatala Matthes, "Cultural Appropria- tion without Cultural Essentialism?," *Social Theory and Practice* 42, no. 2 (2016):

343–66; Dianne Lalonde, "Does Cultural Appropriation Cause Harm?," *Politics, Groups and Identities* 9, no. 2 (2021): 329–46.

33. Erich Fromm and Karl Marx, *Marx's Concept of Man, Including Economic and Philosophical Manuscripts*, trans. T. B. Bottomore (London: Bloomsbury, 1961), 81–160; Desmet and Iyengar, "Adaptation, Appropriation, or What You Will," 14; Rahel Jaeggi, *Alienation*, trans. Frederick Neuhouser and Allen E. Smith, ed. Frederick Neuhouser (New York: Columbia University Press, 2014).

34. Jaeggi, *Alienation*.

35. Michel de Certeau, *The Practice of Everyday Life*, trans. Steven Rendall (Berkeley: University of California Press, 1984); Christian Huck and Stefam Bauernschmidt, eds., *Travelling Goods, Travelling Moods: Varieties of Cultural Appropriation* (Frankfurt: Campus, 2012), 18, 149, 236.

36. For example, bell hooks, "Eating the Other: Desire and Resistance," in *Black Looks: Race and Representation* (Boston: South End Press, 1992), 21–39; Lott, *Love and Theft*; Deloria, *Playing Indian*; Chad Barbour, "When Captain America Was an Indian: Heroic Masculinity, National Identity and Appropriation," *Journal of Popular Culture* 48, no. 2 (2015): 269–84.

37. Sara Ahmed, *Strange Encounters: Embodied Others in Post-Coloniality* (London: Routledge, 2013), 118; Barbour, "When Captain America Was an Indian," 270; Avril Bell, *Relating Indigenous and Settler Identities: Beyond Domination* (London: Palgrave Macmillan, 2014), 34.

38. Anne Goldman, "I Yam What I Yam: Cooking, Culture and Colonialism," in *De/Colonizing the Subject: The Politics of Gender in Women's Autobiography*, ed. Sidonie Smith and Julia Watson (Minneapolis: University of Minnesota Press, 1992), 169–95; Lisa Heldke, *Exotic Appetites: Ruminations of a Food Adventurer* (New York: Routledge, 2003); Ray, "Culinary Difference"; Simona Stano, *Eating the Other: Translations of the Culinary Code* (Newcastle upon Tyne: Cambridge Scholars Publishing, 2015); Sam Grey and Lenore Newman, "Beyond Culinary Colonialism: Indigenous Food Sovereignty, Liberal Multiculturalism, and the Control of Gastronomic Capital," *Agriculture and Human Values* 35 (2018): 717–30.

39. hooks, "Eating the Other."

40. For example, Heldke, *Exotic Appetites*; Sonja Weishaupt, "Cook at Home in Chinese: Mediating Chinese Food for American Kitchens," in *Travelling Goods, Travelling Moods*, 45–59; Grey and Newman, "Beyond Culinary Colonialism"; Erica J. Peters, "Power Struggles and Social Positioning: Culinary Appropriation and Anxiety in Colonial Vietnam," in *Food Anxiety in Globalizing Vietnam*, ed. Judith Ehlert and Nora Katharina Faltmann (Singapore: Springer, 2019); Ronald Ranta, Alejandro Colás, and Daniel Monterescu, eds., *'Going Native?': Settler Colonialism and Food* (London: Palgrave Macmillan, 2022).

41. Ray, "Culinary Difference."

42. Uma Narayan, *Dislocating Cultures: Identities, Traditions, and Third World Feminisms* (London: Routledge, 1997), 180. See also Krishnendu Ray, *The Ethnic Restauranteur* (London: Bloomsbury Academic, 2016), 6–7.

43. Grey and Newman, "Beyond Culinary Colonialism," 718; Ranta, Colás, and Monterescu, *Going Native?*

44. Ian Cook and Philip Crang, "The World on a Plate: Culinary Culture, Displacement, and Geographical Knowledges," *Journal of Material Culture* 1, no. 2 (1996): 131–53; Ian Cook, "Geographies of Food: Mixing," *Progress in Human Geography* 32, no. 6 (2008): 821–33; William Crane, "Cultural Formation and Appropriation in the Era of Merchant Capitalism," *Historical Materialism* 26, no. 2 (2018): 248–50.

45. Bill Ashcroft, *Post-Colonial Transformation* (London: Routledge, 2001), 24; James Clifford, *Routes: Travel and Translation in the Late Twentieth Century* (Cambridge, MA: Harvard University Press, 1997).

46. For example, Cook, "Geographies of Food: Mixing"; Cook and Crang, "The World on a Plate"; Donna R. Gabaccia, *We Are What We Eat: Ethnic Food and the Making of Americans* (Cambridge, MA: Harvard University Press, 1998); Jeffrey M. Pilcher, *Food in World History* (New York: Routledge, 2006); Rachel Laudan, *Cuisine and Empire: Cooking in World History* (Berkeley: University of California Press, 2013).

47. Ziff and Rao, "Introduction to Cultural Appropriation," 3–4; Young, *Cultural Appropriation and the Arts*, 13–17; Huck and Bauernschmidt, "Trans-Culture Appropriation," 244; Rina Arya, "Cultural Appropriation: What It Is and Why It Matters?," *Sociology Compass* 15, no. 10 (2021): 3.

48. Nicholas Dirks, "Is Vice Versa? Historical Anthropologies and Anthropological Histories," in *The Historic Turn in the Human Sciences*, ed. Terrence J. McDonald (Ann Arbor: University of Michigan Press, 1996), 17–51.

49. Anthony F. Buccini and Amy Dahlstrom, "Culinary Change, Disruption, and Death: Do Traditional Cuisines Have a Future?," *Dublin Gastronomy Symposium* (2020): 1–6.

50. Chaddad and Nizri, "How Shakshuka and Other Middle Eastern Dishes."

51. Appadurai, "Gastro-Politics in Hindu South Asia"; Mintz, *Tasting Food, Tasting Freedom.*

52. Hall, "Signification, Representation, Ideology." Although Hall talks about "levels of the social formation" rather than fields, his argument concerning the lack of necessary correspondence between different levels has shaped my thinking on this matter.

53. Cook and Crang, "The World on a Plate," 140–45; Akhil Gupta and James Ferguson, "Beyond 'Culture': Space, Identity and the Politics of Difference," *Cultural Anthropology* 7, no. 1 (1992): 6–23.

162 NOTES TO PAGES 8–10

54. Oded Erez and Nadeem Karkabi, "Sounding Arabic: Postvernacular Modes of Performing the Arabic Language in Popular Music by Israeli Jews," *Popular Music* 38, no. 2 (2019): 298–316.

55. However, many will avoid the term *Palestinian* in this context and use *Arab* instead.

56. Charles S. Peirce, *Philosophical Writings of Peirce*, ed. Justus Buchler (New York: Dover, 1955), 101, 115–19. See also Webb Keane, "Semiotics and the Social Analysis of Material Things," *Language & Communication* 23 (2003): 409–25; Anne Meneley, "Oleo-Signs and Quali-Signs: The Qualities of Olive Oil," *Ethnos* 73, no. 3 (2008): 303–26; Paul Manning, *The Semiotics of Drink and Drinking* (London: Continuum, 2012).

57. Clifford, *Routes*, 7; Manning, *Semiotics of Drink and Drinking*, 21.

58. Keane, "Semiotics and the Social Analysis of Material Things."

59. See also Huck and Bauernschmidt, "Trans-Culture Appropriation," 229–51.

60. Daniel Boyarin, *Unheroic Conduct: The Rise of Heterosexuality and the Invention of the Jewish Man* (Berkeley: University of California Press, 1997), 271–312; Todd Samuel Presner, *Muscular Judaism: The Jewish Body and the Politics of Regeneration* (London: Routledge, 2007); Boaz Neumann, *Land and Desire in Early Zionism*, trans. Haim Watzman (Waltham, MA: Brandeis University Press, 2011); Dafna Hirsch, *'We Are Here to Bring the West': Hygiene Education and Culture Building in the Jewish Society of Mandate Palestine* (Sde Boker: The Ben-Gurion Research Institute for the Study of Israel and Zionism, 2014) (Hebrew).

61. The literature on Zionism as a settler-colonial movement is by now extensive. See, for example, Maxime Rodinson, *Israel: A Colonial-Settler State?* (New York: Monad Press, 1973); Gershon Shafir, *Land, Labor and the Origins of the Israeli-Palestinian Conflict, 1882–1914* (New York: Cambridge University Press, 1989); Gabriel Piterberg, *The Returns of Zionism: Myth, Politics and Scholarship in Israel* (London: Verso, 2008); Salamanca et al., "Past Is Present"; Lorenzo Veracini, "The Other Shift: Settler Colonialism, Israel, and the Occupation," *Journal of Palestine Studies* 42, no. 2 (2013): 26–42; Veracini, "What Can Settler Colonial Studies Offer to an Interpretation of the Conflict in Israel-Palestine?," *Settler Colonial Studies* 5, no. 3 (2015): 268–71; Rashid Khalidi, *The Hundred Years' War on Palestine: A History of Settler Colonialism and Resistance, 1917–2017* (New York: Metropolitan Books, 2020); Hagar Kotef, *The Colonizing Self: Home and Homelessness in Israel/Palestine* (Durham, NC: Duke University Press, 2020). For a genealogy of this paradigm in relation to Zionism and further references, see Areej Sabbagh-Khoury, "Tracing Settler Colonialism: A Genealogy of a Paradigm in the Sociology of Knowledge Production in Israel," *Politics & Society* 50, no. 1 (2022): 44–83. As Sabbagh-Khoury shows, the first to employ this paradigm were Arab scholars, mainly Palestinians.

62. Zreik, "When Does a Settler Become a Native?," 359.

63. Even-Zohar, "The Emergence of a Native Hebrew Culture," 167–84; Zohar Shavit, ed., *History of the Jewish Community in Eretz-Israel since 1882*, Vol. 3, *The Construction of Hebrew Culture in Eretz Israel* (Jerusalem: Bialik Institute, 1999) (Hebrew); Eric Zakim, *To Build and Be Built: Landscape, Literature, and the Construction of Zionist Identity* (Philadelphia: University of Pennsylvania Press, 2006); Arieh Bruce Saposnik, *Becoming Hebrew: The Creation of a Jewish National Culture in Ottoman Palestine* (Oxford: Oxford University Press, 2008); Yaffa Berlovich, ed., *Talking Culture: The First Aliya, and Interperiod Discourse* (Tel Aviv: Hakibbutz Hameuchad, 2010) (Hebrew).

64. Even-Zohar, "The Emergence of a Native Hebrew Culture"; Yael Zerubavel, *Recovered Roots: Collective Memory and the Making of Israeli National Tradition* (Chicago: University of Chicago Press, 1995).

65. Anna Johnston and Alan Lawson, "Settler Colonies," in *A Companion to Postcolonial Studies*, ed. Henry Schwartz and Sangeeta Ray (Malden, MA: Blackwell, 2000), 369. See also Wolfe, *Settler Colonialism*, 208–209; Lorenzo Veracini, *Settler Colonialism: A Theoretical Overview* (Basingstoke: Palgrave Macmillan, 2010), 95.

66. Zerubavel, *Recovered Roots*; Amnon Raz-Karkotzkin, "The Return to the History of Redemption, or: What Is the 'History' One 'Returns' to in the Expression 'The Return to History?'" in *Zionism and the Return to History: A Reassessment*, ed. Shmuel Eisenstadt and Moshe Lissak (Jerusalem: Yad Izhak Ben-Zvi, 1999), 249–76 (Hebrew); Dafna Hirsch, "'We Are Here to Bring the West, Not Only to Ourselves': Zionist Occidentalism and the Discourse of Hygiene in Mandate Palestine," *International Journal of Middle East Studies* 41, no. 4 (2009): 577–94.

67. Lionel Trilling, *Sincerity and Authenticity* (Cambridge, MA: Harvard University Press, 1971); Charles Lindholm, *Culture and Authenticity* (Malden, MA: Blackwell, 2008); Dina Roginsky, "Nationalism and Ambivalence: Ethnicity, Gender and Folklore as Categories of Otherness," *Patterns of Prejudice* 40, no. 3 (2006): 238; Bell, *Relating Indigenous and Settler Identities*, 25–57.

68. Christopher E. Forth, *Masculinity in the Modern West: Gender, Civilization and the Body* (London: Palgrave Macmillan, 2008), 4–5, 141; Gail Bederman, *Manliness and Civilization: A Cultural History of Gender and Race in the United States, 1880–1917* (Chicago: University of Chicago Press, 1995); Michael S. Kimmel, *The History of Men: Essays on the History of American and British Masculinities* (New York: State University of New York Press, 2005).

69. Forth, *Masculinity in the Modern West*, 14, 17, 89–91; Bell, *Relating Indigenous and Settler Identities*.

70. Bell, *Relating Indigenous and Settler Identities*, 26. Italics in the original.

71. There were also contexts in which Zionists attributed inferior masculinity, even effeminacy, to Arab men. Scholarship on masculinity in Israel has

paid more attention to this aspect of the Zionist gendering of Palestinian men. See Simona Sharoni, *Gender and the Israeli-Palestinian Conflict: The Politics of Women's Resistance* (New York: Syracuse University Press, 1995), 41; Danny Kaplan, *Brothers and Others in Arms: The Making of Love and War in Israeli Combat Units* (New York: Haworth Press, 2003), 117; Daniel Monterescu, "Masculinity as a Relational Mode: Palestinian Gender Ideologies and Working-Class Boundaries in an Ethnically Mixed Town," in *Reapproaching Borders: New Perspectives on the Study of Israel-Palestine*, ed. Sandra Sufian and Mark LeVine (Lanham, MD: Rowman and Littlefield, 2007), 177–97; Avner Wishnitzer, "'A Fortress of Ignorance and Cowardice'—The Image of the Arab Warrior in the Eyes of the Israeli Fighters in 1948," *Jama'a* 14 (2006): 91–121 (Hebrew).

72. Ella Shohat, "Sephardim in Israel: Zionism from the Standpoint of Its Jewish Victims," *Social Text* 19/20 (1988): 1–35; Shohat, "The Invention of the Mizrahim," *Journal of Palestine Studies* 29, no. 1 (1999): 5–20; Aziza Khazzoom, "The Great Chain of Orientalism: Jewish Identity, Stigma Management, and Ethnic Exclusion in Israel," *American Sociological Review* 68, no. 4 (2003): 481–510; Yehouda Shenhav and Hannan Hever, "The Arab-Jews: The Metamorphosis of a Concept," *Pa'amim* 125–127 (2011): 57–74 (Hebrew).

73. For example, Roginsky, "Nationalism and Ambivalence"; Yael Guilat, *Yemeni Jewish Silver Craft in the Israeli 'Melting Pot'* (Sde Boker: The Ben-Gurion Research Institute for the Study of Israel and Zionism, 2009) (Hebrew); Noah S. Gerber, *Ourselves or Our Holy Books? The Cultural Discovery of Yemenite Jewry* (Jerusalem: Yad Izhak Ben-Zvi, 2013) (Hebrew).

74. Ronald Ranta and Claudia Raquel Prieto Piastro, "Does Israeli Food Exist? The Multifaceted and Complex Making of a National Food," in *The Emergence of National Food: The Dynamics of Food and Nationalism*, ed. Atsuko Ichijo, Venetia Johannes, and Ronald Ranta (London: Bloomsbury Academic, 2019), 119–29. On the distinction between the level of public representations and symbols and the level of everyday practice in the context of food culture, see Richard Wilk, *Home Cooking in the Global Village: Caribbean Food from Buccaneers to Ecotourists* (Oxford: Berg, 2006), 105–6.

75. Anat Helman, "European Jews in the Levant Heat: Climate and Culture in 1920s and 1930s Tel Aviv," *Journal of Israeli History* 22, no. 1 (2003): 71–90; Orit Rozin, "Food, Identity, and Nation-Building in Israel's Formative Years," *Israel Studies Review* 21, no. 1 (2006): 52–80; Yael Raviv, *Falafel Nation: Cuisine and the Making of National Identity in Israel* (Lincoln: University of Nebraska Press, 2015); Ofra Tene, "Thus You Shall Cook! Analysis of Israeli Cookbooks" (MA thesis, Tel Aviv University, 2000) (Hebrew); Tene, "'The New Immigrant Must Not Only Learn, He Must Also Forget': The Making of Eretz Israeli Ashkenazi Cuisine," in *Jews and Their Foodways* (*Studies in Contemporary Jewry* 28), ed. Anat Helman (New York: Oxford University Press, 2015), 46–64; Sertbulut, "The

Culinary State"; Nir Avieli, *Food and Power: A Culinary Ethnography of Israel* (Berkeley: University of California Press, 2018); Ari Ariel, "Mosaic or Melting Pot: The Transformation of Middle Eastern Jewish Foodways in Israel," in *Global Jewish Foodways*, ed. Hasia R. Diner and Simone Cinotto (Lincoln: University of Nebraska Press, 2018), 91–114; Piastro, *Eating in Israel*. For studies adopting a settler-colonial framework, see Ranta, "Re-Arabizing Israeli Food Culture"; Efrat Gilad, "Meat in the Heat: A History of Tel Aviv under the British Mandate for Palestine (1920s–1940s)" (PhD diss., Graduate Institute Geneva, 2022); Daniel Monterescu and Ariel Handel, "Liquid Indigeneity: Wine, Science, and Colonial Politics in Israel/Palestine," *American Ethnologist* 46, no. 3 (2019): 313–27; Ranta and Monterescu, "Decolonising Israeli Food?," 147–71.

76. Raviv, *Falafel Nation*; Tene, "The New Immigrant Must Not Only Learn"; Erela Teharlev Ben-Shachar, "On Calories, Proteins and Posture: Zionism, Socialism and Consumerism; Learning History from Diet and Fitness Guides, Israel, 1930's–1980's," (PhD diss., Bar Ilan University, 2018); Ariel, "Mosaic or Melting Pot," 91–114; Piastro, *Eating in Israel*, 23–44; Gilad, "Meat in the Heat," 66–81.

77. Jack Goody, "Structuralism, Materialism and the Horse," in *Food and Love: A Cultural History of East and West*, ed. Jack Goody (New York: Verso, 1998), 148–60.

78. Steven Shapin, "'You Are What You Eat': Historical Changes in Ideas about Food and Identity," *Historical Research* 87, no. 237 (2014): 377–92.

79. Rebecca Earle, "'If You Eat Their Food . . .': Diets and Bodies in Early Colonial Spanish America," *American Historical Review* 115, no. 3 (2010): 688–713. Overall, however, colonizers' engagement with native foods was more heterogenous, including some cases of selective, temporary, or adjustive adoption of dishes and ingredients from the indigenous repertoire. See, for example, Jeffrey M. Pilcher, *Que Vivan Los Tamales!: Food and the Making of Mexican Identity* (Albuquerque: University of New Mexico Press, 1998); Shannon Lee Dawdy, "A Wild Taste: Food and Colonialism in Eighteenth-Century Louisiana," *Ethnohistory* 57, no. 3 (2010): 389–414; Blake Singley, "'Hardly Anything Fit for Man to Eat': Food and Colonialism in Australia," *History Australia* 9, no. 3 (2012): 27–42; Charlotte Craw, "Gustatory Redemption? Colonial Appetites, Historical Tales and the Contemporary Consumption of Australian Native Foods," *International Journal of Critical Indigenous Studies* 5, no. 2 (2012): 13–24; Robert Launay, "Maize Avoidance? Colonial French Attitudes towards Native American Foods in the Pays des Illinois (17th–18th Century)," *Food and Foodways* 26, no. 2 (2018): 92–104.

80. Shapin, "'You Are What You Eat.'"

81. Pierre Bourdieu, *Distinction: A Social Critique of the Judgment of Taste*, trans. Richard Nice (Cambridge, MA: Harvard University Press, 1984), 190.

82. Dafna Hirsch, "Hummus Masculinity in Israel," *Food, Culture and Society* 19, no. 2 (2016): 337–59.

83. For example, Paul Rozin, "Sociocultural Influences on Human Food Selection," in *Why We Eat What We Eat: The Psychology of Eating*, ed. Elizabeth Capaldi (Washington, DC: American Psychological Association, 1996), 233–63; Barbara E. Willard, "The American Story of Meat: Discursive Influences on Cultural Eating Practice," *Journal of Popular Culture* 36, no. 1 (2002): 105–18; Priscilla Parkhurst Ferguson, *Accounting for Taste: The Triumph of French Cuisine* (Chicago: University of Chicago Press, 2004); Isabelle De Solier, *Food and the Self: Consumption, Production and Material Culture* (London: Bloomsbury, 2013), 68–73.

84. Krishnendu Ray, *The Migrant's Table: Meals and Memories in Bengali-American Households* (Philadelphia: Temple University, 2004); Ferguson, *Accounting for Taste*, 16; Dietler, "Culinary Encounters," 235.

85. Zrubavel Gilad, *The Palmach Book* (Tel Aviv: Hakibbutz Hameuchad, 1955), 225 (Hebrew).

86. Yigal Alon, *My Father's House* (Tel Aviv: Ministry of Defense Publishing House, 1980), 29, 50, 71–76 (Hebrew).

87. Alona Nitzan-Shiftan, "Seizing Locality in Jerusalem," in *Reapproaching Borders*, 227. See also Johnston and Lawson, "Settler Colonies," 369; Cook and Crang, "The World on a Plate," 140.

88. According to Bourdieu, bodily mimesis has the power to evoke a universe of feelings and experiences. Bourdieu, *Distinction*, 474. See also Andreas Reckwitz, "Practices and their Affects," in *The Nexus of Practices*, ed. Allison Hui, Theodore Schatzki, and Elizabeth Shove (London: Routledge, 2016), 126–37.

89. Kaelyn Stiles, Özlem Altıok, and Michael M. Bell, "The Ghosts of Taste: Food and the Cultural Politics of Authenticity," *Agriculture and Human Values* 28, no. 2 (2011): 234.

90. Bourdieu, *Distinction*, 56; Deborah Lupton, *Food, the Body and the Self* (London: Sage, 1996), 35; Ben Highmore, "Alimentary Agents: Food, Cultural Theory and Multiculturalism," *Journal of Intercultural Studies* 29, no. 4 (2008): 381–98; Fabio Parasecoli, *Gastronativism: Food, Identity Politics, and Globalization* (New York: Columbia University Press, 2022).

91. Dietler, "Culinary Encounters," 222–23.

92. Tahini is a paste made from ground raw or roasted, hulled or unhulled sesame seeds.

93. The biblical word for bread is the Aramaic *pat*, which many have mistakenly assumed to be the source for the contemporary *pita*—the Hebrew word for flatbread. In fact, the source for the Hebrew *pita* is Greek and other Balkan languages, having entered the Hebrew through Ladino (Judeo Spanish). See "Pita," Academy of the Hebrew Language, accessed January 25, 2023, https://

hebrew-academy.org.il/2019/11/13/%D7%A4%D7%99%D7%AA%D7%94 (Hebrew).

94. Menachem Kapeliuk, "Studies in the Bible," *Davar*, January 25, 1957 (Hebrew). The only response to Kapeliuk, which appeared in the same newspaper several months later, disputed his thesis. The responder's argument was that at summertime workers in the field dip their bread in sour foods (*hometz* and *hamutz*, or sour in Hebrew, also derive from the same root), to alleviate the heat, and not in hummus, which is eaten in the winter (due to quick spoilage) and is not intended for dipping. D. Avisar, "On 'Studies in the Bible'," *Davar*, April 21, 1957 (Hebrew).

95. Me'ir Shalev, "Hummus Is Ours," *Yediot Ahronot*, January 1, 2001 (Hebrew).

96. For example, Dani Ishai Behan, "Israelis, and Jews More Broadly, Are Not Appropriating Anything," *Times of Israel—the Blogs*, June 23, 2019, https://blogs .timesofisrael.com/israelis-and-jews-in-general-are-not-appropriating-anything; "Avshalom Kor Explains: Hummus Is the New Hit of Shavuot," accessed November 24, 2022, https://youtu.be/hPWN66y8bnI (Hebrew); Ministry of Education, State Bible Website, "Workers' Meal in the Bible," accessed January 12, 2023, https://did.li/lDuTY (Hebrew).

97. Charles Perry, *Scents and Flavors: A Syrian Cookbook* (New York: New York University Press, 2017), 129–30. The English translation of the title is taken from Nawal Nasrallah, *Treasure Trove of Benefits and Variety at the Table: A Fourteenth-Century Egyptian Cookbook* (Leiden: Brill, 2018), 16. Similar concoctions of mashed chickpeas, tahini, herbs, spices, and nuts appear in two Cairenes cookbooks from the fourteenth century: *Kitab Wasf al-Atʿima al-Muʿtada* (*The Description of Familiar Foods*, 1373) and *Kanz al-Fawāʿid fī Tanwīʿ al-Mawāʿid* (*Treasure Trove of Benefits and Variety at the Table*, exact date unknown), which contains ten different recipes for *ḥimmaṣ kassā* (pounded chickpeas). Here is one example: "Pound chickpeas until they become mushy after boiling them. Take vinegar, olive oil, tahini, *aṭrāf ṭīb* (spice blend), black pepper, mint, Macedonian parsley (*baqdūnis*), a bit of dry thyme, walnuts, hazelnuts, almonds, pistachios, toasted coriander and caraway seeds, lemon preserved in salt (*laymūn māliḥ*), olives and salt as needed. Knead all these ingredients to mix them, and spread them (*yubsaṭ*) [on a plate]. Sprinkle the surface with kassia (*dār Ṣīnī*) and sprinkle it with olive oil. Set it aside overnight and serve it. It will come out good, God willing." Nasrallah, *Treasure Trove*, 381–82. This recipe is almost identical to the one that appears in *Kitab Wasf* (*ḥummuṣ kasā*). See Maxime Rodinson, Arthur John Arberry, and Charles Perry, *Medieval Arab Cookery* (Totnes: Prospect Books, 2001), 383. Most of the recipes in the *Wasf* are based on a Baghdadi cookbook from the thirteenth century, *Kitab al-Tabih*, but the *ḥummuṣ kasā* recipe belongs to a group of recipes that are not part of the *Kitab*.

98. Today *musabbaha* is the name of a dish made of whole cooked chickpeas with tahini.

99. James Grehan, *Everyday Life and Consumer Culture in 18th-Century Damascus* (Seattle: University of Washington Press, 2007), 107–8.

100. Umberto Eco, "How Culture Conditions the Colours We See," in *On Signs*, ed. Marshall Blonsky (Baltimore: Johns Hopkins University Press, 1985), 157–75.

101. Daniel Miller, "Materiality: An Introduction," in *Materiality*, ed. Daniel Miller (Durham, NC: Duke University Press, 2005), 1–40; Diana Coole and Samantha Frost, "Introducing the New Materialisms," in *New Materialisms: Ontology, Agency and Politics*, ed. Diana Coole and Samantha Frost (Durham, NC: Duke University Press, 2010), 1–43; Jeneviève Zubrzycki, "Matter and Meaning: A Cultural Sociology of Nationalism," in *National Matters: Materiality, Culture and Nationalism*, ed. Jeneviève Zubrzycki (Stanford, CA: Stanford University Press, 2017), 4.

102. Coole and Frost, "Introducing the New Materialisms," 26; Dominik Bartmański, "A Temple of Social Hope? Tempelhof Airport in Berlin and Its Transformations," in *National Matters*, 218–21.

103. Bartmański, "A Temple of Social Hope?," 216–40. On materiality and affordances see also Ian Hutchby, "Technologies, Texts and Affordances," *Sociology* 35, no. 2 (2001): 441–56; Ian Hodder, *Entangled: An Archaeology of the Relationships between Humans and Things* (Malden, MA: Blackwell, 2012), 48–50; Manning, *Semiotics of Drink and Drinking*, 11–14; Huck and Bauernschmidt, "Trans-Cultural Appropriation"; Zubrzycki, "Matter and Meaning," 7.

104. Michel Callon, Cécile Méadel, and Vololona Rabeharisoa, "The Economy of Qualities," *Economy and Society* 31, no. 2 (2002): 194–217. See also Steven Shapin, "The Tastes of Wine: Toward a Cultural History," *Rivista di Estetica* 51 (2012): 49–94.

105. Andreas Reckwitz, "The Status of the 'Material' in Theories of Culture: From 'Social Structure' to 'Artefacts,'" *Journal for the Theory of Social Behaviour* 32, no. 2 (2002): 195–217; Reckwitz, "Toward a Theory of Social Practices: A Development in Culturalist Theorizing," *European Journal of Social Theory* 5, no. 2 (2002): 243–63.

106. See also Brad Weiss, *Real Pigs: Shifting Values in the Field of Local Pork* (Durham, NC: Duke University Press, 2016).

107. David Grazien, "Demystifying Authenticity in the Sociology of Culture," in *Routledge Handbook of Cultural Sociology*, ed. Laura Grindstaff, Ming-Cheng M. Lo, and John R. Hall (London: Routledge, 2018), 192.

108. Manning, *Semiotics of Drink and Drinking*, 9.

109. Glenn R. Carroll and Dennis Ray Wheaton, "The Organizational Construction of Authenticity: An Examination of Contemporary Food and Dining in the US," *Research in Organizational Behavior* 29 (2009): 255–82; Lauren

Crossland-Marr and Elizabeth L. Krause, "Theorizing Authenticity: Introduction to Special Section," *Gastronomica* 23, no. 1 (2023): 5–12.

110. Carroll and Wheaton, "Organizational Construction of Authenticity"; Somogy Varga and Charles Guignon, "Authenticity," in *The Stanford Encyclopedia of Philosophy* (Fall 2017 Edition), ed. Edward N. Zalta, accessed June 18, 2023, https://plato.stanford.edu/archives/fall2017/entries/authenticity.

111. Parasecoli, *Gastronativism*, 88–89. See also: Michael B. Beverland, "Crafting Brand Authenticity: The Case of Luxury Wines," *Journal of Management Studies* 42, no. 5 (2005): 1003–29; Josée Johnston and Shyon Baumann, *Foodies: Democracy and Distinction in the Gourmet Foodscape* (New York: Routledge, 2010); Weiss, *Real Pigs*.

112. Panel on the "hummus wars," Al-Sham Arab Food Festival, Haifa, December 8, 2015.

113. Webb Keane, "Subjects and Objects," in *Handbook of Material Culture*, ed. Chris Tilley et al. (London: Sage, 2006), 200; Keane, "Semiotics and the Social Analysis of Material Things."

114. Jeff Pratt, "Food Values: The Local and the Authentic," *Critique of Anthropology* 27, no. 3 (2007): 285–300; Daniel Philippon, "How Local Is Slow Food?," *RCC Perspectives, No. 1, Think Global, Eat Local: Exploring Foodways* (2015): 7–12.

115. Anne Meneley, "Like an Extra Virgin," *American Anthropologist* 109, no. 4 (2007): 684.

116. For example, the American company Tribe stated on its website, "Our hummus is full of chickpeas, a touch of tahini and a whole lot of tradition." Tribe website, accessed August 9, 2023, https://tribehummus.com/flavors.

117. Rachel Laudan, "A Plea for Culinary Modernism: Why We Should Love New, Fast, Processed Food," *Gastronomica* 1, no. 1 (2001), 42–43; Richard Wilk, "From Wild Weeds to Artisanal Cheese," in *Fast Food/Slow Food: The Cultural Economy of the Global Food System*, ed. Richard Wilk (Lanham, MD: Altamira Press, 2006), 16; Deborah Heath and Anne Meneley, "Techne, Technoscience, and the Circulation of Comestible Commodities: An Introduction," *American Anthropologist* 109, no. 4 (2007): 594; Pratt, "Food Values"; Weiss, *Real Pigs*.

118. For example, James L. Watson, ed. *Golden Arches East: McDonald's in East Asia* (Stanford, CA: Stanford University Press, 1997); Melissa L. Caldwell, "Domesticating the French Fry: McDonald's and Consumerism in Moscow," *Journal of Consumer Culture* 4, no. 1 (2004): 5–26; Robert J. Foster, *Coca-Globalization: Following Soft Drinks from New York to New Guinea* (New York: Palgrave Macmillan, 2008); Carolyn de la Peña and Benjamin N. Lawrence, "Foodways, 'Foodism,' or Foodscapes? Navigating the Local/Global and Food/Culture Divide," in *Local Foods Meet Global Foodways: Tasting History*, ed. Carolyn de la Peña and Benjamin N. Lawrence (London: Routledge, 2012), 2–14; David L. Wank and James Farrer, "Chinese Immigrants and Japanese Cuisine in the United

States: A Case of Culinary Glocalization," in *The Globalization of Asian Cuisines: Transnational Networks and Culinary Contact Zones*, ed. James Farrer (New York: Palgrave Macmillan, 2015), 81–99.

119. For example, Penny van Esterik, "From Hunger Foods to Heritage Foods: Challenges to Food Localization in Lao PDR," in *Fast Food/Slow Food*, 83–96; James Farrer, "Introduction: Traveling Cuisines in and out of Asia: Toward A Framework for Studying Culinary Globalization," in *Globalization of Asian Cuisines*, 1.

120. Wilk, "From Wild Weeds to Artisanal Cheese," 19. See also Wilk, *Home Cooking in the Global Village*; David Inglis, "Globalization and Food: The Dialectics of Globality and Locality," in *The Routledge International Handbook of Globalization Studies*, ed. Bryan S. Turner (London: Routledge, 2010), 492–513.

121. Rachel Laudan, "Afterword," in *Local Foods Meet Global Foodways*, 210. See also Stiles, Altıok, and Bell, "The Ghosts of Taste"; Robert Feagan, "The Place of Food: Mapping Out the 'Local' in Local Food Systems," *Progress in Human Geography* 31, no. 1 (2007): 23–42; Michaela DeSoucey and Isabelle Téchoueyres, "Virtue and Valorization: 'Local Food' in the United States and France," *Globalization of Food* (2009): 81–95; Weiss, *Real Pigs*.

122. Stiles, Altıok, and Bell, "The Ghosts of Taste."

123. See, for example, Sidney W. Mintz, *Sweetness and Power: The Place of Sugar in Modern History* (New York: Penguin, 1985); William Roseberry, "The Rise of Yuppie Coffees and the Reimagination of Class in the United States," *American Anthropologist* 98, no. 4 (1996): 762–75; Emiko Ohnuki-Tierney, *Rice as Self: Japanese Identities through Time* (Princeton, NJ: Princeton University Press, 1993); Alison Leitch, "Slow Food and the Politics of Pork Fat: Italian Food and European Identity," *Ethnos* 68, no. 4 (2003): 437–62; Meneley, "Like an Extra Virgin"; Deborah B. Gewertz and Frederick Karl Errington, *Cheap Meat: Flap Food Nations in the Pacific Islands* (Berkeley: University of California Press, 2010).

124. For a list of the archives consulted see the bibliography.

125. At the time when I collected the materials for this study, the digital archive of local Arabic newspapers did not yet exist.

126. Interviews with elderly Palestinians were conducted by Nisreen Mazzawi. Some of the interviews with elderly Mizrahim were conducted by Matan Boord. I have used first name and family name initial to protect the interviewees' privacy.

127. Trevor Graham, *Make Hummus Not War*, Yarra Bank Films, 2012.

128. The survey was conducted by the B. I. and Lucille Cohen Institute for Public Opinion Research at the Gershon Gordon Faculty of Social Sciences, Tel Aviv University. The results were analyzed by Tania Kolobov.

129. Forum for the Study of Society and Culture, the Jerusalem Van Leer Institute, "Epistemology of Mizrahiness in Israel," in *Mizrahim in Israel: A*

Critical Observation into Israel's Ethnicity, ed. Hannan Hever, Yehouda Shenhav, and Pnina Motzfi-Haller (Jerusalem: Van Leer Institute, 2002), 15–27 (Hebrew). Aziza Khazzoom, "Mizrahim, Mizrachiut, and the Future of Israeli Studies," *Israel Studies Forum* 17, no. 2 (2002): 94–106; Ronit Lentin, *Traces of Racial Exception: Racializing Israeli Settler Colonialism* (London: Bloomsbury Academic, 2018).

130. Ferguson, *Accounting for Taste*, 3.

131. Sami Zubaida, "National, Communal, and Global Dimensions in Middle Eastern Food Cultures," in *A Taste of Thyme: Culinary Cultures of the Middle East*, ed. Sami Zubaida and Richard Tapper (London: I. B. Tauris, 2000), 33; Anny Gaul and Graham Auman Pitts, "Introduction: Making Levantine Cuisine," in *Making Levantine Cuisine: Modern Foodways of the Eastern Mediterranean*, ed. Anny Gaul, Graham Auman Pitts, and Vicki Valosik (Austin: University of Texas Press, 2022), 1–22.

1. EARLY CULINARY CONTACTS

* The idea to open each chapter with a hummus recipe from the relevant period was inspired by Wilk, *Home Cooking in the Global Village*.

1. Dorothy Kahn Bar-Adon, "Oriental Gourmet: Lamb, Tahina, Humas," *Palestine Post*, February 2, 1941.

2. Lisa Heldke defines "exotic" as "excitingly unusual." Heldke, *Exotic Appetites*, 17–19.

3. For example, Ian Mosby, *Food Will Win the War: The Politics, Culture, and Science of Food on Canada's Home Front* (Vancouver: UBC Press, 2014), 133–61; Jakob Tanner, "The Rationing System, Food Policy and Nutritional Science during the Second World War: A Comparative View of Switzerland," in *Changing Food Habits: Case Studies from Africa, South America and Europe*, ed. Carola Lenz (Mainz: Harwood Academic, 1999), 211–42.

4. Sidney Mintz distinguishes between "inside meanings," which are the meanings associated with the communal dealings with a certain food, how people came to have it, how it is prepared, whether it is plentiful or scarce, and so on, and "outside meanings," which refer to systems of power, whose actions transcend individuals and local communities and set the outer boundaries, within which people organize and give meaning to their everyday activities. Mintz, *Tasting Food, Tasting Freedom*, 17–32.

5. Palestinian cuisine reflects a confluence of several culinary traditions, most notably Arab, Ottoman, and Persian. Within it, there were regional and cultural variations: between the northern, central, and southern regions; between mountain and coastal plain; between villagers, Bedouins, and city dwellers. Claudia Roden, *The New Book of Middle Eastern Food* (London: Alfred A. Knopf, 2000), 16–30; Reem Kassis, "Even in a Small Country Like Palestine, Cuisine Is

Regional," in *Making Levantine Cuisine: Modern Foodways of the Eastern Mediterranean*, ed. Anny Gaul, Graham Auman Pitts, and Vicki Valosik (Austin: University of Texas Press, 2022), 133–49; Gaul and Pitts, "Introduction," 1–20.

6. Shmuel Avitzur, *Everyday Life in Palestine in the 19th Century* (Tel Aviv: Am Hasefer, 1972), 20, 46 (Hebrew); Nahum Gross, "The Palestine Economy towards the Close of the Ottoman Era," in *The History of the Jewish Community in Eretz-Israel since 1882, The Ottoman Period, Part Two*, ed. Israel Kolatt (Jerusalem: Israel Academy for Sciences and Humanities and Bialik Institute, 2002), 279–308 (Hebrew); Gad G. Gilbar, "The Growing Economic Involvement of Palestine with the West, 1865–1914," in *Palestine in the Late Ottoman Period: Political, Social and Economic Transformation*, ed. David Kushner (Jerusalem: Yad Izhak Ben-Zvi and Brill, 1986), 188–210; Christian Sassmannshausen, "Eating Up: Food Consumption and Social Status in Late Ottoman Greater Syria," in *Insatiable Appetite: Food as Cultural Signifier in the Middle East and Beyond*, ed. Kirill Dmitriev, Julia Hauser, and Bilal Orfali (Leiden: Brill, 2020), 28; Gaul and Pitts, "Introduction."

7. William John Vickers, *A Nutritional Economic Survey of Wartime Palestine, 1942–1943* (Palestine: Department of Health, 1944), 3, 47. According to Vickers, only people of means ate meat on a weekly basis, while the majority did not eat meat or fish at all, or only seldom.

8. Aaron Aaronsohn, *Agricultural and Botanical Explorations in Palestine* (Washington, DC: Government Printing Office, 1910), 29–31. On Aaronsohn's book see Omar Tesdell, "Wild Wheat to Productive Drylands: Global Scientific Practice and the Agroecological Remaking of Palestine," *Geoforum* 78 (2017): 48. The purpose of the book was to recommend the introduction of some of Palestine's flora to the United States.

9. Aaronsohn, *Agricultural and Botanical Explorations*, 29–30. Due to its resilience, chickpea functioned as a summer crop, sown in early spring and picked in the summer. Zvi Shilony, "Random Factors in the Creation of Degania," in *Studies in Geography and History in Honour of Yehoshua Ben-Arieh*, ed. Yossi Ben-Artzi, Israel Bartal, and Elchanan Reiner (Jerusalem: Magness Press, 2000), 434 (Hebrew).

10. Interview with Samira H., Nazareth, April 19, 2012 (interviewer: Nisreen Mazzawi). See also Shukri ʿAraf, *The Land, the People and the Effort* (Tarshiha: Aljil Liltajlid, 1993), 28 (Arabic).

11. Avitzur, *Everyday Life in Palestine*, 48.

12. Gustaf Dalman, *Arbeit und Sitte in Palästina*, Band II, *Der Ackerbau* (Hildesheim: Georg Olms, 1964), 271. Palestinian chef and researcher of Levantine cuisine Muʿin Halabi also mentioned in an interview that mashed chickpeas were often prepared without tahini. Interview with Muʿin Halabi, Haifa, May 26, 2010. See also Bar-Adon, "Oriental Gourmet." Most of the written references to hummus from this period that I came across do not mention garlic.

13. Mustafa Abbasi and David De Vries, "Commodities and Power: Edible Oil and Soap in the History of Arab-Jewish Haifa," in *Haifa before and after 1948: Narratives of a Mixed City*, ed. Mahmoud Yazbak and Yfaat Weiss, Series 6 (The Hague: Institute for Historical Justice and Reconciliation, 2011), 107. In 1945, 1 kg of chickpeas cost 50 mil, whereas 1 kg of tahini cost 215 mil. In comparison, 1 kg of kosher beef cost 458 mil. "Jerusalem Prices mid-April, 1945," Israel State Archives (ISA), 5037/6-m.

14. Interview with Jeries Saba, manager of Jaffa restaurant (with participation of Sami Abu Shehadeh), Jaffa, April 13, 2010; Interview with Janet M., Haifa, January 26, 2012 (interviewer: Nisreen Mazzawi).

15. Interview with Gloria E., Nazareth, February 14, 2012 (interviewer: Nisreen Mazzawi).

16. Hisham Sharabi, "From *Embers and Ashes*," in *Anthology of Modern Palestinian Literature*, ed. Salma Khadra Jayyusi (New York: Columbia University Press, 1992), 698.

17. Interview with Jeries Saba; Interview with Ezra Sherfler, owner of Azura Restaurant, Jerusalem, June 19, 2012 (interviewer: Matan Boord).

18. District Price Controller, Lydda District, "Maximal prices for food and drinks," July 24, 1945, The Historical Archives of the City of Tel Aviv-Yafo (TAHA), 1064/05-152; "Retail prices for food and drinks in establishments," ISA, 6-5223/24-m. In more expensive restaurants a dish of hummus could cost up to 45 mils. A mil was a thousandth of a Palestine pound, which was equivalent in value to the British pound.

19. Zubaida, "National, Communal, and Global Dimensions in Middle Eastern Food Cultures," 33.

20. In the Mandate period, only ten thousand Jewish immigrants arrived from Syria and Lebanon, where hummus was consumed. Yaron Tzur, "The Immigration from Muslim Countries," in *The First Decade: 1948–1958*, ed. Zvi Zameret and Hannah Jablonka (Jerusalem: Yad Izhak Ben-Zvi, 1997), 61 (Hebrew).

21. Boiled chickpeas were served in the "sholem zucher" banquet, to mark the birth of a son, and on Purim eve. In Sephardic, North African and Iraqi cuisines, in contrast, it was an important ingredient, often used in soups and stews. "Nutrition Cycles"; Claudia Roden, *The Book of Jewish Food: An Odyssey from Samarkand and Vilna to the Present Day* (London: Penguin, 1999); Jacob Yehoshua, *The House and the Street in Old Jerusalem* (Jerusalem: Rubin Mass, 1966), 44 (Hebrew); Ken Albala, *Beans: A History* (London: Bloomsbury, 2007), 84.

22. "What Does a Prisoner Eat?," *Davar*, October 17, 1936 (Hebrew).

23. Sarah Bromberg, "The Question of Purposeful Nutrition in Eretz Israel," *Hamazon* 1, no. 1 (1938): 2 (Hebrew).

24. E. W. G. Masterman, "Food and Its Preparation in Modern Palestine," *Biblical World* 17, no. 6 (1901): 416. On the European distaste for Middle Eastern

food, see also Jill Tilsley-Benham, "'Pride and Prejudice,' or Familiarity Breeds Content: A Western Taste of Middle Eastern Food," in *Oxford Symposium on Food and Cookery 1987: Taste, Proceedings*, ed. Tom Jaine (London: Prospect Books, 1988), 198–204.

25. Rachel Seri, *A Tree and Its Branches (The Story of a Yemenite Family)* (Published by the author, 1988) (Hebrew).

26. There are different estimates of the total number of Jews in Palestine in 1914. See Yair Wallach, "Rethinking the Yishuv: Late-Ottoman Palestine's Jewish Communities Revisited," *Journal of Modern Jewish Studies* 16, no. 2 (2017): 277–78.

27. David Sitton, *The Story of a Neighborhood* (Jerusalem: Council of the Sephardi Community, 1977) (Hebrew).

28. Seri, *A Tree and Its Branches*, 39–42; Ranta and Mendel, "Consuming Palestine," 11–12.

29. Hanna Bezalel, *Life Chapters* (Published by the author, 2004), 41 (Hebrew).

30. Seri, *A Tree and Its Branches*, 40–41. Pastelicos are pastries filled with cheese, spinach, or meat.

31. Seri, *A Tree and Its Branches*, 36–38.

32. Seri, *A Tree and Its Branches*, 39.

33. Seri, *A Tree and Its Branches*, 42. In fact, *siniya* is a generic name for dishes cooked in the oven on a tray.

34. Seri, *A Tree and Its Branches*, 42; Yehoshua, *The House and the Street*, 159.

35. Seri, *A Tree and Its Branches*, 57–58. See also Jacob Yehoshua, "Neighborhoods in Old Jerusalem," in *Childhood in Old Jerusalem: Episodes of Life from Days Gone By* (Jerusalem: Rubin Mass, 1978), 155 (Hebrew). Yehoshua writes about Eliyahu Armoza, who used to entertain the Bedouins with whom he traded while his wife prepared for them their favorite food.

36. Seri, *A Tree and Its Branches*, 57–58. See also Yehoshua, "Neighborhoods in Old Jerusalem," 217.

37. Salim Tamari, *Mountain against the Sea: Essays on Palestinian Society and Culture* (Berkeley: University of California Press, 2009), 83; Hillel Cohen, *Year Zero of the Arab–Israeli Conflict 1929*, trans. Haim Watzman (Waltham, MA: Brandeis University Press, 2015); Menachem Klein, *Lives in Common: Arabs and Jews in Jerusalem, Jaffa and Hebron*, trans. Haim Watzman (Oxford: Oxford University Press, 2014); Abigail Jacobson and Moshe Naor, *Oriental Neighbors: Middle Eastern Jews and Arabs in Mandatory Palestine* (Waltham, MA: Brandeis University Press, 2016); Wallach, "Rethinking the Yishuv," 275–94; Israel Bartal, *Tangled Roots: The Emergence of Israeli Culture* (Rhode Island: Brown Judaic Studies, 2020), 9–22; Michelle U. Campos, "Mapping Urban 'Mixing' and Intercommunal Relations in Late Ottoman Jerusalem: A Neighborhood Study," *Comparative Studies in Society and History* 63, no. 1 (2021): 133–69.

38. Yair Wallach, "Jerusalem between Segregation and Integration: Reading Urban Space through the Eyes of Justice Gad Frumkin," in *Modernity, Minority, and the Public Sphere: Jews and Christians in the Middle East*, ed. S. R. Goldstein-Sabbah and H. L. Murre-van den Berg (Leiden: Brill, 2016), 210; Campos, "Mapping Urban 'Mixing'"; Klein, *Lives in Common*.

39. Israel Bartal, *Exile in the Land: The Settlement of Eretz Israel before Zionism* (Jerusalem: Zionist Library by the World Zionist Organization, 1994), 78–79, 81 (Hebrew); Wallach, "Rethinking the Yishuv," 280.

40. Tamari, *Mountain against the Sea*, 150–66; Klein, *Lives in Common*, 19–64. This does not mean that no sense of a shared Jewish identity existed in the Yishuv—the Jewish community of Palestine pre-1948—before Zionism's rise to hegemony. However, as Yair Wallach argues, different social, political, and economic networks in which the Jews operated dictated different categorization systems and collective definitions, and these were not overridden by a single protonational Jewish identity. Wallach, "Rethinking the Yishuv."

41. Yehoshua, *The House and the Street*, 56.

42. Klein, *Lives in Common*, 41; Wallach, "Jerusalem between Segregation and Integration," 211.

43. Ita Yellin, *To My Children: My Memories, Part 1* (Jerusalem: Hama'arav, 1938), 80 (Hebrew).

44. Johann Büssow, *Hamidian Palestine: Politics and Society in the District of Jerusalem 1872–1908* (Leiden: Brill, 2011), 193.

45. Yellin, *To My Children, Part 1*, 57; Ita Yellin, *To My Children: My Memories, Part 2* (Jerusalem: Hama'arav, 1941), 25.

46. Campos, "Mapping Urban 'Mixing,'" 161.

47. Howard Sachar, *Aliyah: The People of Israel* (Cleaveland: World Publishing, 1961), 23, quoted in Ranta and Mendel, "Consuming Palestine," 11.

48. Interview with M., Ta'ami restaurant, Jerusalem, November 25, 2012 (interviewer: Matan Boord); Conversation with Duee from Hummus Duee, Lakhish, April 17, 2010.

49. Wallach, "Jerusalem between Segregation and Integration," 228; Klein, *Lives in Common*.

50. Ora Shem-Or, *Without the Ponytail and the Sarafan* (Tel Aviv: Noga, 1981), 82 (Hebrew).

51. Quoted in Highmore, "Alimentary Agents," 387.

52. Israel Bartal, "On Being Primary: Time and Place in the First Aliyah," in *Talking Culture*, 15–24.

53. On *harathin* see the introduction, footnote 3. Some of these workers were peasants who had lost their grazing or planting rights following the purchase of the land by Jews. Seltenreich, "Jewish or Arab Hired Workers?," 230; Liora Halperin,

The Oldest Guard: Forging the Zionist Settler Past (Stanford, CA: Stanford University Press, 2021), 71.

54. Yossi Ben-Artzi, "Development of the First Aliya Colonies and the Establishment of New Colonies during the Second Aliya Period," in *The Second Aliya*, 151–53 (Hebrew).

55. Aaronsohn noted his success in introducing into his brother's colony in the lower Galilee a chickpea variety from another part of the country, more suitable to the weather conditions than the one that had been grown there. In light of his success, the neighboring colonies hastened to sow large areas with chickpeas. Aaronsohn, *Agricultural and Botanical Explorations*, 30–31.

56. Alon, *My Father's House*, 16, 34, 47.

57. Ever Hadani, *Settlement in the Lower Galilee*, 206.

58. Tzvi Nadav, *Thus We Started* (Tel Aviv: Hakibbutz Hameuchad, 1957), 83, 176 (Hebrew).

59. Hummus also came up in a testimony on culinary transfer in the colonies by Tikva Rosenman (b. 1923), who grew up in the colony of Nes Ziona. The women in her family learned from the wives of the *harathin* how to prepare dishes like hubeiza (mallow) leaves stuffed with rice, labaneh, salty white cheese, hummus, ful, and others. Colony women also learned cooking techniques such as stuffing leaves and vegetables, cooking wild herbs with onion and olive oil, pickling, and baking flat wheat bread in a taboon or sorghum bread—in times of wheat shortage—on a *saj*. According to Rosenman, culinary exchange was bidirectional: Arab workers sometimes bartered various products for dishes made by the colony's women—for example, twenty-five to thirty eggs for a homemade loaf of white bread. Interview with Tikva Rosenman, Nes Ziona, February 11, 2014 (interviewer: Ofra Tene).

60. Saposnik, *Becoming Hebrew*, 180–88; Israel Bartal, "Introduction: 'The Culture of Israel' or 'The Cultures of Israel?,'" in *A Century of Israeli Culture*, ed. Israel Bartal (Jerusalem: Magness Press, 2002), x (Hebrew); Yaffa Berlovich, "The Hebrew Colony: The Beginning of an Eretz Israeli Culture," in *Talking Culture*, 96–98.

61. Berlovich, "The Hebrew Colony," 70–109; Saposnik, *Becoming Hebrew*, 94.

62. Even-Zohar, "The Emergence of a Native Hebrew Culture," 172–74; Berlovich, "The Hebrew Colony," 98; Zerubavel, "Memory, the Rebirth of the Native," 322–23; Halperin, *Oldest Guard*, 100–105.

63. Yaacov Ro'i, "Jewish-Arab Relations in the First Aliyah Colonies," in *The Book of the First Aliyah*, ed. Mordechai Eliav (Jerusalem: Yad Izhak Ben-Zvi, 1982), 246–47 (Hebrew); Even-Zohar, "The Emergence of a Native Hebrew Culture," 173–74; Yair Seltenreich, "The Shaping of the Masculine Image of the Farmers in the Galilee Colonies: The First Period," *Social Issues in Israel* 12 (2011): 11 (Hebrew); Saposnik, *Becoming Hebrew*, 181.

64. Jonathan Frankel, *Prophecy and Politics: Socialism, Nationalism, and the Russian Jews, 1862–1917* (Cambridge: Cambridge University Press, 1981), 366–452; Margalit Shilo, *Experiments in Settlement* (Jerusalem: Yad Izhak Ben-Zvi, 1988) (Hebrew); Shafir, *Land, Labor*; Ben Halpern and Jehuda Reinharz, *Zionism and the Creation of a New Society* (Hanover, NH: Brandeis University Press, 1998), 186, 191, 197.

65. See, for example, Aviva Ufaz, "The Portrait of the Man of Hashomer: Following the Letters of Mendel Portugali," *Cathedra* 48 (1988): 73–89 (Hebrew); Zerubavel, "Memory, the Rebirth of the Native," 324–25; Yaacov N. Goldstein, "The Jewish–Arab Conflict: The First Jewish Underground Defense Organizations and the Arabs," *Middle Eastern Studies* 31, no. 4 (1995): 744–51; Boaz Lev Tov, "Leisure and Popular Culture Patterns of Eretz Israeli Jews in the Years 1882–1914 as a Reflection of Social Changes" (PhD diss., Tel Aviv University, 2007), 180–87 (Hebrew). According to Lev Tov, after the men of Hashomer mastered the performance of a "fantasia" on horseback, they competed with Arabs at their performance (184–85).

66. Tzvi Nadav, "Half a Body Gone," in *The Book of Hashomer*, ed. Izhak Ben-Zvi, Israel Shochat, Matti Megged, and Yohanan Tversky (Tel Aviv: Dvir, 1957), 150–51. (Hebrew)

67. Gur Alroey, "Servants of the Colony or Rude Tyrants? Hundred Years to Hashomer—Historical Perspective," *Cathedra* 133 (2009): 77–104 (Hebrew).

68. Alroey, "Servants of the Colony or Rude Tyrants?" This attitude was one of the reasons why Hashomer had to leave the larger colonies of Hadera and Rehovot in 1913, three years after they had been placed in charge of guarding these colonies. Yaacov Goldstein, "Self-Defense and Guarding: 'Bar Giora' and 'Hashomer' in the Second Aliya," in *The Second Aliya*, 463 (Hebrew).

69. A quote by Avner Shaf'el, a member of Hashomer, who believed in armed struggle both against the Arabs and against Jews who employed Arabs, gives a particularly strong example for the element of revival: "Initially they [the colonists] came here as idealists, who intend to sacrifice themselves for the country and the national future. But the poison of pragmatism slowly consumed their soul, weakened their vitality, and killed their spirit! And now comes a new element, young and fresh, full of life, and ideals and devotion, that wishes to remove life—the flag of our national revival—from their cold, dead hands." Quoted in Alroey, "Servants of the Colony or Rude Tyrants?," 93. Shaf'el himself took his own life.

70. Bracha Havas, *The Second Immigration Wave Book* (Tel Aviv: Am Oved, 1947), 199 (Hebrew); Even-Zohar, "The Emergence of a Native Hebrew Culture," 172; Gilat Gofer, "The Zionist Woman: The Construction of Femininity in the Early Zionist Labor Movement, 1903–1923" (PhD diss., Tel Aviv University, 2009), 110–11 (Hebrew).

71. Havas, *Second Immigration Wave Book*, 199.

72. Havas, *Second Immigration Wave Book*, 489.

73. Yigal Aliovich, "In Days of Conquest," in *Kfar Tavor (Mescha), 1901–1976*, ed. Meir Hareuveni (Kfar Tavor: Yovel, 1976), 99–100 (Hebrew); Muki Tzur, Tair Zvulun, and Hanina Porat, eds., *The Beginning of the Kibbutz* (Tel Aviv: Hakibbutz Hameuchad and Sifriyat Hapo'alim, 1981), 47, 218 (Hebrew); Havas, *Second Immigration Wave Book*, 360.

74. For example, Havas, *Second Immigration Wave Book*, 272–73, 396, 475, 526; Gofer, "Zionist Woman," 95–122.

75. Golda Meir, "First Days in the Group," *Lamerchav*, December 26, 1969 (Hebrew).

76. Tzur et al., *Beginning of the Kibbutz*, 93.

77. "30 'Combine' Harvesters on the Farms," *Davar*, June 5, 1935 (Hebrew); Yaacov Kostrinsky, *Agronomical Surveys on Chickpea and Seed Cycles*, Special Publication no. 34 (Beit Dagan: Department of Scientific Publications, Vulcani Center, 1974), 3 (Hebrew). Chickpeas had to be harvested within a few days of ripening; otherwise, the summer dryness would cause the pods to open and the seeds to fall to the ground. In Arab villages, the entire family was called to task. Because the plants were low, picking had to be done while kneeling. During harvesting, the stems and pods released an acidic fluid that burned the skin. To avoid this, pickers began their work before sunrise, when the plants were still covered in dew, and continued until the heat became unbearable. Shilony, "Random Factors," 434–35.

78. "Agricultural Workers' Diet: Change from Animal to Plant Foods," *Palestine Post*, October 12, 1941; Vickers, *Nutritional Economic Survey*, 79–80.

79. Bar-Adon, "Oriental Gourmet."

80. M. Ben-Yitzhak, "The Wandering Cooks," *Davar*, August 10, 1962 (Hebrew).

81. At its peak, about a quarter of the Jewish population lived in rural settlements. Jacob Metzer, *The Divided Economy of Mandatory Palestine* (Cambridge: Cambridge University Press, 1998), 8–9.

82. Deborah Bernstein and Badi Hasisi, "'Buy and Promote the National Cause': Consumption, Class Formation and Nationalism in Mandate Palestinian Society," *Nations and Nationalism* 14, no. 1 (2008): 127–50; Sherene Seikaly, *Men of Capital: Scarcity and Economy in Mandate Palestine* (Stanford, CA: Stanford University Press, 2015); Amir Ben-Porat, *The Bourgeoisie: The History of the Israeli Bourgeoisie* (Jerusalem: Magnes Press, 1999), 77–80 (Hebrew).

83. Metzer, *Divided Economy*, 7–8; Anat Kidron, "The Influence of the Results of the 1929 Events on Haifa and on Jaffa / Tel Aviv: A Comparative Look," *Israel* 22 (2014): 73 (Hebrew). Seven such cities existed: Jerusalem, Safed, Tiberius,

Haifa, Hebron and Acre (both until 1929), and Jaffa (officially until 1946, but in effect until 1936).

84. Daniel Monterescu and Dan Rabinowitz, eds., *Mixed Towns, Trapped Communities* (Aldershot, UK: Ashgate, 2007), 2.

85. Mark LeVine, *Overthrowing Geography: Jaffa, Tel Aviv, and the Struggle for Palestine, 1880–1948* (Berkeley: University of California Press, 2005); Deborah Bernstein, "Contested Contact: Proximity and Social Control in Pre-1948 Jaffa and Tel-Aviv," in *Mixed Towns, Trapped Communities*, 215–41; Tammy Razi, "'Arab-Jewesses'? Ethnicity, Nationality and Gender in Mandate Tel Aviv," *Theory and Criticism* 38–39 (2011): 137–60 (Hebrew); Kidron, "The Influence," 73–109.

86. Mordechai Ron, *Haifa of My Youth: Everyday Life in Haifa in the 1920s and 1930s* (Jerusalem: Ariel, 1993), 79–80 (Hebrew); Tziona Rabau, *In Tel Aviv on the Sands* (Ramat Gan: Masada, 1973), 93 (Hebrew); Anat Helman, *Young Tel Aviv: A Tale of Two Cities* (Waltham, MA: Brandeis University Press, 2010), 78–89; Liora R. Halperin, *Babel in Zion: Jews, Nationalism, and Language Diversity in Palestine, 1920–1948* (New Haven, CT: Yale University Press, 2015), 72–82; Caroline Kahlenberg, "Peddlers and the Policing of National Indifference in Palestine, 1920–1948," *History Workshop Journal* 90 (2020): 115–41.

87. Shlomo Tivʻoni, *My Friend Had a Vineyard: Musa al-Ful* (Tel Aviv: Hakibbutz Hameuchad, 1978), 53–54 (Hebrew); Seri, *A Tree and Its Branches*, 59; Aharon Chelouche, *From Jalabiya to Tembel Hat: The Story of a Family* (Published by the author, 1991), 81–84 (Hebrew); Ron, *Haifa of My Youth*, 48–52; Bezalel, *Life Chapters*, 163–64.

88. Ami Ayalon, *Reading Palestine: Printing and Literacy, 1900–1948* (Austin: University of Texas Press, 2004), 103–6; Bernstein and Hasisi, "'Buy and Promote,'" 131; Maayan Hilel, "Cultural Changes in Palestinian Arab Society, 1918–1948: Haifa as a Case-Study" (PhD diss., Tel Aviv University, 2018), 83, 166–67 (Hebrew); interview with Samira H. Some cafés hosted illicit activities such as prostitution and drug dealing, and some functioned as centers for political organization. Haim Fireberg, "Tel Aviv: Change, Continuity and the Many Faces of Urban Culture and Society during War (1936–1948)" (PhD diss., Tel Aviv University, 2003), 275; Hilel, "Cultural Changes," 87–89, 219.

89. Manar Hasan and Ami Ayalon, "Arabs and Jews, Leisure and Gender, in Haifa's Public Spaces," in *Haifa Before and After 1948*, 73, 87; Manar Hasan, *The Invisible: Women and the Palestinian Cities* (Jerusalem: Van Leer and Hakibbutz Hameuchad, 2017), 97–98 (Hebrew); Hilel, "Cultural Changes," 218–19, 232, 248–56.

90. Tamari, *Mountain against the Sea*, 181.

91. Julia Chelouche, *The Tree and the Roots* (Tel Aviv: Akad, 1982), 9 (Hebrew).

92. An example for such a menu can be found in the digital collection of the National Library of Israel, in an advertisement for the restaurant of Arafat Mohammed al-Turk in Jaffa. The menu contains twenty-one dishes, including kebab, roasted fish, veal tongues, rice, stuffed vegetables, *malouchia* (jute mallow), beans, green ful, okra, and others. It also includes two cakes, soda pop, tea, and coffee. The name of the restaurant is written both in Arabic and in Hebrew, and another sentence in Hebrew invites the customers to come and try, testifying to the restaurant's attempt to attract Jewish customers. Accessed August 23, 2021, https://web.nli.org.il/sites/NLI/Hebrew/digitallibrary/pages/viewer.aspx?presentorid=NNL_Ephemera&DocID=NNL_Ephemera700121635.

93. Liora Gvion, "Cooking, Food, and Masculinity: Palestinian Men in Israeli Society," *Men and Masculinities* 14, no. 4 (2011): 408–29.

94. "Mata'em," *Filastin*, October 28, 1927 (Arabic). On the place of hygiene and sanitation in the making of middle-class culture, see Seikaly, *Men of Capital*, 53–76. On hygiene and culture building in Jewish society, see Hirsch, "'We Are Here to Bring the West, Not Only to Ourselves,'" 577–94.

95. Hasan and Ayalon, "Arabs and Jews," 69–98; Seikaly, *Men of Capital*, 66; Price Control Office, Galilee District Nazareth, April 27, 1946, Statement of the accused, Sami Haj Said H. Sheikh of Safed, ISA, 5220/13-m. See also interview with Samira H.

96. "Palestine Restaurants are Popular," *Palestine Post*, July 5, 1944.

97. Hasan and Ayalon, "Arabs and Jews"; Hilel, "Cultural Changes," 333–35.

98. Ron, *Haifa of My Youth*, 80; Yaacov Davidon, *Haifa That Was . . .* (Tel Aviv: Bitan, 1983), 57–60 (Hebrew).

99. Hilel, "Cultural Changes," 333–34.

100. Hilel, "Cultural Changes," 333–34.

101. Ron, *Haifa of My Youth*, 92; interview with Janet M.

102. Ron, *Haifa of My Youth*, 91–93.

103. Interview with Janet M. The meaning of the saying is "X knows/understands nothing about Y."

104. Martina Rieker, "Modern Histories of Jerusalem's Old City: Culinary Practices and Popular Mapping(s) of Palestinian Social Spaces," in *Pilgrims, Lepers and Stuffed Cabbage: Essays on Jerusalem's Cultural History*, ed. Issam Nassar and Salim Tamari (Jerusalem: Institute of Jerusalem History, 2005), 87.

105. Tamari, *Mountain against the Sea*, 176–89; Klein, *Lives in Common*, 130–35.

106. Gabriel Strassman, "Oriental Restaurants," *Maariv*, July 21, 1955 (Hebrew).

107. Bar-Adon, "Oriental Gourmet."

108. "Cafés, Restaurants and Canteens," 1947 (exact date undecipherable), Haganah Archive, 105/24.

109. Hilel, "Cultural Changes," 287. In Tel Aviv food shops and restaurants represented a larger share of the businesses (49% and 15.4%, respectively) than in the rest of the *Yishuv* (47.1% and 14.1%, respectively). Fireberg, "Tel Aviv," 85.

110. Levine, *Overthrowing Geography*; Fireberg, "Tel Aviv," 30–31. In 1921 Tel Aviv gained the status of a township and in 1934 of an independent city.

111. Fireberg, "Tel Aviv," 6.

112. "A list of cafés and restaurants in Tel Aviv," July 2, 1939, TAHA 1087/2314; Yaacov Shavit and Gideon Biger, *The History of Tel Aviv*, vol. 2 (Tel Aviv: Ramot, 2007), 270 (Hebrew). Shavit and Biger note 254 cafés, bars, and restaurants in 1941 (far short of the number of names listed in the municipal archive dated to 1939) and 422 in 1946. Fireberg, "Tel Aviv," 272. Fireberg notes 254 cafés, bars, and restaurants at the end of 1941 and 422 in the second half of 1946.

113. Fireberg, "Tel Aviv," 2, 26.

114. Bernstein, "Contested Contact"; Klein, *Lives in Common*, 68–70.

115. Hasan and Ayalon, "Arabs and Jews," 75; Tikva Weinstock, "The East Conquers the Stomachs of the West . . .," *Maariv*, August 2, 1951 (Hebrew); Shlomo Ajami, Letter to Tel Aviv Mayor Israel Rokach, November 30, 1942, TAHA 2315/4. See also Klein, *Lives in Common*, 82; Hilel, "Cultural Changes," 176, 334.

116. Bernstein and Hasisi, "'Buy and Promote,'" 45; Bernstein, "Contested Contact," 224.

117. For example, Ron, *Haifa of My Youth*, 89; Kidron, "The Influence," 73–109; Yaacov Shavit and Gideon Biger, *The History of Tel Aviv*, vol. 1 (Tel Aviv: Ramot, 2001), 99 (Hebrew).

118. "A Short While with the Eaters of Kibbe and Players of Backgammon: Atmosphere Pictures from an Oriental Café in the Heart of Tel Aviv," *Special Journal*, July 26, 1946, 5 (Hebrew). See also Helman, *Young Tel Aviv*, 127–28; Bernstein, "Contested Contact."

119. Kidron, "The Influence," 97. See also Haim Gouri, *The Crazy Book* (Tel Aviv: Am Oved, 1971), 89–92 (Hebrew).

120. Fireberg, "Tel Aviv," 43; Klein, *Lives in Common*, 74. For Haifa, see Hasan and Ayalon, "Arabs and Jews"; Hilel, "Cultural Changes," 334.

121. "A Quick Tour in the Streets of Jaffa on Saturday," *Special Journal*, 5, no. 160, March 8, 1940 (Hebrew); "The Joy of Yom Kippur Turned This Year into Mourning for Restaurant Owners in Jaffa," *Special Journal*, 6, no. 241, October 3, 1941, 6 (Hebrew); Israel Goldschmid-Paz, "Jaffa as It Is: People among the Ruins," *Al Hamishmar*, January 2, 1953 (Hebrew); Shimon Tsabar, "In the Eyes of Tsabar: The Lost Yom Kippur," *Haaretz*, September 26, 1958 (Hebrew). Leavened bread is prohibited on Passover, and therefore Jewish-owned stores do not sell it.

122. Hagor (Haim Gouri), "Thirty Years," *Davar*, December 2, 1977 (Hebrew); Strassman, "Oriental Restaurants." See also Amos Kenan, "Uzi and Co.: They Will Soon Announce That I Was Born," *Haaretz*, October 7, 1949 (Hebrew).

123. Phone conversation with Menachem Talmi, December 20, 2009. Various articles mention Arab restaurants in the Carmel market that were popular among Jews. See, for instance, Tsabar, "In the Eyes of Tsabar"; A. K., "The Last Kebab of Ali Sambo . . .," *Maariv*, May 2, 1948 (Hebrew).

124. Yehoshua Zalivansky, *Tel Avi, Tel Aviv* (Tel Aviv: Y. Golan, 1994), 88 (Hebrew). I thank Asaf David for referring me to this text.

125. Lilian Cornfeld, "Seaside Temptations: Juveniles' Fare at Tel Aviv," *Palestine Post*, October 19, 1939.

126. Head of the Licenses Department to the Municipal Secretary, Mr. Yehuda Nedivi, July 29, 1941, 4/355a (Hebrew); The Municipal Inspection Department to the Tel Aviv Mayor, November 28, 1944, TAHA 4/358b. The Tel Aviv municipality granted vending licenses as a form of welfare.

127. Many of the immigrants from Yemen arrived in Palestine via Egypt and may have learned to prepare it there and then adjusted the recipe to the Palestinian version, made from chickpeas rather than from fava beans. Ari Ariel, "Foodways and the Ethnicization of Yemeni Identity in Israel," *Mashriq & Mahjar: Journal of Middle East and North African Migration* 6, no. 2 (2019): 135. See also the story of Shmuel Yefet's father: https://www.youtube.com/watch?v=nzihYViJFQM, 29.1.2017, accessed May 13, 2019.

128. I have gathered several testimonies from the early 1950s about Mizrahi restaurant owners who learned to prepare hummus from Arab neighbors, acquaintances, or cooks.

129. S. E. Sadow to Dr. Zagoretzky, January 30, 1927, CZA J113/78; Helman, *Young Tel Aviv*, 121.

130. Helman, *Young Tel Aviv*, 121; Alma Igra, "Meatropolis: Tel Aviv's Slaughterhouse and Demarcation of Urban-National Boundaries in Palestine, 1927–1938" (MA thesis, Central European University, 2012), 48–50.

131. Weinstock, "The East Conquers the Stomachs"; Kidron, "The Influence," 73–109. Fireberg, "Tel Aviv," 78. According to Fireberg, the Jewish businesses in Jaffa that were harmed during the revolt included twenty-five "drink dealers and restaurant owners."

132. Fireberg, "Tel Aviv," 89, 194. The help was received from a local Zionist fund that was established in the wake of the revolt for social and security purposes (144–45).

133. Bernstein, "Contested Contact"; Razi, "'Arab-Jewesses?'" See also Shavit and Biger, *History of Tel Aviv*, vol. 2, 238.

134. "An Expensive Cheap Love," *Special Journal* 3, no. 126 (1939): 4 (Hebrew).

135. Boaz Lev Tov, "'The Same Sea': Jews and Palestinians at the Beach in the Late Ottoman and Mandate Periods," in *Entangled Histories in Palestine/Israel*, 48–72; Bernstein, "Contested Contact."

136. Bar-Adon, "Oriental Gourmet."

137. For example, tenants of the Levine House to Mayor Rokach, May 30, 1945, TAHA, 4/357c (Hebrew); A longtime resident of Tel Aviv to the Mayor, December 10, 1945, TAHA 4/359a (Hebrew).

138. Hirsch, "'We are Here to Bring the West.'"

139. Itzhak Banay, "Locked Gates," in *Compilation Marking the Twentieth Anniversary of the Health Associations in Jerusalem*, ed. Puah Menczel Ben-Tovim and Bezalel Bazrawi (Jerusalem: Hadassah, 1947), 58 (Hebrew).

140. David Shacham, *Requiem to Tel Aviv* (Tel Aviv: Sifriyat Hapo'alim, 2010), 55 (Hebrew).

141. Gabriel G. Yaacov, in the name of the organization of falafel vendors to the Tel Aviv mayor, December 18, 1944, TAHA 4/357b (Hebrew); Alperin, internal memo to the municipal secretary, January 29, 1945, TAHA 4/357c (Hebrew); E. Rosenbaum, director of the Department of Education to Haim Alperin, director of the Municipal Inspection Department, no date, TAHA 4/357b (Hebrew); "Strong Accusations by Falafel Vendors," *Special Journal* 9, no. 401 (1944): 3 (Hebrew).

142. Krishnendu Ray describes a similar attraction among Hindu young men to the forbidden meats of the Muslims. Ray, "Culinary Difference."

143. Itamar Ben-Avi, "Falafela'ot," *Doar Hayom*, July 30, 1929 (Hebrew). Ben-Avi used the word *mefulpal* for spicy, which is a play on words: the word comes from the same root as falafel and means "peppered."

144. The Editorial Council, "Our Program," *Doar Hayom*, August 8, 1919 (Hebrew). An avid Jewish nationalist, Ben-Avi was a supporter of Arab-Jewish cooperation in the framework of a federation of independent national cantons. Yosef Nedava, "Preface," in Itamar Ben-Avi, *Dreams and Wars* (Jerusalem: The Public Committee for the Publishing of the Writings of Itamar Ben-Avi, 1978), 10–12 (Hebrew); Aharon Even-Chen, "The Dream of Hebrew Dominion," *Maariv*, September 19, 1975 (Hebrew).

145. Strassman, "Oriental Restaurants."

146. Interview with Yehuda Litani, Jerusalem, March 16, 2010.

147. This poem was published in a 1998 collection of Gouri's poems without an exact date, noting only that the poem was written before his 1949 book *Fire Flowers*. The last two lines of the poem allude to the possibility of destruction, so it seems likely that it was written during the war. Haim Gouri, *The Poems*, vol. 1 (Jerusalem: Bialik Institute, 1998), 20 (Hebrew).

148. Citation from Haim Gouri, "From the Sack: Two Cities," *Lamerchav*, July 6, 1956 (Hebrew).

149. Gouri, *The Crazy Book*.

150. On Hadassah, see Erica B. Simmons, *Hadassah and the Zionist Project* (Oxford: Rowman and Littlefield, 2006); Hirsch, "'We Are Here to Bring the West.'" On WIZO, see Ofra Grinberg and Hanna Herzog, *A Voluntary Women's Organization in an Emerging Society: WIZO's Contribution to the Israeli Society* (Tel Aviv: The Institute for Social Research, Tel Aviv University, 1978) (Hebrew).

151. Hadassah launched its nutrition initiatives in 1923, with the School Luncheon Program, a network of school-based restaurants that provided meals

to needy children while promoting nutrition education and table manners. A similar, smaller-scale program was introduced in Arab schools only in the early 1940s. Hadassah also engaged in public education through its Nutrition Department. See Sarah Bavly, "Proposal for a Hadassah Nutrition Center under the Israeli Government," August 16, 1948, Hadassah Archives at the Center for Jewish History, New York (HANY), RG5/13; Henrietta Szold, "Preface to the Second Edition," in Sarah Bavly, *Our Nutrition: Chapters in the Theory of Nutrition and of Foods* (Jerusalem: Ever, 1951), iii–vii (Hebrew); Vickers, *Nutritional Economic Survey*, 1; Raviv, *Falafel Nation*, 69–70. On similar luncheon programs in other places, see James Vernon, *Hunger: A Modern History* (Cambridge, MA: Harvard University Press, 2007), 161–64; Andrew R. Ruis, *Eating to Learn, Learning to Eat* (New Brunswick, NJ: Rutgers University Press, 2017). WIZO had been active in nutrition since 1927, offering education and cooking courses in urban and rural areas. Its initiatives included home visits to provide personalized cooking guidance. Tsiona Katinsky-Rabau, "WIZO's Instruction Work in Rational Nutrition," *Hamazon* 2, no. 3 (1939): 19–20 (Hebrew); Raviv, *Falafel Nation*, 86–118. Both organizations also published educational material in domestic science and cooking.

152. Yosef Me'ir, "The Theory of Nutrition," in *Medicine and the Public: A Collection of Articles*, ed. M. Tamari (Tel Aviv: Kupat Holim Center, 1955), 163 (Hebrew). See also Helman, "European Jews in the Levant Heat," 76.

153. Akiva Ettinger, "With the Exhibition on the *Yishuv*'s Nutrition," *Davar*, July 19, 1939 (Hebrew).

154. Israel Jacob Kligler, Alexander Geiger, Sarah Bromberg, and David Gurevitch, "An Inquiry Into the Diets of Various Sections of the Urban and Rural Population of Palestine," *Bulletin of the Palestine Economic Society* 5, no. 3 (1931): 5. On the early nutritional studies in Palestine, see Yechiel Guggenheim et al., "The Beginning of Nutritional Studies in Eretz Israel," *Cathedra* 59 (1991): 144–60 (Hebrew).

155. Kligler et al., "An Inquiry," 5; see also Mordechai Brachya/Borochov, *Hygiene: A General Part* (Warsaw: Levin Epstein, 1925), 92 (Hebrew); Mary Swartz Rose, "Racial Food Habits in Relation to Health," *Scientific Monthly* 44, no. 3 (1937): 257–67. Swartz Rose was a teacher at Columbia's Teachers College, where two of the leading Jewish nutritionists in Palestine had studied.

156. Kligler et al., "An inquiry," 5.

157. Kligler et al., "An inquiry," 6.

158. Hamilton Cravens, "The German-American Science of Racial Nutrition, 1870–1920," in *Technical Knowledge in American Culture: Science, Technology, and Medicine since the Early 1800s*, ed. Hamilton Cravens, Alan I. Marcus, and David M. Katzman (Tuscaloosa: University of Alabama Press, 1996), 130; Gyorgy Scrinis, *Nutritionism: The Science and Politics of Dietary Advice* (New York: Columbia University Press, 2013), 51–71.

159. Harvey Levenstein, *Revolution at the Table: The Transformation of the American Diet* (Berkeley: University of California Press, 2003), 147–60; Scrinis, *Nutritionism*, 66.

160. Harmke Kamminga, "'Axes to Grind': Popularizing the Science of Vitamins, 1920s and 1930s," in *Food, Science, Policy and Regulation in the Twentieth Century: International and Comparative Perspectives*, ed. David F. Smith and Jim Phillips (London: Routledge, 2000), 92; Nick Cullather, "The Foreign Policy of the Calorie," *American Historical Review* 112 (2007): 338; Vernon, *Hunger*, 89.

161. Cullather, "The Foreign Policy of the Calorie," 338, 345–46.

162. Vernon, *Hunger*, 106–7.

163. On the study of race and nutrition, see Michael Worboys, "The Discovery of Colonial Malnutrition between the Wars," in *Imperial Medicine and Indigenous Societies*, ed. David Arnold (Manchester: Manchester University Press, 1988), 208–25; Cravens, "The German-American Science," 125–45; Cynthia Brantley, "Kikuyu-Maasai Nutrition and Colonial Science: The Orr and Gilks Study in Late 1920s Kenya Revisited," *International Journal of African Historical Studies* 30, no. 1 (1997): 49–86. Cullather, "The Foreign Policy of the Calorie," 354–55, 359; Vernon, *Hunger*, 104–16.

164. For a similar approach toward Chinese food in the US in this period, see Weishaupt, "Cook at Home in Chinese," 49–51. See also Gabaccia, *We Are What We Eat*, 93–121; Ray, *The Ethnic Restauranteur*, 76.

165. Kligler et al., "An inquiry," 11.

166. Kligler et al., "An inquiry," 9. According to David Arnold, in the nineteenth century, East India surgeons noted that Europeans in India had something to learn from Indian dietary habits, but by the end of the century this attitude had all but disappeared. David Arnold, "The 'Discovery' of Malnutrition and Diet in Colonial India," *Indian Economic & Social History Review* 31, no. 1 (1994): 3, 11–12. See also Vernon, *Hunger*, 108.

167. Brachya/Borochov, *Hygiene*, 126; Yaʿacov Zass, *The Hygiene of the Body and the Mind* (Jerusalem: Hygiena Modernit, 1929), 58 (Hebrew).

168. Bromberg, "The Question of Purposeful Nutrition."

169. See, for example, From the Laboratory of Moshe Wilbushewich, Haifa, "Guide to the Household: On Oil," *Davar*, April 9, 1930 (Hebrew); "WIZO Housekeeping Institute—Recipes for the New Year," *Palestine Post*, January 1, 1938.

170. Dr. Erna Meyer, *How to Cook in Eretz Israel* (Tel Aviv: WIZO, 1936), 8 (Hebrew).

171. Josep L. Barona, "Nutrition and Health: The International Context during the Inter-War Crisis," *Social History of Medicine* 21, no. 1 (2008): 88; Vernon, *Hunger*, 104–17; Alma Igra, "Farm to Pharmacy: Nutrition, Animals and Governance in Britain, 1870–1945" (PhD diss., Columbia University, 2020); Hadassah's part

in social-service work in Palestine: Survey of the work of the Hadassah Nutrition Department during the 1936–46 period, HANY, RG5/13.

172. The committee included physicians; experts on hygiene, nutrition, economy, and agriculture; and representatives of the different institutions. Israel Kligler, "Our Goal," *Hamazon* 1, no. 1 (1938): 1 (Hebrew); "The Nutrition Committee at this Time," *Hamazon* 2, no. 4 (1939): 1–2 (Hebrew).

173. Fireberg, "Tel Aviv," 9; Ben-Shachar, "On Calories, Proteins and Posture," 33–36.

174. Roberto Bachi, Sarah Bavly, and S. V. Berman, *Inquiry into Poverty and Malnutrition among the Jews of Jerusalem* (Jerusalem: Hadassah Emergency Committee, 1943), 7; Raviv, *Falafel Nation*, 220–21; Seikaly, *Men of Capital*, 104.

175. Vickers, *Nutritional Economic Survey*, 44. By May 1941, food prices were already 32 percent over the level of the prewar years. S. Bromberg to A. Duskin, Chairman, Child Welfare Committee, Hadassah, New York, April 30, 1942, HANY, RG5/15.

176. Seikaly, *Men of Capital*, 90–97; Guy Seidman, "Unexceptional for Once: Austerity and Food Rationing in Israel, 1939–1959," *Southern California Interdisciplinary Law Journal* 18 (2008): 117–19; Nimrod Hagiladi, "The Israeli Society and the Black Market from WWII to the Early 1950s" (PhD diss., Hebrew University of Jerusalem, 2011), 33–57. (Hebrew)

177. "Hadassah's Part in Social-Service Work in Palestine: Survey of the Work of the Hadassah Nutrition Department during the 1936–1946 Period," HANY, RG5/13; "Instruction of the Public in Feeding in Times of Emergency," *Davar*, June 9, 1940 (Hebrew); "The Cooking Exhibition," *Haaretz*, June 28, 1940 (Hebrew); Raviv, *Falafel Nation*, 130–40. Some of these activities were funded by the British Food Controller, who aimed to promote government-purchased foods like egg and milk powder. However, Zionist nutrition education infrastructure surpassed that of the British government in both resources and expertise. Raviv, *Falafel Nation*, 139–40; Sherene Seikaly, "Bodies and Needs: Lessons from Palestine," *International Journal of Middle East Studies* 46 (2014): 786.

178. For example, The Nutrition Committee, "Minimum Food for the Yishuv," *Davar*, June 23, 1940 (Hebrew); "Nutrition in Times of War," *Davar*, August 8, 1940 (Hebrew). During the war years, Jewish agricultural cultivation expanded significantly, and production output increased. The area of legume cultivation also increased, by 2,125 acres. Yoav Gelber, "The Consolidation of Jewish Society in Eretz-Israel, 1936–1947," in *The History of the Jewish Community in Eretz-Israel Since 1882: The Period of the British Mandate, Part Two*, ed. Moshe Lissak, Anita Shapira, and Gavriel Cohen (Jerusalem: Israeli Academy for Sciences and Humanities and Bialik Institute, 2001), 406–407 (Hebrew); H. Halperin, "The Production of Food Ingredients in the Country During the War," *Bulletin of the Central Nutrition Committee*, December 1941, CZA A211/157 (Hebrew). Nevertheless,

in 1947 Jewish farms provided only 50 percent of Jewish food consumption; 43 percent came from imports and 7 percent from Arab farms. Hagiladi, "The Israeli Society," 152–53.

179. Dr. Erna Meyer, "For the Housewife," *Haaretz*, November 2, 1942 (Hebrew).

180. Lilian Cornfeld, "We Learn from Our Neighbors," *Palestine Post*, November 12, 1939; Cornfeld, "The Foods of the Oriental Communities," *Hamazon* 2, no. 4 (1939): 12 (Hebrew); Cornfeld, "Our Nutrition in Times of Emergency," *Hamazon* 2, no. 4 (1939): 13–14 (Hebrew); Akiva Ettinger, "With the Exhibition on the Nutrition of the *Yishuv*," *Davar*, July 19, 1939 (Hebrew); "Nutrition in Times of War"; WIZO, "Cheap and Nourishing in Times of Emergency," *Davar*, November 29, 1940 (Hebrew).

181. "Nutrition in Times of War."

182. Cornfeld arrived in Palestine in 1922, age twenty, with the Young Judea youth movement, affiliated with Hadassah. In 1928 she traveled to New York to study nutrition at Columbia. Before she returned to Palestine in 1933, she taught as a part-time lecturer on nutrition there. Giveon Cornfield, *Lilian: Israel's First Lady of Cuisine* (New York: Xlibris, 2012).

183. Cornfeld, "We Learn from Our Neighbors."

184. Cornfeld, "The Foods of the Oriental Communities."

185. An earlier reference to hummus, although not by name, appears in a column published by WIZO in *Palestine Post* in 1938: "'Tchina' is a very healthful and nourishing fat containing 25 per cent protein, while other fats contain practically no protein. It is also very cheap, being about 9 mils the okia. To be properly made, 'Tchina' has to be whipped or stirred for at least one quarter of an hour. It is sometimes combined with a puree of cooked dried peas. It is also poured over a vegetable salad or over cooked eggplant. But it is most popular when served by itself or as a salad with meat." WIZO Housekeeping Institute, "Recipes for the New Year," *Palestine Post*, January 11, 1938. An even earlier reference appeared in the German *Jüdische Rundschau* in 1934 as "Pea Salad" (Erbsensalat), albeit without tahini: B. G., "Koche palästinensisch!" *Jüdische Rundschau* 13 (1934): 6. I thank Viola Rautenberg for sending me this piece.

186. S. Bavly, "Report on the Nutrition Department of the Nathan and Lina Straus Health Centre of Hadassah, Jerusalem," January–December 1945, CZA A520/6; Erna Meyer, "For the Woman and the Home: Kitchen without Meat," *Haaretz*, August 26, 1947 (Hebrew); Shulamit, "Our Nutritional Situation at this Time," *Haaretz*, December 30, 1947 (Hebrew); Hagiladi, "The Israeli Society," 149.

187. Shulamit, "Our Nutritional Situation at this Time."

188. Dr. Sarah Bavly, "An Investigation Into the Nutrition and the Nutritional Levels of the Urban Hebrew Population in Eretz Israel," in *Standard of Living*

and Nutritional Problems in the Urban Hebrew Yishuv, ed. Gershon Zidrovich and Sarah Bavly (Jerusalem: Institute for Economic Research, The Jewish Agency, 1947), 37 (Hebrew); Sarah Bergner-Rabinovich, *Hygiene, Education and Nutrition among Kurdish and Persian Jews in Jerusalem, Compared to Ashkenazim* (Jerusalem: The Eretz Israeli Institute for Folklore and Ethnology, 1948), 30 (Hebrew); Vickers, *Nutritional Economic Survey*, 29; Schedule III (4)/Jewish Families/Average per Unit per Day in Grammes, August 1942, ISA 5117/ 1-m.

189. Sarah Bavly, *Food Habits and Their Changes in Israel* (Jerusalem: Ministry of Education and Culture, 1964).

190. Bavly, *Food Habits and Their Changes*; Agronomist Akiva Ettinger, "What Are the Products That Our Agriculture Provides the Women?" probably 1940, CZA A111/25 (Hebrew); Helman, "European Jews in the Levant Heat," 77; Ofra Tene, *The White Houses will be Filled* (Tel Aviv: Hakibbutz Hameuchad, 2013), 195 (Hebrew). For a similar tendency to adopt foods that were associated with higher social strata among Jewish and Bengali migrants to the US, respectively, see Hasia R. Diner, *Hungering for America: Italian, Irish, and Jewish Foodways in the Age of Migration* (Cambridge, MA: Harvard University Press, 2003), 179–80; Ray, *The Migrant's Table*, 96.

191. Ettinger, "What Are the Products"; Bavly, "Investigation of Nutrition," 36; Tene, *The White Houses*, 196–97.

192. Helman, "European Jews in the Levant Heat," 78; Tene, *The White Houses*, 195–96.

193. Helman, "European Jews in the Levant Heat," 77.

194. Stuffed vegetables were also offered, although these were prevalent beyond the Arab world and could be tempered through spices. Benny Cohen, *From "Carlton" to "Tnuva": Memories and Impressions from Early Restaurants in Tel Aviv* (Kibbutz Dalia: Ma'arechet, 2010), 56. In her 1962 *Israeli Cookery*, Lilian Cornfeld presents a "typical menu" of a cooperative restaurant in Tel Aviv, which was established in 1927 to provide affordable meals to workers. The only two dishes on the menu that were clearly Middle Eastern were tahini and shashlik. Cornfeld, *Israeli Cookery* (Westport, CT: Avi Publishing, 1962), 87.

195. "Is It Really as They Say?," *Davar*, May 17, 1937 (Hebrew). Until that point, pita bread could be bought in the Carmel market, probably baked and sold by Arabs. The article does not mention who were the prospected customers for that pita bread.

196. "Nutrition Cycles: Arab Food," December 5, 1944, HANY, RG5/13. The recipe provided did not contain tahini.

2. "THE EAST CONQUERS THE STOMACHS OF THE WEST"

1. Abu Ghosh was the only Palestinian village in the Jerusalem corridor that collaborated with the Jewish forces. Nevertheless, the Israeli army encouraged

the residents to flee during the war, promising resettlement, which it later prevented, forcibly deporting anyone found on village lands. Eventually an agreement was reached, and the inhabitants of Abu Ghosh were allowed to return to their diminished village. Rebecca Stein, *Itineraries in Conflict: Israelis, Palestinians, and the Political Lives of Tourism* (Durham, NC: Duke University Press, 2008), 101.

2. Yehuda Litani and Na'im 'Araidi, *Not by Hummus Alone: Hummus, Olive Oil, References* (Tel Aviv: D. Dinur and Modan, 2000), 11 (Hebrew).

3. Hasan, *The Invisible*; Itamar Radai, *Palestinians in Jerusalem and Jaffa, 1948: A Tale of Two Cities* (London: Routledge, 2016).

4. Shira Robinson, *Citizen Strangers: Palestinians and the Birth of Israel's Liberal Settler State* (Stanford, CA: Stanford University Press, 2016), 30.

5. Walid Khalidi, *All That Remains: The Palestinian Villages Occupied and Depopulated by Israel in 1948* (Washington, DC: Institution for Palestine Studies, 1992), xxxii.

6. Robinson, *Citizen Strangers*; Leena Dallasheh, "Persevering through Colonial Transition: Nazareth's Palestinian Residents after 1948," *Journal of Palestine Studies* 45, no. 2 (2016): 8.

7. Orit Bashkin, *Impossible Exodus: Iraqi Jews in Israel* (Stanford, CA: Stanford University Press, 2017), 22.

8. Yoav Gelber, "The Consolidation of Jewish Society in Eretz-Israel, 1936–1947," in *The History of the Jewish Community in Eretz-Israel Since 1882: The Period of the British Mandate, Part Two*, ed. Moshe Lissak, Anita Shapira, and Gavriel Cohen (Jerusalem: Israeli Academy for Sciences and Humanities and Bialik Institute, 2001), 304 (Hebrew); Moshe Lissak, "Immigration, Absorption and Society Building in the Jewish Community in Eretz-Israel (1918–1930)," *The History of the Jewish Community in Eretz-Israel Since 1882*, 192 (Hebrew); Sergio DellaPergola, "The Population of Israel in the Third Decade: Trends and Contexts," in *Iyunim Bitkumat Israel: Israel 1967–1977: Continuity and Change* (theme series, vol. 11), ed. Ofer Shiff and Aviva Halamish (Sde Boker: The Ben-Gurion Research Institute for the Study of Israel and Zionism, 2017), 204 (Hebrew).

9. Moshe Lissak, *The Mass Immigration in the Fifties: The Failure of the Melting Pot Policy* (Jerusalem: Bialik Institute, 1999), 9 (Hebrew); Tzur, "The Immigration from Muslim Countries," 61.

10. Mintz, *Sweetness and Power*.

11. Tom Segev, *1949—The First Israelis* (Tel Aviv: Domino Keter, 1984), 281–82 (Hebrew); Seidman, "Unexceptional for Once," 95–130; Orit Rozin, "Craving Meat during Israel's Austerity Period, 1947–1953," in *Jews and Their Foodways*, 65–88; Rozin, *The Rise of the Individual in 1950s Israel: A Challenge to Collectivism* (Waltham, MA: Brandeis University Press, 2011); Anat Helman, *Becoming Israeli: National Ideals and Everyday Life in the 1950s* (Waltham, MA: Brandeis University Press, 2014). The rationing policy was part of the emergency measures that the

Jewish leadership declared already before the war and that placed all economic activity under centralized control. They continued the British emergency measures of WWII. Rozin, "Craving Meat," 65. Similar statist policies were embraced by many postwar European countries. Helman, *Becoming Israeli*, 47.

12. Mordechai Naor, "The Austerity," in *Immigrants and Ma'barot, 1948–1952*, ed. Mordechai Naor (Jerusalem: Yad Izhak Ben-Zvi, 1986), 98 (Hebrew); Dov Gnichovsky, "The Austerity Regime—Economic Aspects," in *Immigrants and Ma'barot 1948–1952*, 111–14 (Hebrew).

13. Rozin, "Craving Meat," 67.

14. Some products were available in limited amounts but did not require coupons.

15. Rozin, "Craving Meat," 73.

16. Albala, *Beans*, 2.

17. In comparison, the weekly ration of meat in summer 1949 was 200 grams, but during some weeks only 125 grams were supplied. "Distribution of Portions in June in Tel Aviv and the District," *Al Hamishmar*, June 11, 1950 (Hebrew); "Portions in Jerusalem," *Al Hamishmar*, May 16, 1951 (Hebrew); Rozin, "Craving Meat," 72.

18. Lilian Cornfeld, "A Woman to Her Mate: What's in the Market," *Maariv*, July 12, 1948 (Hebrew).

19. Avner Yaron, "Sulha in Jaffa—A Modest Version, without Meat and without Rice," *Maariv*, October 7, 1949 (Hebrew). See also Dahn Ben-Amotz, "What's Up: Lunch," *Davar*, June 12, 1953 (Hebrew). On falafel as meat substitute, see "The Bitter Falafel," *Ha'olam Haze*, December 24, 1958 (Hebrew).

20. According to the nutrition plan of 1949, the monthly ration of legumes was 600 grams per person, but actual consumption was only 285 grams. "List of Consumption (Marketing) in November 1950 (Compared to the Nutrition Plan)," Israel State Archive (ISA), 4147/13-c (Hebrew). In 1952, for instance, the total yearly provision of legumes came from import. "The Actual Consumption of Food in 1952 Compared to the Importation Plans, 1952–3 and 1953–4," ISA 4147/13-c (Hebrew).

21. Hila Baharad, "'Low-Temperature Melting Pot': Language, Religion, Education and Inter-Ethnic Relations in the Israeli Transit Camps" (PhD diss., Hebrew University of Jerusalem, 2019), 35–38 (Hebrew). At the peak, in early 1952, there were 194 transitional camps across the country. By the end of the decade most were dismantled, but some continued to exist for decades: the last ones were officially dismantled only in the 1990s (37–38).

22. Segev, *The First Israelis*, 129; Rozin, *The Rise of the Individual*, 158; Gadi Algazi, "The First Act in the Struggle of the *Ma'barot*, 1951–1952: Contestation amid Subjection," in *Entangled Histories*, 152–88; "Immigrants in Rosh Ha'ayin Went on a Hunger Strike," *Al Hamishmar*, May 29, 1950 (Hebrew). According to

this report, twenty camp employees were arrested after having been caught with stolen foodstuffs in their bags.

23. Bryan K. Roby, *The Mizrahi Era of Rebellion: Israel's Forgotten Civil Rights Struggle 1948–1966* (Syracuse, NY: Syracuse University Press, 2015), 113; Bashkin, *Impossible Exodus*, 167.

24. Rozin, *The Rise of the Individual*, 158; Esther Meir-Glitzenstein, "Longing for the Aromas of Baghdad: Food, Emigration and Transformation in the Lives of Iraqi Jews in Israel in the 1950s," in *Jews and Their Foodways*, 97; Bashkin, *Impossible Exodus*, 31. According to Cornfeld, some of the camps had two different menus—one for Ashkenazim and one for Mizrahim—but the only difference between them was in the seasoning. Lilian Cornfeld, "One Cuisine to the Ingathering of the Exiles," *Haaretz*, October 31, 1950 (Hebrew).

25. Yediot Ahronot Service, "Distribution of Foods—According to Ethnic Groups," *Yediot Ahronot*, May 24, 1950 (Hebrew); "A New Method in the Rationing of Food," *Maariv*, May 23, 1950 (Hebrew); Lilian Cornfeld, "Food and Nutrition in the Rationing Regime," *Haaretz*, June 3, 1952 (Hebrew).

26. Sabri Jiryis, *The Arabs in Israel*, trans. Inea Bushnaq (New York: Monthly Review Press, 1976), 80–101; Alexandre (Sandy) Kedar and Oren Yiftachel, "Land Regime and Social Relations in Israel," in *Realizing Property Rights: Swiss Human Rights Book*, ed. Hernando de Soto and Francis Cheneval, 1 (2006): 127–44.

27. In the years of acute food shortages, Palestinian landowners were forced to sell their produce to Jewish marketing concerns at prices that were much lower than those paid to Jewish farmers. Ian Lustick, *Arabs in the Jewish State: Israel's Control of a National Minority* (Austin: University of Texas Press, 1980), 60; Liora Gvion, *Beyond Hummus and Falafel: Social and Political Aspects of Palestinian Food in Israel*, trans. David Wesley and Elana Wesley (Berkeley: University of California Press, 2012); Robinson, *Citizen Strangers*, 30; Gadi Algazi, "Colonial Profits in the Shadow of Military Rule," in *Colonization and Resistance in Israel/Palestine*, ed. Lev Luis Grinberg and Daniel DeMalach (Jerusalem: Van Leer and Hakibbutz Hameuchad, 2023), 164–207 (Hebrew).

28. Robinson, *Citizen Strangers*, 59; Benny Nurieli, "Accumulation and Surveillance: The Military Rule in Lydda, July 1948–July 1949," in *Entangled Histories in Palestine/Israel*, 133–51. Internal refugees are Palestinian refugees who remained under Israeli rule. They received Israeli citizenship but were not allowed to return to their homes and lands. According to Hillel Cohen, twenty thousand Palestinians became internal refugees. Hillel Cohen, *Good Arabs: The Israeli Security Agencies and the Israeli Arabs, 1948–1967*, trans. Haim Watzman (Berkeley: University of California Press, 2010), 96. Lustick gives a higher estimate. Lustick, *Arabs in the Jewish State*, 47, 60.

29. Robinson, *Citizen Strangers*, 75. Only 40 percent of the 160,000 Palestinians who remained under Israeli rule were granted citizenship immediately. For

the remaining 100,000, the process could last up to several years. Yair Bäuml, "The Principles of the Discrimination Policy towards Arabs in Israel, 1948–1968," *Iyunim Bitkumat Israel* 16 (2006): 16 (Hebrew).

30. Robinson, *Citizen Strangers*, 88. Until 1954 food was given to the head of each tribe, and he distributed it among his people. A. Halevy, director of the food unit, to the head of the minority division in the Ministry of Interior, February 22, 1955, ISA 4146/21-c (Hebrew).

31. Lustick, *Arabs in the Jewish State*, 60; Robinson, *Citizen Strangers*, 51, 213 fn. 62; "A Delegation of Arab Villages Demands the Cancellation of Discriminations," *Haaretz*, March 27, 1952 (Hebrew); Deputy director of the food branch, south district, to the management of the food division, Jerusalem, "The supply to Arabs and Bedouins," April 20, 1952, ISA 4146/20-c (Hebrew). The folder contains many letters of complaint in Arabic about the insufficient food rations.

32. Segev, *The First Israelis*, 65; Protocol of the Meeting with the Representative of the Food Controller, January 20, 1949, IDF archive, 94-1255-1953 (Hebrew).

33. Robinson, *Citizen Strangers*, 93–95.

34. Rozin, "Food, Identity, and Nation-Building," 58, 61–64; Rozin, *The Rise of the Individual*, 160, 169.

35. Naor, "The Austerity," 105; Rozin, "Food, Identity, and Nation-Building," 58; Rozin, *The Rise of the Individual*, 26–28; Hagiladi, "Israeli Society."

36. Segev, *The First Israelis*, 299; Algazi, "The First Act in the Struggle of the Ma'barot."

37. Segev, *The First Israelis*, 212.

38. Avi Picard, *Cut to Measure: Israel's Policies Regarding the Aliyah of North African Jews, 1951–1956* (Sde Boker: The Ben-Gurion Research Institute for the Study of Israel and Zionism, 2013) (Hebrew).

39. All austerity measures were revoked by 1959. Seidman, "Unexceptional for Once," 129.

40. Its main sources were the American Foreign Aid, the bonds issued by the Israeli government to American Jewry, and, since September 1952, the reparations from Germany. Segev, *The First Israelis*, 300–303; Nachum Gross, "Israel's Economy," in *The First Decade: 1948–1958*, ed. Zvi Zameret and Hannah Jablonka (Jerusalem: Yad Izhak Ben-Zvi, 1997), 142 (Hebrew).

41. Arnon Golan, "Settlement in the First Decade of the Israeli State," in *The First Decade*, 93 (Hebrew).

42. Dan Giladi, "From Austerity to Economic Growth," in *Israel in the First Decade, section 5* (Ramat Aviv: Open University of Israel, 2002), 42 (Hebrew); Golan, "Settlement in the First Decade," 94; Nachum Gross, "Israel's Economy, 1954–1967," in *The Second Decade: 1958–1968*, ed. Zvi Zameret and Hannah Jablonka (Jerusalem: Yad Izhak Ben-Zvi, 2000), 32–33 (Hebrew). In 1955, 17.5

percent of the workforce was employed in agriculture, compared to 14 percent in the beginning of the decade—itself a high percentage compared to most modern countries at the time, where the agricultural sector only shrank. Amir Ben-Porat, *How Israel Became a Capitalist Society* (Haifa: Pardes, 2011), 161–62 (Hebrew).

43. Picard, *Cut to Measure.*

44. Smadar Sharon, *"And Thus a Homeland Is Conquered": Planning and Settlement in 1950s Lakhish Region* (Haifa: Pardes, 2017) (Hebrew).

45. Kedar and Yiftachel, "Land Regime and Social Relations in Israel," 135–37.

46. At the end of the decade, 20 percent of the development budget was directed to the industry. Giladi, "From Austerity to Economic Growth," 74. On Mizrahim providing cheap labor power to the industry, see Deborah Bernstein and Shlomo Swirski, "The Rapid Economic Development of Israel and the Emergence of the Ethnic Division of Labour," *British Journal of Sociology* 33, no. 1 (1982): 64–85.

47. Giladi, "From Austerity to Economic Growth," 74. According to the daily *Herut*, in the Mandate period production of tahini was entirely in Arab hands whereas by 1949 there were nine tahini factories, only one of which was Arab owned. "Plans for New Factories," *Herut*, February 3, 1949 (Hebrew). See also Our Economic Correspondent, "The 'Tahini' Industry—A New Hebrew Industry," *Herut*, February 7, 1949 (Hebrew); Yosef Kna'an, "The Food Industry in the Country's Economy," *Davar*, August 25, 1954 (Hebrew).

48. Bernstein and Swirski, "Rapid Economic Development of Israel"; Michael Shalev, *Labour and the Political Economy in Israel* (Oxford: Oxford University Press, 1992), 207–08.

49. Ruth Bondi, "It Will Be Good," *Davar*, January 27, 1956 (Hebrew). In Hebrew, the Arabic phrase ʿala kaifak, literally meaning "however you want," came to mean "good," "very good," or "terrific."

50. Lilian Cornfeld, "The Austerity Menu and Its Problems," *Haaretz*, May 17, 1949 (Hebrew); Shulamit, "For the Woman and the Home: From Week to Week," *Haaretz*, May 24, 1949 (Hebrew); Economic Correspondent, "The Restaurant—A Thermometer for 'Pennies,'" *Davar*, January 19, 1953 (Hebrew).

51. Shavit and Biger, *The History of Tel Aviv*, vol. 2, 21-22; Shulamit Levari, "In Tel Aviv's Restaurants: Filth and Rotten Food," *Haaretz*, August 6, 1951 (Hebrew).

52. "The Supply for Restaurants Decreases," *Maariv*, January 18, 1950 (Hebrew); Cornfeld, "The Austerity Menu and Its Problems"; Shulamit, "For the Woman and the Home"; Levari, "In Tel Aviv's Restaurants."

53. "Ordinance Concerning the Prices of Meals and Dishes," *Davar*, July 25, 1949 (Hebrew); "Permission for Serving Dishes in Guesthouses," *Davar*, October 28, 1949 (Hebrew). Among the dishes were hummus, tahini, and falafel. In November 1949, the controller stipulated the maximum price of a falafel portion: twenty-five mils for half a pita, forty grams of fried falafel balls, vegetable salad,

and tahini. "Falafel—Price-Controllable," *Maariv*, November 23, 1949 (Hebrew). Restaurants were subject to control until November 1953, but cheaper restaurants were still obliged to serve a standard meal at an affordable price. The Morning Journalist, "Supervision of Restaurants Was Cancelled," *Haboker*, November 25, 1953 (Hebrew).

54. Anat Helman, *Consumer Culture and Leisure in the Young State of Israel* (Jerusalem: Zalman Shazar Center, 2020), 161 (Hebrew).

55. Weinstock, "The East Conquers the Stomachs"; Levari, "In Tel Aviv's Restaurants."

56. Rozin, "Craving Meat."

57. On the ambivalence of "hospitality" in the context of a relationship of domination, see Smadar Lavie, *The Poetics of Military Occupation* (Berkeley: University of California Press, 1990), 287–88; Dan Rabinowitz, *Overlooking Nazareth: The Ethnography of Exclusion in Galilee* (Cambridge: Cambridge University Press, 1997), 115–18; Stein, *Itineraries in Conflict*.

58. On Jewish tourism to Nazareth, see Yosef Tamir, "No Austerity in Nazareth . . . ," *Maariv*, May 10, 1949 (Hebrew); Special Correspondent, "Christian Nazareth Thanks and Complains," *Haaretz*, November 10, 1949 (Hebrew); D. Nahum, "Went to Nazareth to Eat—A Fish Filet . . . ," *Yediot Ahronot*, April 10, 1950 (Hebrew); Y. Ophir, "Whispering Coals in Nazareth," *Herut*, August 14, 1951 (Hebrew). See also Helman, *Consumer Culture*, 99–102.

59. The military governor of Nazareth refused the command to expel its residents. Prime Minister Ben-Gurion supported his position. Benny Morris, *1948: A History of the First Arab-Israeli War* (New Haven, CT: Yale University Press, 2008), 278–83. Leena Dallasheh, "Troubled Waters: Citizenship and Colonial Zionism in Nazareth," *International Journal of Middle East Studies* 47, no. 3 (2015): 468.

60. Mustafa Abbasi, "'Times of Storm': Nazareth and the Military Government," *Iyunim Bitkumat Israel* 22 (2012): 399–422 (Hebrew); Dallasheh, "Persevering through Colonial Transition," 10.

61. Tamir, "No Austerity in Nazareth." IDF are initials of Israel Defense Forces.

62. Nahum, "Went to Nazareth to Eat."

63. Amos Elon, "The Black Market Is White—in Nazareth," *Haaretz*, January 18, 1951 (Hebrew). According to Elon, restaurant owners bought cheap rationing cards on the black market in Nazareth. Although most diners were Jewish, they submitted the Arab tickets. After the foundation of the state, Nazareth was a major junction for smuggling meat from across the border. Ophir, "Whispering Coals in Nazareth."

64. Amos Elon, "Nazareth in Preparation for Christmas," *Haaretz*, December 26, 1950 (Hebrew). According to Elon, Nazareth's Christian residents received

250 grams of pork per person, owners of hunting permits hunted wild boars, and the agency of the Vatican also distributed special food portions. See also Helman, *Consumer Culture*, 100.

65. Elon, "Nazareth in Preparation for Christmas." On the use of Israeli national artifacts in Palestinian businesses as a way of signaling "safety" to Jewish tourists, see Stein, *Itineraries in Conflict*.

66. Elon, "Nazareth in Preparation for Christmas"; Yaacov Aviel, "Nazareth on Christmas Eve," *Haaretz*, December 29, 1953 (Hebrew).

67. Morris, *1948*, 164–66.

68. Rachel Hoter-Yishay, "In an Arab Café," *Dvar Hapoelet* 7 (1949, July 31): 169–71 (Hebrew).

69. R. Ben-Zvi, "In the Alleys of Old Acre," *Maariv*, September 19, 1950 (Hebrew).

70. Ilan Pappe, *The Ethnic Cleansing of Palestine* (Oxford: Oneworld, 2006), 58–61, 92–96, 200–201, 207–08; Morris, *1948*, 140–47.

71. D. Nahum, "Coffee, Hummus and Menu," *Yediot Ahronot*, December 14, 1949 (Hebrew).

72. Dan Yahav, *Jaffa: Neighborhoods, Suburbs and Arab Cemeteries around Her* (Published by the author, 2018), 19 (Hebrew).

73. Moshe Ben-Shachar, "I Have Seen the Second Jaffa," *Herut*, January 5, 1952 (Hebrew); Israel Goldschmidt-Paz, "Jaffa as It Is: Wiener Schnitzel in Times of Austerity," *Al Hamishmar*, January 8, 1953 (Hebrew); Daniel Monterescu, *Jaffa Shared and Shattered: Contrived Coexistence in Israel/Palestine* (Bloomington: Indiana University Press, 2015), 80–84.

74. Oded Erez, "Becoming Mediterranean: Greek Popular Music and Ethno-Class Politics in Israel, 1952–1982" (PhD diss., UCLA, 2016), 75–77. On the ambivalence of Zionist representations of Jaffa, see Monterescu, *Jaffa Shared and Shattered*, 67–96.

75. Haim Fireberg, "East Meets West: Cafés at the Margins of Tel Aviv, 1936–1960," in *Tel Aviv's Cafés, 1920–1980*, ed. Batya Carmiel (Tel Aviv: Eretz Israel Museum, 2007), 297–98 (Hebrew).

76. Weinstock, "The East Conquers the Stomachs"; Weinstock, "Night Falls on Jaffa," *Maariv*, June 26, 1952 (Hebrew). According to Shulamit Levari, by August 1951 there were ten "grade 3" (middle-priced) restaurants in Jaffa. Levari, "In Tel Aviv's Restaurants."

77. Helman, *Consumer Culture*, 112. See also Fireberg, "East Meets West," 296.

78. Weinstock, "Night Falls on Jaffa." In December 1952, a tour intended to introduce journalists to tourist attractions in Tel Aviv and Jaffa, probably organized by the Tel Aviv municipality, included eating hummus and falafel in an Arab restaurant in Jaffa's Ajami neighborhood. T. L., "Tourists for One Night," *Maariv*, December 7, 1952 (Hebrew).

79. Goldschmidt-Paz, "Jaffa as It Is."

80. A. Shapira, "Oriental Restaurants in Jerusalem," *Zmanim*, October 4, 1954 (Hebrew). On immigrants and food businesses, see Narayan, *Dislocating Cultures*, 180; Gabaccia, *We Are What We Eat*; Diner, *Hungering for America*, 50, 65, 197; Ray, *The Ethnic Restauranteur*, 11–15; Liora Gvion, "Cuisines of Poverty as Means of Empowerment: Arab Food in Israel," *Agriculture and Human Values* 23, no. 3 (2006): 308.

81. Dahn Ben-Amotz, *What's Up* (Jerusalem: Achiasaf, 1965), 61–63 (Hebrew); Tikva Weinstock, "Yokneam 'Swallows' a Ma'bara," *Maariv*, January 11, 1951 (Hebrew); Ministry of Health, "Report on the Situation of the Ma'barot," December 15, 1951, ISA 160/14-c. According to the report, cafés and restaurants were opened in several transitional camps. Opening this kind of venue required a license from the Ministry of Health, which was granted only to "social cases" after inspection of the hygienic conditions.

82. Avner Treinin, "The Settlement Dalet," *Lamerchav*, May 26, 1955 (Hebrew). I thank Gadi Algazi for sending me this story.

83. Lilian Cornfeld, "Secrets from the Oriental Kitchen," *Haaretz*, November 21, 1955 (Hebrew); Strassman, "Oriental Restaurants"; On Tel Aviv, see Weinstock, "The East Conquers the Stomachs." Weinstock estimated the number of Oriental restaurants in Tel Aviv in 1951 at several dozen. On Majdal-Ashkelon and Be'er Sheva, see "The Immigrant Town Majdal-Ashkelon in an Economic and Moral Recession," *Al Hamishmar*, November 16, 1952 (Hebrew); M. Ben-Shachar, "One Day in the Capital of the Negev Desert," *Herut*, March 4, 1953 (Hebrew). On Jerusalem, see A. Mashiach, "Jerusalem—A Day City," *Herut*, March 5, 1958 (Hebrew); Haim Mas, "The Family of Hummus Pioneers in the Capital," *Maariv*, April 14, 1960 (Hebrew). In late 1954 A. Shapira estimated the number of Oriental restaurants in Jerusalem at nine, with two additional ones about to open. Shapira, "Oriental Restaurants in Jerusalem."

84. Interview with Ezra Sherfler, Azura Restaurant, Jerusalem, June 19, 2012 (interviewer: Matan Boord). In 2015 a second branch was opened in Tel Aviv. Both restaurants are operated by Sherfler's sons. See also Gerda Glazer, "The Institute: Azura," *Walla! News*, March 19, 2012, https://food.walla.co.il/item /2517874 (Hebrew).

85. Mashka, Boris Carmi, and Nissim Aloni, "Docks on the Edge of the Sand," *Davar*, April 11, 1958 (Hebrew); Moshe Ben-Sha'ul, "'Che Janet' and Its Fishermen," *Maariv*, October 30, 1959 (Hebrew).

86. Amos Ben-Vered, "Albert's Restaurant," *Haaretz*, April 23, 1958 (Hebrew); Interview with M., waiter and cook in Ta'ami since 1980, Jerusalem, November 25, 2012 (interviewer: Matan Boord); Ta'ami existed until 2019. After Albert's death, it was operated by his sons.

87. The earliest result that came up in a search for the term *mis'ada mizrahit* in the digitalized Hebrew newspaper archive was from 1936 (one result). The next result was from 1943.

88. For example, the Savoya restaurant in Jaffa offered roasted meat, shashlik, hummus, and tahini as well as "other excellent international menus" (advertisement in *Maariv*, March 30, 1953 [Hebrew]), and the Savoy restaurant in Holon offered Oriental dishes along with French and Romanian cuisine (ad in *Maariv*, February 18, 1955 [Hebrew]).

89. While the cuisines of Syria and Lebanon, from which relatively few immigrants hailed, were similar, they differed significantly from those of North Africa, Yemen, Turkey, and Iran. See also Tene, "The New Immigrant Must Not Only Learn," 56.

90. Nathan Dunevich, *A City Dines: One Hundred Years of Dining in Tel Aviv* (Tel Aviv: Achuzat Bayit, 2012), 86 (Hebrew); Dahn Ben-Amotz, "What's Up: The King of Falafel," *Davar*, June 26, 1953 (Hebrew).

91. Interview with Ezra Sherfler; Glazer, "The Institute: Azura."

92. Interview with M., Ta'ami restaurant, Jerusalem, November 25, 2012 (interviewer: Matan Boord).

93. The owner of the Big Rachmo restaurant in Tel Aviv, who arrived in Israel from Egypt in 1957, encountered hummus for the first time in the Jaffa restaurants he used to visit on occasion. He never asked for a recipe: he knew what the ingredients were and experimented until he managed to reach what he considered the perfect formula. The grandparents of Duee from Hummus Duee arrived in Palestine from Iraq in the 1920s and settled in the Old City of Jerusalem, where they learned to prepare hummus from their Arab neighbors. Duee himself learned to prepare it from his mother. A conversation with Duee, near Amazya junction, April 17, 2010.

94. Shapira, "Oriental Restaurants in Jerusalem"; Mas, "The Family of Hummus Pioneers"; Yitzhak White, "Tombstone to Disappeared Cafés," *Yediot Ahronot*, December 7, 1956 (Hebrew); "Unemployment in Tel Aviv Has Exacerbated," *Haaretz*, January 21, 1954 (Hebrew). According to this piece, out of the 300–350 Arab workers from the Galilee and the Little Triangle who were located in the Tel Aviv area, some were employed in "all kinds of 'Oriental' restaurants in Jaffa and at the Tel Aviv seashore." Although this item does not tell in which jobs they were employed, it is likely that at least some of them worked as cooks. See also Interview with Issa D., Ramle, July 12, 2012 (interviewer: Nisreen Mazzawi).

95. Weinstock, "The East Conquers the Stomachs." See also Strassman, "Oriental Restaurants"; Cornfeld, "Secrets from the Oriental Kitchen"; Eliyahu Markovich, "Life in Haifa: The Priest of Hummus and Shashlik," *Haaretz*, October 16, 1959 (Hebrew); "Problems of Absorption and Integration in the Center of the Discussions at the Scientific Conference in Haifa," *Haaretz*, October 20, 1959 (Hebrew).

96. Weinstock, "The East Conquers the Stomachs"; Nahum, "Coffee, Hummus and Menu"; Advertisement: "To the Attention of the Government and Public Opinion!," *Kol Ha'am*, August 18, 1950 (Hebrew); Y. Zakai, "Where Is the

Tahini?," *Maariv*, September 9, 1952 (Hebrew); "Wide Dismissal in the Halva Branch," *Herut*, January 17, 1955 (Hebrew).

97. Shapira, "Oriental Restaurants in Jerusalem."

98. Weinstock, "The East Conquers the Stomachs"; H. G. (Haim Gouri), "At Sa'id's," *Lamerchav*, January 14, 1955 (Hebrew).

99. "To the Attention of the Authorities and the Public Opinion!," *Kol Ha'am*, August 18, 1950 (Hebrew); "In the Meantime Altogether 185 New Files Were Opened and Only a Few Confiscations," *Al Hamishmar*, October 11, 1950 (Hebrew); "Reports on an Action Against the Black Market," *Yediot Ahronot*, October 8, 1950 (Hebrew).

100. Y. H. Tenev, "In the Jurisdiction of the . . . Citizen," *Herut*, September 24, 1950 (Hebrew).

101. Oded Kapeliuk, 39 Ben Yehuda St., to the Tel Aviv Mayor, Mr. Haim Levanon, September 13, 1956, TAHA, 4-2317. The municipal representatives did not always validate these complaints. For instance, in his reply to the complaint of the Rotholz couple from 1 Bikurei Ha'itim Street, October 22, 1959, concerning the stench coming from the Oriental restaurant nearby, the municipal secretary wrote that the Sanitary Department made a special inspection at the complainant's apartment and did not detect any smells that could have been considered a hazard or a nuisance. The Municipal Secretary to Rotholz Family, January 14, 1960, TAHA 2320.

102. Uri Keisari, "Falafel—Israel's National Dish?," *Maariv*, July 27, 1956 (Hebrew).

103. H. G., "At Sa'id's"; Ben-Shachar, "One Day in the Capital of the Negev Desert"; Yuval Elizur, "People in Jerusalem: Meal on Top of a Cemetery," *Haaretz*, October 22, 1956 (Hebrew); Dahn Ben-Amotz, "What's Up," *Davar*, July 1,1955 (Hebrew). See also Helman, *Consumer Culture*, 113. As early as 1949, the food controller's edict, which listed dish prices according to restaurant tiers, included hummus at all five levels. In contrast, falafel was priced at the same rate only in the three lowest tiers of restaurants. "Addition to the Guesthouse Edict 1949," *Haaretz*, December 5, 1949 (Hebrew).

104. N. Ben Iser, "Notes from My Diary: Colonel in the . . . Kitchen," *Yediot Ahronot*, July 2, 1957 (Hebrew).

105. Examples for the second option are: recipe for "Kebab (Arab style ground meat)," WIZO, *The Cookbook* (Tel Aviv: Masada, 1948), 210; Lilian Cornfeld, "To the Woman and the Home: Cooking Arab Style," *Haaretz*, January 24, 1950 (Hebrew); "Menu: 4. Burghul with Lentils (Mjaddara), an Arab dish," *Herut*, June 27, 1956 (Hebrew).

106. Rozin, "Food, Identity and Nation Building," 65–75.

107. Raviv, *Falafel Nation*, 95–106; Helman, *Consumer Culture*, 129; Ranta and Prieto Piastro, "Does Israeli Food Exist?"; Prieto Piastro, *Eating in Israel*.

108. Helman, *Consumer Culture*, 123–31.

109. Baruch Kimmerling, "State Building, Mass Immigration and Establishment of Hegemony (1948–1951)," *Israeli Sociology* 1 (1999): 185 (Hebrew); Ariel, "Mosaic or Melting Pot."

110. WIZO, *The Cookbook*, 3; WIZO Instructors, *Thus We Shall Cook*, 6th ed. (Tel Aviv: Ner, 1965), 3 (Hebrew).

111. Sarah Bavly, "Tradition and Food Habits in the Different Ethnic Communities in Israel," *Mada—A Scientific Journal for All* 4, no. 3–4 (1960): 25, CZA A520/8 (Hebrew).

112. On food choice and cooking as moral choices in the American context, see Helen Zoe Veit, *Modern Food, Moral Food: Self-Control, Science, and the Rise of Modern American Eating in the Early Twentieth Century* (Chapel Hill: University of North Carolina Press, 2013).

113. Dov Yosef, "Introduction," in Lilian Cornfeld, *What Shall I Cook with the Rationing Portions? A Guide* (Published by the author, 1949), 7 (Hebrew).

114. Rozin, *The Rise of the Individual*, 27; Hagiladi, "Israeli Society," 285. For a similar perception in other national contexts, see Amy Bentley, *Eating for Victory: Food Rationing and the Politics of Domesticity* (Urbana: University of Illinois Press, 1998); Ina Zweiniger-Bargielowska, *Austerity in Britain: Rationing, Controls, and Consumption, 1939–1955* (Oxford: Oxford University Press, 2000); Mosby, *Food Will Win the War.*

115. "Israelis Eat Better than Many in Europe," April 5, 1950 (author and title of newspaper are missing), HANY, RG5/14.

116. Kimmerling, "State Building," 178.

117. Rozin, *The Rise of the Individual*, 162–79; Dafna Hirsch and Smadar Sharon, "'Neglectful Mothers': Constructions of Mizrahi Women's Motherhood during the Mandate and Early State Periods," in *Awlad al-Kalb—Children of the Heart: Aspects in the Study of the Missing Babies of Israel*, ed. Tova Gamliel and Nathan Shifriss (Tel Aviv: Resling, 2019), 253–97 (Hebrew).

118. Kimmerling, "State Building"; Henriette Dahan-Kalev, "You're So Pretty—You Don't Look Moroccan," *Israel Studies* 6, no. 1 (2001): 1–14.

119. Dr. Sarah Bavly, "A College of Nutrition and Home Economics in Israel," 1953, HANY, RG/14; Note by Dr. Bavly re School Luncheons in Places of Settlement of New Immigrants, June 19, 1949, HANY, RG5/15.

120. Cornfeld, "One Cuisine to the Ingathering of the Exiles"; Dov Shoval, "Jamila Mizrahi Learns to Light a Primus," *Al Hamishmar*, April 16, 1953 (Hebrew); Amos Elon, "From the 11th to the 20th Century," *Haaretz*, February 16, 1951 (Hebrew). See also Rozin, "Food, Identity and Nation-Building," 68. However, in an article on the Korat Gag (shelter) project, in which mostly Mizrahi children were transferred from the transitional camps to (mostly Ashkenazi) well-off families in the harsh winter of 1950–51, it was written concerning the

children's adjustment to the food and eating manners of their hosts, that "no conspicuous difficulties were detected. It seems that a large section of the children who hailed from Iraq, Egypt, Turkey and Romania were well-educated in their parents' homes and continued to act in their habitual manner." The author added that in some places these children served as an example to the children of the hosting family. Rebecca Sapir, "Korat Gag," *Megamot* 3, no. 1 (1951): 32 (Hebrew).

121. "Immigrant Guides in a Seminar," *Haaretz*, November 21, 1955 (Hebrew). See also Rozin, *The Rise of the Individual*, 137–90; Raviv, *Falafel Nation*, 100–106; Meir-Glitzenstein, "Longing for the Aromas of Baghdad," 100–101; Ariel, "Mosaic or Melting Pot," 96–101; Ariel, "Foodways and the Ethnicization of Yemeni Identity in Israel," 136–37.

122. The main organizations involved in nutrition education among the immigrants were Hadassah, WIZO, the Women Workers' Council, the workers' Sick Fund, the Jewish Agency, the Bureau for the Immigrant of the Ministry of Welfare, and the Institute for Nutrition Education of the Ministry of Supplies and Rationing (later transferred to the Ministry of Education and Culture). Educational activities included cooking courses, public demonstrations, exhibitions, and publication of educational materials. For instance, in 1952, the Institute for Nutrition Education had reached 22,600 women in 886 food demonstrations, 220 cooking lessons, and 51 food exhibits. Ida L. Boneparth, "Digest of Dr. Sarah Bavly's Annual Report on the Activities of the Institute for Nutrition Education," 1-9.1952, HANY, RG5/14. See also Raviv, *Falafel Nation*, 100–106.

123. Walter Strauss, *A Preliminary Investigation into the Food Habits of Oriental Jewish Communities with Special Reference to the Changes Enforced by Immigration to Israel* (Jerusalem: Department of Hygiene, Hebrew University-Hadassah Medical School, 1955), 17.

124. Sarah Bavly, "From the Activities of the Nutrition Department" (published in *Hinuch Vetarbut*, 3 [1955]), CZA A520/7 (Hebrew). In 1959, 50 percent of the schools in which the top two grades comprised more than seventy pupils had teaching kitchens. Sarah Bavly, "Child Feeding Program and Related Nutrition Education," in *Child and Young Welfare in Israel* (Jerusalem: Henrietta Szold Institute, 1960), 188, CZA A520/8.

125. Bavly, "Tradition and Food Habits"; Strauss, *A Preliminary Investigation*, 8; Walter Strauss, *Changes in Food Habits in the Yemenite and Iraqi Communities in Israel* (Israel Institute of Applied Social Research and the Department of Preventive Medicine of the Hebrew University-Hadassah Medical School, 1958), 7. According to Krishnendu Ray, studies on immigration and food show that children advance the adaptation of the immigrants to the local diet. Ray, *The Migrant's Table*, 75–76, 95.

126. Emma-Jayne Abbots, "Approaches to Food and Migration: Rootedness, Being and Belonging," in *The Handbook of Food and Anthropology*, ed. Jacob A. Klein

and James L. Watson (London: Bloomsbury, 2016), 115–32; Diner, *Hungering for America*; Ray, *The Migrant's Table*.

127. Strauss, *A Preliminary Investigation*, 8–10; Margot Kulas, "Cultural Patterns and Ways of Adjustment of Immigrants from the Atlas Mountains," *Megamot 6*, no. 4 (1956): 369 (Hebrew).

128. Dimona, "Bridge to the Immigrants from the East: B. Why Didn't They Understand Regina?," *Al Hamishmar*, August 10, 1956 (Hebrew); Shoshana Levy, *On a Crossroad* (Published by the author, 2001), 86 (Hebrew); Cornfeld, "One Cuisine to the Ingathering of the Exiles"; Strauss, *Changes in Food Habits*, 7; Meir-Glitzenstein, "Longing for the Aromas of Baghdad," 97–99; Raviv, *Falafel Nation*, 104; Bashkin, *Impossible Exodus*, 95. See also Veit, *Modern Food, Moral Food*, 136.

129. According to studies from the period, they drank more milk, ate more vegetables than previously, ate more regular bread than flatbread, and adopted new ingredients like potatoes and noodles. Strauss, *A Preliminary Investigation*, 16; Strauss, *Changes in Food Habits*, 34; Bavly, "Tradition and Food Habits," 8. See also Ariel, "Foodways and the Ethnicization of Yemeni Identity in Israel," 139–144.

130. In an article published in *Al Hamishmar*, a Moroccan woman shared her refusal to eat margarine, describing it as useful only for "greasing the hair when you go for a walk on Saturday!" Instead, her husband went to a nearby Arab village and bought some olive oil. Yermiyahu Shmueli, "The oil shortage is not inescapable," *Al Hamishmar*, October 10, 1950 (Hebrew). On attempts to reconstruct familiar dishes see interview with Lili K., Kfar Vitkin, April 27, 2012 (interviewer: Matan Boord); Seri, *A Tree and Its Branches*, 95–96; Strauss, *Changes in Food Habits*. According to Strauss, "[t]he immigrants themselves stress their health and strength in Yemen and their longing for their 'natural' food." Strauss, *A Preliminary Investigation*, 13. See also Liora Gvion, "Hummus, Couscous, Sushi: Food and Ethnicity in Israeli Society," in *A Full Belly: Rethinking Food and Society in Israel*, ed. Aviad Kleinberg (Tel Aviv: Tel Aviv University and Keter, 2005), 47–50 (Hebrew); Meir-Glitzenstein, "Longing for the Aromas of Baghdad"; Ariel, "Mosaic or Melting Pot," 101–3; Ariel, "Foodways and the Ethnicization of Yemeni Identity in Israel," 137–38.

131. Alex Weingrod, "Change and Continuity in a Moroccan Immigrant Village in Israel," *Middle East Journal* 14, no. 3 (1960): 284; Geula Shayek-al-'Ani, *The Theft of the Rooster: From the Diary of a Transit Camp Girl* (Kiryat Ono: Tsafra, 2011), 27 (Hebrew); Mordechai Naor, ed., *Immigrants and Ma'barot, 1948-1952* (Jerusalem: Yad Izhak Ben-Zvi, 1986), 180 (Hebrew); Interview with Reuven A., January 2, 2012, Jaffa (interviewer: Matan Boord); Rozin, *The Rise of the Individual*, 158.

132. Edward Wellin, "Cultural Factors in Nutrition," *Nutrition Reviews* 13, no. 5 (1955): 129; "Cultural Factors in Food Selection," *Pages for Nutrition* 9, no. 3 (1958): 26–28 (Hebrew); Bavly, "Tradition and Food Habits."

133. Gabaccia, *We Are What We Eat*, 147; Veit, *Modern Food, Moral Food*, 123–56.

134. Ray, *The Ethnic Restauranteur*, 63.

135. hooks, "Eating the Other," 21.

136. Cornfeld, "One Cuisine to the Ingathering of the Exiles"; Henrietta Boas, "Oriental Flavors in Local Food," November 3, 1950 (newspaper title missing), HANY, RG5/14.

137. Cornfeld, "One Cuisine to the Ingathering of the Exiles."

138. Boas, "Oriental Flavors in Local Food."

139. Strauss, *A Preliminary Investigation*, 18.

140. Dahn Ben-Amotz, "What's Up: Gefilte Yang-Yo," *Davar*, May 8, 1953 (Hebrew).

141. *Thou Shall Make Your Guests' Heart Happy* (Jerusalem: The Ministry of Education, College of Nutrition and Home Economics, 1958) (Hebrew). An expanded second edition appeared in 1965, which included recipes from additional ethnic communities. In the introduction to the second edition, it was stated that the ethnic communities were already learning from one another, and yet there was still more to learn.

142. Strauss, *Changes in Food Habits*, 10.

143. Cornfeld, "Cooking Arab Style." See also Raviv, *Falafel Nation*, 70–71.

144. Lilian Cornfeld, "To the Woman and the Home: Tahini—To Diversify Your Menu," *Haaretz*, December 27, 1949 (Hebrew).

145. Lilian Cornfeld, "Secrets from the Oriental Kitchen."

146. In the same year, Dan Almagor had written "The Falafel Song" (also known as "And We Have Falafel") for Israel's tenth anniversary celebrations.

147. http://web.nli.org.il/sites/NLI/Hebrew/collections/israel-collection /israeli_food/1955/Pages/1955-feast.aspx, accessed August 4, 2015 (Hebrew). Lilian Cornfeld, "Tonight Independence Dinner," *Haaretz*, April 26, 1955 (Hebrew); "Independence Day Menu," *Haaretz*, April 9, 1956 (Hebrew). Already in 1951, the committee for the preparation of the Independence Day celebrations suggested a special menu for Independence Day. The menu, which was developed by Cornfeld, included a cake (sweet or salty), an orange juice and milk drink, and lollipops in the colors of the national flag, all of which had symbolic meanings. Cornfeld left room for variations in ingredients and flavoring according to the taste of the different ethnic communities. Lilian Cornfeld, "Suggestion for a Festive Menu for Independence Day," ISA4147/18-c.

148. Anonymous, "For the Woman and the Family: The Festive Dinner," *Davar*, May 3, 1957 (Hebrew).

149. Lilian Cornfeld, "For the Woman and the Home: Delicacies for Purim," *Haaretz*, March 3, 1958 (Hebrew); Cornfeld, "For the Woman and the Home: Bites for Parties," *Haaretz*, December 8, 1958 (Hebrew).

150. Lilian Cornfeld, "For the Woman and the Home: Bites for Entertaining Guests," *Haaretz*, January 6, 1958 (Hebrew).

151. Ministry of Education and Culture, Nutrition Department, "Program of home economics in elementary schools (as restated and reprinted in the year 1959–60)", CZA A520/8 (Hebrew); "Hand to the Mouth," *Maariv*, May 8, 1958 (Hebrew); Tene, "The New Immigrant Must Not Only Learn," 56–57; Helman, *Consumer Culture*, 111, 115; Prieto Piastro, *Eating in Israel*, 51–54.

152. Haganah was the central military organization of the Yishuv, which formed the infrastructure for the establishment of the Israeli army after the foundation of the state.

153. "The Chief of Staff in Kfar Shmaryahu," *Yediot Ahronot*, March 21, 1954 (Hebrew); Dahn Ben-Amotz, "What's Up: Parties Report," *Davar*, April 2, 1954 (Hebrew).

154. Besides hummus and falafel, the refreshments included fresh vegetables, hard-boiled eggs, potato salad, and peanuts.

155. Oz Almog, *The Sabra: The Creation of the New Jew*, trans. Haim Watzman (Berkeley: University of California Press, 2000), 3; Helman, *Becoming Israeli*, 32, 69; Amnon Dankner, *Dahn Ben-Amotz: A Biography* (Jerusalem: Keter, 1992), 165–68 (Hebrew).

156. Netiva Ben-Yehuda, *1948—Between the Countings: A Roman on the Beginning of the War* (Jerusalem: Keter, 1981), 175 (Hebrew). A partial translation of this excerpt appears in Yael Zrubavel, *Desert in the Promised Land* (Stanford, CA: Stanford University Press, 2018), 48. On Palmach members' adoption of Arab cultural items as status symbols, see Almog, *The Sabra*, 198–201.

157. According to Sara Ahmed, by consuming objects that are thought to contain the "truth" of the stranger, the consuming subject both becomes *like* the stranger and establishes itself as other than the stranger—as an agentic subject capable of transformation. Ahmed, *Strange Encounters*, 114–33.

158. Claude Fischler, "Food, Self and Identity," *Social Science Information* 27, no. 2 (1988): 275–92.

159. Ben-Amotz's section What's Up began appearing in the daily *Davar* in 1953. In 1956 it moved to the daily *Maariv*.

160. The Youth Aliyah was a Jewish organization dedicated to transporting Jewish children from Europe to Palestine, to save them from the Nazis.

161. Dahn Ben-Amotz, "What's Up: The Kings Restaurant," *Davar*, May 6, 1955 (Hebrew).

162. Dahn Ben-Amotz, "What's Up: By the Sea," *Davar*, October 7, 1955 (Hebrew). See also Ben-Amotz, "What's Up: Party," *Davar*, February 6, 1953 (Hebrew); Ben-Amotz, "What's Up: Shemesh Paintings," *Davar*, August 27, 1954 (Hebrew); Ben-Amotz, "What's Up," *Maariv*, May 18, 1956 (Hebrew); Ben-Amotz, "What's Up: Karawan's Meeting Place" *Maariv*, July 4, 1958 (Hebrew).

163. Ben-Amotz, "What's Up" Kugel is an Eastern European casserole, usually made from noodles or potatoes.

164. Dahn Ben-Amotz, "What's Up: Karawan's Meeting Place."

165. H. G., "At Sa'id's."

166. "Haim Gouri," *Lexicon of New Hebrew Literature*, Ohio State University, accessed January 11, 2021, https://library.osu.edu/projects/hebrew-lexicon/00108.php.

167. Hagor (Haim Gouri), "Between Nazareth and Nazareth," *Lamerchav*, December 28, 1956 (Hebrew).

168. Hagor (Haim Gouri), "Kawkab-al-Sabach," *Lamerchav*, October 11, 1957 (Hebrew).

169. Johnston and Lawson, "Settler Colonies," 369.

170. Ben-Shachar, "One Day in the Capital of the Negev Desert"; Zvi Rosen, "Is It Really as Bad?," *Davar*, October 3, 1957 (Hebrew). See also A. Zuta, "On What's Certain—You Don't Bet," *Maariv*, April 6, 1958 (Hebrew).

171. Yermiyahu Halpern, "Father Good-for-Nothing," *Herut*, February 4, 1955 (Hebrew); Dahn Ben-Amotz, "What's Up: An Israeli Club," *Davar*, May 31, 1957 (Hebrew); Hagai (Haim Gouri), "What Do You Say? Goodbye, Doctor, Safe Travels!" *Lamerchav*, November 1, 1957 (Hebrew).

3. NATIONALISM IN A CAN

1. Orit Rozin, "Israel and the Right to Travel Abroad 1948–1961," *Israel Studies* 15 (2010): 147–76.

2. Palestine Edible Products Ltd., "Review on Position of Our Business in 1960," Haifa, November 1960, CZA A449/23.

3. Henry Rosenfeld and Shulamit Carmi, "Appropriation of Public Means and a State-Made Middle Class," *Machbarot Leyiun Velebikoret* 3 (1979): 70 (Hebrew); Daniella Ohad Smith, "The 'Designed' Israeli Interior, 1960–1977: Shaping Identity," *Journal of Interior Design* 38, no. 3 (2013): 21–36; Hemi Sheinblat, "'Catching America': The Americanization of Israeli Society, 1958–1967" (PhD diss., Tel Aviv University, 2017) (Hebrew).

4. Gross, "Israel's Economy, 1954–1967," 31; David Horowitz, *The Enigma of Economic Growth: A Case Study of Israel* (New York: Praeger, 1972), 39–40.

5. In the year 1963–64, the upper quintile earned 42.6 percent of the general income, while the three lower quintiles earned only 35.3 percent. While the upper quintile was largely populated by Ashkenazim, the lower quintiles were mostly populated by Mizrahim and Arabs. Rosenfeld and Carmi, "Appropriation of Public Means," 67. See also Ben-Porat, *How Israel Became a Capitalist Society*, 163–64.

6. Cornfeld, *Israeli Cookery*, viii, 68; Efrat Arad, "A Modern 'Baking Oven,'" *Maariv*, January 23, 1963 (Hebrew); Dov Shoval, "A Glimpse into the Mystery

of the Food Basket," *Al Hamishmar*, September 26, 1965 (Hebrew); Sarah Bavly, *Family Expenditure Survey, Part 2: Nutrition Level in Israel, 1968/69* (Jerusalem: Central Bureau of Statistics and Ministry of Education and Culture, 1972) (Hebrew). See also Iris Kalka, "Changing Nutrition Value and Self-Image in Israel," *ICAF Occasional Report* vii (1990), 8; Sheinblat, "'Catching America,'" 43.

7. Horowitz, *Enigma of Economic Growth*, 39; Oz Almog, "From Vegetable Salad and Lebeniya to Hamburger and Sushi: The Coca-Colonization of Israel," *Makom Lemachshava* 2 (1998): 11 (Hebrew); Sheinblat, "'Catching America'"; Shoval, "A Glimpse into the Mystery."

8. Sheinblat, "'Catching America,'" 38, 43.

9. These are merely estimations based on a list that might be incomplete. Moreover, recipes were sometimes published in the form of booklets and leaflets, mainly during periods of food rationing. Here I tried to limit the estimations to cookbooks proper.

10. Miriam Goren, "The March of Israeli Delicacies Marches Again," *Davar*, August 28, 1964 (Hebrew). According to Goren, the number of applicants to cooking schools had doubled, and cooking was added to the Israeli profession market. The first class of graduates—seventeen in number—were immediately snatched to work in hotels and on ships, attesting to the orientation of professional cooking toward the tourism industry.

11. "In the Country and in the World: A Gastronomic Congress of the Confrérie de la Chaîne des Rôtisseurs," *Lamerchav*, October 30, 1968 (Hebrew); Rita Goldstein, "Behind the Scenes: Knights of the Fork and Ladle," *Walla! Food*, July 4, 2013, https://food.walla.co.il/item/2657228 (Hebrew).

12. Menachem Talmi, "The Younes Fashion," *Maariv*, November 15, 1965 (Hebrew). See also Ami Shamir, "The Era of Eateries," *Lamerchav*, February 14, 1964 (Hebrew); Ruth Bondi, *The Taste of Israel 1965* (Jerusalem: Israel Museum, 2015) (Hebrew).

13. The Central Bureau of Statistics, *Food and Drink Services Survey, 1967/68*. A series of special publications, no. 298 (Jerusalem: CBS, 1970), 9 (Hebrew).

14. Dunevich, *A City Dines*; Nathan Dunevich, *Tel Aviv: Sands which Became a Metropolis* (Jerusalem: Schocken, 1959), 124–25 (Hebrew); Almog, "From Vegetable Salad and Lebeniya," 11–12.

15. *Maariv* seems to have been the first newspaper to include restaurant reviews, first by Yosef Lapid (since 1961) and later by journalist and author Menachem Talmi (pen name Ma'ul). Since the mid-1960s, author and artist Amos Kenan (pen name Lokulus) wrote reviews for *Yediot Ahronot*, and Rene R. Mokedi (David Benedict) wrote for *Haaretz* (pen name Estinis). The Labor newspaper *Davar* joined only in late 1968 with a column by journalist and author Ruth Bondi.

16. Kalka, "Changing Nutrition Value," 8.

17. For example, "The Party of the Month: Bnei Mitzva," *Lamerchav*, February 7, 1965 (Hebrew); Aharon Geva, "Hummus with Tahini," *Lamerchav*, November 9, 1967 (Hebrew).

18. "Hummus, Shaslik, Kebab, Pickles," *Davar*, January 6, 1961 (Hebrew); Ma'ul, "Bon Appétit: Haifa! Haifa . . . ," *Maariv*, February 6, 1969 (Hebrew); Ma'ul, "Bon Appétit: Pigeons' Spleen," *Maariv*, October 2, 1969 (Hebrew); Dunevich, *A City Dines*, 181.

19. "Night Clubs—Bars—Restaurants," *Haaretz*, November 25, 1960 (Hebrew); Arie Kinrati, "Thanks God, That Yemenite Kerem Still Exists," *Lamerchav*, November 23, 1961 (Hebrew); Ma'ul, "Bon Appétit: Haifa! Haifa . . ."; Dunevich, *A City Dines*, 188–93.

20. Talmi, "The Younes Fashion"; Dunevich, *A City Dines*, 184–85.

21. For example, Maariv's Reporter in the Corridor, "A New Oriental Restaurant Will Be Established Next to the New Road in Abu Ghosh," *Maariv*, December 29, 1964 (Hebrew); Dunevich, *A City Dines*, 185.

22. Dunevich, *A City Dines*, 287; Erez, "Becoming Mediterranean."

23. Cornfeld, *Israeli Cookery*, 98.

24. For instance, Ora Shem-Or, *Yediot Ahronot*, July 28, 1961 (Hebrew); Idit Neuman, "The Voice of a Bride and All the Expenses," *Yediot Ahronot*, February 1, 1963 (Hebrew).

25. For example, A. Almagor, "To Eat from Happiness and to Cook with Love," *Yediot Ahronot*, November 10, 1964 (Hebrew); Gideon Reicher, "Thus the Knesset Chews," *Yediot Ahronot*, December 8, 1967 (Hebrew).

26. "Breakfast for Purim Eve," *Lamerchav*, March 23, 1967 (Hebrew).

27. Gisela Ardosh, "The Domain of the Individual—a Recipe as You Please: Hummus, Falafel and All the Rest," *Maariv*, July 7, 1969 (Hebrew).

28. Mintz, *Tasting Food*, 96.

29. "Maariv Talks: How Does One Eat Hummus?," *Maariv*, April 18, 1963 (Hebrew); "Mira Avrech Tells about Men and about Women," *Yediot Ahronot*, March 25, 1966 (Hebrew); "The Domain of the Individual: Hummus—to the Elites," *Maariv* September 9, 1968 (Hebrew).

30. Tamar Elor and Motti Regev, "The Establishment of an Israeli Style, 1967–1973," in *Israel 1967–1977: Continuity and Turning (Iyunim Bitkumat Israel: Thematic Series, vol. 11)*, ed. Ofer Shiff and Aviva Halamish (Sde Boker: The Ben-Gurion Research Institute for the Study of Israel and Zionism, 2017), 308–33 (Hebrew); Elke Kaschl, *Dance and Authenticity in Israel and Palestine: Performing the Nation* (Leiden: Brill, 2003); Yael Guilat, "The Yemeni Ideal in Israeli Culture and Art," *Israel Studies* 6, no. 3 (2001): 26–53; Smith, "The 'Designed' Israeli Interior"; Dana Kaplan, "Beautiful Israeli Girls: Aesthetic Labor in the Media between Nation Building and Neoliberalism," unpublished manuscript.

31. Laudan, *Cuisine and Empire*, 323–34; Mary Neuburger, "Dining in Utopia: A Taste of the Bulgarian Black Sea Coast under Socialism," *Gastronomica* 17, no. 4 (2017): 56.

32. Smith, "The 'Designed' Israeli Interior," 24; Guilat, "The Yemeni Ideal"; Dina Roginsky, "Orientalism, the Body, and Cultural Politics in Israel: Sara Levi Tanai and the Inbal Dance Theater," *Nashim: A Journal of Jewish Women's Studies & Gender Issues* 11 (2006): 164–97; Elor and Regev, "The Establishment of an Israeli Style."

33. For a discussion of different creolization methods in Belizean cooking, see Wilk, *Home Cooking in the Global Village*, 112–21.

34. Y. Carmel, "Our Oriental Mania," *Al Hamishmar*, September 14, 1958 (Hebrew). See also Roginsky, "Orientalism, the Body, and Cultural Politics."

35. Amos Noy points at a different representational trope of associating Mizrahim with dangerous and superficial modernity. However, it was much less common than the trope of the primitive Oriental. See Amos Noy, "When Mizrahim Were Modern: Non-Orientalist Representations of Mizrahim in Israel in the 1950s and 1960s," in *The Long History of Mizrahim: New Directions in the Study of Jews from Muslim Countries: In Tribute to Yaron Tzur*, ed. Aviad Moreno et al. (Sde Boker: The Ben-Gurion Research Institute for the Study of Israel and Zionism, 2021), 127–44 (Hebrew).

36. Yaron Tzur, "The Ethnic Problem," in *The Second Decade: 1958–1968*, 116.

37. Guilat, "The Yemeni Ideal," 31, 46.

38. Tzur, "The Ethnic Problem," 116–17.

39. Erez, "Becoming Mediterranean"; Ella Shohat, *Israeli Cinema: East/West and the Politics of Representation* (London: I. B. Tauris, 2010), 116.

40. On tourism as a motivation for the development of a "national cuisine," see Wilk, *Home Cooking in the Global Village*, 177–79; Lindholm, *Culture and Authenticity*, 79–80; Laudan, *Cuisine and Empire*, 324; Neuburger, "Dining in Utopia," 48–60.

41. Lilian Cornfeld, "A Cooking Experts Visits the Country," *Haaretz*, March 12, 1959 (Hebrew); R. Nadav, "The King Tastes Falafel," *Davar*, November 20, 1959 (Hebrew).

42. Ruth Bondi, "It Will Be Good: Sample Menu," *Davar*, February 13, 1959 (Hebrew); "Initiative to Improve the Israeli Menu," *Davar*, October 7, 1962 (Hebrew). According to this piece, 60 percent of the tourists who stayed in luxury hotels complained about the food. See also Helman, *Consumer Culture*, 131–33.

43. Avner Molcho, "Capitalism and 'The American Way' in Israel: Productivity, Management and the Capitalist Ethos in the American Technical Assistance in the 1950s," in *Society and Economy in Israel: Historical and Contemporary*

Perspectives, ed. Avi Bareli, Daniel Gutwein, and Tuvia Friling (Sde Boker: The Ben-Gurion Research Institute for the Study of Israel and Zionism, 2005), 263–94 (Hebrew).

44. "An American Nutrition Expert: It's Time to Invent an Israeli Dish," *Herut*, March 29, 1960 (Hebrew). See also "A Nutrition Expert Praises the Israeli Breakfast," *Davar*, March 31, 1960 (Hebrew); Aharon Geva, "Wilta Came, Smelled—and Was Beaten," *Maariv* April 1, 1960 (Hebrew); "Selected Chapters from a Depressing Report," *Davar*, January 6, 1961 (Hebrew); Dunevich, *A City Dines*, 238.

45. "A Nutrition Expert Praises the Israeli Breakfast."

46. Deborah Namir, "The Man Who Stirs the Knesset Cauldron," *Yediot Ahronot*, December 17, 1968 (Hebrew).

47. Esther Barzel, "To the Woman and the Home: The Secrets of the Master of the Kitchen," *Haaretz*, July 1, 1963 (Hebrew).

48. "Initiative to Improve the Israeli Menu," *Davar*, October 7, 1962 (Hebrew). See also Shaul Hon, "The Next Stage: Ingathering of . . . Cuisines," *Maariv*, November 7, 1962 (Hebrew); "The Queen of the Kitchen without 'Gefilte fish,'" *Davar*, January 18, 1963 (Hebrew); Sarah, "For the Home and the Family: The Queen of the Kitchen Was Crowned with an Apron," *Davar*, February 8, 1963 (Hebrew).

49. "The Queen of the Kitchen without 'Gefilte Fish'"; Talma Tal, "Who Will Get the Crown?," *Maariv*, January 25, 1963 (Hebrew).

50. "The Israeli Queen of the Kitchen Will Earn a Prize of 2,500 IL," *Herut*, January 8, 1963 (Hebrew).

51. "The Israeli Recipe—a Combination of Greek—Iraqi—Middle Eastern Foods," *Herut*, December 21, 1962 (Hebrew).

52. "To the Woman and the Family: Who Will Be the Queen of the Israeli Kitchen?," *Herut*, November 21, 1962 (Hebrew).

53. "The Queen Liked Stuffed Artichoke," *Herut*, February 13, 1963 (Hebrew).

54. Bella Almog, *Israeli Delicacies: Selection of Dishes Submitted to the Contest "Israeli Queen of the Kitchen"* (Jerusalem: March of Israeli Delicacies, 1965); Orna Shemer, "A Conference for Those Who Care How and What to Eat," *Maariv*, December 12, 1966 (Hebrew); Namir, "The Man Who Stirs the Knesset Cauldron"; Tehila Ofer, "Not Only for Women: What Is an Israeli Menu?," *Maariv*, March 13, 1972 (Hebrew). In fact, chicken with oranges was mentioned as a contender for the title of an "Israeli dish" already beforehand. See Nadav, "The King Tastes Falafel."

55. Almagor, "The Falafel Song." For the lyrics (in Hebrew) see https://shironet.mako.co.il/artist?type=lyrics&lang=1&prfid=2329&wrkid=3626, accessed August 9, 2022. See also "The Song of the Decade Celebration Stages," *Maariv*, May 25, 1958 (Hebrew).

56. Bavly, "Tradition and Food Habits in Israel's Ethnic Communities"; Miriam Goren, "Each Ethnic Community and Its Cuisine," *Davar*, March 27, 1964 (Hebrew).

57. Molly Bar-David, *Folkloric Cookbook: Delicacies for Israeli Holidays* (Tel Aviv: Y. & M. Bar-David, 1964) (Hebrew). An English version, titled *The Israeli Cookbook*, appeared in the same year. Two other examples are the booklet *And You Made Your Guests' Heart Happy* (1958), by the Nutrition and Home Economics College of the Ministry of Education, and Cornfeld's *Israeli Cookery* (1962).

58. Shooky Galili, "Recipes from the Past 2: Folkloric Cookbook, 1964," *Hummus for the Masses*, accessed August 18, 2022, https://humus101.com /?p=2076#prettyPhoto (Hebrew).

59. Dafna Mor, "What's Cooking? Independence Day Dinner," *Maariv*, May 6, 1970 (Hebrew).

60. Hizky Shoham, "The Israel BBQ as National Ritual: Performing Unofficial Nationalism, or Finding Meaning in Triviality," *American Journal of Cultural Sociology* 9, no. 1 (2021): 13–42.; Avieli, *Food and Power*, 49–81.

61. Cornfeld, *Israeli Cookery*, 115.

62. Cornfeld, *Israeli Cookery*, 118.

63. Bar-David, *Folkloric Cookbook*, 15. See also Guilat, "The Yemeni Ideal," 45–47.

64. An early example is Uri Keisari, "Falafel—Israel's National Dish?," *Maariv*, July 27, 1956 (Hebrew).

65. "Chef Nikolai: We Have to Develop an Israeli Cuisine," *Davar*, July 26, 1973 (Hebrew); "Israeli or Not—as Long as It Is Tasty," *Davar*, September 12, 1973 (Hebrew).

66. "Israeli or Not—as Long as It Is Tasty." A similar debate took place in the context of folk dances. See Kaschl, *Dance and Authenticity*, 54–55.

67. Cornfeld, *Israeli Cookery*, viii–ix.

68. Cornfeld, *Israeli Cookery*, vii–viii. See also Ruth Bondi, "The Turning Knife," *Davar*, December 13, 1968 (Hebrew). Bondi ironically noted in her column the "worrying ethnic discrimination" in the area of food: while all Ashkenazim ate hummus, tahini, kebab, and French fries, Mizrahim were not that keen on noodle kugel or *kishke* (stuffed intestines), especially since there were very few places in the country that served such dishes, if any.

69. Bavly, "Tradition and Food Habits"; Sarah Bavly, "Food Consumption and Nutritional Status among the Rural Population in Israel, 1959–1960," *Public Health* 5, no. 3 (1962): 365 (Hebrew); Bavly, *Food Habits and Their Changes*. According to these studies, Ashkenazim ate more vegetables; replaced some of the meat with fish, chicken, milk, and eggs; and consumed Arab foods like hummus, falafel, tahini, shashlik, and kebab. Mizrahim consumed more milk than previously, less spices, less white pita bread, and more dark bread, and often replaced rice with noodles or macaroni.

70. Cornfeld, *Israeli Cookery*, 72.

71. "Change in the El Al Airplanes Menu," *Davar*, February 2, 1967 (Hebrew). However, in an item from July 1968, which specified the menu in El Al airplanes, the Mizrahi items disappeared. "The Menu Served in El Al Airplanes," *Hatzofe*, July 23, 1968 (Hebrew).

72. Cornfeld, *Israeli Cookery*, 78–88. See also Raviv, *Falafel Nation*, 157–81; Rozin, "Food, Identity, and Nation-Building," 70–71.

73. "School Meal in Other Countries: 1 Israel," *Education*, September 15, 1961, CZA A520/16.

74. Emmanuel Elnekave, "Kibbutz Youth Are Getting Instruction in 'Urban Consciousness,'" *Yediot Ahronot*, August 21, 1960 (Hebrew); "Not Only for Women: What's Cooking in a Kibbutz?," *Davar*, January 29, 1965 (Hebrew). In the early 1960s, a couple of wandering cooks on a mission to improve the food in kibbutzim introduced Middle Eastern foods like pita bread, tahini, kebab, hummus, and salads into the dining hall menu, but according to the report in *Davar*, the older members could not tolerate it. Eventually the compromise was to serve such dishes once a week, on the same evening when a film was screened. Yitzhak, "The Wandering Cooks."

75. On hotel restaurants, see Raviv, *Falafel Nation*, 159–65. On the military menu, see Raviv, *Falafel Nation*, 168–77. See also Telma advertisement, *Davar*, November 2, 1958 (Hebrew); "Instead of Patties—IDF Soldiers Will Get 'Wimpy,'" *Yediot Ahronot*, November 19, 1968 (Hebrew); Nahum Barne'a, "Bread with Anything," *Davar*, April 11, 1969 (Hebrew); IDF menus, 1972, IDF archive, 9-187-1974 (Hebrew).

76. For example, Moshe Vardi, "Not All Students from Israel Have Fun in the English Capital," *Haboker*, April 29, 1960 (Hebrew); "Our Reporter Announces . . . ," *Al Hamishmar*, August 22, 1960 (Hebrew); Tuvia Carmel, "The Belgian Village—the Advanced Television and an Evening at 'Sabra,'" *Lamerchav*, August 25, 1964 (Hebrew).

77. Zeev Tene, *Short Memory* (Tel Aviv: EnT-T, 2009) (Hebrew).

78. Jack Goody, *Cooking, Cuisine and Class: A Study in Comparative Sociology* (Cambridge: Cambridge University Press, 1982), 154–74; Gabaccia, *We Are What We Eat*; Warren Belasco and Philip Scranton, eds., *Food Nations: Selling Taste in Consumer Societies* (New York: Routledge, 2002).

79. Gabaccia, *We Are What We Eat*, 147–74.

80. Tamar Avidar, "For the Home and the Family: Israeli Food—to Switzerland," *Davar*, July 3, 1959 (Hebrew); L. Ternopoler, "Changes in the Realm of Industry and Export," *Al Hamishmar*, February 19, 1960 (Hebrew); Ch. Weissadler, "With So Many Midwives the Child Was Born Eyeless," *Al Hamishmar*, August 31, 1960 (Hebrew); Dr. Carole Bayer, "The Food Industry in Its Progress," *Davar*, May 10, 1961 (Hebrew); Avi Dafna, "New Developments in the Food Industry,"

Hatzofe, January 19, 1962 (Hebrew); "Nice Progress in the Food Industry," *Haboker*, September 3, 1963 (Hebrew); Aharon Priel, "Increasing the Export is Dependent on Increasing Research and Taking Over the Local Market," *Maariv*, March 19, 1969 (Hebrew).

81. Zvi Lavi, "Hummus Instead of Sabbath Hamin," *Maariv*, December 20, 1964 (Hebrew); Ariel Amiad, "Tasks in Agriculture," *Davar*, June 15, 1964 (Hebrew). The rate of women's employment grew from 27.9 percent of the labor force in 1955 to 39.2 percent in 1980. Yoram Ben-Porath and Reuben Gronau, "Jewish Mother Goes to Work: Trends in the Labor Force Participation of Women in Israel, 1955–1980," *Journal of Labor Economics* 3, no. 1 (1985): 313.

82. David Levi-Faur, *The Visible Hand: State-Directed Industrialization in Israel* (Jerusalem: Yad Izhak Ben-Zvi, 2001), 96 (Hebrew). See also Avi-Dafna, "The Production and Export of Food Is in Constant Growth," *Hatzofe*, December 16, 1960 (Hebrew); Rafael Eldor, "It Is Possible to Increase the Export of Food to the US by 15 Times," *Maariv*, August 1, 1967 (Hebrew).

83. Palestine Edible Products Ltd., "Review on Position of Our Business in 1960." In fact, the Geller Company preceded Telma in manufacturing preserved hummus, "wrapped in aluminum wrapping," already in 1957, but apart from a couple of advertisements for Geller's hummus that appeared in that year, I did not come across any further reference to their hummus. Geller advertisement, *Maariv*, May 12, 1957 (Hebrew).

84. Uri Heiman, *Then and Now—Tozeret Mazon Israelit, 1938–1998* (Haifa: Here and Now, 1998) 12, 14 (Hebrew).

85. Interview with former Telma CEO Giora Teltsch, Haifa, October 21, 2009. Giora's father, Hugo Teltsch, was the CEO who introduced hummus into the company's repertoire.

86. Telma advertisement, *Davar*, December 24, 1958 (Hebrew).

87. "Results December Quarter 1960," CZA A449/23.

88. "Falafel 'Yemeni Style' to Holland and to Finland," *Maariv*, January 11, 1967 (Hebrew); "Advertisement for Telma's Instant Hummus, Yemeni Style," *Davar*, August 22, 1969 (Hebrew); "Advertisement for Telma's Instant Hummus 'ala-Kaifak," *Maariv*, December 1, 1974 (Hebrew). Interestingly, only after 1967 did Arabic enter the names of Telma products.

89. Adina Almog-Perlman, "To the Woman and the Family: Hummus with No Effort," *Herut*, July 21, 1958 (Hebrew); Aharon Priel, "Expanding the Export Depends on Expanding Research and Conquering the Local Market," *Maariv*, March 19, 1969 (Hebrew). Since I have no systematic data on the source of the chickpeas used by Telma, I do not know whether this policy was consistent. In any case, the Israeli food industry at the time was based mostly on local agriculture. Bayer, "The Food Industry in Its Progress." Sesame for the tahini industry, however, was imported.

90. In 1941, 6,464 acres of chickpeas were cultivated on Arab farms and only 1,208 on Jewish farms. Yaacov Kostrinsky, *Agronomical Surveys on Chickpea and Seed Cycles*, Special Publication no. 34 (Beit Dagan: Department of Scientific Publications, Vulcani Center, 1974), 10; Baruch Retig, "Fifty Years of Chickpea Cultivation in Israel," *Hasade* 79, no. 5 October 1998, 350–52 (Hebrew); Central Bureau of Statistics, "Cultivated Area: Dry Farming and Irrigated Field Crops (Dunams), 1959, 1955–1959", ISA 2411/1-c (Hebrew).

91. Moshe J. Pinthus, "The 1959 Revolution in Chickpea Cultivation in Israel," *Hasade* 76, no. 8 (1996): 36–37 (Hebrew).

92. Retig, "Fifty Years of Chickpea Cultivation."

93. Kostrinsky, *Agronomical Surveys*, 10; Shmuel Galili et al., "The History of Chickpea Cultivation and Breeding in Israel," *Israel Journal of Plant Sciences* 65, nos. 3–4 (2018): 189; Isaac Sadomi, "A New Grain Variety at the 'Open Day' in Beit Dagan," *Davar*, June 24, 1976 (Hebrew); Retig, "Fifty Years of Chickpea Cultivation." Experiments in chickpea breeding, sowing, and cultivation continue in Israel to this day.

94. Kostrinsky, *Agronomical Surveys*, 10; Retig, "Fifty Years of Chickpea Cultivation," 530. By 1971, local agriculture produced half of the four thousand tons of chickpeas consumed in the country per annum. "A Possibility for Increasing the Yield of Chickpea in the Negev Was Recently Discovered by Three Researchers from the Faculty of Agriculture in Rehovot," *Davar*, September 23, 1970 (Hebrew). On the dwindling of agricultural lands in the Arab sector, see Bäuml, "The Principles of the Discrimination," 391–413.

95. See Telma's ads in the daily newspaper *Davar* on December 12, 1962, and October 4, 1968, respectively. For Israel's population in 1968, see Arnon Soffer, "Demography and the Shaping of Israel's Borders," *Contemporary Jewry* 10, no. 2 (1989): 93.

96. Telma advertisement, *Davar*, July 3, 1975 (Hebrew); Interview with Teltsch.

97. In 1951, the Arab League declared a ban on Israeli companies and on companies that traded with Israel. On Telma's export of its hummus, see M., "One of Blue Band Telma's Exhibitions in a Fair Abroad," *Lamerchav*, February 13, 1962 (Hebrew). The item notes that Telma won a government certificate of honor, as an outstanding presenter in international exhibitions in the year 1961. See also "Yemeni Style Falafel to Holland and Finland," *Maariv*, January 11, 1967 (Hebrew); Aharon Priel, "Expanding the Export Depends on Expanding Research and Conquering the Local Market," *Maariv*, March 19, 1969 (Hebrew). According to Prof. Amihud Kramer, an American food technologist, industrial hummus and tahini were well received abroad. A. Deutschkron, "Israeli Food—to European Markets," *Maariv*, October 10, 1961 (Hebrew).

98. Interview with Teltsch; Palestine Edible Products Ltd., "Notes to Cumulative Profit and Loss Report for the Telma Factory by Departments, January–July 1979", CZA A449/24 (Hebrew).

99. Yoram Kaniuk, "Mrs. Ashkenazi Goes Shopping," *Davar*, October 9, 1968 (Hebrew).

100. Bavly, *Food Habits and Their Changes*, 12.

101. Telma Advertisements, *Davar*, April 23, 1963, and *Maariv*, August 1, 1972 (Hebrew).

102. Estel Hame'iri, "To the Woman and the Family: Bat Mitzva Party," *Maariv*, January 10, 1964 (Hebrew); "The Party of the Month: Bnei Mitzva."

103. I have come across advertisements for six additional hummus brands: Vita, Mata, Osem, Friman, Yachin, and Sugat.

104. Telma Newsreel commercials can be found at the Herzliya Studios Archive, Herzliya, and a few at the Israeli Film Archive at the Jerusalem Cinematheque, available online at https://jfc.org.il, accessed July 29, 2025.

105. Telma advertisement, *Davar*, December 24, 1958 (Hebrew). Telma being the first to define hummus as an "Israeli national dish" was confirmed by Giora Teltsch.

106. During the 1950s, Yemenites became associated primarily with falafel due to the large number of Yemenites who sold it. Raviv, *Falafel Nation*, 22.

107. Rosemary J. Coombe, "Embodied Trademarks: Mimesis and Alterity on American Commercial Frontiers," *Cultural Anthropology* 11, no. 2 (1996): 208.

108. Telma hummus commercial, Israeli Film Archive, Jerusalem Cinematheque, accessed July 26, 2022, https://jfc.org.il/news_journal/61458-2/98727 -2/?fbclid=IwAR1bcKNJjyF-2VHk-n8VqJT_TwSitxkKeSo_7IuhlKkBmWWKty CkzzzItuo.

109. Advertisement for Telma company's raffle, Israeli Film Archive, Jerusalem Cinematheque.

110. Telma advertisement, *Maariv*, April 28, 1963 (Hebrew).

111. Telma advertisement, *Davar*, August 22, 1969 (Hebrew).

112. Telma advertisement, *Maariv*, May 18, 1984 (Hebrew).

113. Wilk, *Home Cooking in the Global Village*, 93–94. See also Goody, *Cooking, Cuisine and Class*, 166.

114. Helman, "European Jews in the Levant Heat," 75.

115. Raviv, *Falafel Nation*, 157–81.

116. Tamar Avidar, "For the Home and the Family," *Davar*, July 3, 1959 (Hebrew); "An Import Quota of Hundred Thousand Dollars in the Köln Exhibition," *Lamerchav*, July 23, 1961 (Hebrew); "The Swedish Taste Hummus and Falafel," *Lamerchav*, September 3, 1963 (Hebrew); Daniel Bloch, "Hummus and Falafel in Copenhagen," *Davar*, July 20, 1966 (Hebrew); Deborah Namir, "Traffic Report as Souvenir," *Davar*, June 23, 1967 (Hebrew). In a newsreel item from 1962, Telma's

hummus is served as an Israeli national dish at a dinner celebrating the United Nations Day in Tel Aviv. Herzliya Studios Archive, no. 6312.

117. Palestine Edible Products Ltd., "Review on Position of Our Business in 1960"; "Notes to Cumulative Profit and Loss Report for the Telma Factory by Departments, January–July 1979."

118. Cornfeld, *Israeli Cookery*, 115.

119. Litani and ʿAraidi, *Not by Hummus Alone*, 25.

120. Special Reporter, "Pre-Olympic Tour of the Metropolis," *Yediot Ahronot*, September 11, 1964 (Hebrew), my emphasis.

121. Sheila Ryan, "Constructing a New Imperialism: Israel and the West Bank," *MERIP Reports* 9 (1972): 3; Neve Gordon, *Israel's Occupation* (Berkeley: University of California Press, 2008), 6.

122. Ami Shamir, "Careful—the Israelis Are Coming," *Lamerchav*, June 29, 1929 (Hebrew); Yehoshua Meshulach, "Tourism—A Passport to Peace," *Davar*, September 6, 1967 (Hebrew); Ezra Yinov, "Eating in Gaza—During the Day; Suffering Pain—at Night," *Maariv*, September 10, 1967 (Hebrew); Menachem Talmi, "Sabbath Shalom in Qalqilya," *Maariv*, February 2, 1973 (Hebrew); Danny Rubinstein, "Guide to Bargains in the Arab Market," *Davar*, September 21, 1979 (Hebrew). See also Stein, *Itineraries in Conflict*, 2, 11, 111–15.

123. Moshe Dayan, *Milestones: A Biography* (Jerusalem: Idanim and Dvir, 1976), 494 (Hebrew); Gordon, *Israel's Occupation*, 4–5.

124. Amos Kenan, "A Visit to a Restaurant in Hebron," *Yediot Ahronot*, June 22, 1967 (Hebrew).

125. Yinov, "Eating in Gaza—During the Day."

126. Ruth Hefer, "Going to Hang Out: Brotherhood of Nations," *Yediot Ahronot*, July 6, 1972 (Hebrew).

127. Maʾul, "Bon Appétit: Stuffed Pigeons at Maswada's," *Maariv*, June 16, 1971 (Hebrew).

128. "Jews 'Tasted' the Nightlife in the Old City—with the Termination of the Curfew," *Maariv*, August 28, 1967 (Hebrew); Meshulach, "Tourism—A Passport to Peace."

129. Maʾul, "Bon Appétit: At M. Cohen Carefully," *Maariv*, January 22, 1970 (Hebrew).

130. Danny Rubinstein, "Between Rachmo and Abu Shukri—A Journey Following the Hummus," *Davar*, February 2, 1979 (Hebrew).

131. Fotiadis 1995, quoted in Gadi Algazi, "Middling Ages and Living Relics as Objects to Think with: Two Figures of the Historical Imagination," in *Modernity's Classics*, ed. Sarah C. Humphreys and Rudolf G. Wagner (Berlin: Springer, 2013), 325.

132. Hagor (Haim Gouri), "Near the Flower Gate," *Davar*, June 4, 1971 (Hebrew). See also Kenan, "A Visit to a Restaurant in Hebron"; Talmi, "Sabbath Shalom in Qalqilya."

133. Hagor, "Near the Flower Gate."

134. Hagor, "Weekend Notes: Acknowledgements," *Davar*, March 14, 1975 (Hebrew).

135. Ma'ul, "Bon Appétit: At M. Cohen Carefully."

136. Rubinstein, "Between Rachmo and Abu Shukri."

137. For example, Ma'ul, "'Bon Appétit: Al Aharam' in Tul Karem," *Maariv*, November 11, 1970 (Hebrew); Ma'ul, "Bon Appétit: All the Ladino Foods," *Maariv*, January 31, 1973 (Hebrew); Lokulus, "Ful without 'Ceremony,'" *Yediot Ahronot*, October 28, 1976 (Hebrew); Buki Na'e, "A Tour of Samaria," *Maariv*, July 2, 1979 (Hebrew).

138. Na'e, "A Tour of Samaria." For an earlier example, see Hagor, "Between Tira and Kfar Hess," *Lamerchav*, March 5, 1965 (Hebrew).

139. Ma'ul, "Bon Appétit: Haifa! Haifa. . . ." See also Ma'ul, "High-Quality Restaurant," *Maariv*, August 18, 1971 (Hebrew); See Shooky Galili, "Abu Shukri, The Old City of Jerusalem," *Hummus for the Masses*, accessed August 22, 2022, https://humus101.com/?p=157 (Hebrew).

140. Rubinstein, "Between Rachmo and Abu Shukri." Abu Shukri first opened in another location in 1948 and in the 1960s moved to the Via Dolorosa in the Old City of Jerusalem. See Shooky Galili, "Abu Shukri, The Old City of Jerusalem," *Hummus for the Masses*, accessed August 22, 2022, https://humus101.com/?p=157 (Hebrew); The Jerusalem Old City Site, "Abu Shukri," accessed on August 22, 2022, http://www.haatika.co.il/category/%D7%90%D7%91%D7%95 -%D7%A9%D7%95%D7%A7%D7%A8%D7%99 (Hebrew).

141. Summary of the action of the Ministry of Agriculture in the Judea and Samaria area, April 1968, ISA 8134/2-c; Mohammed K. Shadid, "Israeli Policy towards Economic Development in the West Bank and Gaza," in *The Palestinian Economy: Studies in Development under Prolonged Occupation*, ed. George T. Abed (London: Routledge, 1988), 127.

142. Arieh Arad, "Preparing a Five-Year Plan for Judea and Samaria," *Yediot Ahronot*, October 9, 1967 (Hebrew); A. Sadomi, "Farmers Understand Each Other Well," *Lamerchav*, September 12, 1969 (Hebrew); Hezi Carmel, "The Rothschild Foundation Is About to Approve a First Allowance for Developing West Bank Agriculture," *Maariv*, October 26, 1969 (Hebrew); Ryan, "Constructing a New Imperialism," 8–9; A. R. Husseini, "Israel Restructures West Bank Economy: Interview with A. R. Husseini," *MERIP Reports* 60 (1977): 21–23; Hisham Awartani, "Agricultural Development Policies in the West Bank and Gaza," in *The Palestinian Economy*, 154; Leila Farsakh, *Palestinian Labour Migration to*

Israel: Labour, Land and Occupation (London: Routledge, 2005), 92; Gordon, *Israel's Occupation*, 9.

143. Office of the Assistant Minister of Defense, guidelines for the preparation of the budget of the Civil Administration in the new territories for the budget year 1968–69, October 11, 1967, ISA 8134/1-gl (Hebrew); "Cotton—in Samaria for the First Time," *Lamerchav*, February 2, 1969 (Hebrew); "Compiling a Plan for Decreasing the Importation of Foodstuffs," *Maariv*, June 17, 1969 (Hebrew). Chickpeas were imported mainly from various Mediterranean countries.

144. Danny Rubinstein, "Agriculture in the West Bank Prospers," *Davar*, September 2, 1971 (Hebrew); "Kaplan Prize to the Agricultural Headquarters Staff in Judea and Samaria," 1971, ISA 6598/5-c; Ryan, "Constructing a New Imperialism," 8. At that point, chickpeas were one of the products imported into the West Bank. Danny Rubinstein, "Between 7 and 2 the War Stops," *Davar*, March 21, 1969 (Hebrew).

145. Activities committed in Judea and Samaria, September 19, 1969, ISA 8134/2-c (Hebrew); "Hundred Million IL Worth of Commodities Were Marketed in the Framework of the Open Bridges Policy," *Davar*, December 23, 1969 (Hebrew).

146. Ryan, "Constructing a New Imperialism," 9.

147. Awartani, "Agricultural Development Policies," 146; Shlomo Swirski, *The Price of Occupation* (Tel Aviv: Mapa, 2005), 20–25 (Hebrew).

148. Swirski, *The Price of Occupation*, 20, 23; Shadid, "Israeli Policy towards Economic Development," 123.

149. Awartani, "Agricultural Development Policies," 146; Swirski, *The Price of Occupation*, 23.

150. Emile Sahliyeh, "West Bank Industrial and Agricultural Development: The Basic Problems," *Journal of Palestine Studies* 11, no. 2 (1982): 68; "From Metula to Eilat: From the Tin into . . . Ramat Gan," *Maariv*, October 4, 1968 (Hebrew).

151. Awartani, "Agricultural Development Policies," 154.

152. The research literature highlights several factors contributing to the decline of the agricultural sector, including Israeli restrictions on land and water usage, rising costs of resources and labor, and the influx of subsidized Israeli produce into the Palestinian market, which reduced the profitability of local agriculture. See Sahliyeh, "West Bank Industrial and Agricultural Development," 55–69; Awartani, "Agricultural Development Policies," 154; Husseini, "Israel Restructures West Bank Economy"; Farsakh, *Palestinian Labour Migration*, 85–94.

153. Swirski, *The Price of Occupation*, 32; Awartani, "Agricultural Development Policies," 143–45; Farsakh, *Palestinian Labour Migration*.

154. Swirski, *The Price of Occupation*, 39; Farsakh, *Palestinian Labour Migration*, 75.

155. Shlomo Swirski, "On Economy and Society in Times of Empire," *Iyunim Bitkumat Israel* 16 (2006): 579 (Hebrew).

156. Quoted in Rafi Grosglik, "From 'Staged Authenticity' to 'Liquid Authenticity'—Chinese Food in Israel of the 'Glocalization' Era" (MA thesis, Ben Gurion University, 2008), 37 (Hebrew).

157. Oren Soffer, *Mass Communication in Israel: Nationalism, Globalization, and Segmentation* (New York: Berghahn, 2014), 127–28. See also the documentary by Eyal Sagui Bizawe and Sara Tsifroni, *Arabic Movie* (Israel, 2015) (Hebrew and Arabic).

158. Ohad Smith, "The 'Designed' Israeli Interior," 27; Elor and Regev, "The Establishment of an Israeli Style," 315–20.

159. Interview with Amnon Tzaban, Tel Aviv, March 18, 2016; phone interview with Asher Bitansky, January 25, 2016.

160. The original meaning of the Persian word is "something revealed/open/ manifest."

161. Sarit Fuchs, "The Street of Things and Their Opposite," *Maariv*, June 26, 1978 (Hebrew).

162. Gershon Shafir and Yoav Peled, *Being Israeli: The Dynamics of Multiple Citizenship* (Cambridge: Cambridge University Press, 2004), 218; Swirski, "On Economy and Society in Times of Empire," 563; Paul Rivlin, *The Israeli Economy from the Foundation of the State through the 21st Century* (Cambridge: Cambridge University Press, 2011), 41–42.

163. Kalka, "Changing Nutrition Value," 9.

164. Amos Kenan, *The Book of Pleasure* (Tel Aviv: A. Levin-Epstein, 1970) (Hebrew); Yoel Marcus, *The Wine Book* (Haifa: Company for Book Publishing, 1972) (Hebrew); Ron Mayberg, *A Country Eats* (Tel Aviv: Zmora, Bitan, Modan, 1996), 90 (Hebrew).

165. Aviva Goldman, *The Cookbook* (Tel Aviv: Maariv, 1970) (Hebrew).

166. Ruth Sirkis, *From the Kitchen with Love: The Foundations of Cooking and the Secrets of Hosting* (Ramat Gan: R. Sirkis, 1975) (Hebrew). Sirkis first tried to publish her book with Maariv Books in 1966, but they refused on the grounds of its being too fancy, bordering on the luxurious, so eventually she published it herself. Later it was published by one of the leading publishers: Zmora, Bitan, Modan. Emanuela Calò, "Change of Taste in Israeli Food: The Case of 'Italian Cuisine,' 1980–2000" (MA thesis, Tel Aviv University, 2005), 55–56 (Hebrew).

167. Shooky Galili, "Recipes from the Past 3: The Cookbook, 1970," *Hummus for the Masses*, accessed August 30, 2022, https//humus101.com/?p=2319 (Hebrew).

168. Sirkis, *From the Kitchen with Love*, 69.

169. Sami Shalom Chetrit, *The Mizrahi Struggle in Israel: Between Oppression and Liberation, Identification and Alternative, 1948–2003* (Tel Aviv: Am Oved,

2006), 131–32 (Hebrew); Vered Kraus and Yuval Yonay, "The Power and Limits of Ethnonationalism: Palestinians and Eastern Jews in Israel, 1974–1991," *British Journal of Sociology* 51, no. 3 (2000): 525–51; Ben-Porat, *The Bourgeoisie*, 140–42; Ephraim Yuchtman-Yaar, "Differences in Ethnic Patterns of Socioeconomic Achievements in Israel—A Neglected Aspect of Structured Inequality," *International Review of Modern Sociology* 15, no. 1/2 (1985): 99–116; Noah Lewin-Epstein and Moshe Semyonov, "Ethnic Group Mobility in the Israeli Labor Market," *American Sociological Review* 51, no. 3 (1986): 342–52. On mobility among Palestinian citizens, see Aziz Haidar, *The New Arab-Palestinian Middle Class in Israel: Economic, Socio-Cultural and Political Aspects* (Ramat Aviv: Walter-Lebach Institute for Jewish-Arab Coexistence and Tami Steinmetz Center for Peace Research, 2021), 33, 40–50 (Hebrew).

170. Almog, "From Vegetable Salad and Lebeniya," 13. For a similar process among Palestinian citizens, see Gvion, "Cooking, Food, and Masculinity," 419–21. See also Lea Etgar, "The Check Please: The Intifada Visits the Arab Restaurants," *Yediot Ahronot*, October 2, 1988 (Hebrew).

171. Eliezer Strauch, "We Expected a Crisis—But There's Still Some Profit," *Yediot Ahronot*, July 29, 1974 (Hebrew).

172. Dov Gnichovsky, Israel Tomer, and Zvi Vexler, "A Hot Inflationary Summer," *Yediot Ahronot*, July 5, 1974 (Hebrew).

173. Strauch, "We Expected a Crisis"; Lea Etgar, "The High Prices Caused a 25 Percent Decrease in the Number of Visitors in Luxury Restaurants," *Yediot Ahronot*, January 10, 1979 (Hebrew).

174. Orly Azulay, "The Entertainment—for Men Only," *Yediot Ahronot*, August 24, 1979 (Hebrew); Stein, *Itineraries in Conflict*, 116.

175. Azulay, "The Entertainment—for Men Only."

176. Oren Soffer, "The Anomaly of Galei Tzahal: Israel's Army Radio as a Cultural Vanguard and Force for Pluralism," *Historical Journal of Film, Radio and Television* 32, no. 2 (2012): 225.

177. More on Abu Hassan in the next chapter.

178. Phone interview with Micha Levinson, December 14, 2015.

4. THE GOURMETIZATION OF HUMMUS AND THE RETURN OF THE REPRESSED ARAB

1. Dubi Zakai, "The Hummus Road," *Yediot Ahronot*, May 8, 1997 (Hebrew).

2. Shafir and Peled, *Being Israeli*, 231–59; Svirski, "On Economy and Society in Times of Empire"; Uri Ram, *The Globalization of Israel: McWorld in Tel Aviv, Jihad in Jerusalem* (New York: Routledge, 2008), 91; Guy Ben-Porat, "Political Economy: Liberalization and Globalization," in *Israel Since 1980*, ed. Guy Ben-Porat, Yagil Levy, Shlomo Mizrahi, Arye Naor, and Erez Tzfadia (Cambridge: Cambridge University Press, 2008), 91–116.

3. Ram, *Globalization of Israel*, 22–23; Ben-Porat, "Political Economy."

4. Probably the most conspicuous example is satirists Dudu Geva and Kobi Niv's "Ahlan and Sahlan against the Hummus Gang," which appeared in their column in the Jerusalem local newspaper *Kol Ha'ir* and in their comic book *Ridiculous Book* (Jerusalem: Adam, 1981) (Hebrew).

5. According to Dun and Bradstreet, in 2005, there were one thousand hummusiyot operating in Israel, but five hundred of them were at risk of closing. Navit Zomer, "Thousand Hummusiyot in Israel," *Ynet*, January 4, 2005, https://www.ynet.co.il/articles/0,7340,L-3027835,00.html (Hebrew). In 2020, an article on the Monopoli business portal reported six hundred hummusiyot in Israel. Jean Claude Max, "How to open a hummusiya in Israel?," Monopoli, https://bit.ly/3JqRJ3M, accessed March 17, 2023 (Hebrew). Besides hummusiyot, many restaurants also serve hummus.

6. On the masculine gendering of hummus in Israel, see my "Hummus Masculinity in Israel," 337–59.

7. See Litani and 'Araidi, *Not by Hummus Alone*; Ariel Rosenthal, Orly Peli-Bronshtein, and Dan Alexander, *On the Hummus Route* (Published by the authors, 2019); Yaron Gutmark, *Riding for Hummus: Hiking Bike Tracks, Hummus, and Everything in Between* (Published by the author, 2021) (Hebrew); Erez Tikolsker, Ran Atzmon, and Eiran Shoshani, *The Large Hummusiyot Guide* (Published by the authors, 2022) (Hebrew). The hummus blog is Shooky Galili's *Hummus for the Masses*, accessed July 30, 2025, http://humus101.com (Hebrew).

8. Examples of artwork involving hummus are Eliyahu Fatal, *Hummus* (2001–2003); Sharif Waked, *Khumus* (2008); and Boaz Arad, *Hummus* (2013). Examples of songs about hummus are Nigel ha-Admor, "Hummus metamtem" (1993); Benjamin (Banji) Oli'el, "Hummusim" (2010); and Daniel and Noy, "The Hummus Hymn" (2010). Examples of films about hummus are Nadav Rosenblum and Micha Cohen, *Hummus-Chips-Salad* (2009); Eran Vered, *The Unit for Hummus Investigations* (2012); and Oren Rosenfeld, *Hummus! The Movie* (2015). Yehoshua Kenaz's short story "The Black Briefcase" (2008) takes place in a hummusiya.

9. Lupton, *Food, the Body and the Self*, 68–93; Alan Warde, *Consumption, Food and Taste* (London: Sage, 1997), 157; Meneley, "Like an Extra Virgin," 679.

10. Data on vegetarianism and veganism in Israel are partial. According to a survey conducted by the Israeli Ministry of Health in 1999–2001, which included vegetarians and vegans in a single category, the share of both groups in the adult population was 8.5 percent. In a 2010 survey of the Central Bureau of Statistics, only 2.6 percent of the entire population defined themselves as vegetarians or vegans (the difference may result from different definitions of vegetarianism and veganism). See Knesset Research and Information Center, "The Trend of Vegetarianism and Veganism in Israel and in the World," accessed March 19, 2023,

https://bit.ly/3LuK733 (Hebrew). In my own survey (*n* = 500), 3.8 percent testified to being vegetarians and 1.6 percent to being vegans. See also Ori Schwarz, "Identity as a Barrier: Claiming Universality as a Strategy in the Israeli Vegan Movement," *Social Movement Studies* 20, no. 5 (2021): 604.

11. Grosglik, "Global Ethical Culinary Fashion," 165–84; Avital Sebbag, *Five Seasons in the Kitchen: Zen Inspired Vegan Cooking* (Jerusalem: Geffen 2014) (Hebrew).

12. Marion Eugene Ensminger and Audrey H. Ensminger, eds., *Food and Nutrition Encyclopedia*, 2nd edition (Boca Raton: CRC, 1993); Kenneth F. Kiple, ed., *Cambridge World History of Food* (Cambridge: Cambridge University Press, 2000); Benjamin Caballero, ed., *Encyclopedia of Food Sciences and Nutrition* (Kidlington, Oxford: Elsevier Science, 2003); Alan Davidson, ed., *The Oxford Companion to Food* (Oxford: Oxford University Press, 2014).

13. Zohar Kerem et al., "Chickpea Domestication in the Neolithic Levant through the Nutritional Perspective," *Journal of Archaeological Science* 34, no. 8 (2007): 1289–93.

14. Reem Kassis, *The Palestinian Table* (London: Phaidon, 2017), 82.

15. Rabea Eghbariah, "The Struggle for Akoub & Za'atar: On Edible Plants in Palestinian Cuisine and Israeli Plant Protection Laws," in *Studies in Food Law*, ed. Aeyal Gross and Yofi Tirosh (Tel Aviv: The Buchmann Faculty of Law, Tel Aviv University, 2017), 497–533 (Hebrew); Omar Kassis, "Olive Oil and the Taste of Palestine," *Jerusalem Quarterly* 98 (2024): 13, 23.

16. Ram, *Globalization of Israel*, 65–71; Yoram S. Carmeli and Kalman Applebaum, "Introduction," in *Consumption and Market Society in Israel*, ed. Yoram S. Carmeli and Kalman Applebaum (New York: Berg, 2004), 1–2.

17. Carmeli and Applebaum, "Introduction," 3–4; Michael Shalev, "The Welfare State Consensus in Israel: Placing Class Politics in Context," in *Social Justice, Legitimacy and the Welfare State*, ed. Steffen Mau and Benjamin Veghte (Aldershot: Ashgate, 2007), 205–206; Ram, *Globalization of Israel*, 231–34.

18. Bourdieu, *Distinction*; Ben-Porat, *The Bourgeoisie*, 170–76; Dana Kaplan, "Recreational Sexuality, Food, New Age Spirituality: A Cultural Sociology of Middle Class Distinctions," PhD diss., Hebrew University of Jerusalem, 2014, 47.

19. Mike Featherstone, *Consumer Culture and Postmodernism* (London: Sage, 2007), 59; De Solier, *Food and the Self*; Kaplan, "Recreational Sexuality."

20. Or Ezrati, "Israel Aharoni," in *Masters of Culture: Anatomy of Israeli Culture Producers*, ed. Nir Baram (Tel Aviv: Am Oved, 2003), 87 (Hebrew); Calò, "Change of Taste in Israeli Food."

21. Rafi Grosglik and Uri Ram, "Authentic, Speedy and Hybrid: Representations of Chinese food and Cultural Globalization in Israel," *Food, Culture & Society* 16, no. 2 (2013): 223–43; Calò, "Change of Taste in Israeli Food," 61–64; Ezrati, "Israel Aharoni," 92; Dunevich, *A City Dines*, 331–35, 385–403. Food

photography has also changed and included color and documentary-like photographs of food in situ.

22. Almog, "From Vegetable Salad and Lebeniya," 14–19; Calò, "Change of Taste in Israeli Food"; Guy Ben-Porat, *Between State and Synagogue: The Secularization of Contemporary Israel* (Cambridge: Cambridge University Press, 2013), 138–75; Dunevich, *A City Dines*, 385–403. In May 2009, the Pentecost issue of the economic supplement of *Haaretz*, *TheMarker*, was dedicated to the burgeoning market for gourmet food in Israel. Michal Palti, Tali Heruti-Sover, and Amiram Cohen, "The Israeli Gourmet Index: A Decade of Gourmet Growth," *TheMarker*, May 28, 2009 (Hebrew). This process was also manifested in a major increase in the number of cookbooks published in Israel per year. See also Maya Mazor Tregerman, "The Limits of Good Taste: Cookbooks, Popular Culture, and Book Publishing in Global Israel" (MA thesis, University of Haifa, 2008), 10 (Hebrew); Ofra Tene, "From Nationalism and Health to Consumerism and Identity Construction," in *Thoughts on Food*, ed. Ori Bartal, Ronit Vered, and Michal Eitan (Jerusalem: Bezalel Academy of Art and Resling, 2021), 299–300 (Hebrew).

23. The final episode of the third season of *MasterChef* was one of the most viewed TV broadcasts of all time in Israel. Rafi Grosglik and Julia Lerner, "Gastro-emotivism: How MasterChef Israel Produces Therapeutic Collective Belongings," *European Journal of Cultural Studies* 24, no. 5 (2021): 1054.

24. Azri Amram, "Digesting the Massacre: Food Tours in Palestinian Towns in Israel," *Gastronomica* 19, no. 4 (2019): 60–73; Shlomo Guzmen-Carmeli, "Eating the Bubbe: Culinary Encounters between Secular and Haredi Jews in Bnei Brak," *Food and Foodways* 28, no. 2 (2020): 69–90.

25. Tene, "Thus You Shall Cook!," 93; Guy Farhi, "Pita Politics: The Miznon Chain and the Cultural Logic of Late Capitalism," in *Thoughts on Food*, 422–39 (Hebrew). According to Mihalis Mentinis, food has become no less and sometimes more important than sex in defining who we are. Mihalis Mentinis, "Romanticised Chefs and the Psychopolitics of Gastroporn," *Culture & Psychology* 23, no. 1 (2017): 132.

26. Grosglik and Lerner, "Gastro-emotivism," 1053–70.

27. Bourdieu, *Distinction*, 366; Farhi, "Pita Politics."

28. Grosglik and Lerner, "Gastro-emotivism."

29. Shafir and Peled, *Being Israeli*, 90.

30. Uri Cohen and Nissim Leon, "The New Mizrahi Middle Class: Ethnic Mobility and Class Integration in Israel," *Journal of Israeli History* 27, no. 1 (2008): 51–64; Guy Abutbul-Selinger, "Invisible Boundaries within the Middle Class and the Construction of Ethnic Identity," *Identities* 27, no. 2 (2020): 210–28; Rami Adut and Dani Filc, "Constructing a Classed Community in Kiryat Eilon (H-300) in Holon: A 'Popular-Class' Community on Mizrahi 'Building Blocks,'" *Journal of Israeli History* 40, no. 1 (2022): 7–41.

31. Sami Shalom Chetrit, *Intra-Jewish Conflict in Israel: White Jews, Black Jews* (Abingdon, Oxon: Routledge, 2010), 156–60; Avi Picard, "Like a Phoenix: The Renaissance of Sephardic/Mizrahi Identity in Israel in the 1970s and 1980s," *Israel Studies* 22, no. 2 (2017): 1–25.

32. Motti Regev, "To Have a Culture of Our Own: On Israeliness and Its Variants," *Ethnic and Racial Studies* 23, no. 2 (2000): 235.

33. Tene, "From Nationalism and Health," 305–308.

34. Grosglik and Ram, "Authentic, Speedy and Hybrid"; Kaplan, "Recreational Sexuality."

35. Calò, "Change of Taste in Israeli Food"; Tene, "Thus You Shall Cook!"; Grosglik and Ram, "Authentic, Speedy and Hybrid." Exotic, foreign, and ethnic are not rigid and mutually exclusive categories, and their content may vary according to context. Usually the distinction between foreign and ethnic or exotic is based on the global hierarchy of power: cuisines of the less powerful are defined as ethnic or exotic rather than foreign. Here I use it to distinguish between Euro-American cuisines, cuisines from other parts of the world, and those of marginalized ethnic communities in Israel. See Ray, *The Ethnic Restauranteur*; Gvion, "Hummus, Couscous, Sushi."

36. Tene, "From Nationalism and Health," 302–11.

37. I am not arguing that political orientation determines food beliefs. However, it is much less likely for right-wing chefs and food experts to define Arab food as "the most local food of all." Hilik Gurfinkel, "No Longer Amamiko: Arab Cuisine," *Nrg Maariv*, October 3, 2008, https://www.makorrishon.co.il/nrg/online/55/ART1/793/578.html (Hebrew). See also Alon Hadar, "Sabbath Meal: the Battle over Hummus," *Times of Israel*, May 10, 2019, https://www.zman.co.il/659/popup (Hebrew).

38. Eli Landau, "The Wonders of Lebanese Cuisine," *Yediot Ahronot*, November 11, 1998 (Hebrew).

39. Piastro, *Eating in Israel*, 160–61.

40. For example, Tiki Golan, "Politically Correct," *TimeOut*, September 9, 2013, https://bit.ly/3LEmRzi (Hebrew); Maayan Alon, "Much More than Hummus: Ten Culinary Stops in East Jerusalem," *Ynet*, January 28, 2017, http://www.ynet.co.il/articles/0,7340,L-4911478,00.html (Hebrew); Daniel Monterescu, Rafi Grosglik, and Ariel Handel, "How 'Baladi' became the Star of Israeli Cuisine and a Key to Palestinian Identity and Resistance," *Haaretz.com*, December 19, 2022, https://bit.ly/40KywRy. There is no simple definition for *baladi*. Originally indicating local produce, this term became associated with additional values like authenticity and organic agriculture.

41. For example, Yochanan Peled, "A Salad Full of Juice and Imagination," *Davar*, May 26, 1983 (Hebrew).

42. Advertisement for The Pink Ladle restaurant, *Ha'ir*, August 28, 1987 (Hebrew).

43. Israel Aharoni, "Ideological Hummus," *Yediot Ahronot*, January 31, 1997 (Hebrew).

44. Alon Hadar, "A Journey to the Best Hummus in the World," *Nrg Maariv: Culinar blog*, September 30, 2011, https://bit.ly/3nu8bcc (Hebrew).

45. For example, Richard A. Peterson and Roger M. Kern, "Changing Highbrow Taste: From Snob to Omnivore," *American Sociological Review* 61, no. 5 (1996): 900–907; Michèle Ollivier, "Modes of Openness to Cultural Diversity: Humanist, Populist, Practical, and Indifferent," *Poetics* 36, no. 2–3 (2008): 120–47; Alan Warde, David Wright, and Modesto Gayo-Cal, "The Omnivorous Orientation in the UK," *Poetics* 36, no. 2–3 (2008): 148–65; Tally Katz-Gerro, Sharon Raz, and Meir Yaish, "How Do Class, Status, Ethnicity, and Religiosity Shape Cultural Omnivorousness in Israel?," *Journal of Cultural Economics* 33 (2009): 1–17; Omar Lizardo and Sara Skiles, "Reconceptualizing and Theorizing 'Omnivorousness': Genetic and Relational Mechanisms," *Sociological Theory* 30, no. 4 (2012): 263–82.

46. Smadar Shir, "When I Eat, I Make Love with the Plate," *Yediot Ahronot*, July 12, 1998 (Hebrew).

47. Ollivier, "Modes of Openness"; Warde, Wright, and Gayo-Cal, "Omnivorous Orientation"; Lizrado and Skiles, "Reconceptualizing," 269, 275; Kaplan, "Recreational Sexuality," 248.

48. Johnston and Baumann, *Foodies*.

49. Lizrado and Skiles, "Reconceptualizing," 270; De Solier, *Food and the Self*, 61; Peter Naccarato and Kathleen Lebesco, *Culinary Capital* (London: Berg, 2012).

50. Lizrado and Skiles, "Reconceptualizing," 269.

51. Lizrado and Skiles, "Reconceptualizing," 274; Peterson and Kern, "Changing Highbrow Taste"; Johnston and Baumann, *Foodies*; De Solier, *Food and the Self*.

52. Johnston and Baumann, *Foodies*, 69–96; De Solier, *Food and the Self*, 60–61.

53. Johnston and Baumann, *Foodies*, 69–70.

54. Johnston and Baumann, *Foodies*, 94.

55. Among respondents with high cultural capital, only 32.14 percent stated that most of the hummus they eat is packaged hummus, compared to 47.37 percent of those with low cultural capital and 46.07 percent of those with a moderate level of cultural capital.

56. Rita Goldstein, "On Hummus Alone," *Mako*, August 31, 2014, https://www.mako.co.il/food-weekend/Article-d930670b1f01841006.htm (Hebrew).

57. For example, Editorial Board, "Public Opinion: Arab Hummus Is Good Hummus," *Foodis*, accessed October 6, 2014, http://www.foodis.co.il/feature.asp?sec=14&featid=10098 (Hebrew).

58. Before the 1990s, most Jews were unfamiliar with msabbaha and mshawsha. The question whether there is a difference between msabbaha and mshawsha or whether these are different names for the same dish is a favorite topic of debate among hummusologists.

59. Sherry Ansky, "Hummus," *Maariv*, May 5, 1995 (Hebrew).

60. Shooky Galili, "The Third Lebanon War: The Battle over the Hummus," *Ynet*, November 2, 2009, http://www.ynet.co.il/articles/0,7340,L-3798944,00 .html (Hebrew).

61. Erez Tikolsker, post in the Facebook group "Hummusologists Inc.," April 30, 2021, https://www.facebook.com/groups/Msabbaha/permalink/74122 8836518722 (Hebrew). Maccabiah is a multisport competition for Jewish athletes. Out of almost three hundred responses, several disputed the supremacy of Arab hummus, some of them fiercely. Others supported it.

62. Litani and 'Araidi, *Not by Hummus Alone*, 27.

63. Litani and 'Araidi, *Not by Hummus Alone*, 194.

64. For example, Litani and 'Araidi, *Not by Hummus Alone*; Tzur Shezaf, "Hummus—the Real Thing," July 12, 2007, https://shorturl.at/BDB6d (Hebrew). See also *Hummus for the Masses*, http://humus101.com.

65. In earlier periods, racist libels about Arabs contaminating the hummus they sell to Jews—for example, by urinating in it—used to surface from time to time. While seldom heard today, they have not completely disappeared. For example, *Maariv Online*, "The Vicious 'News': 'Abu Hassan Workers Were Arrested after Cooking Chickpeas in the Toilet,'" September 4, 2017, https://www .maariv.co.il/news/viral/Article-598076 (Hebrew).

66. Zakai, "Hummus Road."

67. Of them, 18.5–18.7 percent stated that they strongly agree with these statements, and 25.5–25.9 percent said that they quite agree. Another 15 percent neither agreed nor disagreed. In another survey, conducted by the brand Miki Delicatessen, 95 percent of the respondents said that they had positive associations toward the term "Arab hummus." See Editorial Board, "Public Opinion." Another survey found that 50 percent of the respondents (Israeli Jews) thought that hummus was an Arab dish. Only 25 percent considered it an Israeli dish. Hadar Kane, "The Great Hummus Survey: How Many Israelis Eat Hummus with a Fork, and Which Is Better—with Chickpeas or with Ful?," *TheMarker*, May 9, 2016, https://www.themarker.com/consumer/2016-05-09/ty-article/0000017f -e790-d62c-a1ff-fffbb9ca0000 (Hebrew).

68. Oded Shalom, "Abu Hummus," *Yediot Ahronot*, March 10, 2000 (Hebrew); Michal Palti, "Abu Hassan Died—the Founder of the Legendary Hummusiya," *Haaretz*, October 24, 2007, https://www.haaretz.co.il/misc/2007-10-24 /ty-article/0000017f-e835-da9b-a1ff-ec7fa4440000 (Hebrew).

69. Dudu Geva, "The Wonderful Journey to the Lost Hummus Shrine," reproduced in Sherry Ansky, "The Last Grain," *Nrg Maariv*, June 10, 2010, https:// www.makorrishon.co.il/nrg/online/1/ART/884/458.html (Hebrew).

70. *Hummus Mouse: The Selected Hundred Hummusiyot of Israel* (Tel Aviv: City Mouse, 2010) (Hebrew).

71. Yehuda Litani, "A Very Narrow Bridge, the Hummus," *Haʻir*, August 1, 1997 (Hebrew).

72. Stein, *Itineraries in Conflict*; Amram, "Digesting the Massacre."

73. Amram quotes a survey from 2012 that found that 58 percent of the Jewish respondents stated they avoid entering Palestinian localities in Israel due to fear and distrust of Palestinians. Amram, "Digesting the Massacre," 62.

74. Limor Evron Gilat, "How I Stopped Throwing Hummus Away," *Haaretz*, July 19, 2009 (Hebrew).

75. Liora Gvion, "'From an Arab I Would Expect That . . .': 'MasterChef,' Hegemony and Exclusion," in *Studies in Food Law*, 561–87 (Hebrew); Tiki Golan, "'I Don't Care about Political Definitions': Alaa Musa Opens a Restaurant in Haifa," *Ynet*, March 9, 2018, https://www.ynet.co.il/articles/0,7340,L-5152150,00.html #autoplay (Hebrew).

76. Wolfe, *Settler Colonialism*, 163–214, the quote is on p. 179; Grey and Newman, "Beyond Culinary Colonialism," 720.

77. Bell, *Relating Indigenous and Settler Identities*.

78. For example, Yair Amikam, "Beirut: the End," *Yediot Ahronot*, October 1, 1982 (Hebrew); Eitan Haber, "The Man who Came to Dine in Beirut," *Yediot Ahronot*, June 18, 1982 (Hebrew).

79. Haber, "The Man Who Came to Dine in Beirut."

80. Stein, *Itineraries in Conflict*.

81. For example, Israel Aharoni, "'7 Days' Guide to the Best Restaurants in Jordan," *Yediot Ahronot*, September 2, 1994 (Hebrew); Phyllis Glazer, "Recipes from the Syrian Cuisine," *Yediot Ahronot*, January 12, 2000 (Hebrew); Edna Yis, "An Hour and a Half from Tiberias," *Yediot Ahronot*, December 18, 1995 (Hebrew).

82. Avner Bernheimer, "My Dream Is That Ezer and I Will Sit In the Market in Damascus and Eat Hummus," *Maariv Weekend*, May 21, 1993 (Hebrew); Shoshana Chen, Moshe Ronen, and Shir-li Golan-Meiri, "A Wipe of Health," *Yediot Ahronot*, January 4, 2001 (Hebrew).

83. Emuna Alon, "Maybe in the Sense of Hummus," *Yediot Ahronot*, December 22, 1999 (Hebrew); Uri Elizur, "Golan for Hummus," *Yediot Ahronot*, December 24, 1999 (Hebrew); Elyakim Haetzni, "This Hummus Will Cost Us a Fortune," *Yediot Ahronot*, January 12, 2000 (Hebrew). The allusion here is to the biblical story of Esau, who sold his birthright for lentil stew.

84. John Urry, *Consuming Places* (London: Routledge, 1995), 129–40; Andrew Holden, *Tourism Studies and the Social Sciences* (London: Routledge, 2005), 51–52.

85. These were the words of Zoheir Baʻalul, who moderated the Hummus record event at Abu Ghosh in 2010, on which I expand in the next chapter.

86. Shezaf, "Hummus: The Real Thing."

87. Rosenthal, Peli-Bronshtein, and Alexander, *On the Hummus Route*, 14. The book lists no place of publication but its authors are Israeli.

88. Callie Maidhof, "Settler Nostalgia: Colonizing Temporalities and the Genre of Coexistence," *Cultural Critique* 116, no. 1 (2022): 92–118.

89. One example is the Chefs for Peace organization: https://chefs4peace .weebly.com, accessed April 10, 2023. Another is the Ramadan Nights tours to various Arab villages and towns: https://www.sharedpaths.org.il/activities/, https://ramadan-nights.co.il, and many others, accessed April 10, 2023.

90. Ilan Zvi Baron and Galia Press-Barnathan, "Foodways and Foodwashing: Israeli Cookbooks and the Politics of Culinary Zionism," *International Political Sociology* 15, no. 3 (2021): 338–58.

91. Stein, *Itineraries in Conflict*.

92. For example, Fadi Khoury, "We Don't Want to Go Back to Coexistence That Begins and Ends in a Hummusiya," *Local Conversation*, October 12, 2015, https://bit.ly/3ZTfJD1 (Hebrew); Fadi Maklada, "A Coexistence of Hummus and Garages," *Ynet*, May 25, 2021, https://www.ynet.co.il/news/article/HJoKm89Fd (Hebrew); Samah Salaime, "In Ramadan, Even Feminist Women Return to the Kitchen," *Local Conversation*, July 4, 2015, https://bit.ly/3UiSq4t (Hebrew).

93. For example, "The Operation in Gaza Is Over, the Confiscation of Businesses Owned by Arabs Continues," September 30, 2014, https://www.mako.co.il/news-money/economy-q3_2014/Article -2ce5c5d9b94c841004.htm (Hebrew); Boaz Wolinitz, "Will Food Bring Peace?," *Walla! Food*, December 31, 2015, https://food.walla.co.il/item/2920841 (Hebrew); Rotem Maimon, "Why Did We Decide to Close the Restaurant?," *Haaretz*, June 28, 2016 (Hebrew); Samer Odeh-Karantinji, "Haifa: Boycott and Threats on Arab Businesses," *Hai Po*, https://haipo.co.il/item/20242, accessed July 4, 2023 (Hebrew).

94. Amos Noy, "The Culinary Left," *The Seventh Eye*, January 1, 2010, https://www.the7eye.org.il/40253 (Hebrew).

95. "Hummus Eliyahu—the Wipe with the Groove," accessed April 17, 2023, https://www.humus-eli-yahoo.com; "The Secrets of Hummus Eliyahu with Avi Bitton," accessed April 17, 2023, https://www.youtube.com/watch?v=HQfP okpU6QU.

96. Oren Rosenfeld, *Hummus! The Movie* (Multicom Entertainment, 2015) (English, Hebrew, Arabic).

97. https://www.humus-eli-yahoo.com.

98. Yaron Rowlaschi, "Which Is the Best Hummus in Israel?," *Mako*, May 11, 2016, https://www.mako.co.il/food-weekend/Article-cca2169ba3b7451006 .htm (Hebrew); Yonatan Meital, "Until the Last Pea: The Best Hummusiyot in Tel Aviv," *Haaretz*, accessed July 31, 2025, https://www.haaretz.co.il/food /restaurant-guide/2018-05-13/ty-article/0000017f-f85c-d044-adff-fbfd15b50000 (Hebrew); Oded Pashtazky, "Your Recommendations: The Best Hummus Dishes in the Country," November 5, 2019, https://www.rest.co.il/magazine/ foodnews/30184 (Hebrew); "The Taste of Life and the Holy Grail: The Race after the Perfect Hummus," *Kan News*, August 26, 2022, https://www.youtube.com

/watch?v=POuij6goL5U (Hebrew). For contestations of the claim that Arabs make better hummus than Jews, see the discussion around the following post by Erez Tikolsker, one of the authors of a hummus guide, in the "hummusologists inc." Facebook group: https://www.facebook.com/groups/Msabbaha/permalink /739902209984718, accessed April 18, 2023.

99. Ranta, "Re-Arabizing Israeli Food Culture"; Ranta and Monterescu, "Decolonizing Israeli Food?"; Sertbulut, "The Culinary State," 49–76.

100. Hilik Gurfinkel, "The Cooking in Israel: A Portrait," *Nrg Maariv*, May 9, 2008, https://www.makorrishon.co.il/nrg/online/55/ART1/729/549.html (Hebrew); Dana Melamed, "Mitbach al-Yahud," *Achbar Ha'ir*, February 17, 2011 (Hebrew).

101. When chef Meir Adoni called his kibbeh nayyeh "Palestinian tartar," he became a target for concerted attacks by the ultra-right rapper Yoav Eliasi ("The Shadow") and his followers. Guy Farhi, "Meir Adoni's Tartar Is Too Leftist for 'The Shadow,'" *TimeOut*, October 25, 2017, https://bit.ly/419Jv7U (Hebrew). See also Ranta and Monterescu, "Decolonizing Israeli Food?"

102. For example, Gurfinkel, "The Cooking in Israel: A Portrait"; Melamed, "Mitbach al-Yahud"; Smadar Salomon, "When the Gefilte Met Rosemary," *Fusion*, February 2012, 30–36 (Hebrew).

103. Rotem Maimon, "Israeli Cuisine Is a Success in Europe. What Is the Secret of Its Success?," *Haaretz*, April 11, 2023 (Hebrew). Ranta and Prieto-Piastro, "Does Israeli Food Exist?," 119–29.

104. https://www.neniberlin.de, accessed April 14, 2023; https://sevennorth restaurant.com/en, accessed April 14, 2023.

105. Sarit Sardes-Trotino, "Amba in Times Square," *Mako*, June 12, 2014, https://www.mako.co.il/food-weekend/Article-27ee8f760ea8641006.htm (Hebrew). On the concept of "gastrodiplomacy," see Paul Rockower, "A Guide to Gastrodiplomacy," in *Routledge Handbook of Public Diplomacy*, ed. Nancy Snow and Nicholas J. Cull (London: Routledge, 2020), 205–12.

106. Baron and Press-Barnathan, "Foodways and Foodwashing."

107. Sertbulut, "The Culinary State."

108. Janna Gur, *The Book of New Israeli Food: A Culinary Journey* (Tel Aviv: Al Hashulchan, 2007).

109. For example, Dana Melamed, "Never Mind from Which Ethnic Community," *Ha'ir*, March 22, 2012 (Hebrew); the Galileat food tours and culinary courses initiative: http://www.galileat.com, accessed April 17, 2023; Delicious Israel food tours: https://www.deliciousisrael.com, accessed April 17, 2023; "Israeli Culinary Tours and Experiences" by Via Sabra: https://viasabra.com /israel-culinary-tours/, accessed July 31, 2025.

110. Baron and Press-Barnathan, "Foodways and Foodwashing"; Ahmad, "Freekeh and Fellahin," 45–47.

111. https://www.vibeisrael.com, accessed April 16, 2023.

112. Ilan Lukach, "A Tourist Journey Following Israeli Food," Channel 2 News, June 29, 2012, http://www.mako.co.il/news-channel2/Friday-Newscast/Article -ad7c4fe6b893831018.htm (Hebrew).

113. Danna Herman, "Hummus State of Mind," *Haaretz*, January 5, 2013 (Hebrew).

114. See, for example, the menus of the Tish restaurant in London and the Klezmer-Hois restaurant in Kraków: https://tish.london/menus/, accessed July 31, 2025; http://klezmer.pl/en/our-menu, accessed November 11, 2023. On hummus as part of the Sabbath table in the US, see Shooky Galili, "A Hit in the US: Hummus with Pretzels," *Hummus for the Masses*, June 19, 2007, accessed November 11, 2023, http://humus101.com/?p=110 (Hebrew).

5. MADE WITH LOVE

1. Tour of Strauss's salads factory, Karmiel, August 4, 2010; the quote is taken from Yaron Bornstein, "The Truth about Hummus 2," *Saloona*, August 23, 2010, https://t.ly/rabz (Hebrew).

2. In my survey, the most common mode of hummus consumption—reported by 43 percent of respondents—was eating industrially produced hummus at home. As I noted in the previous chapter, only 13.7 percent of the respondents said that they never bought packaged hummus.

3. Naomi Klein, *No Logo* (New York: Picador, 2002); Douglas B. Holt, "Jack Daniel's America: Iconic Brands as Ideological Parasites and Proselytizers," *Journal of Consumer Culture* 6, no. 3 (2006): 375.

4. Paul Manning and Ann Uplisashvili, "'Our Beer': Ethnographic Brands in Postsocialist Georgia," *American Anthropologist* 109, no. 4 (2007): 640.

5. Michael Shalev, "Have Globalization and Liberalization 'Normalized' Israel's Political Economy?" *Israel Affairs* 5, no. 2–3 (1999): 132; Uri Ram, *The Globalization of Israel: McWorld in Tel Aviv, Jihad in Jerusalem* (New York: Routledge, 2008). Gaining control of local companies has been a common strategy adopted by multinational corporations since the 1970s. See Nuri Zafer Yenal, "Food TNCs, Intellectual Property Investments and Post-Fordist Food Consumption: The Case of Unilever and Nestlé in Turkey," *International Journal of Sociology of Agriculture and Food* 8 (1999): 21–34.

6. Daniel Maman, "Business Groups in the Israeli Economy: Causes for Consolidation and Strengthening," in *The Power of Property: Israeli Society in the Global Age*, ed. Dani Filc and Uri Ram (Jerusalem: Van Leer and Hakibbutz Hameuchad, 2004), 130 (Hebrew).

7. Ram, *The Globalization of Israel*. See also Scott Lash and John Urry, *Economies of Signs and Space* (London: Sage, 1994); Ash Amin, *Post-Fordism: A Reader* (Oxford: Blackwell, 1994).

8. Nitzan Cohen, "Tnuva or Strauss: This Is the Company Which Controls the Food Market," *ICE*, December 21, 2021, https://www.ice.co.il/consumerism /news/article/838678 (Hebrew); Liat Ron, "The Struggle against the Cost of Living: Food Producers Are at the Sight of the Economy Minister," *Walla!*, January 25, 2023, https://finance.walla.co.il/item/3554005 (Hebrew). These companies are either Israeli companies active abroad or multinational corporations active in Israel.

9. For example, Baruch Nadel, "The Content of the Boxes Is Indefinable— Except for Some Human Hair Found in Them," *Yediot Ahronot*, May 28, 1970 (Hebrew).

10. Interview with Zvi Dreizin, Tel Aviv, June 29, 2011.

11. Sever Plocker, "Stomach, Go Stomach!" *Yediot Ahronot*, April 1, 1988 (Hebrew); Arieh Avneri, "A Salad of Prosecutions," *Yediot Ahronot*, May 24, 1988 (Hebrew); Eli Danon, "Company Commander Salads," *Maariv*, February 5, 1988 (Hebrew); Sagit Azari-Wiesel and Dan Ben-David, "The Status of Women in the Labor Market," *Shoresh: Policy Memorandum*, March 2016, https://backend.shoresh.institute/downloads/policy-brief-heb-AzaryViesel -BenDavid-16-03-women-in-LF.pdf (Hebrew); Interview with Ron Antonovsky, Tel Aviv, February 4, 2010.

12. Nurit Arad, "The Discounts War in the Salads Market," *Yediot Ahronot*, December 25, 1985 (Hebrew).

13. Ziva Yariv, "Wiping," *Yediot Ahronot*, January 1, 1988 (Hebrew); Shoshana Chen, "A Storm in a Plate of Hummus," *Yediot Ahronot*, December 5, 2001 (Hebrew).

14. See the Strauss Group website: http://www.strauss-group.com/AboutUs -Overview, accessed May 23, 2023. The factory was established in 1978 by well-known restaurateur Moshe Kruvi, whose restaurants were famous for their steaks and hummus.

15. Howard R. Moskowitz, "The Perfect Is Simply Not Good Enough—Fifty Years of Innovating in the World of Traditional Foods," *Food Control* 138 (2022): 1–7; Malcolm Gladwell, "The Ketchup Conundrum," *New Yorker*, August 29, 2004 (September 6 issue), 128–35; Michael Moss, "The Extraordinary Science of Addictive Junk Food," *New York Times Magazine*, February 20, 2013, https://www .nytimes.com/2013/02/24/magazine/the-extraordinary-science-of-junk-food.html.

16. Phone interview with Howard Moskowitz, May 23, 2023.

17. Interview with Antonovsky; phone interview with Sam Sagui, December 20, 2009.

18. Since Strauss started to produce hummus Achla and until the end of 2001, it invested more than $20 million in publicity. Chen, "A Storm in a Plate of Hummus."

19. Nomination form to the Effie Platinum publicity competition, 2005, http://www.hamil.co.il/upload/tzabar-platinum.doc (Hebrew).

20. In 2006, Strauss was the second-largest Israeli food corporation, with 11 percent market share, and Osem was the third, with 9 percent. Nurit Kadosh, "The Five Biggest Food Companies in Israel Hold 44 percent of the Sales in the Food Market," *Nrg Maariv*, March 22, 2006, https://www.makorrishon.co.il /nrg/online/16/ART1/063/467.html (Hebrew).

21. Kadosh, "The Five Biggest Food Companies."

22. In 2010, Tzabar presented "The Secrets of (Its) Success" on its website as related exclusively to the quality of its products and their development process, while publicity and marketing were not mentioned. In the 2014 version, Tzabar's success was attributed to "maintaining the family-ness, the authentic and homey tastes of the Yanko family, and the international standards of Osem-Nestlé in production, quality assurance, product development and management." See http://www.hummus.co.il, accessed December 22, 2010, and December 26, 2014 (Hebrew). Tzabar's website is currently at https://www.osem-nestle.co.il /brands/%D7%A6%D7%91%D7%A8, accessed July 31, 2025.

23. In documents submitted on behalf of Tzabar to the Effi award competition, Tzabar's marketing strategies received a much more central place in explaining its success. Nomination form to the Effie Platinum publicity competition, 2005; McCann Erickson, "When Love Made It to Hummus," nomination form to the Effie Platinum publicity competition, 2008, http://www.hamil.co.il/upload /zabar-platinum.doc (Hebrew). Another indication of the role of publicity and marketing in the success of the big companies is that in blind taste tests and in open surveys of consumers' satisfaction, their products do not necessarily surpass those of smaller companies. For example, Dafna Lutsky, "Hummus," *Haaretz*, June 21, 2004 (Hebrew); Michal Raz Chaimovitz, "The Hummus Salads Market: Love Miki Delicatessen, Faithful to Achla," *Globes*, May 20, 2013, http:// www.globes.co.il/news/article.aspx?fbdid=1000844846 (Hebrew).

24. Interview with Matti Yahav during a visit to Tzabar's factory, Kiryat Gat, June 1, 2011. See also Yenal, "Food TNCs."

25. Interview with Yahav.

26. Dr. Hezi Gur Mizrahi, "Stupefying Hummus? Israelis Wipe in One Billion Shekels a Year," *Walla!*, February 22, 2023, https://finance.walla.co.il/item /3560625 (Hebrew).

27. According to Yaron Tzur, in blind taste tests of hummus that had spent some time in the refrigerator, people tended to prefer industrial hummus to hummus from a hummusiya.

28. According to industry people, the required level of acidity (lower than pH 4.8) is one of the main causes for the distinct taste of industrial hummus and not, as is often assumed, the preservatives, which are tasteless. Potassium sorbate in

the amount that it is used is indeed tasteless, although some people can sense its presence through a sort of stinging on the tongue. See also a post by food technologist Yaniv Gur Arye in the Hummusologists Inc. Facebook group, July 20, 2019, https://www.facebook.com/groups/Msabbaha/posts/359475294694080 (Hebrew).

29. According to data received from Strauss, dated August 2011.

30. Massimo Montanari, "Taste Is a Cultural Product," in *Food Is Culture*, trans. Albert Sonnenfeld (New York: Columbia University Press, 2004), 61–66.

31. Chen, "A Storm in a Plate of Hummus." I don't have reliable year-by-year data on hummus sales in Israel to allow systematic comparison. In 2013, the total consumption reported was thirty thousand tons (for the barcoded market only), and in 2020, it was over forty thousand tons. Zeela Kotler, "The Symbol of Israeliness: Israelis Eat over 30,000 Tons of Hummus a Year," *Globes*, May 25, 2013, https://www.globes.co.il/news/article.aspx?did=1000845838 (Hebrew); Jean Claude Max, "How to Open a Hummusiya in Israel?," *Monopoli*, accessed March 17, 2023, https://bit.ly/3JqRJ3M (Hebrew).

32. Rina Rosenberg Kendall, "Don't Let Them Smear You," *Haaretz*, March 8, 2011 (Hebrew); Orly and Guy Ltd., "Careful, Processed Food," Channel 2 News, accessed April 29, 2011, http://ong.nana10.co.il/Article/?ArticleID=739219#Scene_1 (Hebrew).

33. Nurit Kadosh, "A New Chapter in the Hummus Wars: After 13 Difficult Years, Strauss Is on the Way Up," *Calcalist*, September 10, 2013, https://www.calcalist.co.il/marketing/articles/0,7340,L-3611913,00.html (Hebrew).

34. Packs of industrial hummus can be quite large (up to one kilogram) and last over a month.

35. Interview with food writer Hilik Gurfinkel (interviewer: Ofra Tene), Tel Aviv, November 29, 2009. See also Rogel Alper, "I Am Afraid Therefore I Am a Duck," *Ha'ir*, May 31, 1996 (Hebrew); Shoshana Chen, Moshe Ronen, and Shir-Li Golan-Me'iri, "A Wipe of Health," *Yediot Aharonot*, January 4, 2001 (Hebrew); Israeli in Portugal, "Hummus, in a Shopping Mall, in Portugal," *Hummus for the Masses*, August 29, 2015, https://humus101.com/?p=5927.

36. I thank Tamar Barkay for this point. When Kolbotek repeated its investigation in 2008, this time focusing on hummusiyot, it failed to attract much public attention, although it did hurt the business of some. See Tal Rosenthal, "They Turned Us into Criminals," *Nrg Maariv*, November 28, 2008, https://www.makorrishon.co.il/nrg/online/54/ART1/817/830.html (Hebrew); Eran Swissa, "The Revenge of the Coliform Bacteria," *Nrg Maariv*, December 7, 2008, https://www.makorrishon.co.il/nrg/online/54/ART1/821/591.html (Hebrew).

37. For example, Yael Garty, "Product Comparison: Which Hummus Is the Healthiest and Which the Most Dietetic?" *Ynet*, September 5, 2008, http://www.ynet.co.il/articles/0,7340,L-3591325,00.html (Hebrew); Orit Ronell, "The Thin

Letters: Tzabar's Hummus," *Nrg Maariv*, October 10, 2008, https://www
.makorrishon.co.il/nrg/online/29/ART1/797/360.html (Hebrew); Gadi Guy,
"What's Inside: Tzabar's Hummus with Pine Nuts—with Love and Oil," *Calcalist*, May 20, 2010, http://www.calcalist.co.il/local/articles/0,7340,L-3404938,00
.html?dcRef=ynet (Hebrew); Yael Dror, "Which Packaged Hummus Salad is the
Healthiest? The Dietician Checked," *Ynet*, June 25, 2012, http://www.ynet.co.il
/articles/0,7340,L-4245555,00.html (Hebrew); Rosenberg Kendall, "Don't Let
Them Smear You."

38. For example, Nurit Kadosh, "The Public Bought Less Salads but Paid
Much More," *Calcalist*, February 14, 2021, https://www.calcalist.co.il/marketing
/articles/0,7340,L-3893557,00.html (Hebrew).

39. "I will not produce a product which I will think my family should not
consume" (interview with Strauss Israel CEO, Zion Balas), *Industrial Zone*, 1,
March 2017, https://www.calameo.com/rb-media/read/004882747e619d719b93c
(Hebrew).

40. This is evident whenever the issue of packaged hummus products comes
up in the Hummusologists Inc. Facebook group.

41. For example, Nurit Kadosh, "They Are Mimics and Copiers," *Nrg Maariv*,
November 22, 2005, https://www.makorrishon.co.il/nrg/online/16/ART1/011/180
.html.

42. Stuart Hall, "What Is This 'Black' in Black Popular Culture?" *Social Justice*
20, no. 1–2(1993): 104–11; Stuart Hall, "The Local and the Global: Globalization
and Ethnicity," in *Dangerous Liaisons: Gender, Nation and Postcolonial Perspectives*, ed. Anne McClintock, Aamir Mufti, and Ella Shohat (Minneapolis: University of Minnesota Press, 1997), 173–87.

43. McCann Erickson, "When Love Made It to Hummus," 2; Kadosh, "A New
Chapter in the Hummus Wars."

44. I thank the Reuveni-Pridan advertising agency for sending me the Achla
commercials.

45. McCann Erickson, "When Love Made It to Hummus."

46. McCann Erickson, Nomination form to the Effie Platinum publicity competition, 2005, https://web.archive.org/web/20110304053525/http://www.hamil
.co.il/upload/zabar-platinum.doc (Hebrew).

47. In fact, various signs of Arabness were part of Strauss's branding from the
start, including the name Achla and a sales promotion campaign involving the
Egyptian ambassador Mohammed Basyouni and his wife, Nagwa. See "Basyouni
Does PR for Strauss," *Hadashot*, August 6, 1992 (Hebrew). Several recent commercials also involve Arab hummus makers alongside Jewish ones.

48. This and other Tzabar commercials are accessible through YouTube. See
https://www.youtube.com/watch?v=aDKPXigFbVk, accessed June 25, 2023
(Hebrew). For a brilliant analysis of this commercial, see Adi Sorek, "Hummus

Is Made with Love: What's between a Hummus Commercial and the Establishment of a Palestinian State," *The Left Bank*, November 17, 2004, https://hagada .org.il/2004/11/17.

49. Ayala Tzoref, "The Marketing Woman of October—Tzabar's Marketing Vice President," *Haaretz*, October 13, 2003 (Hebrew); M. Cohen, "The Niguvim Festival 2004 Is Expected to Attract 100,000 Visitors," *Globes*, August 22, 2004 (Hebrew).

50. McCann Erickson, "The 'Jordanian Nehad' Campaign: Re-breaking the Record of Authenticity," nomination form to the Effie Platinum publicity competition, 2008, https://web.archive.org/web/20130819023336/http://www.hamil .co.il/upload/zabar.doc.

51. Kadosh, "They Are Mimics and Copiers."

52. See, for example, the "premium" product line of Shamir Salads: http:// www.shamirsalads.com/ShowFamilyProducts.asp? MenuID=398 &ParentMenuID=395, accessed May 23, 2011. Below the type of the hummus, it says "home production" in a handwriting font.

53. McCann Erickson, "The 'Jordanian Nehad' Campaign."

54. Conversation with Itzik Dahan, the Tzabar "hummusologist," Jaffa, June 1, 2011.

55. "Tzabar: The King of Hummus from Jordan Arrives to Jaffa," Promo Media Forum, http://www.promomagazine.co.il/pages/show/1658, accessed November 30, 2010.

56. Since the violent year of 2014, Arab hummus makers have almost disappeared from Tzabar's campaigns.

57. Navit Zomer, "Strauss Plans to Establish a Hummus Restaurants Chain," *Ynet*, January 4, 2005, http://www.ynet.co.il/articles/0,7340,L-3027832,00.html (Hebrew).

58. Kadosh, "They Are Mimics and Copiers."

59. Nurit Kadosh, "An Energy Shot," *Nrg Maariv*, February 6, 2008, https:// www.makorrishon.co.il/nrg/online/16/ART1/693/096.html (Hebrew); Nurit Kadosh, "Osem Also Wants Healthy Hummus," *Nrg Maariv*, June 11, 2009, https://www.makorrishon.co.il/nrg/online/16/ART1/902/375.html (Hebrew); Nurit Kadosh, "Following the Investigation of Business: Oil Leaves Hummus 'Achla'," *Nrg Maariv*, February 19, 2009, https://www.makorrishon.co.il/nrg /online/16/ART1/855/661.html (Hebrew).

60. Eran Yas'ur, "Achla Story," Israeli Marketing Association, January 27, 2013, http://www.ishivuk.co.il/articles/863 (Hebrew).

61. This was conveyed to me by senior company people at both Tzabar and Strauss. See also http://www.globes.co.il/news/article.aspx?did=1000845838 #fromelement=hp_folders_821, accessed July 2, 2023 (Hebrew). In general, most of the chickpeas consumed in Israel are imported. In 2023, for example, Israel

imported 16,536 tons of dry chickpeas and produced 3,240 tons. World Integrated Trade Solutions, https://wits.worldbank.org/trade/comtrade/en/country/ALL /year/2023/tradeflow/Imports/partner/WLD/product/071320; FAOSTAT, https://www.fao.org/faostat/en/#data/QCL.

62. Interview with Pini Gottlieb, Petach Tikva, January 6, 2013. One of the obstacles Gottlieb had to deal with was the Jewish halachic law of *shmita*, which decrees that every seventh year the land is to lie fallow and all agricultural work is forbidden. This creates a gap in production and forces Strauss to temporarily change varieties, which requires adjustments.

63. Phone conversation with Yaniv Gur Arye, June 27, 2023.

64. "Achla Taste Starts in the Chickpea Field of Avi Mevorach from Givʻat Koach," https://youtu.be/WfsTLpJIrKA?si=Z_aDPRHe9pSCpn1i, accessed February 13, 2025.

65. Kadosh, "A New Chapter in the Hummus Wars." Tzabar's share of the hummus market still exceeded Strauss's by almost 6 percent.

66. Amy B. Trubek, *The Taste of Place: A Cultural Journey into Terroir* (Berkeley: University of California Press, 2008); Robert Feagan, "The Place of Food: Mapping Out the 'Local' in Local Food Systems," *Progress in Human Geography* 31, no. 1 (2007): 26.

67. Osnat Gueta, "Start Wiping: The First Hummus Festival Starts Today," *Maariv online*, May 9, 2022, https://www.maariv.co.il/food/Article-915904.

68. For example, https://www.youtube.com/watch?v=b3vaGjyjwFE; https:// www.youtube.com/watch?v=hVAkFVDBbXI (Hebrew). Tzabar also has its version of ironic authenticity: one of its commercials featured "Shefita"—a Jewish impersonator of an Arab diva who does Arab-style covers of Hebrew and English songs—a sort of Israeli blackface that can be read as an analogy to Tzabar's hummus. See https://www.youtube.com/watch?v=W7IbyLZGNEE, all accessed on July 3, 2023. On the use of irony in brand management to position viewers as reflexive and "knowing" interpreters, see Adam Arvidsson, "Brands: a Critical Perspective," *Journal of Consumer Culture* 5, no. 2 (2005): 245.

69. Kent Grayson and Radan Martinec, "Consumer Perceptions of Iconicity and Indexicality and Their Influence on Assessments of Authentic Market Offerings," *Journal of Consumer Research* 31, no. 2 (2004): 296–312.

70. On the hummus war, see Ari Ariel, "The Hummus Wars," *Gastronomica* 12, no. 1 (2012): 34–42; Nir Avieli, "The Hummus Wars Revisited: Israeli-Arab Food Politics and Gastromediation," *Gastronomica* 16, no. 3 (2016): 19–30; Peter Heine, *The Culinary Crescent: History of Middle Eastern Cuisine*, trans. Peter Lewis (London: Gingko, 2018), 211–13.

71. AFN staff writers, "American Tastebuds Growing for Hummus," *Australian Food News*, September 25, 2012, https://www.ausfoodnews.com.au/2012/09/25 /american-tastebuds-growing-for-hummus.html; *Pawan Gusain*, "North America

Hummus Market—Industry Trends and Forecast to 2031," Data Bridge, accessed February 10, 2025, https://www.databridgemarketresearch.com/reports/north-america-hummus-market?srsltid=AfmBOopTym6Hdgv_n55eaVY__Q9l-o3p__PKuTvu1eyuUnhpkEE5uIQX.

72. "Hummus Market Size and Trends," Grand View Research, accessed February 10, 2025, https://www.grandviewresearch.com/industry-analysis/hummus-market-report.

73. For a similar phenomenon in a different context, see Jeffrey M. Pilcher, *Planet Taco: A Global History of Mexican Food* (Oxford: Oxford University Press, 2012).

74. In 2018, Sabra's share of the packaged hummus market in the US was 60 percent. Sabra Dipping Company LLC, "A Fresh Look for America's Favorite Hummus," Cision PR Newswire, February 14, 2018, https://www.prnewswire.com/news-releases/a-fresh-look-for-americas-favorite-hummus-300598680.html.

75. Jenny Singer, "Big Hummus Is Watching. It Wants You to Eat More Hummus," *Forward*, October 29, 2019, https://forward.com/life/433902/big-hummus-is-watching-it-wants-you-to-eat-more-hummus.

76. "Dips & Spreads," Strauss Group, accessed May 7, 2023, https://www.strauss-group.com/activity/dips-spreads. In November 2024, Strauss Group sold its holdings in Sabra and Obela—its dips and spreads joint venture operations with PepsiCo in the US and other countries—to Pepsico. "News and Media," Strauss Group, accessed February 11, 2025, https://www.strauss-group.com/newsmention/appointment-of-two-new-directors-to-the-groups-board-2/.

77. Adi Dovrat Meseritz and Ayala Tzoref, "Tzabar CEO: 'We Will Beat Strauss in the U.S.A. as We Beat Them in Israel'; Strauss: 'In Osem, They Are Frustrated by Our Success,'" *TheMarker*, May 10, 2009, https://www.themarker.com/advertising/2009-05-10/ty-article/0000017f-e8ba-df2c-a1ff-fefbe4f80000 (Hebrew); Yoram Gabison, "Achla Story: This Is How Hummus Became an American Health Hit, That Is Also Loved by Celebrities," *TheMarker*, June 4, 2014 (Hebrew); Shany Moses, "Osem Finds Buyer for Beit Hashita Pickles," *Globes*, September 25, 2019, https://en.globes.co.il/en/article-osem-finds-buyer-for-beit-hashita-pickles-1001302067.

78. For example, Pilcher, *Planet Taco*; Jillian R. Cavanaugh and Shalini Shankar, "Producing Authenticity in Global Capitalism: Language, Materiality, and Value," *American Anthropologist* 116, no. 1 (2014): 51–64; Fabio Parasecoli, *Knowing Where it Comes From: Labeling Traditional Foods to Compete in the Global Market* (Iowa: University of Iowa Press, 2017); Danny Hamrick, Michaela DeSoucey, and Nino Bariola, "Distillations of Authenticity: a Comparative Global Value Chain Analysis of Pisco," *Regional Studies* 58, no. 10 (2022): 1792–1803.

79. "Global Wipe," *Yediot Ahronot*, December 7, 1995 (Hebrew); Reuters, "Guinness Record to Israeli Hummus," Ynet, March 9, 2006, http://www.ynet

.co.il/articles/0,7340,L-3225872,00.html (Hebrew); Shooky Galili, "A New Hummus Record: 400 Kilo Hummus," *Hummus for the Masses*, May 20, 2008, https://humus101.com/?p=427#prettyPhoto (Hebrew); Udi Mishel, "Osem Expanding Hummus Activity in UK," *Ynet*, May 8, 2009, https://www.ynetnews.com/articles/0,7340,L-3757522,00.html. See also Avieli, "The Hummus Wars Revisited," 22–23.

80. On the EU schemes of geographical indications and traditional specialties, see Parasecoli, *Knowing Where it Comes From*; Michaela DeSoucey, "Gastronationalism: Food Traditions and Authenticity Politics in the European Union," *American Sociological Review* 75, no. 3 (2010): 432–55.

81. AFP, "Fought Back: Lebanon Defeated Israel in Hummus," *Ynet*, October 24, 2009, http://www.ynet.co.il/articles/0,7340,L-3794596,00.html (Hebrew).

82. Jawadat Ibrahim in a radio interview with Didi Harari, November 8, 2009, http://www.103.fm/programs/Media.aspx?ZrqvnVq= ELLMGD &c41t4nzVQ=EG (Hebrew).

83. Michal Palti, "Mix the Hummus, Tomer," *Haaretz*, December 28, 2005 (Hebrew); Tani Goldstein, "Jawarat [*sic*] Ibrahim: Abu Ghosh Is Not Just Hummus," *Ynet*, January 20, 2006, http://www.ynet.co.il/articles /1,7340,L-3202839,00.html (Hebrew); Jawadat Ibrahim, "Our 'Price Tag,'" *Ynet*, June 19, 2013, http://www.ynet.co.il/articles/0,7340,L-4394138,00.html (Hebrew).

84. The Guinness World Records official website: https://www.guinness worldrecords.com/world-records/largest-serving-of-hummus, accessed on August 1, 2025.

85. Goldstein, "Jawarat [*sic*] Ibrahim"; I thank Trevor Graham, the director of a documentary on the hummus wars, who conducted an interview with Abboud, for this information.

86. Ariel, "The Hummus Wars," 37.

87. In 2019, Miki Delicatessen went out of business. The brand Miki was sold to Shamir Salads, while its hummus factory was sold to the Hebron-based al-Jebrini family, the owners of the largest salads factory in the West Bank, and it began to produce salads for the Israeli market under a different brand name.

88. See also Avieli, "The Hummus Wars Revisited," 24–25.

89. Sarit Sardas-Trotino, "A Storm in a Bowl of Hummus," *Ynet*, November 16, 2009, https://www.ynet.co.il/articles/0,7340,L-3805259,00.html (Hebrew).

90. See also Ariel, "The Hummus Wars," 37.

91. Hadas Ore notes in her dissertation a packaged hummus brand sold in New Zealand under the label "Israeli hummus." Hadas Ore, "'Can Home Come in a Tin Can?': How Jewish-Israeli Women Savour Home in New Zealand," PhD diss., University of Auckland, 2014, 65. In addition, the Israeli connection is reflected in some of the brand names—for example, Yarden and Sabra (which

was at first called Sabra Blue and White). See also Ariel, "The Hummus Wars,"
39; Avieli, "The Hummus Wars Revisited," 22.

92. He said this in an interview with filmmaker Trevor Graham. According
to Abboud, the Lebanese Cortas company began producing canned hummus in
1959—a year after Telma, which also exported its hummus.

93. Graham and I interviewed Yahav together in the Tzabar factory in
Kiryat Gat, on June 1, 2011. On Israeli industrial hummus in the OT, see also
Roy Yerushalmi, "A Ground Story: Everything You Wanted to Know about
Gazan Hummus," *Ynet*, October 23, 2011, http://www.ynet.co.il/articles
/0,7340,L-4137813,00.html (Hebrew); Elior Levi, "To Eat Israeli Hummus
in Gaza," *Ynet*, March 9, 2014, http://www.ynet.co.il/articles/0,7340,L
-4496624,00.html (Hebrew); Doron Paskin, "The Salmonella Effect:
Palestinians Call to Boycott Israeli Food," *Calcalist*, August 21, 2016, https://
www.calcalist.co.il/marketing/articles/0,7340,L-3696023,00.html?dcRef
=ynetCube.

94. For example, Elior Levy, "Israeli Hummus Takes Over Gaza Supermar-
kets," *Ynet*, October 3, 2014, https://www.ynetnews.com/articles/0,7340,L
-4496994,00.html. On the difficulties of exporting Palestinian products, see
Anne Meneley, "Time in a Bottle: The Uneasy Circulation of Palestinian Olive
Oil," *Middle East Report* 248 (2008): 18–23; Flávio Nunes and Loai Aburaida,
"Obstacles to West Bank Industrial Development Caused by the Palestinian
Lack of Control over Its External and Internal Borders," *International Journal of
Management and Applied Science* 4, no. 8 (2018): 5–11.

95. Klein, *No Logo*; Holt, "Jack Daniel's America," 375.

96. On the role of consumers' immaterial labor in creating brands' value, see
Robert J. Foster, "Commodity Futures: Labour, Love and Value," *Anthropology
Today* 21, no. 4 (2005): 11; Arvidsson, "Brands," 235–58.

97. *Hummus Mouse: The Selected Hundred Hummusiyot of Israel* (Tel Aviv: City
Mouse, 2010) (Hebrew).

98. https://web.archive.org/web/20050406095144/http://www.hummus
.co.il/, accessed August 9, 2025 (Hebrew).

99. "Noa Eats: The Hummus Route," accessed June 18, 2023, https://www
.youtube.com/watch?v=vyojGrRH29Q.

100. "The Best Hummus in Israel Chapter 10: Hummus the Level of Yeshayahu
Leibowitz," YouTube, accessed June 25, 2023, https://www.youtube.com/watch
?v=VtMkWrushUo (Hebrew).

101. For example, Kotler, "The Symbol of Israeliness"; Ynet (with Strauss),
"From Hummus to Eggplants: This Is How You Produce Salads without Gluten,"
Ynet, March 18, 2018, https://www.ynet.co.il/articles/0,7340,L-5169047,00.html
(Hebrew); Oren Dagan, "To Grow Chickpeas: You Put a Seed in the Field and
You Don't Know What Will Happen," *Davar*, April 22, 2021, https://www.davar1

.co.il/299500 (Hebrew); Ice Editorial Board, "Strauss Sends Chickpeas into Space: Will It Be Possible to Grow Grains on the Moon?" *ICE*, January 24, 2022, https://www.ice.co.il/research/news/article/841830 (Hebrew); Reut Sahar, "How Is It That in Israel of All Places Grow the Best Chickpeas in the World?" *Ynet*, June 2, 2022, https://www.ynet.co.il/food/foodnews/article/sker5l809 (Hebrew).

102. Douglas B. Holt, "Why Do Brands Cause Trouble? A Dialectical Theory of Consumer Culture and Branding," *Journal of Consumer Research* 29, no. 1 (2002): 70–90; Eva Illouz, "Introduction: Emodities or the Making of Emotional Commodities," in *Emotions as Commodities: Capitalism, Consumption and Authenticity*, ed. Eva Illouz (London: Routledge, 2018), 6.

103. Celia Lury, *Brands: The Logos of the Global Economy* (New York: Routledge, 2004), 57.

104. One often hears from artisanal producers that they make hummus "with love." A few examples are Diana Spechler, "Who Invented Hummus?" *BBC*, December 12, 2017, https://www.bbc.com/travel/article/20171211-who-invented-hummus; Dan Alexander, "A Palestinian, a Lebanese and an Israeli Walk into a Bar," *Hummus*, 14; in the *MasterChef* episode on hummus, broadcast on August 11, 2015, the slogan "hummus is made with love" was repeated several times.

105. Benjamin Orlove and Ella Schmidt, "Swallowing Their Pride: Indigenous and Industrial Beer in Peru and Bolivia," *Theory and Society* 24, no. 2 (1995): 271–98.; Jacob Lahne, "Sensory Science, the Food Industry, and the Objectification of Taste," *Anthropology of Food* 10 (2016), https://doi.org/10.4000/aof.7956.

106. In the survey I conducted, 44 percent of the respondents stated that they, or someone in their household, occasionally prepared hummus, but only 19.3 percent stated that eating homemade hummus was their primary way of eating hummus. In another survey, conducted in 2016, only 13 percent of the respondents stated that they prepared hummus at home from time to time. Hadar Kane, "The Big Hummus Survey," *TheMarker*, May 9, 2016, https://www.themarker.com/consumer/2016-05-09/ty-article/0000017f-e790-d62c-a1ff-fffbb9ca0000 (Hebrew). While I cannot account for this gap, it is certainly the case that several decades ago, preparing hummus at home was rare among Israelis. To this day, a reasonable homemade hummus often receives disproportional accolades.

107. Maria Botsner vs. King's Bounty (Keyad Hamelekh) salads company (2006) Ltd., 2010, http://www.psakdin.co.il/kAnnex/nws_nljo_1.pdf, accessed June 15, 2023 (Hebrew).

108. Strauss even integrated this practice into its commercials, where Raymonde Abecassis is shown adding chickpeas and olive oil to its hummus.

109. See, for example, Frederick Errington, Deborah Gewertz, and Tatsuro Fujikura, *The Noodle Narratives: The Global Rise of an Industrial Food into the Twenty-First Century* (Berkeley: University of California Press, 2013), 5.

110. "Marhaba Festival All the Way Home: Hummus Experts Invite You to Wipe Excellent Hummus with Them," Foodis, July 17, 2011, https://shorturl.at /cRHYV (Hebrew). The festival took place on July 27–28, 2011.

111. In my conversation with Itzik Dahan, Tzabar's "hummusologist," he admitted that it was only very seldom that he encountered an exceptional hummus at people's homes—not even once a year.

112. This campaign took place in January 2014. See https://www.youtube.com /watch?v=2x2gID5U2Bk, accessed on June 27, 2023; "Tzabar Opens for Israelis in Israel and Abroad Hummusiya at Home" (Magnox: advertising content), *Ynet*, January 22, 2014, https://www.ynet.co.il/articles/0,7340,L-4479756,00.html (Hebrew).

113. https://www.facebook.com/hotdudesandhummus, accessed June 25, 2023; Raquel Wildes, "Instagram of the Week: 'Hot Dudes and Hummus' in Israel," *Tablet*, April 28, 2016, https://www.tabletmag.com/sections/news/articles /instagram-of-the-week-hot-dudes-and-hummus-in-israel; Tal Samuel-Azran et al., "Practicing Citizen Diplomacy 2.0: 'The Hot Dudes and Hummus—Israel's Yummiest' Campaign for Israel's Branding," *Place Branding and Public Diplomacy* 15 (2019): 38–49. Not all photos on this page are of Israeli men, but many are.

CONCLUSION

1. Ray, "Culinary Difference," 7.

2. Appadurai, "Gastro-Politics in Hindu South Asia," 495.

3. But see Uncivilized Media, "Eating Stolen Palestinian Food in New York," accessed July 16, 2023, https://www.youtube.com/watch?v=1s6zgGAH7XI.

4. Ahmad, "Freekeh and Fellahin," 39, 42–43.

5. A video of the IDF spokesman in uniform greeting the Muslims for Ramadan, which was posted on the IDF Spokesperson Facebook page in 2017, focused on Arab foods loved by Israelis. See also Israeli soldiers' "hummus challenge": Shooky Galili, "The Hummus Challenge," *The Hummus Blog*, August 19, 2014, https://humus101.com/EN/2014/08/19/the-hummus-challenge. On Hot Dudes and Hummus, see chapter 5. On International Hummus Day, see Ro Yeger, "Israel Gears Up for International Hummus Day," *Jerusalem Post*, May 12, 2015, https://www.jpost.com/Israel-News/Culture/Israel-gears-up-for-International -Hummus-Day-402835; David Shamah, "Hummus Map Shows Off Israeli Tech, and Taste," *Times of Israel*, May 12, 2015, https://www.timesofisrael.com/hummus -map-shows-off-israeli-tech-and-taste.

6. Steven Salaita, "'Israeli' Hummus Is Theft, Not Appropriation," The New Arab, September 4, 2017, https://www.newarab.com/opinion/israeli-hummus-theft -not-appropriation; see also Ben White, "Israel's Obsession with Hummus is About More than Stealing Palestine's Food," *The National*, accessed July 16, 2023, https:// shorturl.at/ehy67; The New Arab, "Cultural Appropriation Fail: Palestinians Mock

Israeli Chef's 'Beef Knafeh,'" *The New Arab*, March 4, 2020, https://www
.newarab.com/news/cultural-appropriation-fail-palestinians-mock-israeli-chefs
-beef-knafeh; Ali Abunimah, "Rachael Ray Cooks Up a Storm by Calling Palestinian Food 'Israeli,'" *Electronic Intifada*, December 26, 2017; Uncivilized Media, "Eating Stolen Palestinian Food in New York."

7. Helga Tawil-Souri, "Where Is the Political in Cultural Studies? In Palestine," *International Journal of Cultural Studies* 14, no. 5 (2011): 467–82.

8. Brenna Bhandar, *Colonial Lives of Property: Law, Land, and Racial Regimes
of Ownership* (Durham, NC: Duke University Press, 2018).

9. Enzel and Luxi, "Talking Doesn't Make You Fat: Hummus for the
Masses," accessed July 20, 2023, https://efratenzel.com/he/enzeluxy/564?pt=127.

10. Daniel Miller, "Coca-Cola: A Black Sweet Drink from Trinidad," in *Material Cultures: Why Some Things Matter*, ed. Daniel Miller (New York: Routledge,
2002), 169–87.

11. Mintz, *Tasting Food, Tasting Freedom*, 33–49.

12. Vered Guttman, "'Gaza Kitchen,' as a Portal," *Washington Post*, April 23,
2008, https://shorturl.at/QU593; Ligaya Mishan, "The Rise of Palestinian Food,"
New York Times, February 12, 2020, https://www.nytimes.com/2020/02/12
/t-magazine/palestinian-food.html.

13. Young, *Cultural Appropriation and the Arts*, 97, 116.

14. Ronit Vered, "A New Generation of Palestinian Chefs Poised to Conquer
the World," *Haaretz.com*, October 25, 2016, https://www.haaretz.com/middle
-east-news/2016-10-25/ty-article-magazine/.premium/new-generation-of
-palestinian-chefs-poised-to-conquer-the-world/0000017f-e0d2-d9aa-afff
-f9da57410000; Mishan, "The Rise of Palestinian Food"; Aina J. Khan, "Preserving a Palestinian Identity in the Kitchen," *New York Times*, October 19, 2022,
https://www.nytimes.com/2022/10/19/world/middleeast/palestinian-culinary
-traditions.html. See also Monterescu and Ranta, "Decolonizing Israeli Food?,"
167; Christiane Dabdoub Nasser, "Recipes Carry Voices and Stories: An Interview with Mirna Bamieh," *Jerusalem Quarterly* 98 (2024): 81; Bascuñan-Wiley
and Schwalb, "Binding Identity," 18; Farah, "Ottolenghi and Tamimi's Cookbook
Jerusalem," 113.

15. Bascuñan-Wiley and Schwalb, "Binding Identity," 18.

16. Ala Hlehel, "Come to the Hummus," accessed July 24, 2023, https://
www.youtube.com/watch?v=frsxQydq5Gs&t=48s. The Hebrew title, which is
extremely difficult to translate, is "ulfa'atey hummus kadima." It is a paraphrase
on a line from the Israeli national anthem, "ulfa'atey mizrah kadima." Combined
with the consecutive line, it refers to Jewish eyes looking to the edge of the East,
where Zion is.

17. Young, *Cultural Appropriation and the Arts*, 3.

18. See, for example, Meneley, "Time in a Bottle"; Meneley, "Blood, Sweat and Tears in a Bottle of Palestinian Extra-Virgin Olive Oil," *Food, Culture & Society* 14, no. 2 (2011): 275–92; Aeyal Gross and Tamar Feldman, "We Didn't Want to Hear the Word Calories: Rethinking Food Security, Food Power, and Food Sovereignty-Lessons from the Gaza Closure," *Berkeley Journal of International Law* 33 (2015): 379–441; Susan J. Massad and Mohammad Hmidat, "Farming, Water, Food Sovereignty and Nutrition in Occupied Palestinian Territories," *International Journal of Food and Nutritional Science* 2, no. 3 (2016): 359–71; Samar Awaad, "Culinary Traditions in the Jerusalem Countryside: Communities Displaced by the 1948 Nakba and Those Who Remained," *Jerusalem Quarterly* 98 (2024): 68–78; Ahmad, "Freekeh and Fellahin," 33–50; Sharif, "How Dough Rises in Gaza," 56–72.

19. Channel 2, "The Journey after the Perfect Hummus," September 23, 2012, https://www.youtube.com/watch?v=aL_OffdfipU.

REFERENCES

ARCHIVES

Central Zionist Archives (CZA)
Hadassah Archives at the Center for Jewish History, New York (HANY)
Haganah Historical Archive
The Historical Archives of the City of Tel Aviv-Yafo (TAHA)
IDF and Defense Establishment Archives
Israel State Archives (ISA)
Newsreel Archives, Herzliya Studio

NEWSPAPERS AND JOURNALS

Al Hamishmar
Davar
Haaretz
Haboker
Hadashot
Ha'ir
Hamazon
Ha'olam Haze
Iton Meyuchad
Kol Ha'am
Lamerchav
Maariv
Palestine Post
Yediot Ahronot

BOOKS AND JOURNAL ARTICLES

Aaronsohn, Aaron. *Agricultural and Botanical Explorations in Palestine.* Washington, DC: Government Printing Office, 1910.

Abbasi, Mustafa. "'Times of Storm': Nazareth and the Military Government." *Iyunim Bitkumat Israel* 22 (2012): 399–422. (Hebrew)

Abbasi, Mustafa, and David De Vries. "Commodities and Power: Edible Oil and Soap in the History of Arab-Jewish Haifa." In *Haifa before and after 1948: Narratives of a Mixed City*, edited by Mahmoud Yazbak and Yfaat Weiss, 99–118. The Hague: Institute for Historical Justice and Reconciliation, 2011.

Abbots, Emma-Jayne. "Approaches to Food and Migration: Rootedness, Being and Belonging." In *The Handbook of Food and Anthropology*, edited by Jacob A. Klein and James L. Watson, 115–32. London: Bloomsbury, 2016.

Abutbul-Selinger, Guy. "Invisible Boundaries within the Middle Class and the Construction of Ethnic Identity." *Identities* 27, no. 2 (2020): 210–28.

Adut, Rami, and Dani Filc. "Constructing a Classed Community in Kiryat Eilon (H-300) in Holon: A 'Popular-Class' Community on Mizrahi 'Building Blocks.'" *Journal of Israeli History* 40, no. 1 (2022): 7–41.

Ahmad, Amanny. "Freekeh and Fellahin: A Symbiotic Relationship of Sumud." *Jerusalem Quarterly* 98 (2024): 33–50.

Ahmed, Sara. *Strange Encounters: Embodied Others in Post-Coloniality.* London: Routledge, 2013.

Albala, Ken. *Beans: A History.* Oxford: Berg, 2007.

Algazi, Gadi. "Colonial Profits in the Shadow of Military Rule." In *Colonization and Resistance in Israel/Palestine*, edited by Lev Luis Grinberg and Daniel DeMalach, 164–207. Jerusalem: Van Leer and Hakibbutz Hameuchad, 2023. (Hebrew)

Algazi, Gadi. "Middling Ages and Living Relics as Objects to Think with: Two Figures of the Historical Imagination." In *Modernity's Classics*, edited by Sarah C. Humphreys and Rudolf G. Wagner, 315–30. Berlin: Springer, 2013.

Algazi, Gadi. "The First Act in the Struggle of the *Maʿbarot*, 1951–1952: Contestation amid Subjection." In *Entangled Histories in Palestine/Israel: Historical and Anthropological Perspectives*, edited by Dafna Hirsch, 152–88. London: Routledge, 2024.

Aliovich, Yigal. "In Days of Conquest." In *Kfar Tavor (Mescha), 1901–1976*, edited by Meir Hareuveni, 99–100. Kfar Tavor: Yovel, 1976. (Hebrew)

Almog, Bella. *Israeli Delicacies: Selection of Dishes Submitted to the Contest "Israeli Queen of the Kitchen."* Jerusalem: March of Israeli Delicacies, 1965.

Almog, Oz. "From Vegetable Salad and Lebeniya to Hamburger and Sushi: The Coca-Colonization of Israel." *Makom Lemachshava Ba-Shaʿar* 2 (1998): 7–19. (Hebrew)

Almog, Oz. *The Sabra: The Creation of the New Jew.* Translated by Haim Watzman. Berkeley: University of California Press, 2000.

Alon, Yigal. *My Father's House.* Tel Aviv: Ministry of Defense Publishing House, 1980. (Hebrew)

Alroey, Gur. "Servants of the Colony or Rude Tyrants? Hundred Years to Hashomer—Historical Perspective." *Cathedra* 133 (2009): 77–104. (Hebrew)

Amin, Ash. *Post-Fordism: A Reader.* Oxford: Blackwell, 1994.

Amram, Azri. "Digesting the Massacre: Food Tours in Palestinian Towns in Israel." *Gastronomica* 19, no. 4 (2019): 60–73.

Appadurai, Arjun. "Gastro-Politics in Hindu South Asia." *American Ethnologist* 8, no. 3 (1981): 494–511.

'Araf, Shukri. *The Land, the People and the Effort.* Tarshiha: Aljil Liltajlid, 1993. (Arabic)

Ariel, Ari. "Foodways and the Ethnicization of Yemeni Identity in Israel." *Mashriq & Mahjar: Journal of Middle East and North African Migration* 6, no. 2 (2019): 130–48.

Ariel, Ari. "The Hummus Wars." *Gastronomica* 12, no. 1 (2012): 34–42.

Ariel, Ari. "Mosaic or Melting Pot: The Transformation of Middle Eastern Jewish Foodways in Israel." In *Global Jewish Foodways*, edited by Hasia R. Diner and Simone Cinotto, 91–114. Lincoln: University of Nebraska Press, 2018.

Arnold, David. "The 'Discovery' of Malnutrition and Diet in Colonial India." *Indian Economic & Social History Review* 31, no. 1 (1994): 1–26.

Arvidsson, Adam. "Brands: A Critical Perspective." *Journal of Consumer Culture* 5, no. 2 (2005): 235–58.

Arya, Rina. "Cultural Appropriation: What It Is and Why It Matters?" *Sociology Compass* 15, no. 10 (2021): 1–11.

Ashcroft, Bill. *Post-Colonial Transformation.* London: Routledge, 2001.

Ashley, Kathleen M., and Véronique Plesch. "The Cultural Processes of 'Appropriation.'" *Journal of Medieval and Early Modern Studies* 32, no. 1 (2002): 1–15.

Avieli, Nir. *Food and Power: A Culinary Ethnography of Israel.* Berkeley: University of California Press, 2018.

Avieli, Nir. "The Hummus Wars Revisited: Israeli-Arab Food Politics and Gastromediation." *Gastronomica* 16, no. 3 (2016): 19–30.

Avitzur, Shmuel. *Everyday Life in Palestine in the 19th Century.* Tel Aviv: Am Hasefer, 1972. (Hebrew)

Awaad, Samar. "Culinary Traditions in the Jerusalem Countryside: Communities Displaced by the 1948 Nakba and Those Who Remained." *Jerusalem Quarterly* 98 (2024): 68–78.

Awartani, Hisham. "Agricultural Development Policies in the West Bank and Gaza." In *The Palestinian Economy: Studies in Development under Prolonged Occupation*, edited by George T. Abed, 139–64. London: Routledge, 1988.

Ayalon, Ami. *Reading Palestine: Printing and Literacy, 1900–1948*. Austin: University of Texas Press, 2004.

Azari-Wiesel, Sagit, and Dan Ben-David. "The Status of Women in the Labor Market." *Shoresh: Policy Memorandum*, March 2016. https://backend.shoresh .institute/downloads/policy-brief-heb-AzaryViesel-BenDavid-16-03-women -in-LF.pdf. (Hebrew)

Bachi, Roberto, Sarah Bavly, and S. V. Berman. *Inquiry into Poverty and Malnutrition among the Jews of Jerusalem*. Jerusalem: Hadassah Emergency Committee, 1943.

Baharad, Hila. "'Low-Temperature Melting Pot': Language, Religion, Education and Inter-Ethnic Relations in the Israeli Transit Camps." PhD diss., Hebrew University of Jerusalem, 2019. (Hebrew)

Banay, Itzhak. "Locked Gates." In *Compilation Marking the Twentieth Anniversary of the Health Associations in Jerusalem*, edited by Puah Menczel Ben-Tovim and Bezalel Bazrawi, 58–59. Jerusalem: Hadassah, 1947. (Hebrew)

Barbour, Chad. "When Captain America Was an Indian: Heroic Masculinity, National Identity and Appropriation." *Journal of Popular Culture* 48, no. 2 (2015): 264–84.

Bar-David, Molly. *Folkloric Cookbook: Delicatessen for Israeli Holidays*. Translated by Varda Mor, Dafna Plotkin, and Esther Frankenberg. Tel Aviv: Y. & M. Bar-David, 1964. (Hebrew)

Baron, Ilan Zvi, and Galia Press-Barnathan. "Foodways and Foodwashing: Israeli Cookbooks and the Politics of Culinary Zionism." *International Political Sociology* 15, no. 3 (2021): 338–58.

Barona, Josep L. "Nutrition and Health: The International Context during the Inter-War Crisis." *Social History of Medicine* 21, no. 1 (2008): 87–105.

Bartal, Israel. "Cossack and Bedouin: A New National Imagery." In *The Second Aliah: Studies*, edited by Israel Bartal, 482–93. Jerusalem: Yad Izhak Ben-Zvi, 1997. (Hebrew)

Bartal, Israel. *Exile in the Land: The Settlement of Eretz Israel before Zionism*. Jerusalem: Zionist Library by the World Zionist Organization, 1994. (Hebrew)

Bartal, Israel. "Introduction: 'The Culture of Israel' or 'The Cultures of Israel'?" In *A Century of Israeli Culture*, edited by Israel Bartal, vii–xvi. Jerusalem: Magnes Press, 2002. (Hebrew)

Bartal, Israel. "On Being Primary: Time and Place in the First Aliyah." In *Talking Culture: The First Aliya, and Interperiod Discourse*, edited by Yaffa Berlovich, 15–24. Tel Aviv: Hakibbutz Hameuchad, 2010. (Hebrew)

Bartal, Israel. *Tangled Roots: The Emergence of Israeli Culture*. Providence, RI: Brown Judaic Studies, 2020.

Bartmański, Dominik. "A Temple of Social Hope? Tempelhof Airport in Berlin and Its Transformations." In *National Matters: Materiality, Culture and*

Nationalism, edited by Jenevieve Zubrzycki, 216–40. Stanford, CA: Stanford University Press, 2017.

Bascuñan-Wiley, Nicholas, and Jessica Schwalb. "Binding Identity: Chilean Palestinian Cookbooks and the Formation of a Diasporic Cuisine." *Jerusalem Quarterly* 99 (2024): 14–32.

Bashkin, Orit. *Impossible Exodus: Iraqi Jews in Israel*. Stanford, CA: Stanford University Press, 2017.

Bäuml, Yair. "The Principles of the Discrimination Policy towards Arabs in Israel, 1948–1968." *Iyunim Bitkumat Israel* 16 (2006): 391–414. (Hebrew)

Bavly, Sarah. *Family Expenditure Survey, Part 2: Nutrition Level in Israel, 1968/69*. Jerusalem: Central Bureau of Statistics and the Ministry of Education and Culture, 1972. (Hebrew)

Bavly, Sarah. "Food Consumption and Nutritional Status among the Rural Population in Israel, 1959–1960." *Public Health* 5, no. 3 (1962): 340–86. (Hebrew)

Bavly, Sarah. *Food Habits and Their Changes in Israel*. Jerusalem: Ministry of Education, 1964.

Bavly, Sarah. "An Investigation into the Nutrition and the Nutritional Levels of the Urban Hebrew Population in Eretz Israel, 1947." In *Standard of Living and Nutritional Problems in the Urban Hebrew Yishuv*, edited by Gershon Zidrovich and Sarah Bavly, 29–53. Jerusalem: Institute for Economic Research, The Jewish Agency, 1947. (Hebrew)

Bavly, Sarah. *Our Nutrition: Chapters in the Theory of Nutrition and of Foods*, vol. 2. Jerusalem: Ever, 1951. (Hebrew)

Bederman, Gail. *Manliness and Civilization: A Cultural History of Gender and Race in the United States, 1880–1917*. Chicago: University of Chicago Press, 1995.

Bell, Avril. *Relating Indigenous and Settler Identities: Beyond Domination*. Houndmills, Basingstoke: Palgrave Macmillan, 2014.

Ben-Artzi, Yossi. "Development of the First Aliya Colonies and the Establishment of New Colonies during the Second Aliya Period." In *The Second Aliya: Studies*, edited by Israel Bartal, 135–69. Jerusalem: Yad Izhak Ben-Zvi, 1997. (Hebrew)

Ben-Porat, Amir. *The Bourgeoisie: The History of the Israeli Bourgeoisie*. Jerusalem: Magnes Press, 1999. (Hebrew)

Ben-Porat, Amir. *How Israel Became a Capitalist Society*. Haifa: Pardes, 2011. (Hebrew)

Ben-Porat, Guy. "Political Economy: Liberalization and Globalization." In *Israel Since 1980*, edited by Guy Ben-Porat, Yagil Levy, Shlomo Mizrahi, Arye Naor, and Erez Tzfadia, 91–116. Cambridge: Cambridge University Press, 2008.

Ben-Porat, Guy. *Between State and Synagogue: The Secularization of Contemporary Israel*. Cambridge: Cambridge University Press, 2013.

Ben-Porath, Yoram, and Reuben Gronau. "Jewish Mother Goes to Work: Trends in the Labor Force Participation of Women in Israel, 1955–1980." *Journal of Labor Economics* 3, no. 1 (1985): 310–27.

Bentley, Amy. *Eating for Victory: Food Rationing and the Politics of Domesticity.* Urbana: University of Illinois Press, 1998.

Ben-Zvi, Izhak. "Hashomer." In *Kfar Tavor (Mescha), 1901–1976,* edited by Meir Hareuveni, 90. Kfar Tavor: Yovel, 1976. (Hebrew)

Bergner-Rabinovich, Sarah. *Hygiene, Education and Nutrition among Kurdish and Persian Jews in Jerusalem, Compared to Ashkenazim.* Jerusalem: Eretz Israeli Institute for Folklore and Ethnology, 1948. (Hebrew)

Berlovich, Yaffa. "The Hebrew Colony: The Beginning of an Eretz Israeli Culture." In *Talking Culture: The First Aliya, an Interperiod Discourse,* edited by Yaffa Berlovich, 70–109. Tel Aviv: Hakibbutz Hameuchad, 2010. (Hebrew)

Berlovich, Yaffa, ed. *Talking Culture: The First Aliya, and Interperiod Discourse.* Tel Aviv: Hakibbutz Hameuchad, 2010. (Hebrew)

Bernstein, Deborah. *Women on the Margins: Gender and Nationalism in Mandate Tel Aviv.* Jerusalem: Yad Izhak Ben-Zvi, 2008. (Hebrew)

Bernstein, Deborah, and Shlomo Swirski. "The Rapid Economic Development of Israel and the Emergence of the Ethnic Division of Labour." *British Journal of Sociology* 33, no. 1 (1982): 64–85.

Bernstein, Deborah, and Badi Hasisi. "'Buy and Promote the National Cause': Consumption, Class Formation and Nationalism in Mandate Palestinian Society." *Nations and Nationalism* 14, no. 1 (2008): 127–50.

Beverland, Michael B. "Crafting Brand Authenticity: The Case of Luxury Wines." *Journal of Management Studies* 42, no. 5 (2005): 1003–29.

Bezalel, Hanna. *Life Chapters.* Published by the author, 2004. (Hebrew)

Bhandar, Brenna. *Colonial Lives of Property: Law, Land, and Racial Regimes of Ownership.* Durham, NC: Duke University Press, 2018.

Bondi, Ruth. *The Taste of Israel 1965.* Jerusalem: Israel Museum, 2015. (Hebrew)

Bourdieu, Pierre. *Distinction: A Social Critique of the Judgment of Taste.* Translated by Richard Nice. Cambridge, MA: Harvard University Press, 1984.

Boyarin, Daniel. *Unheroic Conduct: The Rise of Heterosexuality and the Invention of the Jewish Man.* Berkeley: University of California Press, 1997.

Brachya/Borochov, Mordechai. *Hygiene: A General Part.* Warsaw: Levine-Epstein, 1925. (Hebrew)

Brantley, Cynthia. "Kikuyu-Maasai Nutrition and Colonial Science: The Orr and Gilks Study in Late 1920s Kenya Revisited." *International Journal of African Historical Studies* 30, no. 1 (1997): 49–86.

Bromberg, Sarah. "The Question of Purposeful Nutrition in Eretz Israel." *Hamazon* 1, no. 1 (1938): 2–3. (Hebrew)

Brown, Michael F. *Who Owns Native Culture?* Cambridge, MA: Harvard University Press, 2003.

Buccini, Anthony F., and Amy Dahlstrom. "Culinary Change, Disruption, and Death: Do Traditional Cuisines Have a Future?" *Dublin Gastronomy Symposium* (2020): 1–6. https://doi.org/10.21427/kymj-pk32.

Büssow, Johann. *Hamidian Palestine: Politics and Society in the District of Jerusalem 1872–1908*. Leiden: Brill, 2011.

Caballero, Benjamin, ed. *Encyclopedia of Food Sciences and Nutrition*. Kidlington, Oxford: Elsevier Science, 2003.

Caldwell, Melissa L. "Domesticating the French Fry: McDonald's and Consumerism in Moscow." *Journal of Consumer Culture* 4, no. 1 (2004): 5–26.

Caldwell, Melissa L. "The Taste of Nationalism: Food Politics in Postsocialist Moscow." *Ethnos* 67, no. 3 (2002): 295–319.

Callon, Michel, Cécile Méadel, and Vololona Rabeharisoa. "The Economy of Qualities." *Economy and Society* 31, no. 2 (2002): 194–217.

Calò, Emanuela. "Change of Taste in Israeli Food: The Case of 'Italian Cuisine', 1980–2000." MA thesis, Tel Aviv University, 2005. (Hebrew)

Campos, Michelle U. "Mapping Urban 'Mixing' and Intercommunal Relations in Late Ottoman Jerusalem: A Neighborhood Study." *Comparative Studies in Society and History* 63, no. 1 (2021): 133–69.

Carmeli, Yoram S., and Kalman Applbaum. *Consumption and Market Society in Israel*. Oxford: Berg, 2004.

Carroll, Glenn R., and Dennis Ray Wheaton. "The Organizational Construction of Authenticity: An Examination of Contemporary Food and Dining in the US." *Research in Organizational Behavior* 29 (2009): 255–82.

Cavanaugh, Jillian R., and Shalini Shankar. "Producing Authenticity in Global Capitalism: Language, Materiality, and Value." *American Anthropologist* 116, no. 1 (2014): 51–64.

Chelouche, Aharon. *From Jellabiya to Tembel Hat: The Story of a Family*. Published by the author, 1991. (Hebrew)

Chelouche, Julia. *The Tree and the Roots*. Tel Aviv: Akad, 1982. (Hebrew)

Chetrit, Sami Shalom. *Intra-Jewish Conflict in Israel: White Jews, Black Jews*. Abingdon, Oxon: Routledge, 2010.

Chetrit, Sami Shalom. *The Mizrahi Struggle in Israel, 1948–2003*. Tel Aviv: Am Oved, 2006. (Hebrew)

Chetrit, Sami Shalom. *The Mizrahi Struggle in Israel: Between Oppression and Liberation, Identification and Alternative, 1948–2003*. Tel Aviv: Am Oved, 2006. (Hebrew)

Clifford, James. *Routes: Travel and Translation in the Late Twentieth Century*. Cambridge, MA: Harvard University Press, 1997.

Cohen, Benny. *From "Carlton" to "Tnuva": Memories and Impressions from Early Restaurants in Tel Aviv*. Kibbutz Dalia: Ma'arechet, 2010. (Hebrew)

Cohen, Hillel. *Good Arabs: The Israeli Security Agencies and the Israeli Arabs, 1948–1967*. Translated by Haim Watzman. Berkeley: University of California Press, 2010.

Cohen, Hillel. *Year Zero of the Arab–Israeli Conflict 1929.* Translated by Haim Watzman. Waltham, MA: Brandeis University Press, 2015.

Cohen, Uri, and Nissim Leon. "The New Mizrahi Middle Class: Ethnic Mobility and Class Integration in Israel." *Journal of Israeli History* 27, no. 1 (2008): 51–64.

Cook, Ian. "Geographies of Food: Mixing." *Progress in Human Geography* 32, no. 6 (2008): 821–33.

Cook, Ian, and Philip Crang. "The World on a Plate: Culinary Culture, Displacement and Geographical Knowledges." *Journal of Material Culture* 1, no. 2 (July 1996): 131–53.

Coole, Diana, and Samantha Frost. "Introducing the New Materialisms." In *New Materialisms: Ontology, Agency and Politics,* edited by Diana Coole and Samantha Frost, 1–43. Durham, NC: Duke University Press, 2010.

Coombe, Rosemary J. "Embodied Trademarks: Mimesis and Alterity on American Commercial Frontiers." *Cultural Anthropology* 11, no. 2 (1996): 202–24.

Coombes, Annie E. "The Recalcitrant Object: Culture Contact and the Question of Hybridity." In *Colonial Discourse, Postcolonial Theory,* edited by Francis Barker, Peter Hulme, and Margaret Iversen, 89–114. Manchester: Manchester University Press, 1994.

Cornfeld, Lilian. "The Foods of the Oriental Communities." *Hamazon* 4 (1939): 12. (Hebrew)

Cornfeld, Lilian. *How to Cook at Times of War.* Tel Aviv: Olam Ha'isha, 1942. (Hebrew)

Cornfeld, Lilian. *What Shall I Cook with the Rationing Portions?* Published by the author, 1949. (Hebrew)

Cornfeld, Lilian. *Israeli Cookery.* Westport, CT: Avi Publishing, 1962.

Cornfield, Giveon. *Lilian: Israel's First Lady of Cuisine.* New York: Xlibris, 2012.

Crane, William. "Cultural Formation and Appropriation in the Era of Merchant Capitalism." *Historical Materialism* 26, no. 2 (2018): 242–70.

Cravens, Hamilton. "The German-American Science of Racial Nutrition, 1870–1920." In *Technical Knowledge in American Culture: Science, Technology and Medicine Since the Early 1800,* edited by Hamilton Cravens, David M. Katzman, and Alan I. Marcus, 127–45. Tuscaloosa: University of Alabama Press, 1996.

Craw, Charlotte. "Gustatory Redemption? Colonial Appetites, Historical Tales and the Contemporary Consumption of Australian Native Foods." *International Journal of Critical Indigenous Studies* 5, no. 2 (2012): 13–24.

Crossland-Marr, Lauren, and Elizabeth L. Krause. "Theorizing Authenticity: Introduction to Special Section." *Gastronomica* 23, no. 1 (2023): 5–12.

Cullather, Nick. "The Foreign Policy of the Calorie." *American Historical Review* 112 (2007): 337–64.

Dabdoub Nasser, Christiane. "Discussing Food and Foodways: No Better Time than the Present." *Jerusalem Quarterly* 98 (2024): 6–11.

Dabdoub Nasser, Christiane. "Introduction: Food and the Transmission of Culture: Linking Past, Present and Future." *Jerusalem Quarterly* 99 (2024): 6–13.

Dabdoub Nasser, Christiane. "Recipes Carry Voices and Stories: An Interview with Mirna Bamieh." *Jerusalem Quarterly* 98 (2024): 79–85.

Dahan-Kalev, Henriette. "You're So Pretty—You Don't Look Moroccan." *Israel Studies* 6, no. 1 (2001): 1–14.

Dallasheh, Leena. "Persevering through Colonial Transition: Nazareth's Palestinian Residents after 1948." *Journal of Palestine Studies* 45, no. 2 (2016): 8–23.

Dallasheh, Leena. "Troubled Waters: Citizenship and Colonial Zionism in Nazareth." *International Journal of Middle East Studies* 47, no. 3 (2015): 467–87.

Dalman, Gustaf. *Arbeit und Sitte in Palästina*. Band II, *Der Ackerbau* (Hildesheim: Georg Olms, 1964).

Dankner, Amnon. *Dahn Ben-Amotz: A Biography*. Jerusalem: Keter, 1992. (Hebrew)

Davidson, Alan, ed. *The Oxford Companion to Food*. Oxford: Oxford University Press, 2014.

Dawdy, Shannon Lee. "A Wild Taste: Food and Colonialism in Eighteenth-Century Louisiana." *Ethnohistory* 57, no. 3 (2010): 389–414.

Dayan, Moshe. *Milestones: A Biography*. Jerusalem: Idanim and Dvir, 1976. (Hebrew)

de Certeau, Michel. *The Practice of Everyday Life*. Translated by Steven Rendall. Berkeley: University of California Press, 1984.

De La Peña, Carolyn, and Benjamin N. Lawrence. "Foodways, 'Foodism,' or Foodscapes? Navigating the Local/Global and Food/Culture Divide." In *Local Foods Meet Global Foodways: Tasting History*, edited by Carolyn de la Peña and Benjamin N. Lawrence, 2–14. London: Routledge, 2012.

DellaPergola, Sergio. "The Population of Israel in the Third Decade: Trends and Contexts." In *Israel 1967–1977: Continuity and Turning* (*Iyunim Bitkumat Israel*: Thematic series, vol. 11), edited by Ofer Shiff and Aviva Halamish, 185–220. Sde Boker: The Ben-Gurion Research Institute for the Study of Israel and Zionism, 2017. (Hebrew)

DeMalach, Daniel, and Lev Luis Grinberg. "The Violent Struggle over Land: The Beginning of the Zionist Armed-Settlement Strategy, 1908–1914." In *Entangled Histories in Palestine/Israel: Historical and Anthropological Perspectives*, edited by Dafna Hirsch, 29–47. London: Routledge, 2024.

Desmet, Christy, and Sujata Iyengar. "Adaptation, Appropriation, or What You Will." *Shakespeare* 11, no. 1 (2015): 10–19.

de Solier, Isabelle. *Food and the Self: Consumption, Production and Material Culture*. London: Bloomsbury, 2013.

DeSoucey, Michaela. "Gastronationalism: Food Traditions and Authenticity Politics in the European Union." *American Sociological Review* 75, no. 3 (2010): 432–55.

Dietler, Michael. "Culinary Encounters: Food, Identity, and Colonialism." In *We Are What We Eat: Archaeology, Food, and Identity*, edited by Katheryn C. Twiss, 218–42. Carbondale: Center for Archaeological Investigations, Southern Illinois University, 2006.

Diner, Hasia R. *Hungering for America: Italian, Irish, and Jewish Foodways in the Age of Migration*. Cambridge, MA: Harvard University Press, 2003.

Dinur, Ben Zion, ed. *Book of the History of the Haganah*. Vol. 1, *From Defensiveness to Defense*. Tel Aviv: Zionist Library, 1954. (Hebrew)

Dirks, Nicholas. "Is Vice Versa? Historical Anthropologies and Anthropological Histories." In *The Historic Turn in the Human Sciences*, edited by Terrence J. McDonald, 17–51. Ann Arbor: University of Michigan Press, 1996.

Dorani, Mona. "From Kitchen to Community: Food and Palestinian Marriage Rituals in the Ethnography of Hilma Granqvist." *Jerusalem Quarterly* 99 (2024): 73–84.

Dunevich, Nathan. *A City Dines: One Hundred Years of Dining in Tel Aviv*. Tel Aviv: Achuzat Bayit, 2012. (Hebrew)

Dunevich, Nathan. *Tel Aviv: Sands which Became a Metropolis*. Jerusalem: Schocken, 1959. (Hebrew)

Earle, Rebecca. "'If You Eat Their Food . . .': Diets and Bodies in Early Colonial Spanish America." *American Historical Review* 115, no. 3 (2010): 688–713.

Eco, Umberto. "How Culture Conditions the Colours We See." In *On Signs*, edited by Marshall Blonsky, 157–75. Baltimore: Johns Hopkins University Press, 1985.

Edensor, Tim. *National Identity, Popular Culture and Everyday Life*. Oxford: Berg, 2002.

Eghbariah, Rabea. "The Struggle for Akoub & Za'atar: On Edible Plants in Palestinian Cuisine and Israeli Plant Protection Laws." In *Studies in Food Law*, edited by Aeyal Gross and Yofi Tirosh, 497–533. Tel Aviv: Buchmann Faculty of Law, Tel Aviv University, 2017. (Hebrew)

El-Hadad, Laila M., and Maggie Schmitt. *The Gaza Kitchen: A Palestinian Culinary Journey*. Charlottesville, VA: Just World Books, 2016.

Elor, Tamar, and Motti Regev. "The Establishment of an Israeli Style, 1967–1973." In *Israel 1967–1977: Continuity and Turning (Iyunim Bitkumat Israel*: Thematic series, vol. 11), edited by Ofer Shiff and Aviva Halamish, 308–33. Sde Boker: The Ben-Gurion Research Institute for the Study of Israel and Zionism, 2017. (Hebrew)

Ensminger, Marion Eugene, and Audrey H. Ensminger, eds. *Food and Nutrition Encyclopedia*. 2nd ed. Boca Raton, FL: CRC Press, 1993.

Erez, Oded. "Becoming Mediterranean: Greek Popular Music and Ethno-Class Politics in Israel, 1952–1982." PhD diss., UCLA, 2016.

Erez, Oded, and Nadeem Karkabi. "Sounding Arabic: Postvernacular Modes of Performing the Arabic Language in Popular Music by Israeli Jews." *Popular Music* 38, no. 2 (2019): 298–316.

Errington, Frederick, Tatsuro Fujikura, and Deborah Gewertz. *The Noodle Narratives: The Global Rise of an Industrial Food into the Twenty-First Century.* Berkeley: University of California Press, 2013.

Even-Zohar, Itamar. "The Emergence of a Native Hebrew Culture in Palestine: 1882–1948." *Studies in Zionism* 2, no. 2 (1981): 167–84.

Even-Zohar, Itamar. "Nine Hypotheses on Cultural Interference." *Journal of Turkish Studies* 48 (2017): 387–395.

Ever Hadani. *Settlement in the Lower Galilee: Fifty Years of its History.* Ramat Gan: Masada, 1955. (Hebrew)

Ezrati, Or. "Israel Aharoni." In *Masters of Culture: Anatomy of Israeli Culture Producers*, edited by Nir Baram, 83–95. Tel Aviv: Am Oved, 2003. (Hebrew)

Farah, Reem. "Ottolenghi and Tamimi's Cookbook, Jerusalem: Israel as Frame and Palestine as Subject." *Jerusalem Quarterly* 99 (2024): 106–15.

Farhi, Guy. "Pita Politics: The Miznon Chain and the Cultural Logic of late Capitalism." In *Thoughts on Food*, edited by Ori Bartal, Ronit Vered, and Michal Eitan, 422–39. Jerusalem: Bezalel Academy of Art and Resling, 2021. (Hebrew)

Farrer, James. "Introduction: Traveling Cuisines in and out of Asia: Toward A Framework for Studying Culinary Globalization." In *The Globalization of Asian Cuisines: Transnational Networks and Culinary Contact Zones*, edited by James Farrer, 1–19. New York: Palgrave Macmillan, 2015.

Farsakh, Leila. *Palestinian Labour Migration to Israel: Labour, Land and Occupation.* London: Routledge, 2005.

Feagan, Robert. "The Place of Food: Mapping Out the 'Local' in Local Food Systems." *Progress in Human Geography* 31, no, 1 (2007): 23–42.

Featherstone, Mike. *Consumer Culture and Postmodernism.* London: Sage, 2007.

Ferguson, Priscilla Parkhurst. *Accounting for Taste: The Triumph of French Cuisine.* Chicago: University of Chicago Press, 2004.

Ferguson, Priscilla Parkhurst, and Sharon Zukin. "The Careers of Chefs." In *Eating Culture*, edited by Ron Scapp and Brian Seitz, 92–111. Albany: SUNY Press, 1998.

Fireberg, Haim. "East Meets West: Cafés at the Margins of Tel Aviv, 1936–1960." In *Tel Aviv's Cafés, 1920–1980*, edited by Batya Carmiel, 294–301. Tel Aviv: Eretz Israel Museum, 2007. (Hebrew)

Fireberg, Haim. "Tel Aviv: Change, Continuity and the Many Faces of Urban Culture and Society during War, 1936–1948." PhD diss., Tel Aviv University, 2003. (Hebrew)

Fischler, Claude. "Food, Self and Identity." *Social Science Information* 27, no. 2 (1988): 275–92.

Forth, Christopher E. *Masculinity in the Modern West: Gender, Civilization and the Body*. London: Palgrave Macmillan, 2008.

Foster, Robert J. *Coca-Globalization: Following Soft Drinks from New York to New Guinea*. New York: Palgrave Macmillan, 2008.

Foster, Robert J. "Commodity Futures: Labour, Love and Value." *Anthropology Today* 21, no. 4 (2005): 8–12.

Frankel, Jonathan. *Prophecy and Politics: Socialism, Nationalism, and the Russian Jews, 1862–1917*. Cambridge: Cambridge University Press, 1981.

Fromm, Erich, and Karl Marx. *Marx's Concept of Man, Including Economic and Philosophical Manuscripts*. Translated by T. B. Bottomore. London: Bloomsbury, 1961.

Gabaccia, Donna R. *We Are What We Eat: Ethnic Food and the Making of Americans*. Cambridge, MA: Harvard University Press, 1998.

Galili, Shmuel, Hovav Ran, Evgenia Dor, Joseph Hershenhorn, Arye Harel, Orit Amir-Segev, Aharon Bellalou, Hana Badani, Evgeny Smirnov, and Guy Achdari. "The History of Chickpea Cultivation and Breeding in Israel." *Israel Journal of Plant Sciences* 65, nos. 3–4 (2018): 186-194.

Gaul, Anny, and Graham Auman Pitts. "Introduction: Making Levantine Cuisine." In *Making Levantine Cuisine: Modern Foodways of the Eastern Mediterranean*, edited by Anny Gaul, Graham Auman Pitts, and Vicki Valosik, 1–20. Austin: University of Texas Press, 2021.

Gaul, Anny, Graham Auman Pitts, and Vicki Valosik, eds. *Making Levantine Cuisine: Modern Foodways of the Eastern Mediterranean*. Austin: University of Texas Press, 2021.

Gelber, Yoav. "The Consolidation of Jewish Society in Eretz-Israel, 1936–1947." In *The History of the Jewish Community in Eretz-Israel Since 1882: The Period of the British Mandate, Part Two*, edited by Moshe Lissak, Anita Shapira, and Gavriel Cohen, 303–463. Jerusalem: Israeli Academy for Sciences and Humanities and Bialik Institute, 2001. (Hebrew)

Gerber, Noah S. *Ourselves or Our Holy Books? The Cultural Discovery of Yemenite Jewry*. Jerusalem: Yad Izhak Ben-Zvi, 2013. (Hebrew)

Gewertz, Deborah, and Frederick Errington. *Cheap Meat: Flap Food Nations in the Pacific Islands*. Berkeley: University of California Press, 2010.

Ghandour, Zeina B. "*Falafel* King: Culinary Customs and National Narratives in Palestine (I)." *Feminist Legal Studies* 21 (2013): 281–301.

Gilad, Efrat. "Meat in the Heat: A History of Tel Aviv under the British Mandate for Palestine (1920s–1940s)." PhD diss., Graduate Institute Geneva, 2022.

Gilad, Zrubavel. *The Palmach Book*. Tel Aviv: Hakibbutz Hameuchad, 1955. (Hebrew)

Giladi, Dan. "From Austerity to Economic Growth." In *Israel in the First Decade*, vol. 3, section 5, edited by Benny Neuberger, 9–84. Ramat Aviv: Open University of Israel, 2002. (Hebrew)

Gilbar, Gad G. "The Growing Economic Involvement of Palestine with the West, 1865–1914." In *Palestine in the Late Ottoman Period: Political, Social and Economic Transformation*, edited by David Kushner, 188–210. Jerusalem: Yad Izhak Ben-Zvi and Brill, 1986.

Gnichovsky, Dov. "The Austerity Regime—Economic Aspects." In *Immigrants and Ma'barot, 1948–1952*, edited by Mordechai Naor, 111–14. Jerusalem: Yad Izhak Ben-Zvi, 1986. (Hebrew)

Gofer, Gilat. "The Zionist Woman: The Construction of Femininity in the Early Zionist Labor Movement, 1903–1923." PhD diss., Tel Aviv University, 2009. (Hebrew)

Golan, Arnon. "Settlement in the First Decade of the Israeli State." In *The First Decade: 1948–1958*, edited by Zvi Zameret and Hannah Jablonka, 83–102. Jerusalem: Yad Izhak Ben-Zvi, 1997. (Hebrew)

Goldman, Anne. "I Yam What I Yam: Cooking, Culture and Colonialism." In *De/Colonizing the Subject: The Politics of Gender in Women's Autobiography*, edited by Sidonie Smith and Julia Watson, 169–95. Minneapolis: University of Minnesota Press, 1992.

Goldman, Aviva. *The Cookbook*. Tel Aviv: Maariv, 1970. (Hebrew)

Goldstein, Yaacov. "Self-Defense and Guarding: 'Bar Giora' and 'Hashomer' in the Second Aliya." In *The Second Aliya: Studies*, edited by Israel Bartal, 435–81. Jerusalem: Yad Izhak Ben-Zvi, 1997. (Hebrew)

Goldstein, Yaacov N. "The Jewish–Arab Conflict: The First Jewish Underground Defense Organizations and the Arabs." *Middle Eastern Studies* 31, no. 4 (1995): 744–51.

Goody, Jack. *Cooking, Cuisine and Class: A Study in Comparative Sociology*. Cambridge: Cambridge University Press, 1982.

Goody, Jack. "Structuralism, Materialism and the Horse." In *Food and Love: A Cultural History of East and West*, edited by Jack Goody, 148–60. New York: Verso, 1998.

Gordon, Neve. *Israel's Occupation*. Berkeley: University of California Press, 2008.

Gouri, Haim. *The Crazy Book*. Tel Aviv: Am Oved, 1971. (Hebrew)

Gouri, Haim. *The Poems*, vol. 1. Jerusalem: Bialik Institute, 1998. (Hebrew)

Grayson, Kent, and Radan Martinec. "Consumer Perceptions of Iconicity and Indexicality and Their Influence on Assessments of Authentic Market Offerings." *Journal of Consumer Research* 31, no. 2 (2004): 296–312.

Grazien, David. "Demystifying Authenticity in the Sociology of Culture." In *Routledge Handbook of Cultural Sociology*, edited by Laura Grindstaff, Ming-Cheng M. Lo, and John R. Hall, 168–76. London: Routledge, 2018.

Grehan, James. *Everyday Life and Consumer Culture in 18th-Century Damascus*. Seattle: University of Washington Press, 2007.

Grey, Sam, and Lenore Newman. "Beyond Culinary Colonialism: Indigenous Food Sovereignty, Liberal Multiculturalism, and the Control of Gastronomic Capital." *Agriculture and Human Values* 35 (2018): 717–30.

Grinberg, Ofra, and Hanna Herzog. *A Voluntary Women's Organization in an Emerging Society: WIZO's Contribution to the Israeli Society.* Tel Aviv: Institute for Social Research, Tel Aviv University, 1978. (Hebrew)

Grosglik, Rafi. "From 'Staged Authenticity' to 'Liquid Authenticity'—Chinese Food in Israel of the 'Glocalization' Era." MA thesis, Ben Gurion University, 2008. (Hebrew)

Grosglik, Rafi. "Global Ethical Culinary Fashion and a Local Dish: Organic Hummus in Israel." *Critical Studies in Fashion & Beauty* 2, nos. 1–2 (2011): 165–84.

Grosglik, Rafi. "Organic Hummus in Israel: Global and Local Ingredients and Images." *Sociological Research Online* 16, no. 2 (2011): 88–98.

Grosglik, Rafi, and Julia Lerner. "Gastro-emotivism: How MasterChef Israel Produces Therapeutic Collective Belongings." *European Journal of Cultural Studies* 24, no. 5 (2021): 1053–70.

Grosglik, Rafi, and Uri Ram. "Authentic, Speedy and Hybrid: Representations of Chinese Food and Cultural Globalization in Israel." *Food, Culture & Society* 16, no. 2 (2013): 223–43.

Gross, Aeyal, and Tamar Feldman. "We Didn't Want to Hear the Word Calories: Rethinking Food Security, Food Power, and Food Sovereignty—Lessons from the Gaza Closure." *Berkeley Journal of International Law* 33 (2015): 379–441.

Gross, Nachum. "Israel's Economy." In *The First Decade: 1948–1958*, edited by Zvi Zameret and Hannah Jablonka, 137–50. Jerusalem: Yad Izhak Ben-Zvi, 1997. (Hebrew)

Gross, Nachum. "Israel's Economy, 1954–67." In *The Second Decade, 1958–1968*, edited by Zvi Zameret and Hannah Jablonka, 29–46. Jerusalem: Yad Izhak Ben-Zvi, 2000. (Hebrew)

Gross, Nachum. "The Palestine Economy towards the Close of the Ottoman Era." In *The History of the Jewish Community in Eretz-Israel since 1882, The Ottoman Period, Part Two*, edited by Israel Kolatt, 279–308. Jerusalem: Israel Academy for Sciences and Humanities and Bialik Institute, 2002. (Hebrew)

Guggenheim, Yechiel Karl, Eliyahu Habibi, and Abraham Reshef. "The Beginning of Nutritional Studies in Eretz Israel." *Cathedra* 59 (1991): 144–60. (Hebrew)

Guilat, Yael. "The Yemeni Ideal in Israeli Culture and Art." *Israel Studies* 6, no. 3 (2001): 26–53.

Guilat, Yael. *Yemeni Jewish Silver Craft in the Israeli 'Melting Pot.'* Sde Boker: The Ben-Gurion Research Institute for the Study of Israel and Zionism, 2009. (Hebrew)

Gupta, Akhil, and James Ferguson. "Beyond 'Culture': Space, Identity and the Politics of Difference." *Cultural Anthropology* 7, no. 1 (1992): 6–23.

Gur, Janna. *The Book of New Israeli Food: A Culinary Journey*. Tel Aviv: Al Hashul-chan, 2007.

Gutmark, Yaron. *Riding for Hummus: Hiking Bike Tracks, Hummus, and Everything in Between*. Published by the author, 2021. (Hebrew)

Guzmen-Carmeli, Shlomo. "Eating the Bubbe: Culinary Encounters between Secular and Haredi Jews in Bnei Brak." *Food and Foodways* 28, no. 2 (2020): 69–90.

Gvion, Liora. *Beyond Hummus and Falafel: Social and Political Aspects of Palestinian Food in Israel*. Berkeley: University of California Press, 2012.

Gvion, Liora. "Cooking, Food, and Masculinity: Palestinian Men in Israeli Society." *Men and Masculinities* 14, no. 4 (2011): 408–29.

Gvion, Liora. "Cuisines of Poverty as Means of Empowerment: Arab Food in Israel." *Agriculture and Human Values* 23 (2006): 299–312.

Gvion, Liora. *Culinary Bridges versus Culinary Barriers: Social and Political Aspects of Palestinian Cookery in Israel*. Jerusalem: Carmel, 2006. (Hebrew)

Gvion, Liora. "'From an Arab I Would Expect That . . .': 'MasterChef,' Hegemony and Exclusion." In *Studies in Food Law*, edited by Aeyal Gross and Yofi Tirosh, 561–87. Tel Aviv: Tel Aviv University, Buchmann Faculty of Law, 2017. (Hebrew)

Gvion, Liora. "Hummus, Couscous, Sushi: Food and Ethnicity in Israeli Society." In *A Full Belly: Rethinking Food and Society in Israel*, edited by Aviad Kleinberg, 32–78. Tel Aviv: Tel Aviv University and Keter, 2005. (Hebrew)

Gvion, Liora. "Two Narratives of Israeli Food: 'Jewish' versus 'Ethnic.'" In *Jews and Their Foodways* (Studies in Contemporary Jewry 28), edited by Anat Helman, 126–41. New York: Oxford University Press, 2015.

Hagiladi, Nimrod. "The Israeli Society and the Black Market: From World War II to the Early 1950s." PhD diss., Hebrew University of Jerusalem, 2011.

Haidar, Aziz. *The New Arab-Palestinian Middle Class in Israel: Economic, Socio-Cultural and Political Aspects*. Ramat Aviv: Walter-Lebach Institute for Jewish-Arab Coexistence and Tami Steinmetz Center for Peace Research, 2021. (Hebrew)

Hall, Stuart. "The Local and the Global: Globalization and Ethnicity." In *Dangerous Liaisons: Gender, Nation and Postcolonial Perspectives*, edited by Anne McClintock, Aamir Mufti, and Ella Shohat, 173–87. Minneapolis: University of Minnesota Press, 1997.

Hall, Stuart. "Signification, Representation, Ideology: Althusser and the Post-Structuralist Debates." *Critical Studies in Mass Communication* 2, no. 2 (1985): 91–114.

Hall, Stuart. "What Is This 'Black' in Black Popular Culture?" *Social Justice* 20, nos. 1–2 (1993): 104–11.

Halperin, Liora R. *Babel in Zion: Jews, Nationalism, and Language Diversity in Palestine, 1920–1948*. New Haven, CT: Yale University Press, 2015.

Halperin, Liora R. *The Oldest Guard: Forging the Zionist Settler Past*. Stanford, CA: Stanford University Press, 2021.

Halpern, Ben, and Jehuda Reinharz. *Zionism and the Creation of a New Society.* Hanover, NH: Brandeis University Press, 1998.

Hamrick, Danny, Michaela DeSoucey, and Nino Bariola. "Distillations of Authenticity: A Comparative Global Value Chain Analysis of Pisco." *Regional Studies* 58, no. 10 (2022): 1792–803.

Hart, Rachel. *So Close So Far Away: Jewish-Arab Relations in Jaffa and Tel Aviv, 1881–1930.* Tel Aviv: Resling, 2014. (Hebrew)

Hasan, Manar. *The Invisible: Women and the Palestinian Cities.* Jerusalem: Van Leer and Hakibbutz Hameuchad, 2017. (Hebrew)

Hasan, Manar, and Ami Ayalon. "Arabs and Jews, Leisure and Gender, in Haifa's Public Spaces." In *Haifa Before and After 1948: Narratives of a Mixed City,* edited by Mahmoud Yazbak and Yifaat Weiss, 69–98. Dordrecht: Republic of Letters, 2011.

Havas, Bracha. *The Second Immigration Wave Book.* Tel Aviv: Am Oved, 1947. (Hebrew)

Heath, Deborah, and Anne Meneley. "Techne, Technoscience, and the Circulation of Comestible Commodities: An Introduction." *American Anthropologist* 109, no. 4 (2007): 593–602.

Heiman, Uri. *Then and Now—Tozeret Mazon Israelit, 1938–1998.* Haifa: Here and Now, 1998. (Hebrew)

Heine, Peter. *The Culinary Crescent: A History of Middle Eastern Cuisine.* Translated by Peter Lewis. London: Gingko, 2016.

Heldke, Lisa. *Exotic Appetites: Ruminations of a Food Adventurer.* New York: Routledge, 2003.

Helman, Anat. *Becoming Israeli: National Ideals and Everyday Life in the 1950s.* Waltham, MA: Brandeis University Press, 2014.

Helman, Anat. *Consumer Culture and Leisure in the Young State of Israel.* Jerusalem: Zalman Shazar Center, 2020. (Hebrew)

Helman, Anat. "European Jews in the Levant Heat: Climate and Culture in 1920s and 1930s Tel Aviv." *Journal of Israeli History* 22, no. 1 (2003): 71–90.

Helman, Anat. *Urban Culture in 1920s and 1930s Tel Aviv.* Haifa: University of Haifa Press, 2007.

Helman, Anat. *Young Tel Aviv: A Tale of Two Cities.* Waltham, MA: Brandeis University Press, 2010.

Highmore, Ben. "Alimentary Agents: Food, Cultural Theory and Multiculturalism." *Journal of Intercultural Studies* 29, no. 4 (2008): 381–98.

Hilel, Maayan. "Cultural Changes in Palestinian Arab Society, 1918–1948: Haifa as a Case-Study." PhD diss., Tel Aviv University, 2018.

Hirsch, Dafna. "'Hummus Is Best When It Is Fresh and Made by Arabs': The Gourmetization of Hummus in Israel and the Return of the Repressed Arab." *American Ethnologist* 38, no. 4 (2011): 617–30.

Hirsch, Dafna. "Hummus Masculinity in Israel." *Food, Culture and Society* 19, no. 2 (2016): 337–59.

Hirsch, Dafna. *'We Are Here to Bring the West': Hygiene Education and Culture Building in the Jewish Society of Mandate Palestine*. Sde Boker: The Ben-Gurion Research Institute for the Study of Israel and Zionism, 2014. (Hebrew)

Hirsch, Dafna. "'We Are Here to Bring the West, Not Only to Ourselves': Zionist Occidentalism and the Discourse of Hygiene in Mandate Palestine." *International Journal of Middle East Studies* 41, no. 4 (2009): 577–94.

Hirsch, Dafna, and Ofra Tene. "Hummus: The Making of an Israeli Culinary Cult." *Journal of Consumer Culture* 13, no. 1 (2013): 25–45.

Hirsch, Dafna, and Smadar Sharon. "'Neglectful Mothers': Constructions of Mizrahi Women's Motherhood during the Mandate and Early State Periods." In *Awlad al-Kalb—Children of the Heart: Aspects in the Study of the Missing Babies of Israel*, edited by Tova Gamliel and Nathan Shifriss, 253–97. Tel Aviv: Resling, 2019. (Hebrew)

Hochberg, Gil Z. *In Spite of Partition: Jews, Arabs, and the Limits of Separatist Imagination*. Princeton, NJ: Princeton University Press, 2007.

Hodder, Ian. *Entangled: An Archaeology of the Relationships between Humans and Things*. Malden, MA: Blackwell, 2012.

Holden, Andrew. *Tourism Studies and the Social Sciences*. London: Routledge, 2005.

Holland, Nina. *The World on a Plate: 40 Cuisines, 100 Recipes and the Stories behind Them*. New York: Penguin, 2015.

Hollows, Joanne. "Oliver's Twist: Leisure, Labour and Domestic Masculinity in The Naked Chef." *International Journal of Cultural Studies* 6, no. 2 (2003): 229–48.

Holt, Douglas B. "Jack Daniel's America: Iconic Brands as Ideological Parasites and Proselytizers." *Journal of Consumer Culture* 6, no. 3 (2006): 355–77.

Holt, Douglas B. "Why Do Brands Cause Trouble? A Dialectical Theory of Consumer Culture and Branding." *Journal of Consumer Research* 29, no. 1 (2002): 70–90.

hooks, bell. "Eating the Other: Desire and Resistance." In *Black Looks: Race and Representation*, edited by bell hooks, 21–39. Boston: South End Press, 1992.

Horowitz, David. *The Enigma of Economic Growth: A Case Study of Israel*. New York: Praeger, 1972.

Huck, Christian, and Stefan Bauernschmidt. "Trans-Cultural Appropriation." In *Travelling Goods, Travelling Moods: Varieties of Cultural Appropriation*, edited by Christian Huck and Stefan Bauernschmidt, 229–251. Frankfurt: Campus, 2012.

Huck, Christian, and Stefan Bauernschmidt, eds. *Travelling Goods, Travelling Moods: Varieties of Cultural Appropriation*. Frankfurt: Campus, 2012.

Hummus Mouse: The Selected Hundred Hummusiyot of Israel. Tel Aviv: City Mouse, 2010. (Hebrew)

Husseini, A. R. "Israel Restructures West Bank Economy: Interview with A. R. Husseini." *MERIP Reports* 60 (1977): 21–23.

Hutchby, Ian. "Technologies, Texts and Affordances." *Sociology* 35, no. 2 (2001): 441–56.

Ichijo, Atsuko, Venetia Johannes, and Ronald Ranta, eds. *The Emergence of National Food: The Dynamics of Food and Nationalism*. London: Bloomsbury Academic, 2019.

Igra, Alma. "Farm to Pharmacy: Nutrition, Animals and Governance in Britain, 1870–1945." PhD diss., Columbia University, 2020.

Igra, Alma. "Meatropolis: Tel Aviv's Slaughterhouse and Demarcation of Urban-National Boundaries in Palestine, 1927–1938." MA thesis, Central European University, 2012.

Illouz, Eva. "Introduction: Emodities or the Making of Emotional Commodities." In *Emotions as Commodities: Capitalism, Consumption and Authenticity*, edited by Eva Illouz, 1–29. London: Routledge, 2018.

Inglis, David. "Globalization and Food: The Dialectics of Globality and Locality." In *The Routledge International Handbook of Globalization Studies*, edited by Bryan S. Turner, 492–513. London: Routledge, 2010.

Jacobson, Abigail, and Moshe Naor. *Oriental Neighbors: Middle Eastern Jews and Arabs in Mandatory Palestine*. Waltham, MA: Brandeis University Press, 2016.

Jaeggi, Rahel. *Alienation*. Translated by Frederick Neuhouser and Allen E. Smith, edited by Frederick Neuhouser. New York: Columbia University Press, 2014.

Jiryis, Sabri. *The Arabs in Israel*. Translated by Inea Bushnaq. New York: Monthly Review Press, 1976.

Johnston, Anna, and Alan Lawson. "Settler Colonies." In *A Companion to Postcolonial Studies*, edited by Henry Schwartz and Sangeeta Ray, 360–76. Malden, MA: Blackwell, 2000.

Johnston, Josée, and Shyon Baumann. *Foodies: Democracy and Distinction in the Gourmet Foodscape*. New York: Routledge, 2010.

Julier, Alice. "Appropriation." In *The Practice of the Meal: Food, Families and the Market Place*, edited by Benedetta Cappellini, David Marshall, and Elizabeth Parsons, 101–15. Routledge, 2016.

Kalka, Iris. "Changing Nutrition Value and Self-Image in Israel." *ICAF Occasional Report* vii (1990): 7–10.

Kamminga, Harmke. "'Axes to Grind': Popularizing the Science of Vitamins, 1920s and 1930s." In *Food, Science, Policy and Regulation in the Twentieth Century: International and Comparative Perspectives*, edited by David F. Smith and Jim Phillips, 83–100. London: Routledge, 2000.

Kaplan, Dana. "Beautiful Israeli Girls: Aesthetic Labor in the Media between Nation Building and Neoliberalism." Unpublished manuscript.

Kaplan, Dana. "Recreational Sexuality, Food, New Age Spirituality: A Cultural Sociology of Middle-Class Distinctions." PhD diss., Hebrew University of Jerusalem, 2014.

Kaplan, Danny. *Brothers and Others in Arms: The Making of Love and War in Israeli Combat Units.* New York: Haworth Press, 2003.

Kaschl, Elke. *Dance and Authenticity in Israel and Palestine: Performing the Nation.* Leiden: Brill, 2003.

Kassis, Omar. "Olive Oil and the Taste of Palestine." *Jerusalem Quarterly* 98 (2024): 12–32.

Kassis, Reem. "Even in a Small Country Like Palestine, Cuisine Is Regional." In *Making Levantine Cuisine: Modern Foodways of the Eastern Mediterranean,* edited by Anny Gaul, Graham Auman Pitts, and Vicki Valosik, 133–49. Austin: University of Texas Press, 2022.

Kassis, Reem. *The Palestinian Table.* London: Phaidon, 2017.

Katinsky-Rabau, Tsiona. "WIZO's Instruction Work in Rational Nutrition." *Hamazon* 2, no. 3 (1939): 19–20. (Hebrew)

Katz-Gerro, Tally, and Yossi Shavit. "The Stratification of Leisure and Taste: Classes and Lifestyles in Israel." *European Sociological Review* 14, no. 4 (1998): 369–86.

Katz-Gerro, Tally, Sharon Raz, and Meir Yaish. "How Do Class, Status, Ethnicity, and Religiosity Shape Cultural Omnivorousness in Israel?" *Journal of Cultural Economics* 33 (2009): 1–17.

Keane, Webb. "Semiotics and the Social Analysis of Material Things." *Language & Communication* 23 (2003): 409–25.

Keane, Webb. "Subjects and Objects." In *Handbook of Material Culture,* edited by Christopher Tilley, Susanne Kuechler-Fogden, and Webb Keane, 197–202. London: Sage, 2006.

Kedar, Alexandre (Sandy), and Oren Yiftachel. "Land Regime and Social Relations in Israel." In *Realizing Property Rights: Swiss Human Rights Book,* edited by Hernando de Soto and Francis Cheneval, 127–44. Zurich: Ruffer & Rub, 2006.

Kenan, Amos. *The Book of Pleasure.* Tel Aviv: A. Levin-Epstein, 1970. (Hebrew)

Kerem, Zohar, Simcha Lev-Yadun, Avi Gopher, Pnina Weinberg, and Shahal Abbo. "Chickpea Domestication in the Neolithic Levant through the Nutritional Perspective." *Journal of Archaeological Science* 34 (2007): 1289–93.

Khalidi, Rashid. *The Hundred Years' War on Palestine: A History of Settler Colonialism and Resistance, 1917–2017.* New York: Metropolitan Books, 2020.

Khalidi, Walid. *All That Remains: The Palestinian Villages Occupied and Depopulated by Israel in 1948.* Washington, DC: Institution for Palestine Studies, 1992.

Khazzoom, Aziza. "The Great Chain of Orientalism: Jewish Identity, Stigma Management, and Ethnic Exclusion in Israel." *American Sociological Review* 68, no. 4 (2003): 481–510.

Khazzoom, Aziza. "Mizrahim, Mizrachiut, and the Future of Israeli Studies." *Israel Studies Forum* 17, no. 2 (2002): 94–106.

Kidron, Anat. "The Influence of the Results of the 1929 Events on Haifa and on Jaffa/Tel Aviv: A Comparative Look." *Israel* 22 (2014): 73–109. (Hebrew)

Kimmel, Michael S. *The History of Men: Essays on the History of American and British Masculinities.* New York: State University of New York Press, 2005.

Kimmerling, Baruch. "State Building, Mass Immigration and Establishment of Hegemony (1948–1951)." *Israeli Sociology* 1 (1999): 167–208. (Hebrew)

Kiple, Kenneth F., ed. *Cambridge World History of Food.* Cambridge: Cambridge University Press, 2000.

Klein, Menachem. *Lives in Common: Arabs and Jews in Jerusalem, Jaffa and Hebron.* Translated by Haim Watzman. Oxford: Oxford University Press, 2014.

Klein, Naomi. *No Logo.* New York: Picador, 2002.

Kligler, Israel. "Our Goal." *Hamazon* 1, no. 1 (1938): 1. (Hebrew)

Kligler, Israel Jacob, Alexander Geiger, Sarah Bromberg, and David Gurevitch. *An Inquiry into the Diets of Various Sections of the Urban and Rural Population of Palestine* (Bulletin of the Palestine Economic Society V, no. 3). Tel Aviv: Palestine Economic Society, 1931.

Kopytoff, Igor. "The Cultural Biography of Things: Commoditization as Process." In *The Social Life of Things: Commodities in Cultural Perspective,* edited by Arjun Appadurai, 64–91. Cambridge: Cambridge University Press, 1986.

Kostrinsky, Yaacov. *Agronomical Surveys on Chickpea and Seed Cycles.* Special Publication no. 34. Beit Dagan: Department of Scientific Publications, Vulcani Center, 1974. (Hebrew)

Kotef, Hagar. *The Colonizing Self: Home and Homelessness in Israel/Palestine.* Durham, NC: Duke University Press, 2020.

Kraus, Vered, and Yuval Yonay. "The Power and Limits of Ethnonationalism: Palestinians and Eastern Jews in Israel, 1974–1991." *British Journal of Sociology* 51, no. 3 (2000): 525–51.

Kulas, Margot. "Cultural Patterns and Ways of Adjustment of Immigrants from the Atlas Mountains." *Megamot* 6, no. 4 (1956): 345–76. (Hebrew)

Lahne, Jacob. "Sensory Science, the Food Industry, and the Objectification of Taste." *Anthropology of Food* 10 (2016). https://doi.org/10.4000/aof.7956.

Lalonde, Dianne. "Does Cultural Appropriation Cause Harm?" *Politics, Groups and Identities* 9, no. 2 (2021): 329–46.

Lash, Scott, and John Urry. *Economies of Signs and Space.* London: Sage, 1994.

Laudan, Rachel. *Cuisine and Empire: Cooking in World History.* Berkeley: University of California Press, 2013.

Laudan, Rachel. "A Plea for Culinary Modernism: Why We Should Love New, Fast, Processed Food." *Gastronomica* 1, no. 1 (2001): 36–44.

Launay, Robert. "Maize Avoidance? Colonial French Attitudes towards Native American Foods in the Pays des Illinois (17th–18th Century)." *Food and Foodways* 26, no. 2 (2018): 92–104.

Lavie, Smadar. *The Poetics of Military Occupation.* Berkeley: University of California Press, 1990.

Leitch, Alison. "Slow Food and the Politics of Pork Fat: Italian Food and European Identity." *Ethnos* 68, no. 4 (2003): 437–62.

Lentin, Ronit. *Traces of Racial Exception: Racializing Israeli Settler Colonialism.* London: Bloomsbury Academic, 2018.

Levenstein, Harvey. *Revolution at the Table: The Transformation of the American Diet.* Berkeley: University of California Press, 2003.

Levi-Faur, David. *The Visible Hand: State-Directed Industrialization in Israel.* Jerusalem: Yad Izhak Ben-Zvi, 2001. (Hebrew)

LeVine, Mark. *Overthrowing Geography: Jaffa, Tel Aviv, and the Struggle for Palestine, 1880–1948.* Berkeley: University of California Press, 2005.

Lev Tov, Boaz. "Leisure and Popular Culture Patterns of Eretz Israeli Jews in the Years 1882–1914 as a Reflection of Social Changes." PhD diss., Tel Aviv University, 2007. (Hebrew)

Lev Tov, Boaz. "'The Same Sea': Jews and Palestinians at the Beach in the Late Ottoman and Mandate Periods." In *Entangled Histories in Palestine/Israel: Historical and Anthropological Perspectives,* edited by Dafna Hirsch, 48–72. London: Routledge, 2024.

Levy, Shoshana. *On a Crossroad.* Published by the author, 2001. (Hebrew)

Lewin-Epstein, Noah, and Moshe Semyonov. "Ethnic Group Mobility in the Israeli Labor Market." *American Sociological Review* 51, no. 3 (1986): 342–52.

Lindholm, Charles. *Culture and Authenticity.* Malden, MA: Blackwell, 2008.

Lissak, Moshe. "Immigration, Absorption and Society Building in the Jewish Community in Eretz-Israel (1918–1930)." In *The History of the Jewish Community in Eretz-Israel Since 1882: The Period of the British Mandate, Part Two,* edited by Moshe Lissak, Anita Shapira, and Gavriel Cohen, 173–302. Jerusalem: Israeli Academy for Sciences and Humanities and Bialik Institute, 2001. (Hebrew)

Lissak, Moshe. *The Mass Immigration in the Fifties: The Failure of the Melting Pot Policy.* Jerusalem: Bialik Institute, 1999. (Hebrew)

Litani, Yehuda, and Na'im 'Araidi. *Not by Hummus Alone: Hummus, Olive Oil, References.* Tel Aviv: D. Dinur and Modan, 2000. (Hebrew)

Lizardo, Omar, and Sara Skiles. "Reconceptualizing and Theorizing 'Omnivorousness': Genetic and Relational Mechanisms." *Sociological Theory* 30 (2012): 263–82.

Lott, Eric. *Love and Theft: Blackface Minstrelsy and the American Working Class.* Oxford: Oxford University Press, 1993.

Lupton, Deborah. *Food, the Body and the Self.* London: Sage, 1998.

Lury, Celia. *Brands: The Logos of the Global Economy.* New York: Routledge, 2004.

Lustick, Ian. *Arabs in the Jewish State: Israel's Control of a National Minority.* Austin: University of Texas Press, 1980.

Maidhof, Callie. "Settler Nostalgia: Colonizing Temporalities and the Genre of Coexistence." *Cultural Critique* 116, no. 1 (2022): 92–118.

Maman, Daniel. "Business Groups in the Israeli Economy: Causes for Consolidation and Strengthening." In *The Power of Property: Israeli Society in the Global Age,* edited by Dani Filc and Uri Ram, 116–30. Jerusalem: Van Leer and Hakibbutz Hameuchad, 2004. (Hebrew)

Manning, Paul. *The Semiotics of Drink and Drinking.* London: Continuum, 2012.

Manning, Paul, and Ann Uplisashvili. "'Our Beer': Ethnographic Brands in Postsocialist Georgia." *American Anthropologist* 109, no. 4 (2007): 626–41.

Marcus, Yoel. *The Wine Book.* Haifa: Company for Book Publishing, 1972. (Hebrew)

Massad, Susan J., and Mohammad Hmidat. "Farming, Water, Food Sovereignty and Nutrition in Occupied Palestinian Territories." *International Journal of Food and Nutritional Science* 2, no. 3 (2016): 359–71.

Masterman, E. W. G. "Food and Its Preparation in Modern Palestine." *Biblical World* 17, no. 6 (1901): 407–19.

Matthes, Erich Hatala. "Cultural Appropriation without Cultural Essentialism?" *Social Theory and Practice* 42, no. 2 (2016): 343–66.

Mayberg, Ron. *A Country Eats.* Tel Aviv: Zmora, Bitan, Modan, 1996. (Hebrew)

Mazor Tregerman, Maya. "The Limits of Good Taste: Cookbooks, Popular Culture, and Book Publishing in Global Israel." MA thesis, University of Haifa, 2008. (Hebrew)

Me'ir, Yosef. "The Theory of Nutrition." In *Medicine and the Public: A Collection of Articles,* edited by Moshe Tamari, 163–64. Tel Aviv: Kupat Holim Center, 1955. (Hebrew)

Meir-Glitzenstein, Esther. "Longing for the Aromas of Baghdad: Food, Emigration and Transformation in the Lives of Iraqi Jews in Israel in the 1950s." In *Jews and their Foodways* (Studies in Contemporary Jewry 28), edited by Anat Helman, 89–109. New York: Oxford University Press, 2015.

Mendel, Yonatan, and Ronald Ranta. *From the Arab Other to the Israeli Self: Palestinian Culture in the Making of Israeli National Identity.* Farnham: Ashgate, 2016.

Meneley, Anne. "Blood, Sweat and Tears in a Bottle of Palestinian Extra-Virgin Olive Oil." *Food, Culture & Society* 14, no. 2 (2011): 275–92.

Meneley, Anne. "Like an Extra Virgin." *American Anthropologist* 109, no. 4 (2007): 678–87.

Meneley, Anne. "Oleo-Signs and Quali-Signs: The Qualities of Olive Oil." *Ethnos* 73, no. 3 (2008): 303–26.

Meneley, Anne. "Time in a Bottle: The Uneasy Circulation of Palestinian Olive Oil." *Middle East Report* 248 (2008): 18–23.

Mentinis, Mihalis. "Romanticised Chefs and the Psychopolitics of Gastroporn." *Culture & Psychology* 23, no. 1 (2017): 128–43.

Metzer, Jacob. *The Divided Economy of Mandatory Palestine.* Cambridge: Cambridge University Press, 1998.

Meyer, Erna. *How to Cook in Eretz Israel.* Tel Aviv: WIZO, 1936. (Hebrew)

Miller, Daniel. "Coca-Cola: A Black Sweet Drink from Trinidad." In *Material Cultures: Why Some Things Matter,* edited by Daniel Miller, 169–87. New York: Routledge, 2002.

Mintz, Sidney W. *Sweetness and Power: The Place of Sugar in Modern History.* New York: Penguin, 1985.

Mintz, Sidney W. *Tasting Food, Tasting Freedom: Excursions into Eating, Culture, and the Past.* Boston: Beacon, 1996.

Mokedi, Rene D. *French Dishes and Stews.* Tel Aviv: Yas'ur, 1963. (Hebrew)

Molcho, Avner. "Capitalism and 'the American Way' in Israel: Productivity, Management and the Capitalist Ethos in the American Technical Assistance in the 1950s." In *Society and Economy in Israel: Historical and Contemporary Perspectives,* edited by Avi Bareli, Daniel Gutwein, and Tuvia Friling, 263–94. Sde Boker: The Ben-Gurion Research Institute for the Study of Israel and Zionism, 2005. (Hebrew)

Montanari, Massimo. "Taste Is a Cultural Product." In *Food Is Culture,* 61–66. Translated by Albert Sonnenfeld. New York: Columbia University Press, 2004.

Monterescu, Daniel. *Jaffa Shared and Shattered: Contrived Coexistence in Israel/Palestine.* Bloomington: Indiana University Press, 2015.

Monterescu, Daniel. "Masculinity as a Relational Mode: Palestinian Gender Ideologies and Working-Class Boundaries in an Ethnically Mixed Town." In *Reapproaching Borders: New Perspectives on the Study of Israel-Palestine,* edited by Sandra Sufian and Mark LeVine, 177–97. Lanham, MD: Rowman and Littlefield, 2007.

Monterescu, Daniel, and Ariel Handel. "Liquid Indigeneity: Wine, Science, and Colonial Politics in Israel/Palestine." *American Ethnologist* 46, no. 3 (2019): 313–27.

Monterescu, Daniel, and Dan Rabinowitz, eds. *Mixed Towns, Trapped Communities.* Aldershot, UK: Ashgate, 2007.

Morris, Benny. *1948: A History of the First Arab-Israeli War*. New Haven, CT: Yale University Press, 2008.

Mosby, Ian. *Food Will Win the War: The Politics, Culture, and Science of Food on Canada's Home Front*. Vancouver: UBC Press, 2014.

Moskowitz, Howard R. "The Perfect Is Simply not Good Enough—Fifty Years of Innovating in the World of Traditional Foods." *Food Control* 138 (2022): 1–7.

Naccarato, Peter, and Kathleen Lebesco. *Culinary Capital*. London: Berg, 2012.

Nadav, Tzvi. "Half a Body Gone." In *The Book of Hashomer*, edited by Izhak Ben-Zvi, Israel Shochat, Matti Megged, and Yohanan Tversky, 150–51. Tel Aviv: Dvir, 1957. (Hebrew)

Nadav, Tzvi. *Thus We Started*. Tel Aviv: Hakibbutz Hameuchad, 1957. (Hebrew)

Naor, Mordechai. "The Austerity." In *Immigrants and Ma'barot, 1948–1952*, edited by Mordechai Naor, 97–110. Jerusalem: Yad Izhak Ben-Zvi, 1986. (Hebrew)

Naor, Mordechai, ed. *Immigrants and Ma'barot, 1948-1952*. Jerusalem: Yad Izhak Ben-Zvi, 1986. (Hebrew)

Narayan, Uma. *Dislocating Cultures: Identities, Traditions and Third World Feminism*. New York: Routledge, 1997.

Nasrallah, Nawal. *Treasure Trove of Benefits and Variety at the Table: A Fourteenth-Century Egyptian Cookbook*. Leiden: Brill, 2018.

Nedava, Yosef. "Preface." In *Dreams and Wars*, by Itamar Ben-Avi, 7–14. Jerusalem: Public Committee for the Publishing of the Writings of Itamar Ben-Avi, 1978. (Hebrew)

Nestle, Marion. *Food Politics: How the Food Industry Influences Nutrition and Health*. Berkeley: University of California Press, 2007.

Neumann, Boaz. *Land and Desire in Early Zionism*. Translated by Haim Watzman. Waltham, MA: Brandeis University Press, 2011.

Nitzan-Shiftan, Alona. "Seizing Locality in Jerusalem." In *Reapproaching Borders: New Perspectives on the Study of Israel-Palestine*, edited by Sandra Sufian and Mark LeVine, 223–42. Plymouth: Rowman and Littlefield, 2007.

Noy, Amos. "The Culinary Left." *The Seventh Eye*, January 1, 2001. https://www.the7eye.org.il/40253. (Hebrew)

Noy, Amos. "When Mizrahim Were Modern: Non-Orientalist Representations of Mizrahim in Israel in the 1950s and 1960s." In *The Long History of Mizrahim: New Directions in the Study of Jews from Muslim Countries: In Tribute to Yaron Tzur*, edited by Aviad Moreno, Noah S. Gerber, Esther Meir-Glizenstein, and Ofer Shiff, 127–144. Sde Boker: The Ben-Gurion Research Institute for the Study of Israel and Zionism, 2021. (Hebrew)

Nunes, Flávio, and Loai Aburaida. "Obstacles to West Bank Industrial Development Caused by the Palestinian Lack of Control over Its External and Internal Borders." *International Journal of Management and Applied Science* 4, no. 8 (2018): 5–11.

Nurieli, Benny. "Accumulation and Surveillance: The Military Rule in Lydda, July 1948–July 1949." In *Entangled Histories in Palestine/Israel: Historical and Anthropological Perspectives*, edited by Dafna Hirsch, 133–51. London: Routledge, 2024.

Nute, Kevin. "Toward a Test of Cultural Misappropriation." *International Journal of Critical Cultural Studies* 17, no. 2 (2019): 67–82.

"The Nutrition Committee at This Time." *Hamazon* 2, no. 4 (1939): 1. (Hebrew)

"The Nutrition of the Yishuv at this Time." *Hamazon* 2, no. 3 (1939): 13. (Hebrew)

Ohad Smith, Daniella. "The 'Designed' Israeli Interior, 1960–1977: Shaping Identity." *Journal of Interior Design* 38, no. 3 (2013): 21–36.

Ohnuki-Tierney, Emiko. *Rice as Self: Japanese Identities through Time*. Princeton, NJ: Princeton University Press, 1993.

Ollivier, Michèle. "Modes of Openness to Cultural Diversity: Humanist, Populist, Practical, and Indifferent." *Poetics* 36, nos. 2–3 (2008): 120–47.

Ore, Hadas. "'Can Home Come in a Tin Can?': How Jewish-Israeli Women Savour Home in New Zealand." PhD diss., University of Auckland, 2014.

Orlove, Benjamin, and Ella Schmidt. "Swallowing Their Pride: Indigenous and Industrial Beer in Peru and Bolivia." *Theory and Society* 24, no. 2 (1995): 271–98.

Pappe, Ilan. *The Ethnic Cleansing of Palestine*. Oxford: Oneworld, 2006.

Parasecoli, Fabio. *Gastronativism: Food, Identity Politics, and Globalization*. New York: Columbia University Press, 2022.

Parasecoli, Fabio. *Knowing Where It Comes From: Labeling Traditional Foods to Compete in the Global Market*. Iowa City: University of Iowa Press, 2017.

Paxon, Heather. *The Life of Cheese: Crafting Food and Value in America*. Berkeley: University of California Press, 2013.

Peirce, Charles S. *Philosophical Writings of Peirce*. Edited by Justus Buchler. New York: Dover, 1955.

Perry, Charles. *Scents and Flavors: A Syrian Cookbook*. New York: New York University Press, 2017.

Peters, Erica J. "Power Struggles and Social Positioning: Culinary Appropriation and Anxiety in Colonial Vietnam." In *Food Anxiety in Globalizing Vietnam*, edited by Judith Ehlert and Nora Katharina Faltmann, 43–75. Singapore: Springer, 2019.

Peterson, Richard A., and Roger M. Kern. "Changing Highbrow Taste: from Snob to Omnivore." *American Sociological Review* 61, no. 5 (1996): 900–907.

Philippon, Daniel. "How Local Is Slow Food?" *RCC Perspectives*, No. 1, Think Global, Eat Local: Exploring Foodways (2015): 7–12. https://www.jstor.org/stable/26241300.

Picard, Avi. *Cut to Measure: Israel's Policies Regarding the Aliyah of North African Jews, 1951–1956*. Sde Boker: The Ben-Gurion Research Institute for the Study of Israel and Zionism, 2013. (Hebrew)

Picard, Avi. "Like a Phoenix: The Renaissance of Sephardic/Mizrahi Identity in Israel in the 1970s and 1980s." *Israel Studies* 22, no. 2 (2017): 1–25.

Pilcher, Jeffrey M. *Food in World History.* New York: Routledge, 2006.

Pilcher, Jeffrey M. *Planet Taco: A Global History of Mexican Food.* Oxford: Oxford University Press, 2012.

Pilcher, Jeffrey M. *Que Vivan Los Tamales!: Food and the Making of Mexican Identity.* Albuquerque: University of New Mexico Press, 1998.

Pinthus, Moshe J. "The 1959 Revolution in Chickpea Cultivation in Israel." *Hasade* 76, no. 8 (1996): 36–37. (Hebrew)

Piterberg, Gabriel. *The Returns of Zionism: Myth, Politics and Scholarship in Israel.* London: Verso, 2008.

Pratt, Jeff. "Food Values: The Local and the Authentic." *Critique of Anthropology* 27, no. 3 (2007): 285–300.

Presner, Todd Samuel. *Muscular Judaism: The Jewish Body and the Politics of Regeneration.* London: Routledge, 2007.

Prieto Piastro, Claudia. *Eating in Israel: Nationhood, Gender and Food Culture.* London: Palgrave Macmillan, 2021.

Rabau, Tziona. *In Tel Aviv on the Sands.* Ramat Gan: Masada, 1973. (Hebrew)

Rabinowitz, Dan. *Overlooking Nazareth: The Ethnography of Exclusion in Galilee.* Cambridge: Cambridge University Press, 1997.

Radai, Itamar. *Palestinians in Jerusalem and Jaffa, 1948: A Tale of Two Cities.* London: Routledge, 2016.

Ram, Uri. *The Globalization of Israel: McWorld in Tel Aviv, Jihad in Jerusalem.* New York: Routledge, 2008.

Ranta, Ronald. "Re-Arabizing Israeli Food Culture." *Food, Culture and Society* 18, no. 4 (2015): 611–27.

Ranta, Ronald, Alejandro Colás, and Daniel Monterescu, eds. *'Going Native?': Settler Colonialism and Food.* London: Palgrave Macmillan, 2022.

Ranta, Ronald, and Yonatan Mendel. "Consuming Palestine: Palestine and Palestinians in Israeli Food Culture." *Ethnicities* 14, no. 3 (2014): 412–35.

Ranta, Ronald, and Daniel Monterescu. "Decolonizing Israeli Food? Between Culinary Appropriation and Recognition in Israel/Palestine." In *'Going Native?': Settler Colonialism and Food,* edited by Ronald Ranta, Alejandro Colás, and Daniel Monterescu, 147–72. London: Palgrave Macmillan, 2022.

Ranta, Ronald, and Claudia Raquel Prieto Piastro. "Does Israeli Food Exist? The Multifaceted and Complex Making of a National Food." In *The Emergence of National Food: The Dynamics of Food and Nationalism,* edited by Atsuko Ichijo, Venetia Johannes, and Ronald Ranta, 119–29. London: Bloomsbury Academic, 2019.

Raviv, Yael. *Falafel Nation: Cuisine and the Making of National Identity in Israel.* Lincoln: University of Nebraska Press, 2015.

Ray, Krishnendu. "Culinary Difference: The Difference It Makes." *Graduate Journal of Food Studies* 5, no. 2 (2019): 2–10.

Ray, Krishnendu. *The Ethnic Restauranteur*. London: Bloomsbury Academic, 2016.

Ray, Krishnendu. *The Migrant's Table: Meals and Memories*. Pennsylvania: Temple University Press, 2004.

Razi, Tammy. "'Arab-Jewesses'? Ethnicity, Nationality and Gender in Mandate Tel Aviv." *Theory and Criticism* 38–39 (2011): 137–60. (Hebrew)

Raz-Karkotzkin, Amnon. "The Return to the History of Redemption, or: What Is the 'History' One 'Returns' to in the Expression 'The Return to History'?" In *Zionism and the Return to History: A Reassessment*, edited by Shmuel Eisenstadt and Moshe Lissak, 249–76. Jerusalem: Yad Izhak Ben-Zvi, 1999. (Hebrew)

Reckwitz, Andreas. "Practices and Their Affects." In *The Nexus of Practices*, edited by Allison Hui, Theodore Schatzki, and Elizabeth Shove, 126–37. London: Routledge, 2016.

Reckwitz, Andreas. "The Status of the 'Material' in Theories of Culture: From 'Social Structure' to 'Artefacts.'" *Journal for the Theory of Social Behaviour* 32, no. 2 (2002): 195–217.

Regev, Motti. "To Have a Culture of Our Own: On Israeliness and Its Variants." *Ethnic and Racial Studies* 23, no. 2 (2000): 223–47.

Retig, Baruch. "Fifty Years of Chickpea Cultivation in Israel." *Hasade* 79, no. 5 (October 1998): 350–52 (Hebrew).

Rieker, Martina. "Modern Histories of Jerusalem's Old City: Culinary Practices and Popular Mapping(s) of Palestinian Social Spaces." In *Pilgrims, Lepers and Stuffed Cabbage: Essays on Jerusalem's Cultural History*, edited by Issam Nassar and Salim Tamari, 86–94. Jerusalem: Institute of Jerusalem History, 2005.

Ritzer, George. *McDonaldization: The Reader*. Thousand Oaks, CA: Pine Forge Press, 2010.

Ritzer, George. *The McDonaldization Thesis: Explorations and Extensions*. London: Sage, 1998.

Rivlin, Paul. *The Israeli Economy from the Foundation of the State through the 21st Century*. Cambridge: Cambridge University Press, 2011.

Robinson, Shira. *Citizen Strangers: Palestinians and the Birth of Israel's Liberal Settler State*. Stanford, CA: Stanford University Press, 2016.

Roby, Bryan K. *The Mizrahi Era of Rebellion: Israel's Forgotten Civil Rights Struggle 1948–1966*. Syracuse, NY: Syracuse University Press, 2015.

Rockower, Paul. "A Guide to Gastrodiplomacy." In *Routledge Handbook of Public Diplomacy*, edited by Nancy Snow and Nicholas J. Cull, 205–12. London: Routledge, 2020.

Roden, Claudia. *The Book of Jewish Food: An Odyssey from Samarkand and Vilna to the Present Day.* London: Penguin, 1999.

Roden, Claudia. *The New Book of Middle Eastern Food.* Rev. ed. London: Alfred A. Knopf, 2000.

Rodinson, Maxime. *Israel: A Colonial-Settler State?* New York: Monad Press, 1973.

Rodinson, Maxime, Arthur John Arberry, and Charles Perry. *Medieval Arab Cookery.* Totnes: Prospect Books, 2001.

Roginsky, Dina. "Nationalism and Ambivalence: Ethnicity, Gender and Folklore as Categories of Otherness." *Patterns of Prejudice* 40, no. 3 (2006): 237–58.

Roginsky, Dina. "Orientalism, the Body, and Cultural Politics in Israel: Sara Levi Tanai and the Inbal Dance Theater." *Nashim: A Journal of Jewish Women's Studies & Gender Issues* 11 (2006): 164–97.

Ro'i, Yaacov. "Jewish-Arab Relations in the First Aliyah Colonies." In *The Book of the First Immigration Wave*, vol. 1, edited by Mordechai Eliav, 245–68. Jerusalem: Yad Izhak Ben-Zvi, 1982. (Hebrew)

Ron, Mordechai. *Haifa of My Youth: Everyday Life in Haifa in the 1920s and 1930s.* Jerusalem: Ariel, 1993. (Hebrew)

Roseberry, William. "The Rise of Yuppie Coffees and the Reimagination of Class in the United States." *American Anthropologist* 98, no. 4 (1996): 762–75.

Rosenfeld, Henry, and Shulamit Carmi. "Appropriation of Public Means and a State-Made Middle Class." *Machbarot Leyiun Velebikoret* 3 (1979): 43–84. (Hebrew)

Rosenthal, Ariel, Orly Peli-Bronshtein, and Dan Alexander. *On the Hummus Route.* Published by the authors, 2019.

Rozin, Orit. "Austerity Tel-Aviv: Everyday Life, Supervision, Compliance, and Respectability." In *Tel-Aviv, The First Century: Visions, Designs and Actualities*, edited by Maoz Azaryahu and S. Ilan Troen, 165–90. Bloomington: Indiana University Press, 2011.

Rozin, Orit. "Craving Meat during Israel's Austerity Period, 1947–1953." In *Jews and Their Foodways* (Studies in Contemporary Jewry 28), edited by Anat Helman, 65–88. Oxford: Oxford University Press, 2015.

Rozin, Orit. "Food, Identity, and Nation-Building in Israel's Formative Years." *Israel Studies Forum* 21, no. 1 (2006): 52–80.

Rozin, Orit. "Israel and the Right to Travel Abroad 1948–1961." *Israel Studies* 15 (2010): 147–76.

Rozin, Orit. *The Rise of the Individual in 1950s Israel: A Challenge to Collectivism.* Waltham, MA: Brandeis University Press, 2011.

Rozin, Paul. "Sociocultural Influences on Human Food Selection." *In Why We Eat What We Eat: The Psychology of Eating*, edited by Elizabeth D. Capaldi, 233–63. Washington, DC: American Psychological Association, 1996.

Ruis, Andrew R. *Eating to Learn, Learning to Eat*. New Brunswick, NJ: Rutgers University Press, 2017.

Ryan, Sheila. "Constructing a New Imperialism: Israel and the West Bank." *MERIP Reports* 9 (1972): 3–17.

Sabbagh-Khoury, Areej. "Tracing Settler Colonialism: A Genealogy of a Paradigm in the Sociology of Knowledge Production in Israel." *Politics & Society* 50, no. 1 (2022): 44–83.

Sachar, Howard. *Aliyah: The People of Israel*. Cleveland: World Publishing, 1961.

Sa'di, Ahmad H. "Catastrophe, Memory and Identity: Al-Nakbah as a Component of Palestinian Identity." *Israel Studies* 7, no. 2 (2002): 175–98.

Safadi, Dokhol, and Michal Waxman. *Baladi: Four Seasons in Nazareth*. Rishon LeZion: Yediot Aharonot, 2016. (Hebrew)

Sahliyeh, Emile. "West Bank Industrial and Agricultural Development: The Basic Problems." *Journal of Palestine Studies* 11, no. 2 (1982): 55–69.

Salamanca, Omar Jabary, Mezna Qato, Kareem Rabie, and Sobhi Samour. "Past Is Present: Settler Colonialism in Palestine." *Settler Colonial Studies* 2, no. 1 (2012): 1–8.

Samuel-Azran, Tal, Betti Ilovici, Israel Zari, and Orly Geduild. "Practicing Citizen Diplomacy 2.0: 'The Hot Dudes and Hummus—Israel's Yummiest' Campaign for Israel's Branding." *Place Branding and Public Diplomacy* 15 (2019): 38–49.

Sapir, Rebecca. "Korat Gag." *Megamot* 3, no. 1 (1951): 8–36. (Hebrew)

Saposnik, Arieh Bruce. *Becoming Hebrew: The Creation of a Jewish National Culture in Ottoman Palestine*. Oxford: Oxford University Press, 2008.

Sardes-Terotino, Sarit. "Msabaha, the Chef's Version." *Al HaShulchan* 200 (2007): 70–76. (Hebrew)

Sassmannshausen, Christian. "Eating Up: Food Consumption and Social Status in Late Ottoman Greater Syria." In *Insatiable Appetite: Food as Cultural Signifier in the Middle East and Beyond*, edited by Kirill Dmitriev, Julia Hauser, and Bilal Orfali, 27–49. Leiden: Brill, 2020.

Schlosser, Eric. *Fast Food Nation: The Dark Side of the All-American Meal*. Boston: Houghton Mifflin, 2001.

Schwarz, Ori. "Identity as a Barrier: Claiming Universality as a Strategy in the Israeli Vegan Movement." *Social Movement Studies* 20, no. 5 (2021): 600–618.

Scrinis, Gyorgy. *Nutritionism: The Science and Politics of Dietary Advice*. New York: Columbia University Press, 2013.

Sebbag, Avital. *Five Seasons in the Kitchen: Zen Inspired Vegan Cooking*. Jerusalem: Gefen, 2014. (Hebrew)

Segev, Tom. *1949—The First Israelis*. Jerusalem: Domino, 1984. (Hebrew)

Seidman, Guy. "Unexceptional for Once: Austerity and Food Rationing in Israel, 1939–1959." *Southern California Interdisciplinary Law Journal* 18 (2008): 95–130.

Seikaly, Sherene. "Bodies and Needs: Lessons from Palestine." *International Journal of Middle East Studies* 46, no. 4 (2014): 784–86.

Seikaly, Sherene. *Men of Capital: Scarcity and Economy in Mandate Palestine.* Stanford, CA: Stanford University Press, 2015.

Seltenreich, Yair. "Jewish or Arab Hired Workers? Inner Tensions in a Jewish Settlement in Pre-State Israel." *International Review of Social History* 49, no. 2 (2004): 230.

Seltenreich, Yair. "The Shaping of the Masculine Image of the Farmers in the Galilee Colonies: The First Period." *Social Issues in Israel* 12 (2011): 6–31. (Hebrew)

Seri, Rachel. *A Tree and Its Branches (The Story of a Yemenite Family).* Published by the author, 1988. (Hebrew)

Sertbulut, Zeynep. "The Culinary State: On Politics of Representation and Identity in Israel." *HAGAR Studies in Culture, Policy, and Identities* 10, no. 2 (2012): 49–76.

Shacham, David. *Requiem to Tel Aviv.* Tel Aviv: Sifriyat Hapo'alim, 2010. (Hebrew)

Shadid, Mohammed K. "Israeli Policy towards Economic Development in the West Bank and Gaza." In *The Palestinian Economy: Studies in Development under Prolonged Occupation*, edited by George T. Abed, 121–37. London: Routledge, 1988.

Shafir, Gershon. *Land, Labor and the Origins of the Israeli-Palestinian Conflict, 1882–1914.* New York: Cambridge University Press, 1989.

Shafir, Gershon. "The Meeting of Eastern Europe and Yemen: 'Idealistic Workers' and 'Natural Workers' in Early Zionist Settlement in Palestine." *Ethnic and Racial Studies* 13, no. 2 (1990): 172–97.

Shafir, Gershon, and Yoav Peled. *Being Israeli: The Dynamics of Multiple Citizenship.* Cambridge: Cambridge University Press, 2002.

Shalev, Michael. "Have Globalization and Liberalization 'Normalized' Israel's Political Economy?" *Israel Affairs* 5, nos. 2–3 (1999): 121–55.

Shalev, Michael. *Labour and the Political Economy in Israel.* Oxford: Oxford University Press, 1992.

Shalev, Michael. "The Welfare State Consensus in Israel: Placing Class Politics in Context." In *Social Justice, Legitimacy and the Welfare State*, edited by Steffen Mau and Benjamin Veghte, 193–213. Farnham: Ashgate, 2007.

Shapin, Steven. "The Tastes of Wine: Towards a Cultural History." *Rivista di Estetica* 51 (2012): 49–94.

Shapin, Steven. "'You Are What You Eat': Historical Changes in Ideas about Food and Identity." *Historical Research* 87, no. 237 (2014): 377–92.

Sharabi, Hisham. "From *Embers and Ashes*." In *Anthology of Modern Palestinian Literature*, edited by Salma Khadra Jayyusi, 696–703. New York: Columbia University Press, 1992.

Sharif, Lila. "How Dough Rises in Gaza: Palestine's Foremothers and Recipes against Genocide." *Jerusalem Quarterly* 99 (2024): 56–72.

Sharon, Smadar. *"And Thus a Homeland is Conquered": Planning and Settlement in 1950s Lakhish Region*. Haifa: Pardes, 2017. (Hebrew)

Sharoni, Simona. *Gender and the Israeli-Palestinian Conflict: The Politics of Women's Resistance*. New York: Syracuse University Press, 1995.

Shavit, Yaacov, and Gideon Biger. *The History of Tel Aviv*, vol. 1. Tel Aviv: Ramot, 2001. (Hebrew)

Shavit, Yaacov, and Gideon Biger. *The History of Tel Aviv*, vol. 2. Tel Aviv: Ramot, 2007. (Hebrew)

Shavit, Zohar, ed. *History of the Jewish Community in Eretz-Israel since 1882*. Vol. 3, *The Construction of Hebrew Culture in Eretz Israel*. Jerusalem: Bialik Institute, 1999. (Hebrew)

Shayek-al-'Ani, Geula. *The Theft of the Rooster: From the Diary of a Transit Camp Girl*. Kiryat Ono: Tsafra, 2011. (Hebrew)

Shehadeh, Hanine. "Nourishing Resilience: The Palestinian Kitchen Table and the Healing of Generational Trauma." *Jerusalem Quarterly* 98 (2024): 51–67.

Sheinblat, Hemi. "'Catching America': The Americanization of Israeli Society, 1958–1967." PhD diss., Tel Aviv University, 2017.

Shem-Or, Ora. *Without the Ponytail and the Sarafan*. Tel Aviv: Noga, 1981. (Hebrew)

Shenhav, Yehouda, and Hannan Hever. "The Arab-Jews: The Metamorphosis of a Concept." *Pa'amim* 125–127 (2011): 57–74. (Hebrew)

Shilo, Margalit. *Experiments in Settlement*. Jerusalem: Yad Izhak Ben-Zvi, 1988. (Hebrew)

Shilony, Zvi. "Random Factors in the Creation of Degania." In *Studies in Geography and History in Honour of Yehoshua Ben-Arieh*, edited by Yossi Ben-Artzi, Israel Bartal, and Elchanan Reiner, 437–408. Jerusalem: Magnes Press, 2000. (Hebrew)

Shoham, Hizky. "'Buy Local' or 'Buy Jewish'? Separatist Consumption in Interwar Palestine." *International Journal of Middle East Studies* 45 (2013): 469–89.

Shoham, Hizky. "The Israel BBQ as National Ritual: Performing Unofficial Nationalism, or Finding Meaning in Triviality." *American Journal of Cultural Sociology* 9, no. 1 (2021): 13–42.

Shohat, Ella. "The Invention of the Mizrahim." *Journal of Palestine Studies* 29, no. 1 (1999): 5–20.

Shohat, Ella. *Israeli Cinema: East/West and the Politics of Representation*. London: I. B. Tauris, 2010.

Shohat, Ella. "Sephardim in Israel: Zionism from the Standpoint of Its Jewish Victims." *Social Text* 7, nos. 1–2 (1988): 1–36.

Simmons, Erica B. *Hadassah and the Zionist Project*. Oxford: Rowman and Littlefield, 2006.

Singley, Blake. "'Hardly Anything Fit for Man to Eat': Food and Colonialism in Australia." *History Australia* 9, no. 3 (2012): 27–42.

Sirkis, Ruth. *From the Kitchen with Love: The Foundations of Cooking and the Secrets of Hosting*. Ramat Gan: R. Sirkis, 1975. (Hebrew)

Sitton, David. *The Story of a Neighborhood*. Jerusalem: Council of the Sephardi Community, 1977. (Hebrew)

Soffer, Arnon. "Demography and the Shaping of Israel's Borders." *Contemporary Jewry* 10, no. 2 (1989): 91–105.

Soffer, Oren. "The Anomaly of Galei Tzahal: Israel's Army Radio as a Cultural Vanguard and Force for Pluralism." *Historical Journal of Film, Radio and Television* 32, no. 2 (2012): 225–43.

Soffer, Oren. *Mass Communication in Israel: Nationalism, Globalization, and Segmentation*. New York: Berghahn, 2014.

Stano, Simona. *Eating the Other: Translations of the Culinary Code*. Newcastle upon Tyne: Cambridge Scholars Publishing, 2015.

Stavsky, Moshe. *The Arab Village*. Tel Aviv: Am Oved, 1946. (Hebrew)

Stein, Rebecca L. *Itineraries in Conflict: Israelis, Palestinians and the Political Lives of Tourism*. Durham, NC: Duke University Press, 2008.

Stern, Bat-Sheva Margalit. "'Mothers at the Front': The Struggle for 'Buying Local' and the Confrontation between Gender and National Interests." *Israel* 11 (2007): 91–120. (Hebrew)

Stiles, Kaelyn, Özlem Altıok, and Michael M. Bell. "The Ghosts of Taste: Food and the Cultural Politics of Authenticity." *Agriculture and Human Values* 28, no. 2 (2011): 225–36.

Strauss, Walter. *A Preliminary Investigation into the Food Habits of Oriental Jewish Communities with Special Reference to the Changes Enforced by Immigration to Israel*. Jerusalem: Department of Hygiene, Hebrew University–Hadassah Medical School, 1955.

Strauss, Walter, Mala Shatan-Herzberg, and Esther Borten. *Nutritional Survey in Israel: Second Interim Report—Surveys of 1951 and 1952–3*. Jerusalem: Department of Hygiene, Hebrew University–Hadassah Medical School, 1954.

Swartz Rose, Mary. "Racial Food Habits in Relation to Health." *Scientific Monthly* 44, no. 3 (1937): 257–67.

Swirski, Shlomo. "Israel in the Global Sphere." In *The Power of Property: Israeli Society in the Global Age*, edited by Dani Filc and Uri Ram, 57–83. Jerusalem: Van Leer and Hakibbutz Hameuchad, 2004. (Hebrew)

Swirski, Shlomo. *The Price of Occupation*. Tel Aviv: Mapa, 2005. (Hebrew)

Swirski, Shlomo. "On Economy and Society in Times of Empire." *Iyunim Bitkumat Israel* 16 (2006): 549–93. (Hebrew)

Tamari, Salim. *Mountain against the Sea: Essays on Palestinian Society and Culture*. Berkeley: University of California Press, 2009.

Tanner, Jakob. "The Rationing System, Food Policy and Nutritional Science during the Second World War: A Comparative View of Switzerland." In *Changing Food Habits: Case Studies from Africa, South America and Europe*, edited by Carola Lenz, 211–42. Mainz: Harwood Academic, 1999.

Tawil-Souri, Helga. "Where Is the Political in Cultural Studies? In Palestine." *International Journal of Cultural Studies* 14, no. 5 (2011): 467–82.

Teharlev Ben-Shachar, Erela. "On Calories, Proteins and Posture: Zionism, Socialism and Consumerism—Learning History from Diet and Fitness Guides, Israel, 1930s–1980s." PhD diss., Bar Ilan University, 2018.

Tene, Ofra. "From Nationalism and Health to Consumerism and Identity Construction." In *Thoughts on Food*, edited by Ori Bartal, Ronit Vered, and Michal Eitan, 282–319. Jerusalem: Bezalel Academy of Art and Resling, 2021. (Hebrew)

Tene, Ofra. "'The New Immigrant Must Not Only Learn, He Must Also Forget': The Making of Eretz Israeli Ashkenazi Cuisine." In *Jews and Their Foodways* (Studies in Contemporary Jewry 28), edited by Anat Helman, 46–64. New York: Oxford University Press, 2015.

Tene, Ofra. "Thus You Shall Cook! Analysis of Israeli Cookbooks." MA thesis, Tel Aviv University, 2000.

Tene, Ofra. *The White Houses Will Be Filled*. Tel Aviv: Hakibbutz Hameuchad, 2013. (Hebrew)

Tene, Zeev. *Short Memory*. Tel Aviv: EnT-T, 2009. (Hebrew)

Terrio, Susan J. "Crafting *Grand Cru* Chocolates in Contemporary France." In *The Cultural Politics of Food and Eating*, edited by James L. Watson and Melissa L. Caldwell, 144–62. Malden, MA: Blackwell, 2005.

Tesdell, Omar. "Wild Wheat to Productive Drylands: Global Scientific Practice and the Agroecological Remaking of Palestine." *Geoforum* 78 (2017): 43–51.

Thomas, Nicholas. *Entangled Objects: Exchange, Material Culture, and Colonialism in the Pacific*. Cambridge, MA: Harvard University Press, 1991.

Thou Shall Make Your Guests' Heart Happy. Jerusalem: Ministry of Education, College of Nutrition and Home Economics, 1958. (Hebrew)

Tikolsker, Erez, Ran Atzmon, and Eiran Shoshani. *The Large Hummusiyot Guide*. Published by the authors, 2022. (Hebrew)

Tilsley-Benham, Jill. "'Pride and Prejudice,' or Familiarity Breeds Content: A Western Taste of Middle Eastern Food." In *Oxford Symposium on Food and Cookery 1987: Taste, Proceedings*, edited by Tom Jaine, 198–204. London: Prospect Books, 1988.

Tiv'oni, Shlomo. *My Friend Had a Vineyard: Musa al-Ful*. Tel Aviv: Hakibbutz Hameuchad, 1978. (Hebrew)

Trilling, Lionel. *Sincerity and Authenticity*. Cambridge, MA: Harvard University Press, 1971.

Trubek, Amy B. *The Taste of Place: A Cultural Journey into Terroir*. Berkeley: University of California Press, 2008.

Tzur, Muki, Tair Zvulun, and Hanina Porat, eds. *The Beginning of the Kibbutz*. Tel Aviv: Hakibbutz Hameuchad and Sifriyat Hapoalim, 1981. (Hebrew)

Tzur, Yaron. "The Immigration from Muslim Countries." In *The First Decade: 1948–1958*, edited by Zvi Zameret and Hannah Jablonka, 82–57. Jerusalem: Yad Izhak Ben-Zvi, 1997. (Hebrew)

Tzur, Yaron. "The Ethnic Problem." In *The Second Decade: 1958–1968*, edited by Zvi Zameret and Hannah Jablonka, 101–24. Jerusalem: Yad Izhak Ben-Zvi, 2000. (Hebrew)

Ufaz, Aviva. "The Portrait of the Man of Hashomer: Following the Letters of Mendel Portugali." *Cathedra* 48 (1988): 73–89. (Hebrew)

Urry, John. *Consuming Places*. London: Routledge, 1995.

van Esterik, Penny. "From Hunger Foods to Heritage Foods: Challenges to Food Localization in Lao PDR." In *Fast Food / Slow Food: The Cultural Economy of the Global Food System*, edited by Richard Wilk, 83–96. Lanham, MD: Altamira, 2006.

Varga, Somogy, and Charles Guignon. "Authenticity." In *The Stanford Encyclopedia of Philosophy* (Fall 2017 Edition), edited by Edward N. Zalta. https://plato.stanford.edu/archives/fall2017/entries/authenticity.

Veit, Helen Zoe. *Modern Food, Moral Food: Self-Control, Science, and the Rise of Modern American Eating in the Early Twentieth Century*. Chapel Hill: University of North Carolina Press, 2013.

Veracini, Lorenzo. "The Other Shift: Settler Colonialism, Israel, and the Occupation." *Journal of Palestine Studies* 42, no. 2 (2013): 26–42.

Veracini, Lorenzo. "The Predicaments of Settler Gastrocolonialism." In *'Going Native?': Settler Colonialism and Food*, edited by Ronald Ranta, Alejandro Colás, and Daniel Monterescu, 247–59. London: Palgrave Macmillan, 2022.

Veracini, Lorenzo. *Settler Colonialism: A Theoretical Overview*. Basingstoke: Palgrave Macmillan, 2010.

Veracini, Lorenzo. "What Can Settler Colonial Studies Offer to an Interpretation of the Conflict in Israel-Palestine?" *Settler Colonial Studies* 5, no. 3 (2015): 268–71.

Vernon, James. *Hunger: A Modern History*. Cambridge, MA: Harvard University Press, 2007.

Vickers, William John. *A Nutritional Economic Survey of Wartime Palestine, 1942–1943*. Palestine: Department of Health, 1944.

Wallach, Yair. "Jerusalem between Segregation and Integration: Reading Urban Space through the Eyes of Justice Gad Frumkin." In *Modernity, Minority, and the Public Sphere: Jews and Christians in the Middle East,* edited by S. R. Goldstein-Sabbah and H. L. Murre-van den Berg, 205–33. Leiden: Brill, 2016.

Wallach, Yair. "Rethinking the Yishuv: Late-Ottoman Palestine's Jewish Communities Revisited." *Journal of Modern Jewish Studies* 16, no. 2 (2017): 275–94.

Wank, David L., and James Farrer. "Chinese Immigrants and Japanese Cuisine in the United States: A Case of Culinary Glocalization." In *The Globalization of Asian Cuisines: Transnational Networks and Culinary Contact Zones,* edited by James Farrer, 81–99. New York: Palgrave Macmillan, 2015.

Warde, Alan. *Consumption, Food and Taste.* London: Sage, 1997.

Warde, Alan, David Wright, and Modesto Gayo-Cal. "The Omnivorous Orientation in the UK." *Poetics* 36, no. 2–3 (2008): 148–65.

Watson, James L., ed. *Golden Arches East: McDonald's in East Asia.* Stanford, CA: Stanford University Press, 1997.

Weingrod, Alex. "Change and Continuity in a Moroccan Immigrant Village in Israel." *Middle East Journal* 14, no. 3 (1960): 277–91.

Weishaupt, Sonja. "Cook at Home in Chinese: Mediating Chinese Food for American Kitchens." In *Travelling Goods, Travelling Moods: Varieties of Cultural Appropriation (1850–1950),* edited by Christian Huck and Stefan Bauernschmidt, 45–59. Frankfurt: Campus Verlag, 2012.

Weiss, Brad. "Configuring the Authentic Value of Real Food: Farm-to-Fork, Snout-to-Tail, and Local Food Movements." *American Ethnologist* 39, no. 3 (2012): 614–26.

Weiss, Brad. *Real Pigs: Shifting Values in the Field of Local Pork.* Durham, NC: Duke University Press, 2016.

Wilk, Richard, ed. *Fast Food / Slow Food: The Cultural Economy of the Global Food System.* Lanham, MD: Altamira Press, 2006.

Wilk, Richard. "From Wild Weeds to Artisanal Cheese." In *Fast Food / Slow Food: The Cultural Economy of the Global Food System,* edited by Richard Wilk, 13–27. Lanham, MD: Altamira Press, 2006.

Wilk, Richard. *Home Cooking in the Global Village: Caribbean Food from Buccaneers to Ecotourists.* Oxford: Berg, 2006.

Willard, Barbara E. "The American Story of Meat: Discursive Influences on Cultural Eating Practice." *Journal of Popular Culture* 36, no. 1 (2002): 105–18.

Wishnitzer, Avner. "'A Fortress of Ignorance and Cowardice'—The Image of the Arab Warrior in the Eyes of the Israeli Fighters in 1948." *Jama'a* 14 (2006): 91–121. (Hebrew)

WIZO Instructors. *Thus We Shall Cook.* 6th ed. Tel Aviv: Ner, 1965. (Hebrew)

Wolfe, Patrick. *Settler Colonialism and the Transformation of Anthropology: The Politics and Poetics of an Ethnographic Event.* London: Cassell, 1999.

Yahav, Dan. *Jaffa: Neighborhoods, Suburbs and Arab Cemeteries around Her.* Published by the author, 2018. (Hebrew)

Yavaş, Nesrin. "Safeguarding Traditional Palestinian Food Culture: The Case of the Arab American Play *Food and Fadwa*." *Millî Folklore* 135 (2022): 148–59.

Yehoshua, Jacob. *Childhood in Old Jerusalem: Episodes of Life from Days Gone By, Part 4: Neighborhoods in Old Jerusalem*. Jerusalem: Rubin Mass, 1978. (Hebrew)

Yehoshua, Jacob. *The House and the Street in Old Jerusalem*. Jerusalem: Rubin Mass, 1966. (Hebrew)

Yellin, Ita. *To My Children: My Memories, Part 1*. Jerusalem: Hamaʿarav, 1938. (Hebrew)

Yellin, Ita. *To My Children: My Memories, Part 2*. Jerusalem: Hamaʿarav, 1941. (Hebrew)

Young, James O. *Cultural Appropriation and the Arts*. Malden, MA: Blackwell, 2008.

Yuchtman-Yaar, Ephraim. "Differences in Ethnic Patterns of Socioeconomic Achievements in Israel—A Neglected Aspect of Structured Inequality." *International Review of Modern Sociology* 15, nos. 1/2 (1985): 99–116.

Zafer Yenal, Nuri. "Food TNCs, Intellectual Property Investments and Post-Fordist Food Consumption: The Case of Unilever and Nestlé in Turkey." *International Journal of Sociology of Agriculture and Food* 8 (1999): 21–34.

Zakim, Eric. *To Build and Be Built: Landscape, Literature, and the Construction of Zionist Identity*. Philadelphia: University of Pennsylvania Press, 2006.

Zalivansky, Yehoshua. *Tel Avi, Tel Aviv*. Tel Aviv: Y. Golan, 1994. (Hebrew)

Zass, Yaʿacov. *The Hygiene of the Body and Mind*. Jerusalem: Modern Hygiene, 1929. (Hebrew)

Zayad, Luma. "Systematic Cultural Appropriation and the Israeli-Palestinian Conflict." *DePaul Journal of Art, Technology and Intellectual Property Law* 28, no. 2 (2018): 81–125.

Zerubavel, Yael. *Desert in the Promised Land*. Stanford, CA: Stanford University Press, 2018.

Zerubavel, Yael. "Memory, the Rebirth of the Native, and the 'Hebrew Bedouin' Identity." *Social Research: An International Quarterly* 75, no. 1 (2008): 322–23.

Zerubavel, Yael. *Recovered Roots: Collective Memory and the Making of Israeli National Tradition*. Chicago: University of Chicago Press, 1995.

Ziff, Bruce, and Pratima V. Rao. "Introduction to Cultural Appropriation: A Framework for Analysis." In *Borrowed Power: Essays on Cultural Appropriation*, edited by Bruce Ziff and Pratima V. Rao, 1–27. New Brunswick, NJ: Rutgers University Press, 1997.

Zreik, Raef. "When Does a Settler Become a Native? (With Apologies to Mamdani)." *Constellations* 23, no. 3 (2016): 351–64.

Zubaida, Sami. "National, Communal, and Global Dimensions in Middle Eastern Food Culture." In *A Taste of Thyme: Culinary Cultures of the Middle*

East, edited by Sami Zubaida and Richard Tapper, 33–45. London: I. B. Tauris, 2000.

Zubaida, Sami, and Richard Tapper, eds. *A Taste of Thyme: Culinary Cultures of the Middle East*. London: I. B. Tauris, 2000.

Zubrzycki, Jenevieve. "Matter and Meaning: A Cultural Sociology of Nationalism." In *National Matters: Materiality, Culture and Nationalism*, edited by Jenevieve Zubrzycki, 1–17. Stanford, CA: Stanford University Press, 2017.

Zweiniger-Bargielowska, Ina. *Austerity in Britain: Rationing, Controls, and Consumption, 1939–1955*. Oxford: Oxford University Press, 2000.

FILMS

Bizawe, Eyal Sagui, and Sara Tsifroni. *Arabic Movie*. Israel, 2015. (Hebrew and Arabic)

Graham, Trevor. *Make Hummus Not War*. Yarra Bank Films, 2012. (English)

Rosenblum, Nadav and Micha Cohen. *Hummus-Chips-Salad*. Jerusalem: Bezalel Academy of Art and Design, 2009. (Hebrew)

Rosenfeld, Oren. *Hummus! The Movie*. Multicom Entertainment, 2015. (English, Hebrew, Arabic)

Vered, Eran. *The Unit for Hummus Investigations*. Israel, 2012. (Hebrew)

INDEX

Italicized page numbers refer to image captions.

Aaronsohn, Aaron, 29, 176n55

Abboud, Fadi, 139, 140, 143

Abject, 34

Abu Ghosh, 22, 53, 75, 118, 119, 134, 139, 140–142, *143*, 188–189n1

Abu Hassan, vii, 103, 113, *113*, 116–117, 120, *112*

Abu Hassan al-Baghdadi, 154

Abu Shukri (Abu Ghosh), 134

Abu Shukri (Haifa), 64, 100–101

Abu Shukri (Jerusalem) 98–99, 100–101

Abulhawa, Susan, 5

Acre, 29, 54, 60, *61*, 81, 134

Agriculture, 5, 21, 22, 23, 29, 34–37, 49, 55, 57, 76, 80, 89–91, 99–100, 135, 136, 154, 192–193n42, 212n94; Palestinian, 29, 89–91, 99–100, 102, 154

Aharoni, Israel, 100, 113

Al Hamishmar, 83

al-Han, Nehad, 134–135

Almagor, Dan, 4, 86

Alon, Yigal, 13–14, 35

Aloni, Reuven, 72

Aloni, Shulamit, 72

Alroey, Gur, 36

Ansky, Sherry, 115, 118

Antonovsky, Ron, 130

Apartheid, 125

Appropriation, viii, 6, 9, 10, 14, 15, 20, 118, 149, 153; as cultural erasure, x, 4, 5, 7, 9, 150; Culinary, viii, 1, 3, 4, 5, 6, 7, 8, 15, 21, 26, 72, 84, 85–86, 87, 91, 109, 128, 138, 148, 149, 150, 151, 152, 153; Cultural, viii, x, 3, 4, 5, 6, 7, 9, 11, 35–36, 150, 152–153; Land, 153

Arab Boycott, 40, 77, 105, 143

Arab food. *see* Middle Eastern food

Arabness, 2, 9, 11, 16, 24, 73, 78, 146, 151

'Araidi, Na'im, *107*, 115

Ariel, Ari, 140

Artisanal food, 18, 19–21, 24–25, 78, 110, 112, 114, 127–128, 131–132, 133, 136, 137, 144–145, 146, 153

Ashkenazi Jews, vii, 2, 9, 10, 11, 23, 24, 25, 27, 28, 32, 33–34, 35, 36, 37, 41, 43, 46, 48, 51, 52, 54, 55, 56, 58, 62, 63, 64, 65, 66, 67, 68, 69, 70, 71, 72, 73, 74, 81, 82, 83, 86, 87, 88, 89, 91, 93, 98, 100, 102, 112, 123, 151, 204n5, 209nn68–69

Association of Lebanese Industrialists, 139
Avigdorov, Gad, 1–2, 3, 14
Austerity, 55–56, 58, 59, 62, 67, 69, 78. *see also* Food rationing
Authenticity: and matter, 15, 16–17; Authentic food, ix, 7, 15, 17, 18, 74, 109, 112, 114, 222n40; Authentic ethnic cultures, 106, 111, 114; Authentic human existence, 11; Authentic hummus, 17, 18, 24, 76, 80, 95, 98, 106, 115, 116, 117, 118, 119, 123, 128, 133, 134, 137–138, 146, 148, 152, 153; Authentic Orient, 46, 74, 83; Authentic restaurant, 62, 74, 75, 81, 117; Branding authenticity, 21, 95, 101, 112, 123, 128, 133–134, 135–136, 138, 140, 144–145, 152; Discourse of, 11, 16, 18–19, 21, 106, 114, 123, 137, 138; Fabricated, 135; Iconic, 138; Indexical, 138; Indigenous, 9, 10, 11, 14, 73, 77, 119, 151; industrially produced, 20, 24, 127, 128, 148

Baba ghanoush, 29
Baladi, 99, 112, 222n40
Balkan, 32, 41, 62, 83
Bar-Giora, 1
Bar-Ilan, Wilta, 83–84
Baron, Ilan Zvi, 124
Baumann, Shyon, 113–114
Bavly, Sarah, 67, 68, 88, 91
BDS movement, 143
Beans, 30, 36, 39, 50, 51, 62, 64, 89, 135
Bedouin, 11, 36, 48, 57, 125
Bell, Avril, 11
Ben-Amotz, Dahn, 72, 73–74, 75, 75–76, 101
Ben-Avi, Itamar, 43–44, 183n144
Ben-Gurion, David, 65, 65
Ben-Yehuda, Netiva, 73

Birthright Israel (*Taglit*), 125
Bitansky, Asher, 100–101
Black market, 49, 57, 64, 194n63
Bondi, Ruth, 58, 205n15, 209n68
Bourdieu, Pierre, 12, 13, 14, 109, 132
British government. *see* British Mandate
British Mandate, 29, 33, 37–38, 39–40, 49; Nutrition campaigns, 51, 186n177
Bromberg, Sarah, 48
Bulgur, 29, 35, 49–51, 64, 88

Capitalism, x, 4, 37, 129, 149
Certeau, Michel de, 6
Chaddad, Rafram, 8
Chef Nikolai. *see* Niran Yitzhak
Chickpeas: Agricultural production of, 3, 21, 22, 29, 34, 36, 89–91, 99, 108, 135–136, 172n9, 176n55, 178n77, 212n90, 212n94, 233n61; as food, 2, 4, 15–16, 17–18, 19, 27, 29, 30, 31, 34, 35, 36, 38, 41, 51, 53, 60, 64, 88, 89, 101, 104, 114, 115, 127, 131, 145, 146, 154, 167n97; Hamle Malan, 38, 39; import of, 21, 22, 99, 135, 216nn143–144, 233–234n61
Class: 6, 12, 14, 51, 65, 79, 102, 110, 118; creative class, 109, 111; Ethno-class distinction. See Ethnicity – Ethno-class distinction; Middle class, vii, 28, 37, 40, 43, 62, 79, 80, 81, 102, 111; New middle class, 109, 111, 112, 113
Cohen, Jacques, 134
Colonialism: and food, 3, 6, 12, 27, 153, 154; colonial domination, 6, 150, 152; colonial mimicry, 14; culinary, viii, 7; cultural, viii, 150; of refugees, 10; settler colonialism (*see* Settler Colonialism)
Colonization, viii, 2, 7, 8, 12, 50, 54, 59, 150, 153–154; Zionist, 3, 4, 9, 34. *see also* Land – colonization

Commodification, 3, 6, 7, 15, 19–20, 56, 111–112, 128, 139, 149, 154
Cornfeld, Lilian, 27, 41, 51, 56, 69–70, 71, 72, 86–87, 96, 187n182
Cuisine, 6, 7, 11, 56, 70, 78, 82, 85, 91, 111, 112–113, 150, 152, 154; Industrial, 88; Israeli, 48, 80, 82, 83, 84, 85, 87, 96, 123–124, 150, 151; Levantine, 18, 26, 28, 41, 124; National, 5, 24, 66, 70, 78, 123, 150; Nouvelle, 109, 112, 123; Palestinian, 8, 26, 109, 124, 152, 171n5
Culinary appropriation. *see* Appropriation – Culinary
Culinary cult, 2, 3, 19, 24, 107, 128, 144
Culinary traditions, 5, 6, 7, 18, 20, 47–48, 65, 69, 70, 81, 84–85, 114, 115, 124, 127, 152, 171n5
Cultural appropriation. *see* Appropriation – Cultural
Cultural exchange, 7, 70
Cultural food colonialism, 6, 27. *see also* Appropriation – Culinary, Eating the Other
Cultural homogenization, 66–67
Cultural omnivorousness, 113–114
Culture building, 9, 10, 11, 35, 66, 149

Dabdoub Nasser, Christiane, 5
Dalman, Gustaf, 29
Daud, Habib, 18
Davar, 31, 37, 50, 71–72, 77
Dayan, Moshe, 72, 80, 97
Decolonization, x, 153, 155n7
Diaspora, 2, 10, 12, 44, 54, 71, 73, 74, 79, 86, 92, 115, 124
Diet. *see* Nutrition
Dietary laws – Jewish. *see* Kashrut
Dietler, Michael, 15
Dirks, Nicholas, 8
Displacement, 4
Doar Hayom, 43–44

Dreizin, Zvi, 129
Druze, 125
Dugan, Dennis, vii

Eastern Europe, 2, 10, 27, 34, 35, 65, 70, 74–75, 86, 92, 125
Eating the Other, 5, 6, 7, 73, 119. *see also* Appropriation – Culinary, Cultural food colonialism
Economic exploitation, 5, 150
Egypt, 63, 121
El-Haddad, Laila, 4, 152
Elon, Amos, 59–60
Erez, Oded, 83
Ethiopia, 135, 136
Ethnic cleansing. *see* Ethnicity – Ethnic cleansing
Ethnicity, 6, 14, 25, 79; Boundaries, 7, 37; Ethnic cleansing, xi, 14, 153; Cultures, 106, 111–112; Diversity, 31, 32, 33 48; Food, 6, 65, 69, 82, 102, 111, 112, 113, 124; relations, x, 11, 32, 33, 37, 40, 54–55, 56, 58, 65, 67–68, 79, 83, 94–95, 102, 111; Ethno-class distinction, ix, 51
European food, 2, 32, 34, 35, 42, 52, 58, 64, 66, 68, 69, 70, 71, 72, 74, 75, 86, 92, 125
Even-Zohar, Itamar, viii
Evron Gilat, Limor, 118
Exoticism 6, 18, 31, 44, 45, 46, 59, 62, 77, 97
Exotic food, 27, 28, 46, 75, 81, 109, 111

Fallâh, 1–2, 11, 14, 48
Falafel, 4, 17, 23, 28, 29, 42, 43, 44, 51, 55, 56, 58, 59, 63, 64, 65, 66, 70, 71, 72, 82, 86, 87, 89, 91, 96, 125, 152, 183n143, 193n53, 198n103; Appropriation, 72, 77, 150; as a national dish, 4, 5, 65, 86, 96–97, 106, 152, 156n9; as street food, 38, 41, 43, 52, 65, 80

Fast food, 20, 81
Fatah, 99
Ferguson, Priscilla Parkhurst, viii, 26
Filastin, 38, 40
Food industry, 5, 9, 20, 21, 22, 24, 78,
    79, 80, 88–89, 93, 96, 125, 127, 152
Food rationing, 23, 28, 36, 49, 54–58, 66,
    68, 69, 151, 189n11. *see also* Austerity
"Food washing", 125
Foodies, 106, 108, 112, 114, 123, 128, 132,
    135, 138
Ful, 17, 30, 34, 38, 39, 42, 43, 46, 64, 113

Gabaccia, Donna, 88
Galilee, 29, 35
Galili, Shooky, 115, *144*
Garlic, 4, 29, 53, 104, 114, 127
Gastronationalism, 125, 138
Gaza Strip, 4, 24, 76, 78, 80, 96, 97, 102,
    121, 144, 150, 153–154
Geva, Dudu, 116, 219n4
Gottlieb, Pini, 135–136
Gouri, Haim, 41, 45–46, 73–74, 76–77,
    98
Gourmetization, 24, 104, 105, 109. *see
    also* Hummus: gourmetization of
Graham, Trevor, 22, 143
Great Arab Revolt, 40, 49
Greece, 80, 81, 83, 84
Grehan, James, 16
Gur Arye, Yaniv, 136, 145
Gur, Janna, 124
Gutman, Uri, 87

Haaretz, 44, 49, 51, 69, 71, 118, 122
Hadashot, 112
Hadassah, 46, 183–184n151
Haganah, 39–40, 72, 76, 203n152

Haifa, 18, 35, 37, 38–39, 40, 41, 45, 54,
    60, 64, 74, 77, 81, 98, 153
Ha'ir, 112, 117
Halabi, Mu'in, 18, 19
Hall, Stuart, 133
Harathin, 1, 14, 34, 156n3
Hashomer, 1, 36
Helman, Anat, 58, 62, 95
Herut, 84
Hildesheimer, Arnold, 89
Himtsa, 55. *see* also Hummus
Hlehel, Ala, 153
Holocaust, 11
hooks, bell, 6, 69
Hummus / hummus bi-tahine:*
    Advertisements, 42, 64, 78, 90,
    91–92, 93, *94*, 95, 112, *120*, 127–128,
    131, 133, 134, 135, 136, 145, 146, 148, 150,
    154, 213n103, 232n47; Appropriation,
    21, 109, 148, 149, 150, 152; Arab-made,
    24, 28, 80, 100, 105, 106, 109, 115–116,
    117–118, 119, 121, 122–123, 134, 135,
    138, 148, 151; Artisanal / handmade,
    19, 21, 24, 29, 63, 78, 91, 95, 96, 98,
    101–102, 114, 116, 127, 128, 131, 132,
    133, 136, 137, 138, 144, 145, 146, 153; as
    culinary cult, 2, 3, 19, 24, 106, 107, 116,
    128, 144, 152; as healthy food, 91, 108,
    144, 152; as Israeli national symbol,
    5, 19, 20, 24, 78, 79, 82, 84, 86, 92,
    96, 97, 106, 145, 149, 152; as street
    food, 38, 43, 52; as superfood, 108;
    Coexistence, 24, 98, 119, 120–121,
    122, 139, 141–142; Festivals, 18, 22,
    72, 134, 137, 146, *147*; Food culture,
    100, 106, 119, 153; Globalization of,
    2, 19, 20, 21, 24, 108, 125, 128, 129, 138,
    140; Gourmetization of, 24, 104,

---

*Hummus is mentioned on almost every page of this book; in the index, it is only mentioned in the specified contexts.

105, 111, 112, 113, 114–116; Guinness
record, 138, *141*, *144*; *Hamshuka*, 123;
Industrial, 19, 20, 21, 22, 24, 78, 79–
80, 88, 89, 90–91, 94, 95, 96, 98, 99,
102, 114, 127, 128, 129, 130–131, 132, 133,
134, 135, 136, 137, 138, 140, 143, 144,
145, 146, 148, 151, 152, 153; Popularity,
vii, 4, 52, 54, 55, 58, 66, 72, 75, 81, 89,
91–92, 96, 105, 107, 108, 109, 145, 149;
Wars, 24, 138, 139, 140, 143
Hummusiya, 13, 14, 17, 19, 97, 101, 103,
107, 115, 116, 117, 118, 121, 122–123,
127–128, 131–132, 133–135, 136, 137, 145,
146, 148, 219n5
Hummusologists, 107, 115, 118, 132, 133,
145
Humtsa. see Himtsa
Hygiene. *see* Sanitation

Ibrahim, Jawadat, 139–142
IDF, 59, 76, 103, 116, 150
Indigeneity, ix, 4–5, 6, 7, 11, 12, 13,
25, 28, 35, 72, 150 (*see also* Native,
Settler-indigenous relations); and
authenticity, 10, 14, 15, 73, 77, 119, 151;
and masculinity, ix, 2, 10, 11, 15, 23
Indigenization of the settlers, x, 4, 9,
10, 11, 12, 77, 96, 118, 151
Industrial food, 20, 47, 58, 80, 79, 80,
88, 89, 96, 129
Intifada: First, 97; Second, 121
Islamic world, 11, 54
Iton Meyuchad, 42

Jaffa, viii–ix, 33, 37, 38, 40–42, 45–46,
54, 56, 62–63, 75, 81, 98, 103, 114,
116–117, 135, *147*
Jerusalem, 32, 33, 34, 37, 39–40, 41, 43,
53, 63–64, 70, 76, 80, 81, 82, 97–98,
105, 113, 117, 118, 119, 124, 127; Old
City, 32, 33, 41, 97, 100, *106*, 125, 154

Jewish Agency, 49, 56; Institute for
Economic Research, 49
Jewish Colonization Association, 34
Johnston, Anna, 10, 77
Johnston, Josée, 113–114
Jordan, 16, 119, 134

Kahn Bar-Adon, Dorothy, 27, 28, 37
Kapeliuk, Menachem, 15, 65
Karawan, Ali. *See* Abu Hassan
Karmiel, 22, 127
Kashrut / Kosher, 17, 20, 26, 42, 84, 85,
108, 122, 139, 153
Kassis, Reem, 109
Keane, Webb, 9, 18–19
Kebab, 42, 45, 58, 59, 60, 64, 72, 74,
75, 76, 86, 87, 180n92, 209nn68–69,
210n74n74
Kenan, Amos, 97, 101, 205n15
Kiryat Gat, 22
Kol Ha'ir, 119
Kristeva, Julia, 34

Labaneh, 17, 35, 109
Land, 5, 9, 10, 11, 12, 14, 20, 28, 46, 49,
54, 57, 72, 73, 112, 115, 121, 124, 128, 151,
154; Acquisition, 1, 36; Colonization,
viii, 2, 3; Cultivation, 90, 154;
Dispossession, 4, 57, 152, 153; Theft,
viii, 100, 153, 154
Landau, Eli, 112
Laudan, Rachel, 21
Lawson, Allan, 10, 77
Lebanon, 16, 24, 119, 120, 138–139, 140,
143, 197n89
Legumes, 28, 29, 35, 36, 49, 51, 56, 108,
186n178, 190n20
LeMerchav, 76
Lentils, 2, 3, 31, 34, 35, 36, 50, 88
Levant, 16, 18, 21, 26, 28, 31, 41, 54, 65,
67, 121, 124

Likud, 105, 111
Litani, Yehuda, 45, 53, 96, 107, 115, 117, 119
Lizardo, Omar, 114
Localism, 21, 24, 84, 95, 96, 105, 106, 123, 128, 133, 135, 144
Lydda, 54
Lyons Bar-David, Molly, 86

Maariv, 56, 75, 82, 86, 93, 94, 118, 205n15
Ma'barot, 56, 63, 83, 190n21, 196n81, 199n120
Ma'dhar, 1
Maghreb. *see* North Africa
Majar, Albert, 63–64
Manning, Paul, 129
Mapai, 76, 111
Marx, Karl, 6
Masculinity, vii, 2, 9, 10, 11, 13, 35, 36, 54, 73, 75, 77, 86, 133, 135, 163n71. *see also* Indigeneity - masculinity
Masterman E. W. G., 31
Materialization, 16, 19
Mediterranean diet, 108. *see also* Nutrition
Meged, Eyal, 118
Meir, Golda, 36
Me'ir, Yosef, 46
Meneley, Anne, 20
Mescha, 1, 3, 14, 35
Meyer, Erna, 48, 49, *50*
Middle Eastern food, 11, 18, 23, 26, 27, 28, 32, 33, 34, 37, 41, 42, 43, 48, 49, 51, 54, 55, 58, 63, 64, 65, 68, 69, 70, 71, 72, 73, 79, 81, 82, 84, 86, 87, 88, 92, 102, 112, 123, 124, 139, 141
Mintz, Sidney, ix, 55, 82, 152
Mizrahi Jews, ix, 8, 11, 22, 23, 25, 26, 31, 32, 33, 34, 40, 41, 42, 43, 48, 50–51, 52, 54, 55, 56, 58, 62, 63–64, 65, 67, 68, 69, 70, 73, 74, 76, 77, 79, 81, 83, 86, 88, 91, 93, 94, 95, 96, 100, 102, 111, 123, 133, 134, 135, 149, 151, 204n5, 209nn68–69

Mizrahi food. *see* Middle Eastern Food
Mjaddara, 2–3, 30, 35, 49, 51, 64, 66
Moskowitz, Howard, 130
Msakhan, 109
Mshawsha, 115, 223n58
Musabbaha, 16, 115, 116, 168n98, 223n58

Nablus, 113, 120
Nakba, 54
Narayan, Uma, 7
Nationalism, 9–10, 12, 23, 32, 38, 42, 43, 78, 86, 124, 125, 140. *see also* Patriotism, Cuisine - national
Native, x, 3, 4, 7, 10, 11, 12, 28, 31, 35, 36, 73, 74, 77, 150. *see also* Indigeneity
Nazareth, 42, 54, 59–60, 64, 71, 76, 84, 113, 194n58, 194n63
New Jew ("sabra"), 10, 15, 23, 34, 35, 72–73, 74, 75, 77, 79, 151
Niran, Yitzhak, 87
Nishri, Tzvi, 36
Nitzan-Shiftan, Alona, 14
Nizri, Yigal, 8
North Africa, 23, 25, 54, 57, 62, 69, 70
Noy, Amos, 121
Nutrition, 12, 36, 46–48, 49–52, 54, 66, 67, 70, 83, 87, 88, 108, 118; Discourse, 47, 69; Education, 22, 23, 28, 46, 47, 49, 51, 54, 55, 65, 67, 68, 69–70, 71, 183–184n151, 200n122; Policy, 49, 70, 190n20 (*see also* Food policy); Science, 12, 47, 48

Occupation, 24, 59, 60, 76, 78, 80, 96, 97, 99, 100, 124, 125, 152
Occupied Territories, ix, 22, 97–98, 99, 102, 107, 111, 119, 143. *see also* Gaza Strip, West Bank
Oil, 15, 19, 27, 35, 39, 50, 51, 53, 60, 62, 70, 77, 132, 136; as Palestinian national symbol, 109; Canola oil, 135; Olive oil, 16, 17, 29, 31, 35, 39, 41,

45, 46, 99, 104, *107*, 109, 113, 114, 119, 122, 127, 146
Orient / Oriental, 10, 11, 21, 23, 26, 27, 33, 37, 39, 40, 41, 42–43, 45, 46, 48, 50, 51, 53, 55, 58–59, 62–65, 66, 68, 70–71, 72, 74, 75, 76, 77, 78, 81, 82, 83, 86, 87–88, 91, 92, 93, *94*, 95, 96, 98, 101, 102, 111, 112, 115, 119, 120, 151
Oriental food. *see* Middle Eastern food
Oser, Avraham, 89
Oslo Accords, 106, 119, 121
Ottoman period, 38

Palestine, 1–2, 10–11, 16, 18, 22, 23, 25, 27, 29, 31, 32, 33, 35, 38–39, 42, 46, 47, 48, 74, 98, 153; Mandatory Palestine, 22, 25, 28, 29, 33, 37, 38, 45, 49, 151
Palestine Edible Products Ltd., 89, 96
Palestinian Arabs. *see* Palestinians
Palestinian/s, viii, x, 3, 4, 7, 8, 9, 10, 13, 18, 22, 25, 26, 29, 32–33, 37, 38, 39, 40, 42, 53, 54, 56–57, 58, 59, 62, 79, 82, 87, 97, 98, 99–100, 102, 111, 115, 117, 121, 124, 125, 139, 143, 144, 150, 151, 153, 154, 191nn28–29, 225n73; Citizens of Israel, 100, 142; Culture, 4, 5, 8, 106, 125, 150, 153; Dehumanization of, 5; Cuisine/ food / foodways, 5, 8, 13, 23, 24, 26, 28, 29, 30, 31, 32, 35, 45, 46, 52, 63, 71, 72, 78, 80, 96, 98, 101, 105, 106, 109, 112, 116, 118, 119, 123–124, 125, 149–150, 152, 154, 171n5; National symbols, viii, 3, 109; Resistance to Zionism, 33
Palestinian food, ix, 2, 3, 4, 5, 7, 8, 12, 15, 22, 23, 26, 27, 28, 29, 31, 32, 34, 35, 43, 45, 46, 48, 52, 55, 58, 62, 65, 66, 71, 72, 73, 75, 76, 77, 79, 84, 85, 86, 87, 100, 106, 109, 112, 118, 119, 123, 124, 138, 149, 150, 152, 153, 171n5
Palmach, 13–14, 45, 72–73, 74, 76–77

Parasecoli, Fabio, 18
Patriotism, 133, 139, 140, 141, 142
Performative Consumption, 3, 9, 14, 15, 28, 54, 73, 77
Pickles, 15, 32, 39, 56, 87, 91, 97, 114
Pita, 4, 13, 31, 52, 62, 70, 74, 82, 86, 91, 94, 95, 104, 127, 166n93, 188n195, 193n53, 209n69, 210n74
Press-Barnathan, Galia, 124

Qualisign, 9, 16, 151

Race, 6, 10, 25, 47, 67
Ramallah, 97
Ray, Krishnendu, 7, 149
Reparations from Germany, 79
Rozin, Orit, 59, 66

Saguy, Sam, 130
Salaita, Steven, 4, 150, 154
Sanitation, 38, 43, 67, 68, 81, 95, 96, 129, 130, 132
Sansour, Vivien, 152
Schmitt, Maggie, 4
Semiotics, 2, 3, 9, 15, 19, 20, 132. *see also* Qualisign
Sephardi Jews, 32, 33, 41, 43, 62, 64
Seri, Rachel, 31
Sesame, 29, 38, 99, 127, 135–136, 211n89
Settler colonialism, x, 4–5, 9–10, 11, 12, 119, 125, 149, 154; and the elimination of the native, 4, 7, 150; Settler-indigenous relations, 5, 10–11, 77, 118–119, 151; Zionism as settler colonialism (*see* Zionism – as settler colonialism)
Shani, Eyal, 118, 124
Shapin, Steven, 12
Sharabi, Hisham, 29
Shem-Or, Ora, 34
Sherfler, Ezra, 63, 64
Shezaf, Tzur, 121
Shmu'eli, Eliyahu, 122

Sirkis, Ruth, 101
Skiles, Sara, 114
Social media, 4, 22, 107, 109, 113, 115, 116,
    125, 127, 145, 148, 150
Stein, Rebecca, 119
Strauss, Walter, 68, 70
Sulha, 56, 134
Sumud, 5
Syria, 15, 16, 32, 39, 119–121, 197n89

Tahini, 2, 15–16, 17, 19, 23, 27, 29–30, 31,
    33, 35, 36, 37, 39, 45, 48, 49, 51, 52, 53,
    58, 64, 65, 66, 70, 71, 72, 75–76, 77, 82,
    84, 86, 87, 88, 89, 91, 95, 97, 104, 108,
    113, 115, 122, 123, 127, 131, 135–136, 137,
    146, 166n92, 187n185, 193n47, 211n89
Talmi, Menachem, 41, 80, 81, 97, 98
Taste Perception, 133, 145
Tel Aviv, vii, ix, xii, 37, 40–43, 44, 52,
    58, 62–63, 65, 74, 76, 80–81, 95, 97,
    100, 104, 116, 117, 119, 120, 121, 124,
    128, 134, 137, 139
Tene, Ofra, 105, 112, 127
Tene, Zeev, 88, 96
Third space, 81
Tikolsker, Erez, 115
Tourism, 24, 37, 59–60, 79, 81, 82, 83–84,
    85, 97–98, 105, 118, 119, 121, 153, 195n78
Transitional camps. *see Ma'barot*
Turkey, 25, 32, 54, 63
Tzaban, Amnon, 100–101
Tzur, Yaron, 19, 127

United States, 70, 88, 138
Uplisashvili, Ann, 129

Veganism, 108, 219n10
Vegetarianism, 13, 59, 108, 219n10

Weinstock, Tikva, 62, 64
West Bank, ix, 24, 76, 78, 80, 96, 97, 99,
    102, 122, 144, 154
Westernization, x, 4, 10, 11, 12, 33
Wilk, Richard, 20, 95
WIZO, 46, 48, 53, 66, 68, 88,
    183–184n151
Wolfe, Patrick, 118
World War I, 2, 32
World War II, 41, 49, 101

Yahav, Matti, 131, 135, 144
Yehoshua, Jacob, 33
Yellin, Ita, 33
Yemen, 32, 41, 43, 54, 69–70, 71, 81,
    83, 86, 89, 93–95, 102, 136, 182n127,
    213n106
Yosef, Dov, 66, 67
Young, James, 153
Youth Aliyah, 74, 203n160

Za'atar, 29, 35, 38, 46, 109, 131, 146
Zalivansky, Yehoshua, 41
Zionism, x, 1, 5, 11, 12, 13, 15, 23, 28,
    32, 33, 37, 47–49, 76, 105, 128,
    154; as nationalism, 10; as settler
    colonialism, 3–4, 10; Resistance to
    Zionism, 33; Zionist colonization,
    3, 4, 9, 34; Zionist culture building,
    10, 11, 72, 124, 151; Zionist ideology,
    9, 46, 79
Zreik, Raef, 10
Zubaida, Sami, 30
1948 War, 13, 45, 54, 73, 76
1956 War, 78
1967 War, 76, 84, 97, 101, 105
1973 War, 76, 101, 102
1982 War, 119, 121

DAFNA HIRSCH is an Associate Professor at the Department of Sociology, Political Science and Communication, the Open University of Israel. She is author of *"We Are Here to Bring the West": Hygiene Education and Nation Building in the Jewish Society of Mandate Palestine* (2014) and editor of *Entangled Histories in Palestine/Israel: Historical and Anthropological Perspectives* (2024). She lives in Tel Aviv.